Basic Language

Messages and Meanings

I

Basic Language

Messages and Meanings

Text and Grammar Handbook

I

Authors:
Harry A. Greene
Kate Ashley Loomis
Norma W. Biedenharn
Pauline C. Davis

Basic Language Coordinator:
Norma W. Biedenharn

1817

HARPER & ROW, PUBLISHERS
New York   Hagerstown   San Francisco   London

Editorial Credits: Senior Editor, Carolyn Quinn;
Associate Editor, Barbara Klinger.
The publisher gratefully acknowledges
Dr. Edward R. Levy for his
assistance in the development and
preparation of material in this text.

Illustrations by Muriel and Jim Collins
and Lou Cunette

1979 Printing

Standard Book Number 06-530106-4
798081RRD98765432

Some of the material in this book was previously published under
the titles of *Building Better English 7 Torch Edition, The New
Building Better English 7 Fourth Edition, The New Building Better English 7,
Building Better English 7, Building Better English in Every Way;* copyright ©
1972, 1968, 1965, 1961, 1958, 1952, 1947, 1944 by Harper & Row, Publishers, Inc.

Preface

In the Basic Language: Messages and Meanings series, the authors and the publisher reaffirm their belief that effective instruction in English must be founded upon a basic-skills approach.

In line with that belief, the grammar chapters have been designed to reinforce valuable principles and practices of traditional grammar. All grammar material included was chosen because it does one or both of these things:

1. It offers useful terms, explanations, and practices that can be of tangible help to the students.

2. It reinforces the fundamentals of English grammatical structure. The material on grammatical structure is used as the basis for sentence-combining techniques in composition.

Another notable feature of this series is its treatment of vocabulary development with emphasis on word derivation, roots, prefixes, and suffixes as clues to meaning. In addition, the work on vocabulary development, testing, and reasoning offers helpful preparation for college entrance examinations.

Other features that distinguish the series are:

1. The content reflects careful, logical organization. Hit or miss instruction has no place in the Basic Language series. The content shows an orderly, definite progression from one book of the series to the next. Furthermore, the arrangement of the material makes it readily adaptable to varied types of curricula.

2. Each of the four areas of communication—speaking, listening, reading, and writing—receives ample treatment, not merely token recognition.

3. Instruction is clear and specific, with rules, definitions, and guides easily distinguishable from introductions and exercises. The practice material is useful, varied, and appealing; it makes provision for individual differences. There is consistent maintenance of skills throughout. In addition, a thorough testing program that covers the mechanics of expression is available.

4. An integral part of the texts is concrete provision for applying English skills to the students' work in all subjects and to their lives outside school.

5. The makers of this series believe that young people do not object to hard work if they understand what to do and how to go about doing it.

Even a brief examination of Basic Language: Messages and Meanings will reveal how closely these books adhere to the preceding criteria. A careful analysis should convince students and teachers who use this series that the study of English can be a productive and pleasurable experience.

The Publishers

CONTENTS

Section II: Reading

Section IV: Handbook of Grammar and Usage

Speaking and Listening

THE ENGLISH LANGUAGE:
ITS VOCABULARY

1. The Changing Nature of English

"CANST FIND THOSE PHANTASTICALL VOCABLES IN THY WORD TREASURE?"

RADAR
DACRON
SPUTNIK
BLACK HOLE

READ AND THINK ABOUT . . .

In 1934 the words *radar* and *Dacron* were not in the dictionary. *Sputnik* and *Telstar* still had not made it by 1957. By 1968 terms such as *lunar excursion module* and *black hole* had not yet appeared. In 1973 expressions such as *air bag, petrodollars, work ethic,* and *health food* had still not been entered. On the other hand, *siege* (meaning "seat") and *reve* (meaning "take away"), once common words in English speech, have disappeared from today's language. It is altogether likely that two hundred years from now many words in your own vocabulary will sound strange to your descendants.

In this chapter you will explore the growth of the English language, from its beginnings about fifteen hundred years ago down to the present here in the United States. Then you will learn something about how words change meaning as they continue to be used.

INTRODUCTORY LEARNING ACTIVITIES

A. In this chapter you will be tracing the origins of many words. In doing so, you will need to know what languages many abbreviations stand for. Using your school dictionary or a larger one, find out what languages the abbreviations below represent. Make a list and file it in your notebook.

1. OE (*or* AS)	6. Gk. (*or* Gr.)	11. Am. Ind. (*or* AmerInd.)
2. ME	7. L (*or* Lat.)	12. Scand.
3. Am. (*or* Amer.)	8. OF (*or* OFr.)	13. LG
4. F (*or* Fr.)	9. Pg. (*or* Port.)	14. LL
5. G (*or* Ger.)	10. Sp. (*or* Span.)	15. NL

B. In your investigations you may come across abbreviations for other languages, and you will want to know what they mean. Find the section in your own dictionary, or the dictionary in your classroom, that gives the abbreviations for various languages. Write the meanings of *IE, MHG, Skt.* or *Sans., Gmc., AF* or *Anglo-Fr., Am.Sp.* or *AmerSp.,* and *VL.*

C. Look up *archaic* in your dictionary. Make sure you understand its meaning with regard to language. (1) Write the meanings of the words below. (2) Indicate for each word whether the dictionary labels it *archaic.*

1. sirrah	3. gramercy	5. anon	7. enow
2. belike	4. wert	6. methinks	8. quoth

ENRICHMENT

Try to figure out what the italicized words mean. Their context (other words in the sentences) will help. Check in an unabridged dictionary to see how close you came.

1. I tell you, *certes,* he is a fine gentleman.
2. Truly, risking his life was an act of *hardiment!*
3. Please wait. I'll be with you *eftsoon.*
4. Our car bumped over the *ruggy* road.

5. *Sith* you doubt my word, I shall take my leave.
6. I am going, *maugre* your opposition!

2. The Origin of English

About 500 B.C., the British Isles were inhabited by a tribe from central Europe called the Brythons. They were peace-loving people who spoke a Celtic language. The word *Britain* is derived from the name of that tribe.

During the next nine hundred years, Britain was conquered twice — first by the Romans (about A.D. 43) and then by the Angles, Saxons, and Jutes (about A.D. 400). Under Roman rule, the Celts learned to speak Latin as well as their own language. The Anglo-Saxons, as the later conquerors became known, were from northern Germany and Denmark. They spoke Germanic dialects. The Celts fled to what is now Wales and north to Scotland in the face of this latest invasion. Their language is the basis of today's Gaelic and Welsh.

Since the Celts had fled, the language of the invading Anglo-Saxons eventually became the language you now speak. The word "English" comes from *Engle-isc* (Angle-ish), a term that came to represent all versions of the language, whether spoken by Angles, Saxons, or Jutes. The Anglo-Saxons called their adopted homeland *Engle-land* (Angle-land).

LEARNING ACTIVITIES

A. On a map of Great Britain, find the following cities: *Dover, Dorchester, Newcastle, Chester, Carlisle, Exeter, Carnarvon.* They were established as military posts by the Roman conquerors. What do their locations suggest about why they were chosen as sites for garrisons?

B. Suppose that England had been named for either the Saxons or the Jutes, instead of the Angles. What do you suppose the language and the country would have been called? Discuss in class.

3. The Old English Period

LATIN INFLUENCE

The Roman occupation of Britain lasted for almost four hundred years. Yet, except for a few place names, very little of the Latin language found its way into Old English, the name given to the tongue spoken by the Anglo-Saxons.

Of the Latin "loan words" (borrowed words) that did become part of Old English, some of the commonly used ones were brought by the Anglo-Saxon invaders themselves. They had learned those words during the years of the Roman occupation of northern Europe. Most of the Latin loan words brought to England by the Anglo-Saxons have to do with food, fighting, and trade. Following are a few examples.

Latin	Old English	Modern English
moneta	mynet (coin)	mint
pondo	pund	pound
vinum	win	wine
butyrum	butere	butter
cuprum	coper	copper
caupo	ceap (bargain)	cheap
discus	disc	dish

A second round of Latin borrowings came with the arrival of missionaries from Rome who brought Christianity to the pagan Anglo-Saxons, A.D. 597. With Christianity came the Bible and church services. Both of these were in Latin. The missionaries also introduced the Roman alphabet and set up schools where reading and writing were taught in both Latin and English.

Only a few writings from this period now exist, one of which is the famous epic poem *Beowulf.* From these writings it is clear that the Anglo-Saxons were borrowing Latin words for the new ideas and experiences that came with Christianity. Some such words are *priest, angel, mass, disciple, anthem, stole,* and *temple.*

The Anglo-Saxons expanded their vocabulary by making up their own words, in addition to borrowing Latin words for new ideas. Thus, the Anglo-Saxon *god,* the word for any of the pagan gods, became *God,* a substitution for the Latin *Deus.* The Latin *astronomus* (astronomer) comes from two words which mean "star-knower"; the Anglo-Saxons combined *tugol* (star) and *wittig* (knower) to form their own word for "astronomer" — *tugol-wittig.*

Old English was once thought to be a primitive sort of language, but research has made clear that it was just as capable of expressing fine shades of meaning as any other language.

LEARNING ACTIVITIES

A. Many of the Anglo-Saxon words we still use have to do with home, family, and daily life. Can you figure out what the following words are in modern English? (CLUE: Some vowel sounds have changed.) Discuss in class.

1. grene	6. hund	11. wif	16. snaw
2. sumor	7. tunge	12. fisc	17. niht
3. lytel	8. witnes	13. waerm	18. lippe
4. hus	9. dohtor	14. cild	19. thynne
5. eorthe	10. heorte	15. bryd	20. twelf

B. Study the following list of words related to religion. Using a school or college dictionary, find the *AS* form of each and the language from which it came. (The history, or source, of a word is shown in the dictionary in brackets, like this: [   ]. The symbol < means "came from.") Discuss in class.

1. alms	3. noon	5. deacon	7. cross
2. nun	4. shrine	6. shrive	8. altar

C. Many words having to do with measurement come from words that stand for parts of the human body. Since the body is a natural standard, early people used it as a basis against which they could measure other things. Other measurement words come from names for simple, everyday objects. Using a school or college dictionary, find the meaning of the original words from which the following terms of measurement came. On a separate piece of paper, write down which of the following words have a Latin origin: *cubit, fathom, furlong, dram.*

D. Names for insects often originated from, or were related to, Anglo-Saxon action words. Look in your dictionary and find out what action was associated with each of the following insect names: *fly, spider, beetle.* Make this an oral activity.

ENRICHMENT

The Anglo-Saxon literature that has survived is filled with imaginative comparisons or descriptive expressions called *kennings.* The sea, for example, is called the "whale-road"; an evil monster is a "death-shadow."

Using your imagination, see whether you can match the numbered Anglo-Saxon kennings below with the literal words for which they stand: *ship, sword, sea, sun, battle, friend, deer, spear, vile monster, hero.*

1. flood-domain	6. wave-walker
2. shoulder-comrade	7. heath-rover
3. shaft-of-slaughter	8. contest-crash
4. hard-edge	9. folk-defender
5. shepherd-of-evils	10. bright God's beacon

Afterward, try making up an imaginative compound expression of your own for each of the ten words.

DANISH INFLUENCE

During the eighth century, a fierce seagoing people known as the Danes (they came from what are now the Scandinavian countries) opened a long attack on England. Actually related to the Anglo-Saxons, they also spoke a Germanic language—Old Norse. Education and government practically came to a standstill while the warfare continued, year after year after year. The war finally ended in 878. However, fresh invasions by the Scandinavians continued, and in 1014, Svein, king of Denmark, became king of England. For the next thirty years, England was ruled by Danish kings.

As a result, a great number of Danish words found their way into the English vocabulary. Most of them are from the language of everyday life. What would English be without such words as *root, law, skirt, rotten, thrive, gate, egg, take, skill, sky, ill, scowl, ugly,* and *die*? To the Danes, too, English is indebted for three little pronouns of great value: the plural pronouns *they, their,* and *them.*

Since the Danes and the Anglo-Saxons spoke closely related languages, they naturally had some very like-sounding words for certain things. The Anglo-Saxon farmer, for example, called one of his garden tools a *raca;* his Danish neighbor called it a *reka.*

As the Danes learned to speak English, they usually dropped their own word in favor of the English word. In some cases, however, *both* words survived—by beginning to differ in meaning. Thus, *skirt* and *shirt,* both of which meant "shirt," became distinct from each other: the Danish word came to mean the lower garment and the Anglo-Saxon word referred to the upper garment.

LEARNING ACTIVITIES

A. Here is a list of words introduced into English by the Danes. In your dictionary, find (1) the Old Norse (sometimes called Old Icelandic or Scandinavian) word from which the English word derives and (2) the original meaning, if it was different.

1. score	6. skill	11. whirl
2. fellow	7. cast (*verb*)	12. outlaw
3. scold	8. ugly	13. snub
4. scuffle	9. window	14. gasp
5. scare	10. slaughter	15. boon

B. With the help of your dictionary, (1) explain the present difference in meaning between words of the following pairs and (2) give the language origin of each word. Write out; discuss in class.

1. shatter — scatter
2. ditch — dike
3. drag — draw
4. lawful — legal
5. from — fro

ENRICHMENT

With the help of an encyclopedia, make an oral report on King Canute and the Danish invasions.

4. The Middle English Period

FRENCH INFLUENCE

The Middle English period dates from the Battle of Hastings. In that battle, fought on October 14, 1066, Harold, the last Saxon king, was defeated and killed by an invader from Normandy (now part of France). That man was Duke William, known as the Conqueror.

The Norman Conquest, as it is called, resulted in a period of about four hundred years when truly remarkable changes took place in the English language. During that time, Old French (the ancestor of today's French) was the language of the nobility, of law courts and government, of culture and learning, and of the Church. English, as a written language, was neglected. It survived primarily as a spoken language during this period.

In time, however, the French began to absorb more and more the ways and words of the people they were living among. By 1300, French had ceased to be the first language of the educated upper class. In fact, toward the end of that century, Geoffrey Chaucer wrote his *Canterbury Tales* not in French, but in English. *Canterbury Tales* was the first British literary masterpiece.

Not surprisingly, many French words had in the meantime found their way into English. Among the important kinds of French words brought into the vocabulary of English were the following:

1. *Words dealing with law and government*

   EXAMPLES: judge, justice, bar, jury, fraud, libel, slander, crown, state, empire, royal, parliament, assembly

2. *Words having to do with religion*

   EXAMPLES: baptize, sacrament, preach, sermon, prayer, crucifix

3. *Words dealing with social life and customs*

   EXAMPLES: lace, embroidery, tassels, plumes, satin, fur
   dinner, supper, oranges, lemons, veal, poultry
   cushions, chairs, couches, blankets, chandelier
   sculpture, music, literature, poetry, stories

All in all, as far as the English language is concerned, it is impossible to overestimate the importance of the arrival of the Normans in England.

LEARNING ACTIVITIES

A. In each of the following word pairs, indicate which word is from Anglo-Saxon and which was borrowed from the French. Go over your work in class.

1. beef — ox
2. veal — calf
3. seethe — boil
4. stench — odor
5. wedlock — marriage
6. doom — judgment
7. freedom — liberty
8. house — mansion

B. Give oral sentences that show the difference in the way the words in the pairs in *A* are used today.

C. The following are Old French loan words, but the French had borrowed them, too. With the help of the dictionary, find the original source and original meaning of each word. Write out your answers; then compare them in class.

1. gender
2. grammar
3. noun
4. clause
5. study
6. volume
7. poet
8. pen
9. coffin
10. escape
11. language
12. soldier

D. As the language grew, some French words replaced English ones; some French words with English synonyms dropped out. In still other cases, both an English word and a French synonym survived, but each came to have somewhat different meanings.

Here are six such pairs. (1) Identify the source, English or French, of each word. (2) Explain any differences in meaning. Make this an oral activity.

1. flower — blossom
2. shun — avoid
3. wish — desire
4. body — corpse
5. ship — vessel
6. spring — fountain

ENRICHMENT

These lines are from "The Knight's Tale" in Geoffrey Chaucer's *Canterbury Tales*. Though written in the English of almost six hundred years ago, the lines are ones that you should be able to "translate" into present-day language. Try it!

EXAMPLE: *Som man desyreth for to han richesse.*
   Some men long to have riches.

1. Of Athenes he was lord and governour,
   And in his tyme swich a conquerour,
   That gretter was ther noon under the sonne.

2. His baner he desplayeth, and forth rood
   To Thibes-ward, and al his hoste bisyde.
3. How greet a sorwe suffreth now Arcite!
4. The brighte swerdes wenten to and fro
   So hidously, that with the leaste strook
   It seemed as it wolde felle an ook.
5. "I yow foryeve al hooly this trespas,
   At requeste of the quene that kneleth here."
6. Of fyve and twenty yeer his age I caste.
7. His longe heer was kembd bihinde his bak.
8. His voys was as a trompe thunderinge.
9. Up springen speres twenty foot on highte;
   Out goon the swerdes as the silver brighte.

5. The Modern English Period

READ AND DO . . .

By the time of Chaucer's death in 1400, everyone in England was speaking and writing in English, including the upper class; in fact, to speak French was an achievement. There was never again a doubt that English was here to stay.

In 1474 William Caxton introduced the printing press into England—an event that really marks the beginning of the Modern English period. For the sake of convenience, however, 1500 is the date generally given. Before the time of the printing press, English had had very few standards of vocabulary or spelling; indeed, it was sometimes hard for the English to understand one another.

Caxton, a Londoner, spoke the London dialect, which was already becoming the most widely used one. He was followed by other printers in using it, and the London dialect soon became the standard for the formal writing and speaking of English. In this way, the introduction of printing helped to standardize (give consistent form to) English.

As books became more numerous, the English developed a thirst for learning. Up to this time, most Latin words had made their way into English through French, which itself had developed from Latin. Now English writers and scholars went out of their way to introduce words into English directly from Latin and Greek. In the period from about 1500 to 1650, English became enriched by many useful words of Latin and Greek origin. These loan words include *pedestrian, educate, dedicate, contradict, esteem, paragraph, scene, studious,* and *maturity.*

Sometimes, in their urge to introduce words into the language from Latin and Greek, the English overdid it a little. Such "far out" borrowings as *obtestate, splendidous, adjuvate,* and *attemptate* were condemned by critics and leading writers. One such critic was Ben Jonson, a friend of William Shakespeare and, like him, a famous playwright. In one of his plays he poked fun at the users of such outlandish "inkhorn" terms.

Italian and Spanish (like French, related to Latin) were also sources of new words, especially since the English thought of Italy and Spain as representing the height of fashion and refinement. From the Italian came *sonnet, balcony, violin, grotto, stanza,* and *gala;* from the Spanish and the Portuguese (another language related to Latin), English borrowed *anchovy, bravado, desperado,* and *bastinado.*

LEARNING ACTIVITIES

A. The following words have come into English from the Greek language. Find in your dictionary the Greek word from which each of them came. How does today's English meaning compare with the meaning of the Greek root word? Talk the words over in class.

1. skeleton	4. idea	7. crater	10. elastic
2. eclipse	5. angel	8. athlete	11. tactics
3. anonymous	6. acrobat	9. orchestra	12. planet

B. If Ben Jonson were alive today, do you think he would consider *astronaut* and *bioflavonoid* modern inkhorn terms? Look up their origins in a dictionary; discuss in class.

C. One of the great changes in English since the time of Shakespeare and Jonson is that spelling has become more standardized, or uniform. Here are some spellings as they appeared in an early edition of Shakespeare's play *Hamlet.* How are these words spelled today? Write the modern spellings.

1. propheticke	5. stiffely	9. musicke	13. saurse
2. juyce	6. bookes	10. anckle	14. frends
3. sodaine	7. coppied	11. soveraigne	15. heerein
4. blossomes	8. falshood	12. entreatie	

ENRICHMENT

William Shakespeare was born over four hundred years ago, but by his time English had developed to the point that even today it is much the same as when he wrote. The differences are mostly in such things as verb forms and pronoun forms that have changed and in the order of the words in a sentence.

If you substitute today's verbs and pronouns and rearrange the order of the words in some cases, Shakespeare's lines sound very modern. Prove that fact by substituting modern verbs and pronouns in these quotations from his historical play *Henry IV, Part Two.*

1. Saw you the field? Came you from Shrewsbury?
2. Art thou not ashamed to be called captain?
3.   How doth my son and brother?
   Thou tremblest; and the whiteness in thy cheek
   Is apter than thy tongue to tell thy errand.
4. Thou'lt forget me when I am gone.
5. How chance thou art not with the prince thy brother?
   He loves thee, and thou dost neglect him, Thomas.
6. Heard he the good news yet?
7. Thou hast stolen that which after some few hours
   Were thine without offence.
8. Then get thee gone and dig my grave thyself.
9. Come hither, Harry, sit thou by my bed.
10. Indeed, I think the young king loves you not.
11. Thy life did manifest thou lov'dst me not,
    And thou wilt have me die assured of it.
12. A famous rebel art thou, Colevile.
13. Thou hid'st a thousand daggers in thy thoughts,
    Which thou hast whetted on thy stony heart.
14. Thou bring'st me happiness and peace, son John.
15. When thou dost hear I am as I have been,
    Approach me, and thou shalt be as thou wast.
16. What wouldst thou think of me if I should weep?
17. Why art thou not at Windsor with him, Thomas?
18. Thy wish was father, Harry, to that thought.
19. I stay too long by thee, I weary thee.

6. The Language in America

Just as the Angles, Saxons, and Jutes, a thousand years before, had brought to England a strange tongue that was to become the English language, so the English explorers and the settlers brought the English language to America. Although they did not realize it at first, they were laying the foundations of a different version of English—what can be called the American language.

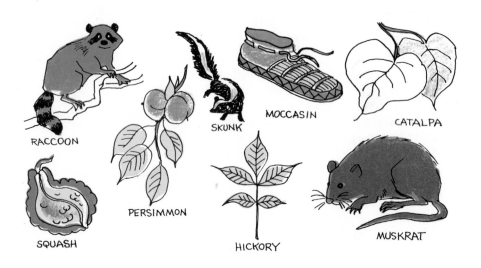

RACCOON PERSIMMON SKUNK MOCCASIN CATALPA SQUASH HICKORY MUSKRAT

Captain John Smith was among the first colonizers who added Native American words to English. These were words that described plants and animals the English had never seen before. By 1612 the colonists had borrowed words such as *raccoon, moose, opossum,* and *persimmon* from the Algonquin language; *raccoon* was originally *rahaugcum.* Before 1700 other settlers added more Native American words, including *skunk, moccasin, squash, hickory, catalpa, terrapin,* and *muskrat.* Most of these words, of course, did not appear at first in their present form, but they were quickly shortened and changed to suit English speakers.

The English also borrowed from other nationalities who had colonies in America. From the Dutch in New Amsterdam (later New York), they took the words (and probably the recipes for) *cookie, cruller, cole slaw, waffle,* and *pot cheese;* they also took *boss, spook,* and *Santa Claus.* Direct borrowings from the French settlers came into English in the eighteenth century: *chowder, levee, portage, prairie, crevasse.*

African languages contributed *goober* (a Southern word for "peanut") from *nguba,* and *gumbo* from *kingombo. Mosquito, cannibal,* and *cockroach* came from the Spanish; later, the Spanish-Americans added *poncho, ranch, burro, lariat,* and other words having to do with cattle raising and ranch life.

Backwoods settlers substituted rough-sounding terms for the tamer words they knew in England: *swampland, clearing, underbrush, bottom land, bluff, barrens, divide, rapids.* They built *log houses, spaded* the soil, ate *mush* and *roasting ears,* wore *snowshoes* in a *cold snap,* shot at *grizzly bears,* and frequently *flew off the handle.*

LEARNING ACTIVITIES

A. Look up the origins of these words. If your dictionary includes it, give the meaning of the source word. Write your answers.

1. bayou	5. hominy	9. pecan	13. bronco
2. caribou	6. sauerkraut	10. buccaneer	14. dollar
3. corral	7. tornado	11. lasso	15. rodeo
4. snoop	8. pemmican	12. tepee	16. sombrero

B. How many of these typically American words do you know? Match the words in the left column with the definitions on the right. Write down the matched pairs. The unabridged dictionary will help you.

1. galluses	a) a frying pan
2. to carry	b) cottage cheese
3. spider	c) suspenders
4. veranda	d) to carry something
5. buttery	e) a brook
6. to back	f) an Indian pony
7. to tote	g) to escort or conduct
8. cayuse	h) porch
9. branch	i) larder, pantry
10. smearcase	j) to address an envelope

A language, as has been pointed out, is a kind of history of the people who speak it. What can you learn about American history when you look up the following Americanisms? Consult more than one source, if possible. Discuss in class.

1. adobe	7. clearing	13. jerkwater
2. prairie	8. sweatshop	14. jaywalker
3. hoecake	9. carpetbagger	15. hot dog
4. forty-niner	10. skyscraper	16. sourdough
5. stampede	11. tycoon	17. sawbuck
6. stoop (porch)	12. leatherneck	18. vamoose

7. Other Sources of Words

How does a new word come into being? You have already seen many ways. Some words are borrowed from other languages; some are made up from parts of other languages. Sometimes words simply arise from nobody knows where. Many words that we use today "sprang up" at various times in Middle or Modern English. They were not borrowed from any other language, nor did they exist in Old English. Because they met an obvious need, they lasted as contributing members of our vocabulary.

Lad and *lass*, for example, were completely new words in thirteenth-century Middle English. The familiar *dad* was first recorded in writing in the sixteenth century. *Chum* goes back only as far as the seventeenth century, and *fuss*, only to the eighteenth century. *Slum* is a nineteenth-century creation, which is not surprising, since the bad effects of the Industrial Revolution were then beginning to be seen and felt in the cities of Europe.

Other words have been created by writers who took two well-known words and "blended" them into one new word. The word *smog*, for example, is a blend of *smoke* and *fog*. *Brunch* is the word for a meal that is neither breakfast nor lunch, but is a late breakfast eaten near lunchtime.

A. Of the words in each of the following pairs, one is of either Anglo-Saxon or Latin origin. Look up each of the pairs to see which word derives from a traceable source word and which word goes back only to Middle or Modern English.

1. job — work
2. blink — flicker
3. huge — big
4. jump — leap
5. wager — bet
6. crack — chink
7. pleasure — fun
8. child — tot (*noun*)
9. drizzle — mist
10. storm — blizzard
11. jaunt — journey
12. fit — adapt

B. From the unnumbered list of words, choose the two words from which each of the numbered blend words was created. Write the two words on your paper. Then compare answers in class.

1. chortle	motor	hotel
2. twirl	broadcast	snort
3. motel	twist	splash
4. newscast	chuckle	transfer
5. travelogue	happen	whirl
6. transistor	news	sputter
7. splutter	resistor	monologue
8. happenstance	travel	circumstance

ENRICHMENT

Try your hand at creating some new blend words of your own. You might create new names for things in your classroom or for possible new inventions or foods of the future.

8. Words Change Meaning

No dictionary can ever be completely up-to-date because growth and change in the meanings of words are continuous. Words enter the language. Some of them die out. A few keep the same meaning for hundreds of years. Most of them change their meanings.

When a word dies out, it does so because a new word comes along to take over the meaning that had belonged to the old word. When a word survives, one of three things may happen: (1) it may keep its old meaning intact; (2) it may add a new meaning and still keep the old one—the new and old meanings coexist; (3) it may change its meaning entirely, and the new meaning will take over as the old one is dropped. Patterns of change develop over a long period of time as meanings are either added or dropped.

WIDENING AND NARROWING OF MEANING

A word may change its meaning by becoming more general and less specific than it once was. This pattern of change is called *widening of meaning*. For example, the word *thing* in Anglo-Saxon used to refer to a gathering—in particular, a legal body of persons such as a court of law. Gradually the word came to include the idea of the case or issue brought to the court. Later, it widened to include the meaning of any action, statement, object, or idea. This growth of meaning was from something quite specific to something associated with it and then to something much more general. Today *thing* can refer to almost any object or idea. You can speak of "some *things*" or "*something* in general."

The word *picture* came from the Latin word meaning "to paint." Today it refers to anything visual, from a painting, drawing, or sketch to a photograph or even a "motion" picture. It can also carry an even wider, more general meaning, that of a large overview of a situation—as in the statement, "I get the *picture*."

Another word that began as a reference to something particular is the word *place*. Originally a term for the open market-place, or square, in a European town, its meaning has widened to refer to any physical space. It can also mean a position or a situation. You can say, "I feel like walking *someplace*," or "I stopped reading at this *place* on the page." You can also say, "This is the *place* where I was born," or even "It's not your *place* to say that."

A word can also develop in the opposite way. It can start out as a very general term and later come to be applied in a specific way. This pattern of change is called *narrowing of meaning*. The word *deer*, in Anglo-Saxon *deor*, is derived from

the Germanic word *Tier,* meaning "animal." For a long time it had that meaning in English. Today *deer* refers only to one specific kind of wild animal. Thus the word has narrowed in meaning.

In the Middle Ages the word *doctor* meant anyone who had studied at a university and received the degree of Doctor of Philosophy, whether that person had studied law, philosophy, or medicine. Today the word refers mainly to medical doctors. Here, too, the meaning has narrowed.

The word *person* (for a long time pronounced "par-son") came to mean not just any person, but one special person in a town—the one who could read and write, the minister who led the congregation. Thus developed the word we know today as *parson.* As *parson* split off to take care of its special area of meaning, the word *person* continued to exist with the meaning we know today.

Changes of meaning go on all the time. In present-day English, Americans use the word *bug* to mean any insect. In British usage, *insect* must be used for that general meaning, because *bug* means the bedbug.

LEARNING ACTIVITIES

A. Each of the words below is followed by two meanings, an early one and a more modern one. Decide how you think those meanings have changed over the time the word has been in use. Identify the meaning change as either widening or narrowing of meaning. Make this an oral activity.

1. meat—(1) any kind of food; (2) the edible flesh of animals
2. infant—(1) one who does not speak; (2) a baby
3. home—(1) the safe and comfortable place or atmosphere where one lives; (2) the physical house or apartment one lives in
4. manufacture—(1) to make by hand; (2) to produce in large quantities by human or machine labor
5. rent—(1) income from any source; (2) income from the use of one's property by others
6. stove—(1) a living room with heat; (2) a device for burning fuel for heat or cooking
7. town—(1) a fence around a garden or yard; (2) a group of houses and buildings where a large group of people live

8. nickel—(1) a hard, silver-white metal; (2) a coin made of copper and nickel equal in value to five cents
9. odyssey—(1) a long, Greek epic poem by Homer that describes the ten years' travels of Odysseus; (2) any series of wanderings and adventures
10. cafeteria—(1) a coffee shop, a place where coffee was drunk; (2) a self-service restaurant
11. companion—(1) one who shares bread (or a meal); (2) a friend who shares experiences with someone
12. luthier—(1) maker of lutes; (2) maker of stringed instruments

B. Using your school dictionary, look up the modern meaning of each of the following words. Compare that modern meaning with the original meaning of the word, given here in parentheses. Write on your paper whether you think the modern meaning illustrates a widening or a narrowing of the old meaning. Compare your answers in class.

1. bedlam (shortened name of an insane asylum in London, the Hospital of St. Mary of Bethlehem)
2. stereotype (a printing term for a metal plate cast from a mold of type)
3. garage (a storehouse for anything)
4. veal (calf)
5. champagne (a region of France)
6. corn (any kind of cereal grain)
7. undertaker (anyone who undertook to do something for someone else for money)
8. broadcast (to sow seeds widely in all directions)
9. devil's advocate (an official appointed by the Roman Catholic Church specifically to argue the case against elevating someone to sainthood)
10. alibi (a legal plea that someone was somewhere else, other than at the scene of a crime)

LOWERING AND RAISING OF MEANING

When words change, they sometimes take on meanings that are less noble or flattering than their original meanings were. The word *silly*, for example, once meant "holy" or "blessed." Today it is clearly not a term of praise. Similarly, *stench* once referred to any odor. Today it is associated only with a particularly offensive odor. To *garble* something once was to purify it by sifting out dirt or other impurities. Now it means

"WHAT A BEAUTIFUL STENCH THIS HAS."

to confuse or mix up information or statements, either un-intentionally or purposely.

Each of these words has shifted from a meaning people generally think of in a positive or neutral way to one that they generally regard as negative or unpleasant. A shift from a positive or a neutral meaning to a negative one is called a *lowering of meaning.*

Shifts in meaning can also go the other way. Words can become *raised in meaning.* To be *nice,* for example, once meant to be ignorant. Now the term, though quite vague, has the quality of approval. *Fond* once meant to be a fool; today it means "loving or affectionate." Both these descriptive terms have risen in meaning.

Examples of raising of meaning give interesting pictures of the social life of times past. A marshal and a steward today hold jobs that are quite respectable. Originally, however, the marshal was the "mare's fellow"—the groom who cared for the horses and shod them. Likewise, the steward was the keeper of the pigsty. The word *governor* came from a Greek word for boat pilot. Today the governor does quite a different kind of "piloting," for he or she is responsible for directing the welfare of a state.

The word from which the modern term *knight* originated in Anglo-Saxon meant a young servant relatively low on the social scale. Gradually the term came to refer to those given high rank for doing good deeds or for protecting royalty.

LEARNING ACTIVITIES

A. Each of the words below is followed by two meanings, an early one and a more modern one. Decide how you think those meanings have changed over the time the word has been in use. Identify the meaning change as either raising or lowering of meaning. Make this an oral activity.

1. brave — (1) scoundrel-like, mean; (2) courageous
2. naughty — (1) evil, wicked; (2) disobedient
3. cheat — (1) someone who looked after forfeited estates; (2) someone who defrauds or swindles
4. boor — (1) a farmer; (2) a rude, ill-mannered person
5. smug — (1) neat; (2) self-satisfied
6. sturdy — (1) harsh, stubborn; (2) strong, firm
7. cunning — (1) knowledgeable about something; (2) clever so as to deceive
8. knave — (1) a young boy; (2) a dishonest person
9. constable — (1) keeper of the stable; (2) a police officer
10. blackguard — (1) a member of the kitchen staff in a castle; (2) a contemptible person
11. homely — (1) simple, suited to the home; (2) ugly, plain
12. poison — (1) any potion or drink, often a medicine; (2) a drug or substance that destroys life

B. Using your school dictionary, look up the modern meaning of each of the following words. Compare that modern meaning with the original meaning of the word, given here in parentheses. Write on your paper whether you think the modern meaning illustrates a raising or a lowering of the old meaning. Compare your answers in class.

1. gossip (godparent)
2. churl (peasant)
3. peculiar (of one's own, as private property)
4. amateur (a lover of something, motivated by pleasure rather than profit)
5. petty (small, little)
6. chamberlain (servant who waited on members of the nobility in the bedchamber)
7. scavenger (a customs inspector)
8. villain (a farm hand)

ENRICHMENT*

One of the most interesting ways in which English words widened their meanings is illustrated in the development, during the Middle Ages, of words for groups of animals or insects. Inventing such terms began as a word game among people of leisure. Many of the terms were quite imaginative and even poetic, and "people of gentle birth" were expected to know them all. Thus, they were recorded in special manuscripts called *books of courtesy.* The terms numbered over a hundred, and many of these survive in the language today. Some familiar examples are a *flock* of sheep, a brace of pheasants.

A. Copy the numbered list of words below. Then, using a college dictionary, look up the words to see which of the animal groups in the right-hand column (identified by letters) each term describes. On your own paper, write the name of the animal or insect beside the term it applies to, until all the items in the columns have been matched. Some group terms may be associated with more than one species of animal. Some kinds of animals may be associated with two terms.

1. skein	*a*) partridges
2. pride	*b*) chicks
3. drove	*c*) seals
4. gam	*d*) geese
5. clutch	*e*) lions
6. school	*f*) locusts
7. skulk	*g*) sheep
8. pod	*h*) bees
9. covey	*i*) fish
10. swarm	*j*) foxes
11. plague	*k*) whales
12. gaggle	*l*) cattle

B. Players of the medieval word game invented many terms for groups of people, too. Among the early ones used, some of them quite humorous, were the following: a *congregation* of people, a *stalk* of foresters, a *slate* of candidates, an *eloquence* of lawyers, and a *skulk* of thieves. Modern writers continue to find this medieval word game interesting and enjoyable. New terms for groups of people of various occupations continue to be invented. Some of the newest contributions include a *shush* of librarians, a *horde* of misers, a *galaxy* of astronomers, a *nucleus* of physicists, and a *wince* of dentists. Try your hand at creating terms of your own for groups you are familiar with in your school or neighborhood or for other groups of professional people — doctors, teachers, coaches, and so on.

---

* Based on material from *An Exaltation of Larks* by James Lipton; copyright © 1968 by James Lipton. Published by Grossman Publishers, Inc., New York.

BUILDING GOOD LISTENING HABITS

1. Learning to Listen

READ AND THINK ABOUT . . .

It would seem that there are some people who have never learned to listen. Such people are so wrapped up in what they have to say that they cannot bother to listen to anyone else.

It is not much fun trying to carry on a conversation with someone who does not listen. Remember that fact the next time you are doing the listening, and really listen!

Listening is a skill. Because it is a skill, you must practice if you are to become really good at it. There is a difference between hearing and listening, though that idea may never have occurred to you before. Think about this, for instance: you can hear a new song being sung, but if you want to learn the words, you must really listen with your mind as well as with your ears. Listening means giving your full attention to a sound, whether that sound is an assignment by a teacher, directions from your parents, a play being called by a quarterback, or the song of a cardinal or a thrush. Hearing is, in other words, mostly a matter of the ear; listening is a matter of the ear *and* the mind.

GUIDES TO GOOD LISTENING

1. Think of the other person; keep your mind on what he or she is saying, and not on your own affairs.

2. Listen not only with your ears, but with your mind. As you listen, ask yourself such questions as these:

   a) What points or facts is the speaker trying to express?
   b) Is he or she sticking to those points?
   c) If someone should ask me later what was said, what things would I want to remember to tell? Would I be able to give both main points and important details?
   d) Where did the speaker get his or her information?
   e) Do I agree with the opinions expressed by the speaker? If not, why not?
   f) What questions would I like to ask? (When you have a chance, ask them!)

3. Show interest, even when you do not agree with what is being said. The interest expressed on your face will help the speaker to do a better job than he or she can do if you just sit back with a polite smile.

4. Do not try to listen and do something else at the same time. Listening needs your full attention.

Learn about words!

You will find the above heading often as you study this book. It calls your attention to certain words in the lesson — words with interesting histories. Remember that the history, or source, of a word is shown in the dictionary in brackets, like this: [   ]. Here are the first words for you to trace. They are taken from Learning Activity *C*.

sentence   fact   statement

LEARNING ACTIVITIES

A. Choose two members of the class to dramatize the conversation on page 27. Discuss what a person might do to become a better listener. (Guides 3 and 4 of the Guides for Holding Discussions, page 35, will help you to have a good discussion.)

B. Discuss this question in class: *Are there times when it is all right to interrupt?* If you think so, be ready to give an example and to tell how the interruption might be made courteously.

C. Write on a piece of paper a sentence containing facts about yourself or members of your family. Take turns at reading the statements aloud; read each sentence only once. Call on a classmate to repeat the statement word for word.

ENRICHMENT

A. Make a list of kinds of work that require good listening ability. Explain to the class why each kind of work on the list requires listening skill.

B. (1) Write an account of how you once got into difficulty by not listening. For help in paragraphing, turn to the guides on page 162. (2) Proofread your paper for errors in capitalization, punctuation, and spelling. (3) Using the Guides for Reading Aloud, page 59, prepare your story and read it to the class.

C. Prepare a short oral or written report on *sound*. You may need to use reference books and science books to get the information. If so, see the Guides to the Use of Reference Books, page 132. Let the Guides for Making a Long Report, page 143, aid you in preparing the report.

2. Listening to Learn

What "attention getters" besides those pictured above can you think of?

How do teachers get your attention when they want you to listen?

Do you listen attentively?

How much learning, do you think, comes through listening?

You learn when you listen to radio or television programs. You learn as you listen to reports or to announcements in class or in assembly. You learn a person's name when you are introduced. (How many times have you only heard a name and not really listened to it?) You learn as you listen to teachers giving directions and making explanations. You learn as you listen during class and group discussions, as well as during club meetings. You learn as you listen in conversations with your friends and family.

Yes, much learning comes — or can come — through listening. Let the following guides help you to form the habit of careful listening.

GUIDES FOR LISTENING TO LEARN

1. Listen carefully to oral directions and explanations.

   a) Take notes; they will help you to remember.
   b) Ask questions if necessary. If you are courteous, the speaker is not likely to mind being interrupted.
   c) Know the order in which directions are to be carried out.

2. Listen with full attention to assignments. Write in your notebook as much about the assignment as you can.

   a) Know the purpose of the assignment.
   b) Know how much material is to be covered.
   c) Know exactly how you are to do the work.
   d) Know when the assignment is due.

3. As reports are given in class, keep your mind on what is being said. Jot down anything that you want to be sure not to forget.

4. When an announcement is made, think about what it means to you in particular and to your class as a group.

5. During discussions, think about the ideas that are being presented. Apply guide 2 of the Guides to Good Listening, page 28.

LEARNING ACTIVITIES

A. In class, discuss the various postures and poses that people may assume when they are not listening attentively. Think of names for them, such as "Slumbering Slouch." List these names on the board.

B. In your small groups, make a list of situations, in school and out, in which you are a listener. Compare the lists in class.

C. For the rest of the day, be alert for ways that people attempt to get and hold your attention. Watch your classmates, teachers, members of your family, and radio and television speakers for examples that you can bring to class tomorrow. List the ways on the board.

D. (1) In a social studies or science book, find a paragraph containing five or six different facts. (2) Prepare a question dealing with each fact. (3) Read the paragraphs in your small groups. (4) Call on students to jot down answers to your questions as you read them. (5) Exchange papers for checking to see how many in your audience really listened.

USING ENGLISH IN ALL CLASSES

Listen carefully to the next lesson assignment in another class. Later, try to write out what the teacher said in making the assignment.

ENRICHMENT

Write a paragraph describing a situation in which a person can hear many sounds but must listen to only one or a few of the sounds. For instance, tell how one of the following might need this skill: *astronaut, hunter, doctor, detective.* For help with the writing, see the Guides for Writing a Paragraph, page 162. Read the paragraphs in class.

3. Building Good TV, Radio, and Film Habits

INTRODUCTORY ACTIVITY . . .

Suppose that a boy or a girl from some foreign country were to visit you for a month or so. Naturally you would want that visitor to get a good impression of you, your home, your hometown, and your country. What radio, television, and film entertainment would you feel proud to offer?

Consider only programs or films that you yourself have seen. Then, on a sheet of paper, list the following:

1. Three radio or television programs (aside from news broadcasts) that you honestly think would be worth your visitor's attention.

2. Three motion pictures that you feel would give a true-to-life idea of the United States.

When they have been completed, discuss the lists.

GUIDES FOR GOOD LISTENING AND VIEWING

1. See what newspaper critics say about motion pictures, television shows, and radio programs. These critics are likely to be more dependable than the advertising previews are.

2. Think critically about a program after you have heard it. Did it give you real pleasure or useful and interesting information; or did it leave you feeling let-down, discontented, bored?

3. Branch out; see what entertainment is being offered that you do not know about. Get variety into your listening and viewing.

LEARNING ACTIVITIES

A. List on the board the television and radio programs that members of the class follow regularly. Discuss the list in terms of variety or lack of variety. Be sure to include programs broadcast on noncommercial television.

B. In small groups discuss motion pictures that members have seen. Use guides 3 and 4 of the Guides for Holding Discussions, page 35. Make a group list of the reasons given for liking some films and disliking others. Be sure to write the reasons in complete sentences. Choose one person from each group to read the lists to the class. How much agreement is there?

C. (1) Bring to class newspaper clippings reviewing television shows, radio programs, and motion pictures. For comparison, clip also the advertisements for the same shows or programs. Have the clippings mounted on the bulletin board. (2) Write a paragraph pointing out the differences between a critic's review and the advertisement. If you saw the performance, tell whether you agree with the advertisement, with the critic, or with neither. Include other ideas you had about the performance. (3) Check your work by the Guides for Writing a Paragraph, page 162. Proofread your paragraph for errors in capitalization, punctuation, and spelling. (4) Exchange paragraphs for criticism.

TALKING WITH—AND TO—
OTHER PEOPLE

1. Holding Discussions

Can *you* answer the question? Is a table needed at all?
What *is* needed for a round-table discussion?

One of the best ways to practice good discussion habits is to
have a round-table discussion. You do not need a round table,
though. "Round-table" just means that the talking circulates
about the group and that everyone has a part in it. Sitting in a
circle or around a table seems to help, probably because everyone has a chance to see everyone else speak.

Although the words *conversation* and *discussion* are often used as if they mean the same thing, there are differences:

> A *conversation* is usually just an exchange of information about people or events.
>
> A *discussion* usually involves (1) a difference of opinion and (2) an attempt to solve a problem.

Many times, of course, a conversation will turn into a discussion.

GUIDES FOR HOLDING DISCUSSIONS

1. Select a topic.
   a) Be sure that it is of interest to the group.
   b) Choose a topic on which members of the group (1) have opinions and (2) can find information.
2. Choose one person to act as leader of the discussion. If you are the leader, follow these special guides:
   a) Call upon the various members of the group. (You may want to prepare a list of questions to ask them.)
   b) Keep the discussion moving.
   c) Hold the speakers to the point.
   d) Keep the discussion from becoming an angry argument.
3. Plan your part as a member of the group. Know what you will say and how you will say it.
   a) Jot down what you know about the topic.
   b) Look over your list and pick out the ideas that seem most important and most interesting.
   c) Arrange these ideas in the order in which you will speak of them. (The Guides for Outlining, pages 106–107, will help you.)
   d) Do not memorize what you will say.
4. Have the discussion.
   a) Be a good listener. (See the guides on page 28.)
   b) When you talk, speak plainly so that everyone can understand your words.
   c) Speak up with your ideas, but do not take more than your share of the time.
   d) Be thoughtful.
      (1) Do not interrupt a speaker.
      (2) If you disagree, do so politely. For example, say, "Ellen, I agree with you on most things, but . . ."

LEARNING ACTIVITIES

A. Divide the class into groups of seven or eight students. Have each small group get together in a corner of the classroom and, after choosing a leader, carry on a short round-table discussion on this topic: *How much control should parents have over the selection of television programs in the home?* After the discussions, the leaders will report the conclusions of their groups to the class. (For help in this activity, use the Guides to Speaking Clearly and Correctly, page 44.)

B. Let each small group plan, outside of class, a ten-minute round-table discussion to present to the class. Use the guides both in planning and in holding your discussion. Choose one of the following topics, unless you can think of another one that you would rather use.

1. How many school activities should seventh graders take part in?
2. Why do some people have trouble making friends, while other people seem to make friends easily?
3. How can we help students who are new in our class or our school?
4. What are the biggest problems in getting along with one's family?
5. What new areas might be included in our school curriculum?

After each discussion, take two or three minutes for the audience to point out good and bad features of the discussion.

USING ENGLISH IN ALL CLASSES

A. Perhaps your social studies teacher will let you have a round-table discussion in class on some topic of current interest or on one connected with whatever you are studying now. Plan the discussion carefully. Afterward, rate yourself and others by the Guides for Holding Discussions, page 35, and also by the Guides to Good Listening, page 28.

B. Science class is another good place for a round-table discussion if the teacher is willing. Plan it according to the Guides for Holding Discussions. Afterward, talk about the discussion in English class and rate it. Be sure to point out good features as well as poor ones.

FOLLOW-UP

Keep a record in your notebook of how you rate yourself on the items in point 4 of the Guides for Holding Discussions, page 35. Grade your performance, using marks such as *A, B, C, D*. Try to check yourself once a week on a discussion in one of your classes or on a discussion held outside school.

2. Building Good Conversation Habits

Have you ever lost your voice for a while? If so, you cannot have forgotten how hard on you it was to be able to speak only in a whisper. Why? The reason is that talking is the most common way that you have of expressing yourself to other people and of getting acquainted with them.

You cannot tell just by looking at a person that he or she enjoys swimming or has a movie camera or has been to Hawaii or builds model airplanes. But through talking, you may learn all those bits of information and many others that will make you want to know that person better. You may find out, too, that someone who may have made a poor first impression on you really is very much worth knowing.

GUIDES FOR CARRYING ON CONVERSATIONS

1. Never say things that might hurt or embarrass people around you.
2. If you disagree with something that is said, do so courteously.
3. Be patient; that is, do not interrupt a speaker. If you do not understand something that is said, wait until the speaker has finished and then ask a courteous question.
4. Include everyone in the group in your conversation. Look at each person in your group, not at just one or two of them.
5. Ask questions that will bring out the special interests of the others in your group; they may not care very much about *you* as a topic.

Learn about words!

The following words, taken from Learning Activity *A*, have interesting histories. Use your dictionary to find the story behind each word.

aunt   plan   ukulele   walk

LEARNING ACTIVITIES

A. Among the worst conversation habits you can have is that of being thoughtless of other people. Read silently and then dramatize the following three conversations.

CONVERSATION 1:

SUE: Mary and I went on a three-mile hike out in the country this morning.

JIMMY: Where did you go?

MARY: We went to Hipple's Grove.

JIMMY: To Hipple's Grove? Well, then you didn't walk three miles. Don't you know that Hipple's Grove is just one mile west of the schoolhouse corner? I thought everyone knew that.

MARY: Yes, we know it.

JIMMY: Well, then you walked only *two* miles, one out and one back.

SUE: But we didn't start from the schoolhouse corner; we started and finished at Mary's house. That's a half mile east of the schoolhouse.

JIMMY: Oh!

CONVERSATION 2:

JACK: Did you see the ball game yesterday afternoon?

BETH: Yes, I went with Sally and Fred. That pitcher for Salem was really good. He's the best pitcher I've ever seen.

JACK: You thought Simmons was good? I guess you haven't seen many real ball games. Why, he's terrible! He doesn't even have a good curve ball. Anybody should be able to tell that!

CONVERSATION 3:

(The place is the school playground on Friday morning. The characters are Jean, Alice, Maria, Kristin, Maya, Evelyn, Martha, Anne.)

JEAN: Don't forget our plan for tomorrow, Alice. You and Maria and Kristin come over to my house about ten, and we'll start from there.

ALICE: I hope it's cool. I'd like to wear the new red jacket my aunt sent me.

MARIA: If you wear your jacket, I think I'll wear my red sweater.

KRISTIN: Mother said she'd make some bread-and-butter sandwiches, and then we can buy some wieners.

MAYA: Are you girls going on a hike?

JEAN: I'll bring my ukulele, and don't you forget to bring your camera, Alice. Maybe we can take some pictures.

ALICE: I won't forget it. Come on; there's the bell.

B. Think about the following questions. Then discuss your answers in class. Be sure to keep in mind point 4 of the Guides for Holding Discussions, page 35.

1. In the first conversation, how does Jimmy impress you? In what way is he thoughtless? How could Jimmy have disagreed about the distance and yet done so courteously?

2. In the second conversation, what do you think of Jack? What is thoughtless in his remarks? How could Jack have shown courteously that he did not agree with Beth's opinion of the pitcher?

3. In the third conversation, what is thoughtless on the part of Jean, Alice, and Maria? Why do you suppose that Evelyn, Martha, and Anne kept still? (*Clue:* What happened to Maya?)

C. Act out the conversations again, only change them so that the *thoughtless talkers* become *thoughtful talkers*. They may still disagree with or doubt what is being said, but they will do so courteously.

D. Discuss the following questions in class. Be careful to apply point 4 of the Guides for Holding Discussions on page 35.

1. Why do you think that people often are less considerate when they are talking with their families than when talking with friends? Are they justified? If not, what can be done to improve the situation?

2. Do you ever have trouble in finding something to talk about to certain people? Why? What do you think you can do to get over that trouble?

E. Separate the class into small groups and hold conversations in which you compare your experiences in connection with one or more of the following topics. Keep in mind the Guides for Carrying On Conversations, page 37.

Picnics	Playing Badminton	Earning Money
Visits	Fourth of July Parade	Nicknames
Camping	Working on a Farm	New Classmates
Trips	Differences in Schools	Pets
Brothers	Changing Neighborhoods	Vacations
Sisters	Likes and Dislikes	Company

FOLLOW-UP

Think about the conversations that you have had today, at home or at school. Rate yourself as *good, fair,* or *poor* on each of the Guides for Carrying On Conversations, page 37. Write in your notebook any points that you need to work on; then concentrate on those points. From time to time, rate yourself again to see whether you are improving.

3. Facing an Audience Alone

Only one of the above speakers has good posture. Which one is it?

Which speakers are doing things that probably would keep an audience from paying close attention to what they are saying?

The human mind and body work closely together. If either one is not under control, the other is affected. A speaker who has not learned to feel "at home" before an audience cannot keep his or her mind on the subject. What is more, the audience cannot be expected to pay much attention to the speech.

Feeling at ease as a speaker — being poised — is something that can be learned. The following activities provide help toward that goal.

LEARNING ACTIVITIES

A. (1) When the teacher has called your name, or when you have volunteered for your turn, walk to the front of the room at an ordinary rate of speed. If you sit near the front of the room, walk to the back of the room first and then to the front of the room, going down one aisle and up the next. (2) When you get to the front of the room, turn to face the audience, but do not say anything. (3) Stand there for one minute and look at the different people in the audience. Your teacher or someone else will tell you when the minute is up. (4) Then, still taking your time, walk back to your seat. (5) After you sit down, list on a piece of paper as many things as you can remember noticing as you stood looking at the class. Do not look around; write from memory. Jot down such things as who was looking out the window, how many people were wearing glasses, and so on. Write until the next person has reached the front of the room. Then stop at once. Turn your paper face down. (6) After everyone has had a turn, compare your lists in class.

B. Repeat Activity *A*, only add to it. As you turn to face the audience this time, follow these additional instructions: (1) Let your hands drop easily to your sides. Do not put them behind you. (2) Stand with one foot slightly ahead of the other, and at a slight angle to it. Standing in this way will mean that your weight is evenly distributed so that you will not seesaw from side to side. Do not get behind or near furniture; there is too much temptation to use it for support. Do not lean against the wall or the board; leaning makes you look frightened and unsure of yourself. (3) When you are standing according to those directions, take a good look at the audience. This will also give the audience a chance to get a good look at you.

C. Repeat *B*, only this time let your classmates ask you three or four questions about yourself. Each person who wishes to ask a question will raise his or her hand, and you will call upon anyone you choose, one after the other. Keep the following points in mind:

1. People who do not know you very well will probably ask the best questions, since they really will want to learn things about you that your best friends already know. Those friends will cooperate by keeping their hands down while you are the speaker.

2. The audience should not ask questions to which they already know the answers.

3. The questions should be of the sort that you can answer at once, without having to stop to think: *when your birthday is, how old you are, how many brothers and sisters you have, who your nearest neighbors are, what pets you have, what your hobby is, . . .* In other words, they should be *fact* questions about you and your family.

4. In asking questions, be sure that you never ask any that you yourself would not like to answer. (In other words, be courteous and kind.)

5. Make each reply a sentence. Do not say, "Jack Allen Smith," but rather, "My full name is Jack Allen Smith."

After you have answered the questions, return to your seat. Take your time. Be careful not to start for your seat until you have finished speaking.

D. Actions help to make clear or more definite what a speaker is saying. Demonstrate that fact by showing what facial expressions and actions would fit the following lines. *Do not say the lines;* let the class decide which ones you are illustrating.

1. Please, won't you help me?
2. Hey! Come on back!
3. What is that up there?
4. Hello there! I'm delighted to see you.
5. How do you like my new shoes?
6. Listen to me!
7. What a mess this is!
8. I don't want anything to do with it!
9. Boy! Am I tired!
10. Who? You mean *me?*

4. Using Your Voice Well

MAKING YOUR OWN VOICE PLEASING AND EFFECTIVE

TALK IT OVER . . .

In class or in your small groups, discuss this question: "If you could trade your speaking voice for that of some radio or television performer, whose voice would you choose, and why?" Keep in mind that this would be the voice that you would have to use *all the time,* not just for a few minutes before an audience. List on the board the different reasons given for liking certain voices. What conclusions can you draw?

GUIDES TO A PLEASING, EFFECTIVE VOICE

1. Really open your mouth so that full, round tones can come out. (Your music teacher can help you.)
2. Avoid shrill, high-pitched tones. They are easily heard, but they are hard on the listener.
3. Avoid hoarse, harsh tones. They, too, bother the listener.
4. Vary your tone, emphasis, loudness, and speed in whatever ways will (*a*) make your meaning clear and (*b*) have on your listeners the effect that you want.

LEARNING ACTIVITIES

A. (*This exercise may be done at home.*) If your school does not have a recording machine, test the sound of your voice in this way: (1) Stand facing into a corner of a room, with your hands cupped behind your ears. (2) Speak a few words, perhaps your name, age, grade, and address. The way that your voice sounds to you will then be much the way that it sounds to other people. What you hear may surprise you. (3) If you do not like what you hear, try speaking in different tones.

B. Here are some sentences that make different impressions, depending upon how the lines are spoken. Take turns reading the sentences to indicate the feelings suggested in parentheses. (Do not tell your listeners which feeling you have in mind; let them decide.)

1. Don't leave. (*anger, fear, worry, sarcasm, sympathy*)
2. He turned out to be a fine friend. (*satisfaction, disgust, surprise*)
3. I wouldn't say that. (*indignation, worry, embarrassment, sarcasm*)
4. There they go. (*fear, envy, surprise, relief*)
5. He didn't believe a word I said. (*surprise, indignation, anger*)
6. She's my best friend. (*sarcasm, pride, satisfaction*)
7. I wonder what she meant. (*worry, puzzlement*)

C. Read the following sentence: *Give me that red apple.* By emphasizing a different word each time, say the sentence to give the following ideas:

1. I haven't the money to pay for it.
2. Don't give it to anyone else.
3. I want that one, not the one next to it.
4. I don't want the yellow one.
5. I'm not interested in the plums.

ENRICHMENT

In your reading or literature book, find a short poem or paragraph to read aloud to the class. Practice beforehand several times so that your delivery will show that you know and understand the Guides to a Pleasing, Effective Voice, page 42. If you choose a poem, the guides on page 48 may be helpful.

USING ENGLISH OUTSIDE SCHOOL

If you would like to improve the sound and range of your voice, practice much at home. Try saying the notes of the scale up and down, as high and as low as you can go without straining your voice. Repeat, using the words of a sentence, such as "I want to see what I can do." Practice imitating radio or television voices that you think are especially pleasing.

SAYING WORDS CLEARLY AND CORRECTLY

READ AND DO . . .

How good are your speech habits? Test them by repeating quickly, several times in succession, a tongue twister such as "A big black dog bit a big black bear." You will discover that the faster you say the words, the more mistakes you make.

GUIDES TO SPEAKING CLEARLY AND CORRECTLY

1. Use tongue, lips, and teeth to make your words come out plainly. Lazy lips turn "didn't you" into "dincha" and "want to" into "wanna," for example.
2. Breathe regularly and smoothly. Take a breath when you pause for punctuation.
3. Do not let your voice fade at the end of a sentence.
4. Finish one word before you begin the next, or your listeners may misunderstand you. For instance, you may think that you are saying, "He works on an iceboat," but your listener may hear this: "He works on a nice boat."
5. Be careful to pronounce words correctly. Make the dictionary your right-hand helper in checking and improving your pronunciation. (Pages 117–128 tell you how to use the dictionary.)

Learn about words!

The following words, taken from Learning Activity *D*, have interesting histories. Use your dictionary to find the story behind each word.

rage   polite   worry   charge

LEARNING ACTIVITIES

A. Careless speech is especially noticeable when a word that ends in *d* or *t* comes just before "you" or "your." (1) With a partner, practice the following combinations until you are sure that you are speaking each word separately. (2) Take turns in class at giving oral sentences containing these words.

didn't you	(not *didncha* or *didnchoo*)
can't you	(not *cancha* or *canchoo*)
won't you	(not *woncha* or *wonchoo*)
don't you	(not *doncha* or *donchoo*)
did you	(not *dija* or *dijoo*)
had you	(not *haja* or *hajoo*)
told you	(not *tolja* or *toljoo*)

B. Many little words are mispronounced because of a wrong vowel sound. The nine numbered words below are such words. (1) Practice pronouncing them in unison. (2) Take turns at reading the sentences that follow the words. (3) Make, and then practice saying, sentences of your own, using at least three of the listed words in each sentence.

	Rhyme	*Not a Rhyme*
1. can	ran	tin
2. catch	match	stretch
3. for	war	her
4. get	let	hit
5. just	must	best or list
6. meant	bent	hint
7. such	much	rich or stretch
8. when	den	chin
9. our	power	car

(*Practice sentences*)
 1. *Can* you *catch just* one game *for our* team?
 2. *Such* a plan would have *meant* that we could *get* there *when* you did.

C. In your literature book or in a library book, find a short sentence (one of about ten words) that has several words ending in *d*, *g* (but not *ing*), *k*, or *t* sounds. When you are called upon, go to the front of the room, turn your back to the class, and read your sentence in your ordinary speaking voice. If persons at the back of the room can repeat the sentence exactly, you are speaking plainly.

D. If the italicized words in the following sentences are not separated clearly, what might the listener think the speaker is saying? Take turns at reading the sentences. Your listeners will tell whether they think that your reading might be misunderstood.

EXAMPLE: Ted has *a name* like mine. (Ted has *an aim* like mine.)

1. I have *a notion* of my own.
2. *Her rage* really surprised me, but I tried to be polite.
3. I'd worry if I had to live in *an icehouse.*
4. *Our rally* is open to the public, free of charge.
5. Would you like to trade *your ache* for a different one?
6. *What all* people need is friendship.
7. May I have *some more?*
8. I have *an arrowhead.*
9. My name is *Ellen Elson.*
10. I should like you to meet *Stan LeRoy.*

E. Have a contest among the class, having each person read the following tongue twister aloud as fast as he or she can. After all have read, choose those who have made the fewest errors.

> Betty Batter bought some butter.
> "But," she said, "this butter's bitter.
> If I put it in my batter,
> It will make my batter bitter."
> So she bought some better butter,
> And she put the better butter in the bitter batter,
> And made the bitter batter better.

ENRICHMENT

In your school library, find other tongue twisters. Bring them to class and practice reciting them rapidly.

5. Enjoying Choral Reading

INTRODUCTORY ACTIVITY . . .

If you are lucky, you have already had fun with *choral reading;* that is, you have read poetry aloud as a class or in smaller groups. In that case, you know that poetry can do many things for you. A poem may hold you breathless with excitement as it tells an action-filled story. It may sing a song that keeps repeating itself in your mind. Always, the aim is to stir your imagination. Read the following poem together as marked, applying the italicized directions at the right.

In Time of Silver Rain

Group 1
In time of silver rain   [*Quietly.*]
The earth
Puts forth new life again,

Group 2
Green grasses grow   [*With energy.*]
And flowers lift their heads,

Group 3
And over all the plain   [*Strongly.*]
The wonder spreads   [*Slowly, deliberately.*]

Group 1
Of life,   [*Quiet but joyous.*]

Group 2
of life,   [*More volume.*]

Group 3
of life!   [*With great energy.*]

Group 1
In time of silver rain   [*Lightly, quickly.*]
The butterflies lift silken wings
To catch a rainbow cry,

Group 2
And trees put forth   [*With energy.*]
New leaves to sing
In joy beneath the sky

Group 3
As down the roadway passing boys
And girls go singing, too,

Group 1
In time of silver rain   [*Quietly.*]

Group 2
When spring
And life

Group 3
are new.

— LANGSTON HUGHES*

You can have fun reading poems together even if doing so is new to you. Following the simple guides below will help you to get real satisfaction out of reading together.

GUIDES FOR CHORAL READING

1. Read the poem carefully; look up the meanings of any words you do not know.

2. Talk over what you think the basic mood of the poem is.

3. Break a poem into as many group and solo parts as will help you to express it well.

4. Let your voices show the mood of the poem.

   a) Speak sad, gloomy, or serious lines, as a rule, in low-pitched tones and at a slow rate.

   b) Speak light, amusing, or exciting lines with a higher pitch and at a faster rate.

5. Speak clearly; do not run words together.

6. Practice to get the "feel" of the poem. Establish a rhythm and tempo so that the words will be easily and clearly spoken by each group.

LEARNING ACTIVITIES

A. Here is a short poem that is good for two groups that "answer" each other. Practice reading it so that you can say it from memory.

A WORD

Group 1
A word is dead   [*Quietly, wonderingly.*]
When it is said,
Some say.

Group 2
I say it just   [*Firmly, with joy.*]
Begins to live
That day.

—EMILY DICKINSON*

* "A Word," poem 1212, from *The Complete Poems of Emily Dickinson* edited by Thomas H. Johnson; copyright, © 1960, by Mary L. Hampson. Adapted for choral reading and reprinted by permission of Little, Brown and Company, Boston.

B. Here is a good "mood" poem. As you read it, your hearers should feel the depth and the mystery of a great river. Read it as marked. Practice until you can say it from memory.

TIDE IN THE RIVER

All

Tide in the river,   [*Make it slow and*
Tide in the river,   *rhythmic.*]
Tide in the river runs deep.

I saw a shiver   [*Say the first two lines*
Pass over the river   *lightly and quickly. Make*
As the tide turned in its sleep.   *the last line slow and soft.*]

— ELEANOR FARJEON*

C. (1) Divide the class into two equal groups. (2) In each group, study the following picture poem to get the "feel" of it. (3) Assign the solo parts and practice reading the poem, following the suggestions at the right of the lines. (4) Listen carefully as the other group reads. (5) Discuss the performances critically but courteously. (See guide 4 on page 35.)

FIVE EYES

Deep Voices
In Hans' old mill his three black cats   [*Slowly. Low pitch,*
Watch the bins for the thieving rats.   *all one tone.*]

Light Voices
Whisker and claw, they crouch in the night,   [*High and fast.*]
Their fire eyes smouldering green and bright: [*Draw out* green.]

Solo 1   *Solo 2*
Squeaks from the flour sacks,   squeaks from where   [*High, quick voices.*]

Deep Voices
The cold wind stirs on the empty stair,   [*Slow.*]

Light Voices
Squeaking and scampering, everywhere.   [*Fast.*]

Solo 1   *Solo 2*
Then down they pounce,   now in, now out,

Light Voices
At whisking tail, and sniffing snout;

---

* "Tide in the River," adapted for choral reading, from *Gypsy and Ginger* by Eleanor Farjeon. Published by E. P. Dutton & Co., Inc., New York, 1920.

Deep Voices
While lean old Hans he snores away   [*Draw out* snores.]

Light Voices
Till peep of light at break of day;   [*High and soft.*]

Deep Voices
Then up he climbs to his creaking mill,   [*Make it* creak.]

Light Voices
Out come his cats all grey with meal —   [*Quickly.*]

Solo 1   Solo 2   Solo 3
Jekkel,   and Jessup,   and one-eyed Jill.   [*Pause between solos.*]

—Walter de la Mare*

D. Read the following poem as marked. It offers practice in small group and unison choral reading. Study it, assign parts, and prepare the poem for reading. Although simple and straightforward, it demands good, strong delivery.

To the Wayfarer

Solo Voice (Narrator)
This is a poem that is placed on trees   [*Straightforward, simple.*]
    in the forests of Portugal

All
Ye who pass by and would raise your hand   [*Strong, quiet warning.*]
    against me, hearken ere you harm me.

Small Group 1
I am the heat of your hearth on the cold   [*Build each of these next*
    winter nights,   *three lines.*]

Small Group 2
the friendly shade screening you from
    summer sun,

Small Group 3
and my fruits are refreshing draughts,
    quenching your thirst as you journey on.

Small Group 1
I am the beam that holds your house,   [*Build these four lines.*]

---

* "Five Eyes," adapted for choral reading, from *Peacock Pie: A Book of Rhymes* by Walter de la Mare. Published by Constable and Company Ltd., London, 1921.

Small Group 2
the board of your table,

Small Group 3
the bed on which you lie,

Small Group 4
the timber that builds your boat.

Small Group 1
I am the handle of your hoe,   *[Build these four lines.]*

Small Group 2
the door of your homestead,

Small Group 3
the wood of your cradle,

Small Group 4
and the shell of your coffin.

Groups 1 and 2
I am the bread of kindness and the   *[Simple, slow delivery.]*
   flower of beauty.

Groups 3 and 4
Ye who pass by, listen to my prayer: *[A statement, not a plea.]*

All
harm me not.   *[Strong, quiet, final warning.]*

— AUTHOR UNKNOWN*

E. Read the following poems and discuss in class how you feel the various parts could be interpreted. After you decide on a plan, assign parts, and practice reading each poem aloud.

GROWTH

Solo Voice
age three

Group 1
there was no past for me

Solo Voice
age five

* "To the Wayfarer," adapted for choral reading, from *The Arbuthnot Anthology of Children's Literature;* copyright © 1976 Scott, Foresman and Company, Glenview, Illinois.

Group 2
my past went back to yesterday

Solo Voice
age seven

Group 3
my past went back to topknotted samurai*

Solo Voice
age eleven

Group 4
my past went back to dinosaurs

Solo Voice
age fourteen

Groups 1 and 2
my past agreed with the texts at school

Solo Voice
age sixteen

Groups 3 and 4
I look at the infinity of my past with fear

Solo Voice
age eighteen

All
I know not a thing about time

— TANIKAWA SHUNTARŌ†

THAT WAS SUMMER

All
Have you ever smelled summer?
Sure you have.

Group 1
Remember that time
when you were tired of running
or doing nothing much

---

* Member or members of the military class in feudal Japan; an honored profession.

† "Growth" by Tanikawa Shuntarō, translated by Harold P. Wright. Originally published in *Chelses*, 30/31, 1972. Reprinted by permission of The Asia Society, New York.

Group 2

and you were hot
and you flopped right down on the ground?
Remember how the warm soil smelled

Solo 1

and the grass?
That was summer.

Group 2

Remember that time
when you were trying to climb
higher in the tree
and you didn't know how

Group 1

and your foot was hurting in the fork
but you were holding tight
to the branch?

Four Voices

Remember how the bark smelled then —
all dusty dry, but nice?
That was summer.

Group 1

Remember that time
when the storm blew up quick
and you stood under a ledge
and watched the rain till it stopped

Group 2

and when it stopped
you walked out again to the sidewalk,

Solo 2

the quiet sidewalk?

Group 2

Remember how the pavement smelled —

Solo 3

all steamy warm and wet?
That was summer.

Group 1

If you try very hard
can you remember that time
when you played outside all day
and you came home for dinner
and had to take a bath right away,

Solo 4

right away?

Group 2

It took you a long time to pull
your shirt over your head.

Four Voices

Do you remember smelling the sunshine?

Group 1

That

All

was summer.

— MARCI RIDLON*

F. Here is a longer poem, one that almost says itself. (1) Read the introduction; (2) read the poem silently; (3) assign parts; (4) practice reading.

[*Sir Francis Drake was a great English fighter who defeated the Spanish in many sea battles during the early days of settlement in the New World. Drake was a pirate, but he loved England. When he lay dying, far away from home, he said to his men, "Take my drum to England. Hang it in Plymouth on the old sea wall. If England needs me, no matter when, strike that drum—and I'll come, living or dead!" More than two hundred years later, England was fighting for its life against the French. A new hero, Lord Horatio Nelson, with a shriveled arm and only one eye, came to England's rescue and won a great sea battle over the French.* . . . Or WAS it really Lord Nelson?]

THE ADMIRAL'S GHOST

Group 1

I tell you a tale tonight   [*Softly, slowly,*
  Which a seaman told to me,   *mysteriously.*]
With eyes that gleamed in the lanthorn †light [*Draw out*
  And a voice as low as the sea.   gleamed.]

Group 2

You could almost hear the stars   [*Very softly;*
  Twinkling up in the sky,   *slowly.*]

Group 1

And the old moon woke and moaned in the spars, [*Draw out*
  And the same old waves went by,   moaned.]

---

* "That Was Summer" by Marci Ridlon; copyright © 1969 by Marci Ridlon. Adapted for choral reading and reprinted by permission of the author.
†**lanthorn:** old spelling of *lantern.*

Group 2

Singing the same old song   *[Slowly and*
  As ages and ages ago,   *smoothly.]*

Group 1

While he froze my blood in that deepsea night   *[Low; draw out*
  With the things that he seemed to know.   froze.]

Group 2

A bare foot pattered on deck;   *[Quickly.]*

Group 1

  Ropes creaked — then all grew still,   *[Pause after*
And he pointed his finger straight in my face   creaked.]
  And growled, as a sea dog will.

Solo 1

"Do 'ee know who Nelson was?   *[Half-whisper.]*
  That pore little shriveled form
With the patch on his eye and the pinned-up sleeve
  And a soul like a North Sea storm?   *[Strongly.]*

Solo 2

"Ask of the Devonshire *men!   *[Slowly and*
  They know, and they'll tell you true;   *seriously.]*
He wasn't the pore little chawed-up chap
  That Hardy †thought he knew.

Solo 3

"He wasn't the man you think!   *[Faster.]*
  His patch was a dern disguise!   *[Mysteriously.]*
For he knew that they'd find him out, d'you see,
  If they looked him in both his eyes.

Solo 4

"He was twice as big as he seemed;   *[Seriously.]*
  But his clothes were cunningly made,   *[Pause after*
He'd both of his hairy arms all right!   made *and*
  The sleeve was a trick of the trade.   right.]

Solo 5

"You've heard of sperrits, ‡no doubt;   *[Mysteriously*
  Well, there's more in the matter than that!   *and very*
But he wasn't the patch and he wasn't the sleeve,   *seriously.]*
  And he wasn't the lace cocked-hat.

***Devonshire** (dev′ən shir): Sir Francis Drake's home was in that part of England.
†**Hardy:** He was Nelson's flag-captain on the *Victory* in the Battle of Trafalgar, the fight referred to in the introduction.
‡**sperrits:** spirits; ghosts.

Group 2

"Nelson was just—a Ghost!   [*Half-whisper.*]

Group 1

You may laugh! But the Devonshire men   [*Show that you*
They knew that he'd come when England called,   *really believe*
And they know that he'll come again.   *the lines.*]

Solo 6

"I'll tell you the way it was   [*Confidentially.*]
   (For none of the landsmen know),
And to tell it right you must go a'starn
   Two hundred years or so.

·   ·   ·   ·   ·   ·   ·   ·   ·   ·   ·   ·   ·   ·   ·

Solo 7

"The waves were lapping and slapping   [*Slowly and*
   The same as they are today;   *softly.*]
And Drake lay dying aboard his ship   [*Solemnly.*]
   In Nombre Dios Bay.*

Group 2

"The scent of the foreign flowers   [*Softly and*
   Came floating all around;   *lightly.*]

Group 1

'But I'd give my soul for the smell of the pitch,'   [*Emphatically.*]
   Says he, 'in Plymouth Sound.†
"'What shall I do,' says he,   [*Seriously.*]
   'When the guns begin to roar,   [*Make them roar!*]
An' England wants me, and me not there   [*Anxiously.*]
   To shatter her foes once more?'

Solo 8

("You've heard what he said, maybe,   [*Quietly and*
   But I'll mark you the points again;‡   *seriously.*]
For I want you to box your compass right
   And get my story plain.)

Group 1

"'You must take my drum,' he says,   [*Slowly and*
   'To the old sea wall at home;   *solemnly.*]
And if ever you strike that drum,' he says,   [*Faster; pause*
   'Why, strike me blind, I'll come!   *after* blind.]

---

* **Nombre Dios** (nôm′brä dē ōs′) **Bay:** bay on north coast of Panama.
† **Plymouth Sound:** Plymouth was Drake's home port.
‡ **I'll mark you the points again:** I'll tell you again.

"'If England needs me, dead
   Or living, I'll rise that day!
I'll rise from the darkness under the sea
   Ten thousand miles away.'

     Solo 9

"That's what he said; and he died;
   And his pirates, listenin' roun'
With their crimson doublets and jewelled swords
   That flashed as the sun went down,

     Group 2

"They sewed him up in his shroud
   With a round-shot top and toe,
To sink him under the salt sharp sea
   Where all good seamen go.

     Group 1

"They lowered him down in the deep
   And there in the sunset light
They boomed a broadside over his grave,
   As meaning to say 'Good night.'

     Group 2

"They sailed away in the dark
   To the dear little isle they knew;

     Group 1

And they hung his drum by the old sea wall
   The same as he told them to.

• • • • • • • • • • • • •

     Group 2

"Two hundred years went by,
   And the guns began to roar,
And England was fighting hard for her life,
   As ever she fought of yore.

     Solo 10

"'It's only my dead that count,'
   She said, as she says today;
'It isn't the ships and it isn't the guns
   'Ull * sweep Trafalgar's Bay.' †

*'Ull:** that will.

†**Trafalgar's** (trə fal'gərz) **Bay:** off the southwest coast of Spain; the scene of
  the naval battle (1805) in which the British defeated the French and the
  Spanish fleets to make Britain ruler of the seas. Nelson met his death here.

Right-margin directions:

[*Do not drop
voices or pause
after* dead.]
[*Draw it out.*]

[*Pause after*
said.]
[*Draw out* crimson
and jewelled.]

[*Make the
picture sharp
and clear.*]

[*Slowly and
solemnly.*]
[*Make it* boom.]

[*Softly.*]

[*Slowly and
seriously.*]

[*Draw it out.*]
[*Make them roar.*]

[*Seriously.*]

Solo 11

"Do you guess who Nelson was?   [*Mysteriously;*
    You may laugh, but it's true as true!   *pause after the*
There was more in that pore little chawed-up chap   *first* was.]
    Than ever his best friend knew.

Group 1

"The foe was creepin' close   [*Softly and*
    In the dark to our white-cliffed isle;   *breathlessly.*]

Group 2

They were ready to leap at England's throat,   [*Make them* leap.]
    When—O, you may smile, you may smile;   [*Pause after* when.]

Group 1

"But—ask of the Devonshire men;   [*Mysteriously;*
    For they heard in the dead of night   *pause after* But.]

Group 2

The roll of a drum, and they saw *him* pass   [*Draw out* roll.]
    On a ship all shining white.   [*Draw out* shining.]

Solo 12

"He stretched out his dead cold face   [*Make it* dead
    And he sailed in the grand old way!   *and* cold.]
The fishes had taken an eye and an arm,
    But he swept Trafalgar's Bay.

All

"Nelson—was Francis Drake!   [*Triumphantly;*
    O, what matters the uniform,   *long pause*
Or the patch on your eye or your pinned-up sleeve,   *after* Nelson.]
    If your soul's like a North Sea storm?"

—ALFRED NOYES*

FOLLOW-UP

Set aside at least part of one English or literature period a week for enjoying poems through choral reading. Let a different committee be responsible each week for choosing a selection and planning how it is to be read. Use poems from your literature book or others that you find. Here are the titles of some poems that are fun to do. The card catalogue in the library (see page 136) will help you find these poems.

* "The Admiral's Ghost," adapted for choral reading, from *Collected Poems in One Volume* by Alfred Noyes. Published by J. B. Lippincott Company, Philadelphia, 1906.

"The Mouse That Gnawed the Oak Tree Down" by Vachel Lindsay
"P. T. Barnum" by Rosemary and Stephen V. Benet
"Rhyme of Johnny Appleseed" by Nancy Byrd Turner
"The Sniffle" by Ogden Nash
"Matilda" by Hilaire Belloc
"Tubby Hook" by Arthur Guiterman
"What is pink? a rose is pink" by Christina Rossetti

6. Reading Aloud

READ AND THINK ABOUT . . .

Did you ever daydream about holding an audience spell-bound? Not everyone can be an audience spellbinder, but the following guides can help you to become a better oral reader.

GUIDES FOR READING ALOUD

1. First read the material silently; be sure that you understand the meaning. Notice the punctuation marks, for they are clues to meaning. (They also indicate good places to catch your breath.)

2. Use the dictionary to check the pronunciation of any words that you are not sure of. Say them over until you *are* sure.

3. If possible, get a friend or a relative to hear you practice.

4. Except for some special purpose, read at a medium rate. You may read easy material faster than hard. Remember, though, that the faster you read, the more distinctly you must say each sound.

5. In reading to entertain—for instance, if you are reading to a little brother or sister—be as dramatic as you can.

    a) Look for words that are clues to the impression the author wants to make. Say those words in a way that will help to give the right effect.

    b) Speak in a different voice for each character.

    c) Suit your speed to the mood. Speed up for exciting action; slow down for gloomy or peaceful scenes.

6. If you get "stuck," just stop—and then go on. Do not back up or say the same words over and over.

7. Hold the book or paper so that the audience can see your face as you read. Look at them, or they will feel that you are reading only to yourself.

LEARNING ACTIVITIES

A. Here are some famous lines from literature. (1) Talk about them in class or in your small groups to decide what point the author is making. (2) Take turns reading the lines aloud. (3) Listen closely so that you can express an opinion about one another's performance and can offer suggestions for better bringing out the author's meaning. Remember to look first for what is good about a classmate's reading.

1. Tolerance is good for all, or it is good for none. — EDMUND BURKE
2. Those who do not complain are never pitied. — JANE AUSTEN
3. Live always in the best company when you read. — SYDNEY SMITH
4. Civility costs nothing and buys everything.
   — LADY MARY WORTLEY MONTAGU
5. A community is like a ship; everyone ought to be prepared to take the helm. — HENRIK IBSEN
6. The reward of a thing well done, is to have done it.
   — RALPH WALDO EMERSON
7. Nature has given us two ears but only one mouth.
   — BENJAMIN DISRAELI
8. Give what you have. To someone, it may be better than you dare to think. — HENRY WADSWORTH LONGFELLOW
9. Animals are such agreeable friends — they ask no questions, they pass no criticisms. — GEORGE ELIOT
10. Parents are apt to be foreigners to their sons and daughters.
    — GEORGE WILLIAM CURTIS
11. Some people are so fond of ill-luck that they run half-way to meet it.
    — DOUGLAS JERROLD
12. What small potatoes we all are, compared with what we might be!
    — CHARLES DUDLEY WARNER
13. No one can make you feel inferior without your consent.
    — ELEANOR ROOSEVELT
14. A sharp tongue is the only edge tool that grows keener with constant use. — WASHINGTON IRVING
15. Education makes a people easy to lead, but difficult to drive; easy to govern, but impossible to enslave. — LORD BROUGHAM

B. Examine the following paragraph from Robert Louis Stevenson's *Treasure Island.* (1) Look first for any unfamiliar words; find out what they mean. (2) Look for words that give clues to the impression that the author wants to give. (3) Note the punctuation; see how it helps you to get the meaning. (4) Decide which words or sentences should be spoken faster than the rest. (5) Take turns at reading the paragraph aloud.

> . . . I suddenly put my hand upon my mother's arm; for I had heard in the silent, frosty air a sound that brought my heart into my mouth — the tap-tapping of the blind man's stick upon the

frozen road. It drew nearer and nearer, while we sat holding our breath. Then it struck sharp on the inn door, and then we could hear the handle being turned, and the bolt rattling as the wretched being tried to enter; and then there was a long time of silence. . . . At last the tapping recommenced, and to our indescribable joy and gratitude, died slowly away. . . .

C. All the paragraphs in this activity are taken from *Treasure Island.* Choose one paragraph and prepare to read it to the class. (1) Study the paragraph by yourself, as the class did in *B*. (2) Practice at home until you can look often at your audience. (3) Read the paragraphs in class or in your small groups. (4) Talk over the various readings, naming their good points as well as ones that could be strengthened. (Keeping your eyes closed as you listen to the readings will help you to judge them well.)

1. I remember him as if it were yesterday, as he came plodding to the inn door, his sea chest following behind him in a hand-barrow; a tall, strong, heavy, nut-brown man; his tarry pigtail falling over the shoulders of his soiled blue coat; his hands ragged and scarred, with black, broken nails; and the saber cut across one cheek, a dirty, livid-white. I remember him looking round the cove and whistling to himself as he did so, and then breaking out in that old sea-song that he sang so often afterwards:

> Fifteen men on the dead man's chest —
> Yo-ho-ho, and a bottle of rum!

in a high, old tottering voice. . . .

2. So things passed, until, the day after the funeral, and about three o'clock of a bitter, foggy, frosty afternoon, I was standing at the door for a moment, full of sad thoughts about my father, when I saw someone drawing slowly near along the road. He was plainly blind, for he tapped before him with a stick, and wore a great green shade over his eyes and nose; and he was hunched, as if with age or weakness, and wore a huge, old tattered sea cloak with a hood, that made him appear positively deformed. I never saw in my life a more dreadful-looking figure.

3. My heart was beating finely when my mother and I set forth in the cold night. . . . A full moon was beginning to rise, and peered redly through the upper edges of the fog, and this increased our haste, for it was plain, before we came forth again, that all would be as bright as day, and our departure exposed to the eyes of any watchers. We slipped along the hedges, noiseless and swift, nor did we see or hear anything to increase our terrors, till, to our relief, the door of the "Admiral Benbow" had closed upon us.

4. In I got bodily into the apple barrel, and found there was scarce an apple left; but, sitting down there in the dark, what with the sound of the waters and rocking movement of the ship, I had either fallen asleep, or was on the point of doing so, when a heavy man sat down with rather a clash close by. The barrel shook as he leaned his shoulders against it, and I was just about to jump out when the man began to speak. It was Silver's voice, and, before I had heard a dozen words, I would not have shown myself for all the world, but lay there, trembling, for from these dozen words I understood that the lives of all the honest men on board depended upon me alone.

D. Poetry is especially full of good "picture" words that suggest the mood or feeling that the author wants to give. (1) Study the following quotations from famous authors, noting especially the picture words. (2) Take turns reading the lines. (3) Listen with closed eyes; be ready to say what you think the reader feels are the picture words.

1. . . . and over them the sea-wind sang
   Shrill, chill, with flakes of foam. — ALFRED, LORD TENNYSON
2. The days were like hot coals; the very ground
   was burned to ashes; . . . — HENRY WADSWORTH LONGFELLOW
3. A sea shell is a palace
   Where many echoes dwell, . . . — DOROTHY VENA JOHNSON*
4. Over the cobbles he clattered and clashed in the dark inn-yard,
   And he tapped with his whip on the shutters, but all was
      locked and barred. — ALFRED NOYES
5. Deep asleep, deep asleep,
   Deep asleep it lies,
   The still lake of Semmerwater
   Under the still skies. — WILLIAM WATSON
6. A poem should be motionless in time
   As the moon climbs. — ARCHIBALD MACLEISH†
7. The misted early mornings will be cold;
   The little puddles will be roofed with glass. — ELINOR WYLIE‡
8. Strong gongs groaning as the guns boom far,
   Don John of Austria is going to the war, . . .
                                      — GILBERT KEITH CHESTERTON

* From "Palace" by Dorothy Vena Johnson. Reprinted from *Golden Slippers* compiled by Arna Bontemps, published by Harper & Brothers, New York, 1941.

† From "Ars Poetica" from *New & Collected Poems, 1917-1976* by Archibald MacLeish; copyright © 1976 by Archibald MacLeish. Published by Houghton Mifflin Company, Boston.

‡ From "Wild Peaches" from *Collected Poems of Elinor Wylie;* copyright 1932 by Alfred A. Knopf, Inc., New York.

Begin a special section in your notebook in which you put lines of poetry that make you see pictures or that appeal to you for their sound. Reread them often—and soon they will be in your memory to stay.

7. Making and Using a Speech Chart

READ AND DO . . .

Make and file in your notebook a speech chart similar to the following one. Draw as many columns as your sheet of paper will allow.

(Do not write in this book.)

Speech Chart

Name   Date

Speech Number	1	2	3	4	5	
1. Waited until audience was ready?						
2. Looked at the audience?						
3. Stood properly?						
4. Knew what to do with hands?						
5. Finished before starting to seat?						
6. Spoke in a pleasant voice?						
7. Spoke distinctly and not too fast?						
8. Used correct pronunciation?						
9. Had interesting material?						
10. Knew material well?						

RATING THE SPEAKER

Prepare a supply of slips of paper about 2½ x 3 inches. Keep them on hand for use as follows:

1. When a person gives a talk, write his or her name at the top of a slip.
2. Write on each slip the words and numbers shown on the left-hand sample below.
3. When a speaker begins, put your pencil down and *listen*.
4. When the person has finished, rate him or her on the slip.
    a) Use the following key: *G*—good; *F*—fair; *P*—poor. Remember, be as fair and accurate as you can. It does not help to mark a friend *good* when you know that he or she is poor.
    b) Jot down at the bottom of the slip any special comments.
    c) Sign your name or your initials at the foot of the slip. The right-hand example shows how a marked slip will look.
5. Pass the slips to the speaker after each speech. He or she should not look at them, but should place them face down until all the speeches are over.

Speaker _____		Speaker *Regina* _____	
1.	6.	1. G	6. P
2.	7.	2. G	7. P
3.	8.	3. F	8.
4.	9.	4. F	9.
5.	10.	5. G	10.

Comments:

Comments:
You are doing better at looking at the audience.

N.C.

MARKING AND USING YOUR SPEECH CHART

Your teacher will probably give you the last five minutes or so of the period for marking your Speech Chart.

1. Take the slips handed to you and go over them carefully.
2. Use them as a guide in rating yourself on your own Speech Chart. For example, if you had ten *G*'s, eight *F*'s, and no *P*'s on one point, mark yourself *F+*.
3. When you next prepare a speech, choose and work on one point on which you received a low mark.
4. Next time, choose another weak point and work on that. Practice to master one weakness at a time.

Never compare your record with that of others. Always compare your score with your own past record, and work hard for improvement. If you are improving, you are doing well.

LEARNING ACTIVITIES

A. You will be given five minutes in which to plan a short talk about yourself. Jot down such things as your favorite color, foods, sports, hobbies, pets, and so on. At the end of the five minutes, you will be called upon to talk. Remember to take your time, to look at the audience, and to stand correctly. Go over the Guides to a Pleasing, Effective Voice, page 42.

Members of the audience should rate each speech by items on the Speech Chart and then pass the slips of paper to the speaker. When you are given time, mark your Speech Chart. Notice where you need to improve.

B. Prepare a short talk on a book that you have read or a motion picture that you have seen recently. Work especially on some point that your Speech Chart shows you are weak in. Mark your chart again after this talk, as in Activity *A*. In what ways have you improved? If you have not improved, do not be discouraged. You *can* improve if you keep trying.

SPEAKING IN LIFE SITUATIONS

1. Making Clear Explanations

One Saturday a girl was out in the backyard showing a friend the willow whistle she had just made. When asked how she had done it, she said, "Oh, it's easy. You just take a piece of green willow, cut a slot in one end of the stick, slide the bark off, deepen the slot, and slide the bark back on. That's all there is to it."

The following day the friend came back. He complained, "I can't make a whistle like yours. The bark keeps splitting."

The whistle maker said, "It's easy, but maybe I didn't give enough details. I'll try again, and draw a few pictures.

"(1) Cut a piece of green willow about five inches long and a half-inch thick. (2) With a knife, cut around the stick about two inches from one end. Cut just through the bark, no deeper. (3) Cut a slanting notch as shown in drawing 3 one inch from the same end. (4) With the handle of your knife, tap the bark lightly on the short end of the stick until you have loosened the bark enough to slide it off the stick all in one piece. (5) Slice a layer about an eighth of an inch thick from the short end to the notch, as in drawing 5. (6) Deepen the notch as shown in drawing 6. (7) Moisten the stick, slide the bark back on, and your whistle is ready."

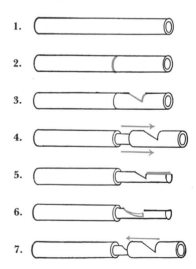

In what ways is the second explanation more helpful than the first one?

Many times you will need to explain something orally. The suggestions in the guides that follow will aid you in making clear, concise explanations that will satisfy your listeners.

GUIDES FOR GIVING CLEAR ORAL EXPLANATIONS

1. Be sure that you yourself understand and see clearly the thing that you are trying to explain. If you do not have all the facts necessary for a clear explanation, find them.

2. Make an outline that includes *in the right order* every necessary step or detail. (See pages 106–107 for help in outlining. A topic outline probably will be easiest to make and use.)

3. Put your explanation into words that your hearers can understand. Explain any words that you think may be puzzling.

4. As you give the explanation, follow your outline *exactly.*

5. Use drawings or charts wherever they will help.

6. In explaining orally, give listeners a chance to ask questions.

LEARNING ACTIVITIES

Directions: Here are some exercises in making explanations. Activity *A* will test how well you can make explanations right now. The others offer practice in improving your ability to make explanations.

A. Below is a list of topics. You probably know something about most of them. Choose a topic and prepare to explain it at the end of ten minutes. Rate the explanations by the Speech Chart, page 63.

Explain how one of these is handled in your school. You may prefer to explain something else suggested by this list.

1. Absences and tardinesses	8. Bells and buzzers
2. The school library	9. Gym classes
3. The grading system	10. Clubs
4. Vacations and holidays	11. The school paper
5. The seating arrangement of your classroom	12. Fire drills
6. The school band	13. Assembly periods
7. The school patrol	14. The lunch hour
	15. The playground

B. In an oral explanation, tell how to make one of the items listed below, or something suggested to you by the list. *Choose something that you actually have made.* Plan and practice the explanation at home. Make an outline to help you (see the Guides for Outlining, pages 106–107). If possible, try the explanation on someone at home before you give it to the class. Apply the Guides to a Pleasing, Effective Voice, page 42, as you practice.

1. A neckerchief slide
2. An apron
3. Hand puppets
4. A birdhouse
5. A kite
6. A pocket telescope
7. A toy or puzzle
8. A knife sheath
9. A pair of stilts
10. Taffy
11. A stencil design
12. A dog bed
13. A relief map
14. A rabbit pen
15. A crystal radio
16. A crossword puzzle

C. In your small groups, explain how to do one of the things listed or something suggested by the list. Be certain that you know what each step is and just how one step follows another. Make a topic outline to help you, using the Guides for Outlining, pages 106–107. If possible, try your explanation first on someone at home. The listeners should rate the explanations by the Speech Chart, page 63.

1. Raising rabbits, chickens, hamsters . . .
2. Playing a certain game
3. Getting volunteers to help in a school or community project
4. Developing a roll of film
5. Earning merit badges in scouting
6. Repairing a bicycle tire
7. Blazing a trail
8. Teaching a dog tricks
9. Painting a room
10. Tying different kinds of knots
11. Making a bed
12. Cooking with charcoal
13. Cleaning fish
14. Building a campfire
15. Using a light meter
16. Preparing a seed bed
17. Mowing a lawn
18. Playing a musical instrument
19. Washing a pet
20. Collecting rocks

USING ENGLISH IN ALL CLASSES

If you must soon give an explanation of some problem or experiment in social studies, science, or arithmetic, let your English class help you to prepare a really good report. Use the Guides for Giving Clear Oral Explanations, page 67. Practice the explanation in English class; ask your classmates to suggest improvements that you might make before you give it in your other class.

2. Giving Oral Directions

A special explanation that you often need to make is the kind in which you give directions for reaching a certain place. If you have ever been lost, you know how important good directions are.

GUIDES FOR GIVING ORAL DIRECTIONS ACCURATELY

1. Find out first of all whether the person has his or her directions straight. *North, south,* and so on will not mean a thing if he or she is turned around. For example, it is better to say "Turn left" or "Turn right" than to say "Turn north."

2. Begin the instructions from the spot where the person will start.

3. Take each step in order.

4. Mention any landmarks or buildings that will serve as guides.

5. Make a sketch if you can do so clearly and accurately.

6. When giving oral directions, ask the person to repeat the directions after you to see that he or she has understood them correctly.

7. Give directions only if you are sure of the way. If not, say so politely.

LEARNING ACTIVITIES

A. Read the two sets of numbered directions. Which would be easier to follow? Which set agrees with the guides above? How does the other fail to agree with the guides? Be definite, and point out examples in a class discussion.

1. Our picnic will be in Turner's Woods. To get there from the schoolhouse, drive toward Route 58. Stay on Route 58 for quite a while, going east. Oh, no, I mean *north.* At last you will come to a dirt road. Take this till you come to Turner's Woods. Oh, I forgot to tell you, you'll cross Salt Creek when you're on Route 58.

2. Our picnic will be in Turner's Woods. To get there from the schoolhouse, leave by the main door and drive to the right.

The first stop street you will come to is Route 58. Turn left onto Route 58 and stay on it for about three miles, until you cross Salt Creek. A half mile farther on, you will reach a dirt road that goes to the right. This is not a crossroad. Take this dirt road for a half mile. The entrance to Turner's Woods is on the left side of the road and is marked.

B. Divide the class into pairs and let each pair choose one of the places listed below. Have each member of the pair, working alone, get ready to give directions to that place. Ask one member of the pair to leave the room while the other gives his or her directions. Then call in the second person to give his or her directions. The class will then discuss the two sets of directions, applying the Guides for Giving Oral Directions Accurately. Be critical but courteous; apply the points under guide 4, page 35.

1. The public library
2. A certain bank
3. The post office
4. A hospital
5. A nearby town
6. A neighboring farm
7. A swimming pool
8. The school nearest yours
9. The nearest filling station
10. Your own home
11. A park
12. The nearest shopping center
13. The police station
14. A certain picnic spot
15. A bus or railway station
16. The nearest drugstore

3. Following Oral Instructions

"I THOUGHT I DID WHAT LYNNE TOLD ME TO DO."

THINK IT OVER . . .

You have just spent some time in learning to *give* careful instructions and directions. It is just as important, and sometimes harder, to know how to *follow* instructions.

GUIDES FOR FOLLOWING ORAL INSTRUCTIONS

1. Be sure that you understand the purpose of the instructions.
2. Listen carefully. See guides 1 and 2 of the Guides for Listening to Learn, page 31.
3. Be sure that you understand exactly what you are to do, and how you are to do it. Ask questions if you do not understand.
4. Check every step to be sure that you did it correctly.

LEARNING ACTIVITY

For one week keep a daily record for each piece of work that you are given instructions for doing. Put a star beside each one that you completed exactly according to instructions. Your list need not be detailed. Something like this should be enough:

> January 17
> * arithmetic assignment
> science experiment
> errand for Mother
> * gym exercises

Follow the same plan the next week. Then compare the two lists to see whether you have improved. If not, keep on with the plan. Bring your lists to class and compare them.

4. Using the Telephone

READ AND THINK ABOUT . . .

Late one night Jim Reynolds awoke to the sound of his mother's voice calling him urgently. When he went to her room, he found her in great pain. "Jim," she said, "I have appendicitis. You'll have to call Dr. Blake."

Jim hurried to the telephone, wishing his father were not out of town. Anxious as he was, he took time to look up Dr. Blake's number; then he made his call.

Jim: (dialing) 623-4085
Dr. Blake: Dr. Blake speaking.

JIM: Dr. Blake, this is Jim Reynolds, Dale Reynolds's son. I'm sorry to call you so late at night, but Mother has a bad attack of appendicitis.

DR. BLAKE: I'll call an ambulance for her and meet you at City Hospital in fifteen minutes. Don't let your mother move until the ambulance gets there.

JIM: Thank you, Doctor. Good-by.

When he made that call, Jim showed that he had learned good telephone habits. Guides for building such habits are listed here. How well do you follow them?

GUIDES FOR TELEPHONING

1. Be careful to dial the right numbers. It is rude to make someone answer the telephone unnecessarily.

2. Speak clearly and slowly enough so that everything you say can be understood correctly. Keep your mouth about a half-inch from the mouthpiece.

3. Tell who you are.

4. Know beforehand exactly what you are going to say so that you will not waste time.

5. Be polite. Say "I'm sorry" and "Thank you" and "Please" and "You're welcome."

6. Be pleasant. Never lose your temper either with the person you are calling or with the operator, if you need help in locating a number or are calling person-to-person.

7. Call at times that will be convenient for those whom you are telephoning. Try not to interrupt their work, sleep, or meals.

8. When you answer the telephone and the call is for someone who is out or is unable to come to the telephone, say, "May I take a message?" Keep a pencil and a pad of paper near the telephone. After jotting down the information, repeat it to check whether you have taken the message accurately.

9. Turn down the radio or TV before using the telephone.

Telephoning is conversing. How to improve conversation skills is covered in section 2 of Chapter 3, pages 37–39. Summed up, the guides above repeat what is emphasized in that section on conversing: "Be thoughtful of others."

LEARNING ACTIVITIES

A. Read Jim's telephone conversation again. Which of the Guides for Telephoning did he follow? Which ones did he not follow? Did he have good reasons? Discuss those questions in class.

B. Plan a short explanatory talk on telephone manners. In your planning, review the Guides to Speaking Clearly and Correctly, page 44. Apply the Guides for Giving Clear Oral Explanations, page 67.

C. Working in small groups, dramatize one or more of the following calls, or any others that you would like to practice. In each call, use two or three persons: the person calling, the one being called, and the operator, if necessary. Each group should also be a committee to discuss the performance of one other group. The performers should be rated by the Guides to a Pleasing, Effective Voice, page 42, as well as by the Guides for Telephoning.

1. You are at home alone when a friend of your mother's calls to say that a meeting has been postponed. She tells why the change has been made, when and where the meeting actually will take place, and the time at which she will call for your mother. She adds, "Tell your mother to call me this afternoon if she has any questions." Jot down the information as she gives it. Afterward, repeat the message to see whether you have forgotten anything.

2. Your family plans to drive to a nearby park for a picnic supper. Call a friend and invite him or her to go with you. Be ready to supply any information that your friend may need, such as when you are going, when you will return, what you plan to wear, . . .

3. Call someone to make arrangements for a class trip. Be sure to write down all the details so that you can report accurately.

4. Call one of the following to get or to give some necessary information. If you are calling for information, jot down before you call exactly what you want to ask. Take down what you are told so that there will be no chance for a mistake.

a) A dry cleaner or a laundry	*f)* Your dentist
b) An airline	*g)* Your doctor
c) A motion-picture theater	*h)* A newspaper office
d) The electric company	*i)* A garage
e) A camera store	*j)* The zoo

ENRICHMENT

If you can, bring to class copies of any telephone directories. Notice their organization, the instructions for placing calls, and any other information given on the introductory pages. Read those pages carefully now, and then quiz one another until you are familiar with the help that they offer.

USING ENGLISH OUTSIDE SCHOOL

In class, work out a chart covering good telephone methods and manners. Make a copy for yourself. Fasten this above the telephone at home on a level with your eyes as you are telephoning. Seeing those points listed right there can help make good telephone manners a habit.

5. Introducing and Being Introduced

THINK IT OVER . . .

It is unnecessary to feel embarrassed when introducing people or being introduced, for the proper ways to make and to respond to introductions are simple. The following guides will help you to feel at ease in all introductory situations.

GUIDES FOR MAKING INTRODUCTIONS

1. Say *first* the name of the person you wish to honor.

   a) *Mother,* this is Shirley Hauser. (*A young person is introduced to an older one.*)

   b) *Mr. Jonas,* may I present Don Scott? (*This style is formal.*)

   c) *Ms. Smith,* I'd like you to meet my father. (*A man is introduced to a woman.*)

   d) Jack, this is our new classmate, Ted Vartelas. Ted, this is Jack Evans. (*These two boys are about the same age; either name may come first.*)

   Notice that in *a* and *c,* the speaker need not give his or her mother's or father's last name, since it will be taken for granted that their names are the same. In *d* both last names must be given.

2. Say each name so plainly that there will be no excuse for anyone to say, "I'm sorry, but I didn't hear your name."

3. If you are being introduced, listen carefully for the other person's name. Try to use it in your conversation.

4. If you are introducing two people who will be expected to go on talking for a time, help them to get the conversation started. For example, in connection with *d* above, you might say, "Ted shares your hobby, Jack. Tell him about the model plane I saw you making last night, Ted."

5. When you are introduced, say, "How do you do." It is a good idea to add the person's name to show that you understood it correctly, as "How do you do, Mrs. Blackmore." If you like, say, "I've been hoping to meet you," or something similar.

6. If you are a boy or a man, shake hands when you are introduced to another boy or man. Formerly, girls and women did not shake hands when boys or men were introduced to them. Today, however, handshaking is more common for women, especially in business situations. In any case, when someone extends his or her hand, you should accept it.

7. If you are a boy, rise for all introductions. Girls need to rise only when they are introduced to older people.

8. Never say, "Jane, meet Fred Smith," or "Jack, shake hands with Mary Brown," or "Pleased to meet you."

9. Never point to the people whom you are introducing.

10. To introduce one person to a group, say, "This is Irma Beck." Then indicate each person in the group and state his or her name.

A. In groups of three, dramatize the following introductions. In some of the introductions, have one of the persons seated.

1. Your father and a teacher (woman)
2. Your mother and a teacher (man)
3. Your cousin and your best friend
4. Your grandmother and one of your friends
5. A boy and a girl near your own age

The audience will judge each introduction. Did the people being introduced say and do the right things? Did the person who was making the introductions do so correctly? Be courteous and helpful.

B. If you feel that you need more practice, write possible introductions on slips of paper. Exchange these with your neighbors and make the introductions, choosing the people that you need to take the various parts.

6. Parliamentary Procedure

Well-run club or class meetings are likely to follow what are known as the rules of *parliamentary procedure*. Use the following section to help your class or club hold successful meetings.

Step 1

"The meeting will come to order. Will the secretary please read the minutes of the previous meeting."

Step 2

"The Speakers Club held its weekly meeting on January 27, 1978, in room 37 of Willard Junior High School. The meeting was called to order at 10:05 A.M. by Gary Katz, president. The secretary, Susan Brown, read the minutes of the January 20 meeting. They were approved. Steve Peppas, program committee chairperson, reported that Captain Ames of the fire department would be unable to speak at our February 3 meeting, but would come on February 17. Sue Ellis moved that the club write a thank-you letter to Mr. Gentry, Mildred's father, for his help with last week's program. The motion was carried. A committee of three— Sue Ellis, Jack Hess, and Bob Larsen—was appointed to write the letter. The program for the day was a choral-reading presentation of the poem 'The Height of the Ridiculous.' The meeting was adjourned at 10:45 A.M. Signed, Susan Brown, Secretary."

Step 3

"Are there any corrections to the minutes? . . . The minutes stand approved as read. Are there any committee reports? . . . If not, is there any old business? . . . Since there is no old business, we shall take up new business. Since this is the first Friday of the month, it is time to elect new officers. Nominations are now in order for president."

Step 4

"Mr. President."
             "Helen."
"I nominate Ella Jackson."
  "Ella Jackson has been nominated."

"Mr. President."
             "Jack."
"I nominate Judy Higgins."
       "Judy Higgins has
        been nominated."

Step 5

"Mr. President."
           "Fred."
"I move that nominations be closed."

"I second the motion."

"It has been moved and seconded that nominations for president be closed. Those in favor say *aye*. . . . Those opposed say *no*. . . . The motion is carried. The secretary will pass out slips of paper. Write on the paper the name of the person you want for president."

Step 6

"Ella Jackson has been elected president."

"Nominations are now in order for vice-president."

ELECTING OFFICERS

When you form a club, the first thing to do is to hold a meeting to elect officers. The first two officers to be elected are the president and the vice-president.

After the vice-president has been elected, a new secretary is elected. A new officer takes over the duties as soon as he or she is elected. The newly elected president, Ella Jackson, took over as chairperson of the meeting illustrated here. The new secretary, when elected, will take over the minutes from the past secretary.

GUIDES FOR ELECTING OFFICERS

1. Vote for a person because of his or her fitness for the job, not just because he or she is a good friend.

2. Choose a president who can carry out the duties well. Know what those duties are.

   a) To call the meeting to order
   b) To give all members an equal chance to talk
   c) To state motions and put them to a vote
   d) To vote only if his or her vote will make a tie or break a tie
   e) To appoint committees
   f) To keep out of the discussion

3. Since the vice-president takes charge when the president is absent, choose a vice-president who would make a good president.

4. Choose an efficient secretary, keeping in mind what the duties are.

   a) To take clear, exact notes of meetings, and to put those notes into clear, exact minutes
   b) To read the minutes at the beginning of the meeting
   c) To carry on club correspondence

5. Vote secretly by ballot.

   NOTE: A majority of all the votes cast is needed to elect an officer. (DEFINITION) **A** *majority* **is more than half of all the votes cast.** A candidate may receive more votes than anyone else but still may not have a majority. For example, suppose John has 16 votes; Tom, 10; and Phil, 7. John has more votes than anyone else, but he does not have over half the total number of votes cast (33). He would need 17 for a majority.

LEARNING ACTIVITIES

A. Go over the following questions in class. On the board, write complete answers. To check, turn back to the drawings on pages 76–78.

1. When during the meeting does the president stand?
2. What is the correct order in which to take up *committee reports, old business, reading of minutes, new business?*
3. How does a person get permission to speak? How does the chairperson give that permission?
4. Does a member stand or sit while making a nomination?
5. Are nominations seconded?
6. Does a member stand or sit to make a motion?
7. With what three words does a motion begin?
8. When does a member not need to get permission to speak?
9. How is voting for officers done?
10. How is voting on a motion done (in the sample meeting)?

B. Using your answers in *A* as a guide, plan and dramatize an election of officers for an imaginary club.

CARRYING ON CLUB WORK

The sample meeting illustrated on pages 76–78 is continued here. The new officers have taken over the running of the meeting.

Step 7

"Is there any more new business?"
"Madam President."

"Arnie."

"I move that we ask Ms. Roberta Aiken to show her movies of Europe at our next meeting."

"I second the motion."

"It has been moved and seconded that we ask Ms. Roberta Aiken to show her movies of Europe next week. Is there any discussion?"

The club members take turns at giving reasons for being for or against the motion. Then the chairperson asks, "Are you ready for the question?" If someone calls out, "Question!" the chairperson puts the motion to a vote. ("Question!" means "Let's vote on it.")

Step 8

"Question!"

"It has been moved and seconded that we ask Ms. Roberta Aiken to show her movies of Europe at our next meeting. All in favor say aye. . . . All opposed, no. . . . The motion is carried."

"Madam President."

"Karen."

"I move that the meeting be adjourned."

"I second the motion."

"It is moved and seconded that the meeting be adjourned. All in favor say aye. . . . All opposed, no. . . . The meeting is adjourned."

● THESE ARE THE FACTS ABOUT CONDUCTING CLUB MEETINGS

1. The chairperson usually sits to conduct business except when (a) calling the meeting to order and (b) stating the motion and calling for a vote.

2. As a rule, a member must rise and get permission to speak. He or she may, however, remain seated and speak without permission when he or she (a) seconds a motion or (b) calls for a vote by saying, "Question!"

3. A meeting should follow this order:

   a) Call to order
   b) Reading and approval of the minutes
   c) Committee reports
   d) Unfinished business
   e) New business
   f) Program (if any)
   g) Adjournment

4. The most common method of voting is by saying "Aye" or "No." (Aye is pronounced "eye" and means "yes.")

LEARNING ACTIVITIES

A. Assign parts and dramatize the club meeting that is illustrated on pages 76–80. Be sure to rise and to sit at the right times.

B. (1) Write the minutes for the pictured club meeting. (2) Proofread your paper for careless mistakes in capitalization, punctuation, spelling, and sentence sense. (3) Compare your minutes in class. (4) Decide whether each set of minutes has included all the information needed.

C. Dramatize a meeting of your own in which at least six motions are made and voted on. Afterward, have the minutes read.

Section II:

Reading

READING AND LEARNING

"DID YOU READ ABOUT THE COMET?"

"GEE, I READ THE NEWSPAPER, BUT I DIDN'T SEE THAT."

TALK IT OVER . . .

Is the student really inaccurate in saying that he "read" the newspaper? In other words, should reading involve more than the eyes? If so, what else should he be using?

Is it important to be able to read? Teachers have told you that it is, ever since you entered the first grade. How well have they convinced you? If you still have doubts, consider the following facts.

If you did not know how to read, most street and highway signs would be a mystery to you. You could have no really personal mail, because someone else would have to read your letters to you. You could not look up anyone's telephone number. You would miss many good television and radio programs because you would be unable to read the schedules. You would miss the point in most cartoons, and even comic books would puzzle you. What other situations can you can think of that call for the ability to read?

1. Reading for Different Purposes

Though you may never have thought about the matter, you read for different purposes.

1. Sometimes you read for fun—just to enjoy a story. This usually is *rapid reading*. It is likely to be easy for you.

2. Sometimes you do not read a whole page but just glance over it to find some definite piece of information. This kind of reading is called *skimming*. Here you focus your eyes only on certain words, dates, or numbers. For example, suppose you want to find out in what year Henry (Hank) Aaron hit his greatest number of home runs. You do not need to read all the available information about him; instead, you run your eyes quickly over the pages, stopping only when you see a date.

3. Sometimes you read to get *all* the information from a page. This is *careful reading* and will go much more slowly than the other two types. You need to do this kind of reading often when you study.

The suggestions in this chapter can help you to do your studying faster and to remember better what you study. If you use these suggestions regularly, you should find that you have more time for extra activities, and that your school grades are improving.

LEARNING ACTIVITIES

A. In an oral discussion, decide which kind of reading would probably be the chief type to use in each of the following situations. Be sure to apply guides 3 and 4 of the Guides for Holding Discussions, page 35.

1. Using a telephone directory
2. Carrying out a science experiment
3. Reading a mystery novel
4. Following instructions for putting a toy together
5. Making a list of important dates in a biography

6. Finding a word in the dictionary
7. Reading the comics
8. Doing a mathematics assignment
9. Using a new cookbook recipe
10. Reading magazine stories

B. Here is an activity to carry out in the class period. It will give you practice in skimming. Your teacher will allow you ten minutes only. (1) Number your paper from 1 to 8. (2) By skimming the indicated pages of this book, find and jot down the answers to the following questions. (3) Go over the questions orally. If you failed to find all or most of the answers, you need practice in skimming.

1. How many capital letters are there on page 159?
2. According to the Index, on what page are prepositions defined?
3. Skim the Table of Contents to learn the title of the tenth chapter of this book.
4. How many lines are there in the poem that begins on page 49?
5. How many commas are there on page 85?
6. Which spelling rule on page 254 deals with words that end in *o*?
7. Which item on the Speech Chart, page 63, deals with the hands?
8. What book title is mentioned on page 60?

2. Improving Reading Habits

Although you have been reading for years, you may have some bad habits that need correcting. How well do you follow each of the following guides?

GUIDES TO BETTER READING

1. Do not point to the words as you read. Pointing slows you down, because you read single words instead of groups of words.
2. Try to avoid moving your lips or your throat muscles.
3. Practice to increase the number of words that your eyes can see at a time.
4. Read with your mind as well as with your eyes; that is, think about the meaning of what your eyes see.

Turn to a page in a book that you have not read before. Begin reading the page to yourself. Have a partner watch you as you read to see (1) whether at any time you point to words, (2) whether you tend to move your lips or throat muscles, (3) whether your eyes move rapidly or slowly, and (4) whether your eyes make many or few pauses per line.

After your partner has checked your reading habits, change places and watch her or him in the same manner.

3. Getting the Central Idea

"I THOUGHT THE TOPIC SENTENCE ALWAYS CAME AT THE BEGINNING."

READ AND TALK ABOUT . . .

The other day a teacher overheard two students arguing about paragraphs. Here are a few of the things they said. Which of their remarks are not true?

"A paragraph has to have at least three sentences."
"A paragraph should not have more than a hundred words."
"Paragraphs are there just to make reading look easier."
"Every paragraph has to have a topic sentence."
"The topic sentence is always at the beginning of a paragraph."

Actually, every one of those five remarks is untrue.

The students need not have argued if they had learned the following things about paragraphs.

1. A *paragraph* is a unit of writing that is built around one main idea. That idea is the *central idea* of the paragraph. It is often, but not always, expressed in one sentence of the paragraph.

2. The *topic sentence* is the sentence that states the central idea of a paragraph. Topic sentences are especially useful in paragraphs of explanation or description.

3. Topic sentences may come at the beginning of a paragraph, at the end of a paragraph, or even in the middle. Most often, however, the topic sentence comes at the beginning.

In order to find out which sentence of a paragraph is the topic sentence, you must read the paragraph carefully to determine the central idea and to see just how each sentence relates to that idea. Here is a paragraph that has its topic sentence at the beginning. Observe how the other sentences relate to that sentence, which is printed in italics.

> *When actually meeting in the forest, tigers have ways of communicating.* When they approach each other on the trail, for example, or when a tigress returns to her cubs, they greet each other by touching cheeks and even rubbing the whole side of their bodies against each other. The same expression of friendliness is shown by a house cat when it rubs itself against the leg of a person. Just before this greeting, the tiger often makes a soft puffing sound as it blows air several times out of its mouth and nostrils. This also shows friendliness. If a person at a zoo makes this sound in front of the tiger cage, the cat may reply and approach the bars.
>
> —GEORGE B. SCHALLER AND MILLICENT E. SELSAM*

In this paragraph the first sentence states a general fact, that tigers have ways of communicating with each other. The statement arouses curiosity. What are those ways? The sen-

---

* Adapted from *The Tiger: Its Life in the Wild* by George B. Schaller and Millicent E. Selsam; copyright © 1969 by George B. Schaller and Millicent E. Selsam. Published by Harper & Row, Publishers, Inc., New York.

tences that follow offer details in support of the general statement. Touching cheeks, rubbing sides, and blowing air out of the nostrils are given as examples of the ways tigers communicate. Thus, the first sentence is the topic sentence of the paragraph because it "covers" the details that the rest of the sentences present.

Read the following paragraph, in which the topic sentence is neither the first nor last sentence.

> Under the guidance of professional farmer-soldiers, the whole of the Inca realm—which included Andes, desert, and Upper Amazon—became a great center of plant domestication. *It has been estimated that more kinds of food and medicinal plants were systematically cultivated here than in any other sizable area in the world!* One has only to mention the obvious: corn—that is, maize—(20 varieties); potatoes (240 varieties); sweet potatoes, yams, squash, beans of infinite variety; manioc (from which comes our farina and tapioca); peanuts, cashews, pineapples, chocolate, avocados, tomatoes, peppers, papaya, strawberries, blackberries. These plants were so many and so varied and so long domesticated in the Old World that one forgets that all of these were "American" in origin.
>
> —Victor W. von Hagen*

In this paragraph, the first sentence states the fact that the Incas grew many domestic plants. The second sentence states a more general idea—that the Incas grew more kinds of plants than were grown in any other part of the world. Succeeding sentences provide evidence for that statement. The final sentence echoes the idea of the topic sentence for emphasis. Thus, the *second* sentence is the topic sentence for the paragraph because it states the central idea.

Now read the paragraph below, which has its topic sentence as the final sentence in the paragraph.

> One calm summer evening an Illinois family was eating supper when a tornado struck the area suddenly. It lifted the roof and walls of the house away but did not disturb the supper table. In Arkansas a family sitting on the front porch of their

---

* Adapted from *Realm of the Incas* by Victor W. von Hagen; copyright © 1957 by Victor W. von Hagen. Reprinted by permission of The New American Library of World Literature, Inc., New York.

house saw the house blow away while the porch stayed behind. In Minnesota a tornado blew a trunk full of clothes from one house to the attic of another house two blocks away. *Whenever there are tornadoes, one will hear of strange and almost unbelievable results of these storms.*

— BERTHA MORRIS PARKER*

The first two sentences of this paragraph give details about what happened to an Illinois family during a tornado. The third sentence deals with a similar occurrence in Arkansas; the fourth deals with what happened during another tornado in Minnesota. The final sentence points up the central idea that all of these incidents together suggest: tornadoes have "strange and almost unbelievable results." Thus, the final sentence is the topic sentence.

Learn about words!

The following words, taken from Activity *A* below, have interesting histories. Use your dictionary to find the story behind each word.

insect   sequoia   cathedral

LEARNING ACTIVITIES

A. Volunteer to read any one of the following paragraphs aloud to the class. Reviewing the Guides for Reading Aloud, page 59, will help you. After a paragraph has been read, talk it over. Decide for yourself what the central idea is. Name the topic sentence and show how each sentence in the paragraph has a connection with it.

1. Insects that are our friends do not deserve any credit for being helpful. Neither do insects that are our enemies deserve blame for harming us. Insects live their own lives, and in doing so, simply happen to interfere with us human beings. The cockroach that comes into our kitchens is not trying to take our food

---

* Adapted from *Ways of the Weather* by Bertha Morris Parker; copyright ©
1957 by Harper & Row, Publishers, Inc., New York.

away from us—it is simply getting the food that it needs for itself. The honeybee that stores up honey is laying away food for its own use, and not for ours.

—BERTHA MORRIS PARKER AND ROBERT E. GREGG*

2. If the 1849 gold seeker did not go to California by sea, there were several land trails that might be taken. First, there was the trail to Oregon. This well-known trail led from Independence, Missouri, to the present state of Idaho. From there, the traveler could then turn southward to California. Another trail led from Independence to Santa Fe, crossed what are now New Mexico and Arizona, and entered southern California. Still other trails went through Texas to El Paso and crossed southern New Mexico and Arizona.

—CLARENCE L. VER STEEG†

3. The oldest living things on earth are trees. Some of California's sequoias have for four thousand years looked down on the changes in the landscape and the comings and goings of mankind. They sprouted from tiny seeds about the time the Egyptian pyramids were being built. They were sturdy young saplings when Moses led the Israelites to the Promised Land. Today these giant patriarchs seem as remote and inaccessible as the rocks and mountain cliffs on which they grow, like cathedral columns holding up the sky. It is hard to imagine them playing any part in the lives of mere humans or being in any way affected by the creatures that pass at their feet.

—ANNE OPHELIA DOWDEN‡

4. Family life for the Jordans revolved around two basic areas—religion and music. God was ever-present, and though they did not have much money, they were secure in the belief that they were cared for and loved. Music, too, was ever-present. Both Benjamin and Arlyne Jordan sang and played musical instruments, and they encouraged the musical abilities of their daughters. Barbara's favorite instrument was the guitar.

—JAMES HASKINS**

B. Match the four topic sentences below with the four lettered paragraphs that follow them; that is, decide which topic sentences belong with which paragraphs.

1. The earth has had several ice ages.
2. In time, as snows fall and glaciers grow, the ice starts to flow.
3. An ice age is a time when sheets of ice thousands of feet thick spread out over large parts of the continents.
4. An ice age has a drastic effect on ocean levels.

*a.*_____ It begins when heavy snows fall in the colder parts of the world: in polar lands and among the peaks and slopes of lofty mountains. The snows of winter are so heavy that the summer sun cannot melt them all, and so, year after year, the snow builds up. The weight of new snow packs the old into ice. These masses of ice are called glaciers.

*b.*_____ Giant rivers of ice reach slowly down from the mountains into the valleys. Tremendously thick sheets of ice flow out from polar lands. Then, after thousands of years have passed, a change occurs, and the glaciers start to melt and shrink. They draw back to the polar lands, back to the mountain heights, releasing great floods of meltwater.

*c.*_____ The last one, which is often called the Ice Age, began about 1.5 million years ago, and it had four main stages. Four times great glaciers advanced over the land, melted, and shrank back. The last advance started some 65,000 years ago. By 18,000 years ago nearly a third of the earth's land lay under thick sheets of ice. Then the ice began to melt. By 10,000 years ago large parts of the Northern Hemisphere were free of ice. By 6,000 years ago, the glaciers had almost shrunk back to where they are today.

*d.*_____ The reason is that the oceans are the chief source of moisture for the heavy snows that fall. At a time when glaciers are growing, the snows of thousands of winters accumulate on land. With a vast quantity of water from the oceans locked up in land ice, ocean levels drop. During the glacial advances of the Ice Age, ocean levels were several hundred feet lower than they are today. Large areas now under water were then dry land.

—Patricia Lauber*

C. Choose a paragraph from one of your other schoolbooks and read it to the class. Look over the Guides for Reading Aloud, page 59, before

* Adapted from *Who Discovered America?* by Patricia Lauber; copyright ©
1970 by Patricia Lauber. Published by Random House, Inc., New York.

doing the reading. Call on a classmate to tell what the central thought is and to give his or her reasons for thinking so. Use the Guides to Good Listening on page 28.

ENRICHMENT

Search through newspapers and magazines for good examples of paragraphs that have topic sentences. Underline the topic sentences. Bring the paragraphs to class and use them as the basis for group discussion. Post the best examples on the bulletin board. Try to find paragraphs in which the topic sentence occurs (1) at the beginning, (2) in the middle, and (3) at the end.

USING ENGLISH IN ALL CLASSES

From one of your other books, bring to class an example of a paragraph that you think does a good job of developing its topic sentence. Read that topic sentence to the class, and tell how the other sentences develop it.

4. Using Key Words As a Study Help

READ AND THINK ABOUT . . .

You have been studying topic sentences, the sentences that tell you what a paragraph is about. Not every paragraph, however, has a topic sentence. Stories, for example, have many paragraphs without a sentence that states the central idea. In such a paragraph, you must figure out the central idea for yourself. To do so, you need to be able to find and use the *key words* in the paragraph.

What are key words? Keys unlock doors; key words unlock paragraph meaning. If you have those key words, you can get along without the rest of the words in the paragraph and still be able to know and tell the main information in it.

Read the following paragraph, paying special attention to the words in italics.

> In the summer of *1847*, Captain John Augustus *Sutter* decided to build a sawmill. He *hired* James Wilson *Marshall* to *build* a *mill* on the banks of the American River in *California*. The mill rose without incident until the next year, *1848*. One January evening, Marshall turned the water from the millpond into the tailrace to wash the channel free of loose dirt. In the morning, when he returned, his eye was caught by the gleam of *yellow metal* at the bottom of the clear *water*. When he pounded this soft metal, it flattened easily like *gold*.*

In the preceding paragraph, the italicized words might be called key words. They are *1847, Sutter, hired, Marshall, build, mill, California, 1848, yellow metal, water, gold.*

The paragraph has no topic sentence, but the key words suggest this central thought: "Gold was discovered in California in 1848." If you want to add a bit more than the central thought, the key words will even help you to recall important details:

> The discoverer, Marshall, built the mill for his employer, Captain Sutter, in 1847.

The following guides will help you to review and remember the important information in lessons that you read.

* Adapted from *The California Gold Rush* by the editors of *American Heritage;* copyright © 1961 by American Heritage Publishing Co., Inc.

GUIDES FOR USING KEY WORDS AS A STUDY HELP

FOR PARAGRAPHS WITHOUT TOPIC SENTENCES

1. Skim each sentence in a paragraph that has no topic sentence.
2. Jot down the most important words, that is, the *key words*.
3. Build a sentence that gives the central thought suggested by those words.
4. Go back over the paragraph to see whether your central thought is accurate.
5. Under the central thought write brief sentences giving any important details also suggested by the key words.

FOR PARAGRAPHS WITH TOPIC SENTENCES

1. Copy the topic sentence.
2. Jot down the other key words in the paragraph.
3. Build short sentences that give the important details suggested by those key words.

Learn about words!

The following words, taken from the guides above, have strange or interesting histories. Use your dictionary to find the story behind each word.

jot   skim   detail   accurate

LEARNING ACTIVITIES

A. The five paragraphs in this activity do not have topic sentences. (1) Find and jot down what you think are key words in each paragraph. (2) Write a topic sentence for each one, using as many of your key words as you need. (3) Write another sentence, giving main details suggested by the key words. (4) Compare work in class or in your small groups. Some key words you choose in a paragraph may differ, but each of you should express the same *idea* in your topic sentence for that paragraph.

1. Estevanico was born in Azamor, Morocco, probably before 1500. Spanish soldiers captured him during an attack on that city in 1513, and he became the slave of Don Andrés Dorantes de Carranza, a nobleman of Castile. Except for his size and strength, there was little in his appearance to set him apart from other slaves. Yet his courage and ability enabled him to become

the first man of African birth whose name is known to American history. A member of the first party to cross the wide part of the North American continent, he discovered Arizona and is remembered as one of the great adventurers of all time.

—J. NORMAN HEARD*

2. Even Columbus noticed the power of the Gulf Stream in 1492. In 1513 another early explorer, Juan Ponce de León, tried to sail south down the coast of what is now Florida. In spite of a brisk wind and ideal sailing conditions, his ships were carried backward by the strong current. Only by crossing the stream and getting out of its current, could he go south. But it was Benjamin Franklin, in 1769, who, using a wooden bucket and a thermometer, was the first to plot the Gulf Stream accurately.

—DOROTHY TELFER†

3. In the tropics, there is very little change in the weather. On the other hand, in such regions as the western plains of the United States and Canada, the only thing certain about the weather is that it will be uncertain. The summers are often very hot, and the winter temperatures may go down to fifty or sixty degrees below zero. Some years there will be in these regions a fair amount of rain, but these may be followed by five or six years of drought.

—BERTHA MORRIS PARKER AND RALPH BUCHSBAUM‡

4. The first houses in Plymouth were very quickly built and probably looked like the wigwams of the Indians. As soon as they could, the Pilgrims began to cut down trees and saw them into beams and boards. They used these to build houses, the first of them just shacks. The roofs were made of brush and straw, and the floors of dirt. Solid shutters, without glass, formed the doors and windows. When they were closed, the only light came through the cracks.

—EUGENE C. BARKER, FRANCES CAVANAH,
AND WALTER P. WEBB**

* From "The Odyssey of Estevanico" from *The Black Frontiersmen* by J. Norman Heard; copyright © 1969 by J. Norman Heard. Published by The John Day Company, New York.

† From *Exploring the World of Oceanography* by Dorothy Telfer; copyright © 1968 by Regensteiner Publishing Enterprises, Inc. Published by Childrens Press, Chicago.

‡ Adapted from *Balance in Nature* by Bertha Morris Parker and Ralph Buchsbaum; copyright © 1958 by Harper & Row, Publishers, Inc., New York.

** Adapted from *Our New Land* by Eugene C. Barker, Frances Cavanah, and Walter P. Webb; copyright © 1961 by Harper & Row, Publishers, Inc., New York.

5. None of the houses of the Pilgrim settlers had bathrooms; in fact, none even had running water. Windows and doors were without screens, and in the summertime flies and mosquitoes swarmed everywhere. There were, of course, no gas stoves and no electricity. People lighted their houses with whale-oil lamps and pine knots, or with tallow candles that they made at home.

— EUGENE C. BARKER, FRANCES CAVANAH,
AND WALTER P. WEBB*

B. (1) Reread each of the four paragraphs on pages 91–92. (2) Copy each topic sentence. (3) Under it, jot down the key words in the rest of the paragraph. (4) Build a sentence or more that states important details based upon these key words. (5) Compare work in class.

C. (1) Read the first paragraph of "The Speed of Light," page 100. As you read, jot down the key words on a piece of paper. (2) Close your book and, using the key words, reconstruct the paragraph in your own words. (3) Read your paragraphs in class.

ENRICHMENT

As would be expected, the list of key words in a paragraph will vary somewhat from student to student. Even though many students will include the same words, some students will include more words than are really necessary. Following is such an "overcomplete" list.

Using your imagination, write a paragraph suggested to you by these key words:

> Winter . . . 1777–78 . . . Washington . . . soldiers . . . starved . . . froze . . . Valley Forge . . . log huts . . . little protection . . . cold winds . . . many . . . rags . . . uniforms . . . worn out . . . hundreds . . . no shoes . . . some . . . wrapped . . . rags . . . others . . . barefoot . . . bloody footprints . . . snow . . . many . . . sick . . . died.

If two or more in the class do this assignment, your teacher may let you read your paragraphs aloud to show how they may differ in details.

USING ENGLISH IN ALL CLASSES

A. Here is an assignment that will test your reading ability and the listening skill of your audience. (1) In your social studies or history or geography book find a paragraph that has no topic sentence. (2) Read it to the class. (3) Ask classmates to jot down what they think are the key

---

* Adapted from *Our New Land* by Eugene C. Barker, Frances Cavanah, and Walter P. Webb; copyright © 1961 by Harper & Row, Publishers, Inc., New York.

words and the central thought. (4) When you have finished, call on someone to read his or her list of key words and statement of the central
thought. If there is disagreement, take time to go over the paragraph again.
Apply guides 3 and 4 of the Guides for Holding Discussions, page 35.

B. If you have a reading assignment in some other class for tomorrow,
try, as you read, to pick out the central thought in each paragraph. (If
there is a topic sentence, copy that; if there is none, use key words to help
you frame your own central thought.) This is a very good way to study a
lesson. Jot these central thoughts down on paper to see whether they tell
you the main points in the assignment.

If some of you have the same assignment, compare the central thoughts
that you jotted down. If you do not agree, go over the paragraphs together
to see whether you can reach an agreement.

5. Learning by Summarizing

THINK IT OVER . . .

What is a "summary"?
How would you go about making one?

Probably at one time or another, you, like the man in the
drawing, have said, "To make a long story short . . ." That is exactly what a summary is: telling in a few words the most important points of a story or an article.

You have had practice in finding central thoughts and key words. Making a summary is based upon those two things — central ideas and key words. The guides that follow explain how to use them sensibly in summarizing material made up of several paragraphs.

GUIDES TO MAKING A SUMMARY

1. Pick out the main idea of each paragraph. Let topic sentences and key words help you.
2. Write each main idea in your own words, being as brief as possible.
3. Put all the main-idea sentences together in one paragraph.
4. Go back over your paragraph. Cut any words or ideas that are not important.

Learn about words!

The following words, taken from Learning Activity *A*, have interesting histories. Use your dictionary to find the story behind each word.

require   orbit   revolve   energy

LEARNING ACTIVITIES

A. Go over the following article, "The Speed of Light," and its summary carefully. Then check the summary, using the Guides to Making a Summary. In class, decide (1) whether all the main ideas are included in the summary, (2) whether any unimportant ideas are included, and (3) whether the summary could be condensed even more. In the article, paragraphs are numbered. In the summary, sentences are numbered to show which sentences come from which paragraphs.

THE SPEED OF LIGHT

1. The key to the nature of light is provided by the things that light can *do*. Since it causes heat, moves the winds, and makes plants grow, light must be some kind of energy closely connected with motion.

2. An important clue was uncovered in the seventeenth century when telescopes revealed that Jupiter had at least four moons. As astronomers watched the moons revolve about Jupiter, they noticed that each moon had a definite period, or time, of revolution around the planet. But there was a most peculiar thing about the revolutions of the moons of Jupiter. They seemed to revolve a bit faster as the earth approached Jupiter and to slow down as the earth moved away from the planet. For a half year, as the earth moved closer to Jupiter, the moons would speed up. For the next half year, as the earth moved away, the moons revolved more slowly.

3. In 1676, the Dutch scientist Olaus Roemer offered a startling explanation for this curious fact. He thought that light traveled at a certain speed and therefore required time to cross the vast distance between Jupiter and the earth. When the earth was farthest away from Jupiter, the light arriving at the earth from Jupiter required an extra fifteen minutes to cross the additional distance.

4. Roemer made some calculations. Knowing the distance across the earth's orbit and the time required for the light to cross it, he was able to calculate the speed of light. His answer was quite close to the figure of 186,000 miles a second, which we accept today as the speed of light.

5. Since Roemer, other methods have been used to measure the speed of light. A number of scientists have timed the passage of a beam of light as it passed between two places on earth. The most famous of these experiments was performed in 1902 by the American scientist Albert Michelson. He accurately timed a light beam as it traveled from one mountaintop to another, then bounced off a mirror and returned to the starting point. The forty-four-mile distance was covered in less than a thousandth of a second. Michelson's measurements were so accurate that he was able to express the speed of light as 186,265 miles per second with an error of probably not more than a few miles per second.

— Hy Ruchlis*

Summary of "The Speed of Light"

(1) Light is a kind of energy connected with motion. (2) In the seventeenth century, astronomers watching the revolutions of the four moons of Jupiter found that the moons seemed to re-

---

volve faster as the earth approached Jupiter, but would revolve more slowly as the earth moved away. (3) In 1676, Dutch scientist Olaus Roemer suggested that light traveled at a certain speed and therefore required more time to cross the extra distance when Jupiter was farthest away from the earth. (4) Roemer calculated the speed of light to be 186,000 miles per second. (5) In 1902, the American scientist Albert Michelson, using a mirror and a light beam traveling from one mountaintop to another and reflected back, accurately calculated the speed of light to be 186,265 miles per second.

B. There is some needless repetition in the summary sentences for "The Speed of Light," pages 101–102. Condense the thoughts of the summary into three sentences, two sentences, or (possibly) one sentence. Study the summary sentences carefully first; do not omit necessary information.

C. (1) Divide the class into several discussion groups, with four or five people in each group. (2) Read silently through the following article to get the general idea. (3) Then in your small groups, read the article aloud. Check one another's reading by guides 4–7 of the Guides for Reading Aloud, page 59. For some words that are new to you, you may find clues in the way that they are used. (See the Guides for Getting Meaning from Context, page 112.) If other words give no clues, use the dictionary. Decide in your group which meaning makes the best sense in the sentence that you are reading. (4) Go back over the article together, but this time pick out the important information and put it into as many sentences as you need to tell it clearly. Have someone act as secretary to write the sentences as they are made. (5) Choose one person to read your summary to the class. As the various summaries are read, listen carefully to see whether all groups agreed on what the important information in the article is.

THE GREAT FORESTS

At first glance, a forest appears to be a haphazard collection of trees, shrubs, vines, and flowers. There may be several dozen species of trees in even a small forest, and they seem to grow at random. The shrubs are carelessly scattered over the forest floor, and the vines cling to any convenient tree. Yet, destroy a a forest by fire or ax, and in several centuries it will be replaced by a forest of almost exactly the same kind. The forest may make what appear to be numerous false starts. At first there arise trees and plants different from those that originally grew in that location. But all of these temporary stages point in one direction: the rebirth of the forest along its original lines. The dominant trees will be almost an exact replica of the old forest, and they will have as companions very much the same plants and animals that are unique to that kind of forest.

Every forest passes through a series of stages before it reaches the final stage. In southern New England the stages are not the same as in northern New England.

The first stage begins with the open field. For example, when a Connecticut farmer abandons a field, numerous kinds of plants attempt to invade it. It is captured, though, by plants which can germinate most quickly and which can survive the sunlight and drying winds of an open field. These plants provide a nursery for the next stage in the succession.

This second stage produces a new forest of white pine and birch. For a while the white pines rule this young forest, but they eventually eliminate themselves: their seedlings cannot survive in the dense shade of the older pines. Only trees whose seedlings can endure the lack of sunlight, for example certain oaks and maples, manage to grow in the shade of the white pines. As the pines fall prey to one or another of the hazards of forest life, they leave openings in the forest which are filled by the oaks and maples. This is the third stage.

As the forest matures, the oaks and maples, along with the remnant of the white pine pioneers, grow so tall that they shut out even the small amount of sunlight needed for their own seedlings. When that happens, their career as rulers of this third forest stage is at an end. For growing on the dark forest

floor are the seedlings of such trees as hemlock and beech. It may be scores of years before the oaks and maples surrender their rule, but eventually the hemlocks and beeches become the dominant species. The forest reaches its climax in this final stage, for the only seedlings that can survive in the darkness are those of the dominant trees.

— PETER FARB*

D. Now try your hand at making a summary alone. (1) Read carefully through the Guides to Making a Summary, page 100. (2) Then read and summarize the following article. (Use a dictionary to look up words you do not know.) (3) Proofread your paragraph for careless errors in capitalization, punctuation, spelling, and sentence sense. (4) Be prepared to read your summary to the class.

FLOODS

A flood is a terrible thing. People are forced to flee for their lives. Their homes, their furniture, their beds must be left to the mercy of muddy, oily water. A few people refuse to leave their homes and stay staunchly to meet the flood. Busily they move their furniture to the second floor. As the water rises, they are forced to climb out on the roof.

The icy flood pushes in the windows and doors. Sometimes, groaning and crumbling, the house caves in, dumping its occupants into the swirling waters with little chance of rescue. The people who were prudent enough to escape to high ground are crowded into schools, churches, and refugee camps.

* Adapted from *The Face of North America* by Peter Farb; copyright © 1963 by Peter Farb. Published by Harper & Row, Publishers, Inc., New York.

Hourly, the coast guard brings additions to this miserable company. Many are ill from exposure; some have been injured. Doctors and nurses work day and night. After dark, emergency operations must be performed by the light of a candle or a lantern. There is no electricity: the floodwaters have covered the power plants.

The greatest problem is drinking water. In all this sea of water, people cannot find a drop to drink. The river is so poisoned with sewage that no one would dare to drink from it. Now with dead animals floating past and with purification plants under water, to drink from the river would be suicide. Pure water must be brought in, yet transportation over railroads and highways is paralyzed. Epidemics of disease threaten.

After the flood there comes the dirty job of cleaning up. Merchants, returning to their stores, find their stock ruined. People, returning to their homes, may find a barn on their front lawn or a dead horse against the kitchen door. Inside, the wallpaper has peeled, glued chairs and tables have fallen apart, the rug oozes with slime, and the mattress is saturated with filthy water.

Wells must be cleaned, and for weeks their water will be unfit to drink. Automobile motors and the machines of factories will have to be taken completely apart and cleaned of caked mud and rust. The decaying bodies of dead animals will have to be gathered and burned. Yes, the flood is a terrible thing.

—MURL DEUSING*

E. Bring to class a short article from a magazine or an editorial from a newspaper. Write a summary of it, letting the Guides to Making a Summary help you. Check your paper by the Writing Chart, page 151. Read the summaries in your small groups. As a listener, be sure that you understand clearly what each article is about. If you do not, tell the one who wrote the summary what you think needs to be made clearer.

USING ENGLISH IN ALL CLASSES

In preparing your next reading assignment in science or social studies, make a summary of the lesson. If some of you have the same assignment, compare your results. Discuss them if you do not agree. You will find that what you study is much easier to understand and remember if you make a summary of the important facts.

* Adapted from *Soil, Water, and Man* by Murl Deusing; copyright © 1968 by Western Publishing Company, Inc., Racine, Wisconsin. Reprinted by permission,

Listen carefully to a talk on television or on radio or to any other speaker that you have a chance to hear. Write a summary and read it to the class or to your small group. Call upon someone to tell in her or his own words what you have said.

6. Outlining: A Help to Clear Thinking

Have you ever watched the building of a house? If you have, you know that a framework is built upon a firm foundation, and that the walls, floors, ceilings, and roof are fastened to that framework. You do not see the framework in the finished house, but it is there.

In the same way, a well-written paragraph, story, or article has a framework. *Making an outline* of the material that you read will help you to understand that material. By making an outline of the material, you are finding its framework.

There are two kinds of outlines: (1) *sentence outlines,* in which every point is a complete sentence, and (2) *topic outlines,* in which there are no sentences at all. A sentence outline really summarizes what the writer says and is therefore more useful than a topic outline whenever you must refer to it sometime in the future. A topic outline, on the other hand, just states the topics about which the writer says something. It is most useful when it is to be used soon after it has been made.

GUIDES FOR OUTLINING

1. Read carefully through the material to be outlined.
2. Decide what the main idea of each paragraph is. State it as a topic or as a sentence. (Look for topic sentences, central thoughts, and key words.)
3. Use these main ideas as chief points; label them *I, II,* and so on.
4. Decide whether there are at least two points that give important information about a main point. Such points are *subpoints.*

5. List these subpoints under the right main point and label them *A, B,* and so on.

6. Decide whether at least two *details* tell more about a subpoint.

7. List these details under the right subpoint and label them *1, 2,* and so on.

8. Remember, never put only one subpoint under a main point or one detail under a subpoint.

9. Capitalize and punctuate properly.

   a) Use a period after each division numeral or letter.
   b) Capitalize the first word of each point.
   c) Use a period after each point in a sentence outline; use no period after a point in a topic outline.

10. Use only sentences *or* topics, not both, in the same outline.

SENTENCE OUTLINE	TOPIC OUTLINE
I. This is a main point.	I. Main point
A. This is an important subpoint.	A. Important subpoint
B. This is an important subpoint.	B. Important subpoint
1. This is a detail.	1. Detail
2. This is a detail.	2. Detail
3. This is a detail.	3. Detail
II. This is a main point.	II. Main point

Read the following selection about how animals protect themselves; then study the *sentence outline* and the *topic outline* that come immediately after it. Notice that there are seven main points in the outline, one for each paragraph of the selection, and that they are marked by Roman numerals. Note that the subpoints are indicated by capital letters and that the details are indicated by Arabic numerals.

Note also that every main point has at least two subdivisions. Each numeral and each letter is followed by a period, as in the forms shown under guide 10 above. Observe how the main topics, subpoints, and details "line up" in both outlines. *The only difference is that one is made up of sentences; the other is not.*

Study the differences between the information given in the two outlines. Always remember that a topic outline merely *suggests* ideas; a sentence outline actually *states* the ideas. It will be as useful a month or a year later as when it was first written. The topic outline may be a real puzzle after a month or more has gone by.

How Animals Protect Themselves

Animals, like other forms of life, have enemies from which they must find ways to protect themselves. The following paragraphs tell about some of those ways.

Being able to move fast is the best way that many animals have of protecting themselves from their enemies. Some animals — the swallow for one — have no other way.

Many animals have what is known as "protective coloring"; that is, their color changes to match their surroundings. Some animals, the arctic foxes, for example, change color with the seasons. Other animals change oftener. The common tree toad is one of these that do. It changes from gray to green, for example, if it moves from the trunk of a tree to a green leaf.

The walking-stick insect is protected by its resemblance to a twig. The dead-leaf butterfly escapes being seen by its enemies because it looks like a dried leaf. This means of protection is called "protective resemblance."

Many animals wear armor of one kind or another. Shellfish such as clams, oysters, and scallops are enclosed in shells. So are beetles and turtles. The tough hide of the elephant and the hippopotamus is not easily penetrated. The armadillo has its head and body encased in armor made up of many small bony plates.

Some animals carry weapons. The spines, or quills, of the porcupine can inflict painful wounds. The swordfish has a long, dangerous, swordlike beak. Lions, tigers, and leopards have deadly claws. Other animals protect themselves by poison. The sea anemone, for instance, has poison darts. Bees and wasps inject poison with their stings. The black widow spider poisons as it bites. Some animals protect themselves by giving out a bad odor. The skunk is a good example.

Animals may have habits that help protect them from their enemies. The opossum, for instance, plays dead. The hog-nosed snake protects itself in the same way. Many animals escape their enemies by doing their hunting at night.

— Bertha Morris Parker*

How Animals Protect Themselves *(sentence outline)*

I. Animals must be able to protect themselves from enemies.
II. Some animals, such as the swallow, must depend on their speed.
III. Some animals have protective coloring.
   A. The arctic foxes change color with the seasons.
   B. Some animals, such as the tree toad, change more often.

* Adapted from *Adaptation to Environment* by Bertha Morris Parker; copyright © 1959 by Harper & Row, Publishers, Inc., New York.

IV. Some animals have protective resemblance.
    A. The walking-stick insect looks like a twig.
    B. The dead-leaf butterfly looks like a dead leaf.
V. Many animals have armor.
    A. Shellfish, turtles, and beetles have protective shells.
    B. The elephant and hippopotamus have tough hides.
    C. The armadillo has strong, bony plates.
VI. Some animals carry weapons.
    A. The porcupine has spines.
    B. The swordfish has its sword.
    C. Lions, tigers, and leopards have claws.
    D. Some use poison.
        1. The sea anemone shoots out poison darts.
        2. Bees and wasps inject poison with their stings.
        3. The black widow spider's bite is poisonous.
    E. Some animals, such as the skunk, give out a bad odor.
VII. Animals have habits that protect them.
    A. The opossum and the hog-nosed snake play dead.
    B. Many animals escape enemies by hunting at night.

How Animals Protect Themselves *(topic outline)*

    I. Need for protection from enemies
    II. Speed, a method of protection
    III. Protective coloring
        A. Arctic foxes
        B. Tree toad
    IV. Protective resemblance
        A. Walking-stick
        B. Dead-leaf butterfly
    V. Armor
        A. Protective shells
        B. Tough hides
        C. Bony plates
    VI. Weapons
        A. Spines
        B. Swords
        C. Claws
        D. Poison
            1. Darts
            2. Stings
            3. Bites
        E. Bad odor
    VII. Protective habits
        A. Playing dead
        B. Hunting at night

LEARNING ACTIVITIES

A. In your small groups, make a sentence outline of "The Great Forests," pages 103–104. Have outlines put on the board and compared.

B. Now make an outline by yourself. (1) Turn to the article on page 104 ("Floods") and make a sentence outline of the important information in it. (2) Proofread for careless errors in capitalizing and punctuating. (3) Have several outlines put on the board or read in class.

C. (1) Find an interesting article, a page or so long, in a magazine. (2) Make a topic outline of the article and then prepare a talk based upon that outline. (3) Examine your Speech Chart, page 63, to see which points need special work on your part. (4) Practice this talk before a mirror at home, and then ask a friend to listen to you. (5) As each speech is given in class, rate it on a speech slip (page 64). (6) Afterwards mark your own Speech Chart.

USING ENGLISH IN ALL CLASSES

As you study your next assignment in any class, outline the important facts. If any of you have the same assignment, compare outlines.

LEARNING NEW WORDS

"IF THESE WORDS ARE ENGLISH, I MUST BE READING THEM UPSIDE DOWN."

READ AND THINK ABOUT . . .

What do you do in your reading when you come to words that you do not know?

What are you doing to improve your vocabulary?

If you have ever been out in a heavy fog, you will remember that everything around you was blurred and hard to make out. When the fog lifted, everything looked different, so clear and plain that you could not possibly mistake one thing for another.

In the same way, the things that you read may be blurred and hard for you to understand just because you come across words that puzzle you. To get a clear idea of what you read, you must know what the words mean.

1. Learning Words from Context

Sometimes you can guess correctly at the meaning of a word from its *context,* that is, from the other words used with it in the sentence or in nearby sentences. The following guides will help you to use context clues in your reading.

GUIDES FOR GETTING MEANING FROM CONTEXT

1. Watch for a word that explains or defines the unfamiliar word.

   I found the old woman waiting on the **gallery**, or, as it is called here, the *porch.*

   On the tree trunk, I noticed a strange **excresence**, a gray, thorny *lump.* (*Lump* is an appositive. See Rule 4, page 228.)

2. Watch for a word that gives a clear hint as to the meaning of the unfamiliar word.

   It seemed that nothing could **slake** her *thirst.* (*Thirst* suggests that *slake* probably means "satisfy.")

3. If no single word gives a clue, look (*a*) at the sentence as a whole, or (*b*) at a sentence or sentences nearby.

   a) The **famished** man seized the loaf of bread and began to gnaw on it hungrily. (The whole sentence suggests that *famished* means "starving.")

   b) The man stared at me **wrathfully**. I could see that he was *hot-tempered.* (*Hot-tempered* suggests that *wrathfully* means "angrily.")

LEARNING ACTIVITIES

A. (1) Read the following paragraphs, paying special attention to the words in italics. (2) Copy the paragraphs, but for the italicized words select substitutes from the list that follows the paragraphs. The paragraphs have in them context clues that should help you to choose the right words. (3) Compare your choices in class. (4) Point out context clues that helped you to choose certain words.

One day in July I had climbed to the *summit* of a high, bare ridge, and sat down on a *prominent* point to rest and to *sweep* the landscape with my glasses. Below me, in rolling *undulations,* stretched the forest, with numerous open parks. At one side the ribbon of Pacific Creek wound its way toward the valley, the upper Jackson Hole, the distant parts dimmed in the *haze* of a quiet summer day. And before me, *emerging* from the mist of the valley, rose the Tetons.

At first there was little sign of active life. Then a movement in a green meadow just below me caught my eye, and I stiffened to *alert* attention as an elk came out of the shadow of a pine and began grazing. I caught other small movements, then *discerned* other shapes *obscured* in the shadow of the forest edge, and to my amazement I became aware of a whole herd of elk resting in the shade.

—OLAUS J. MURIE*

1. saw	4. view	7. top
2. appearing	5. hidden	8. projecting
3. smoky air	6. waves	9. wide-awake

B. Using any context clues that you can find, decide what you think is the meaning of each italicized word in the following sentences, all taken from *A Tale of Two Cities* by Charles Dickens. Make this an oral activity.

1. The air among the houses was of so strong a *piscatory* flavor that one might have supposed that sick fish went up to be dipped in it, as sick people went down to be dipped in the sea.
2. They had not *traversed* many steps of the long main staircase when he stopped, . . .
3. Mr. Lorry was already out when Carton got back, and it was easy to *surmise* where the good old man was gone.
4. It was as if the wind and rain had *lulled* at last, after a long and fearful storm.
5. "I would ride over any of you very willingly, and *exterminate* you from the earth."
6. The *wicket* opened on a stone staircase, leading upward.
7. "Now, I told you so," said the spy, casting a *reproachful* look at his sister; "if any trouble comes of this, it's your doing."

C. (1) Rewrite the following paragraph, replacing each word in italics with one word or more suggested to you by context clues. (2) Proofread for careless errors in copying. (3) In class, compare your work. (4) List on the board the various words substituted for the italicized ones. With the help of the dictionary, if necessary, decide which substitutes best give the meaning intended.

* From "The Elk of Jackson Hole" by Olaus J. Murie from *Ants, Indians, and Little Dinosaurs* edited by Alan Ternes; copyright © 1975 The American Museum of Natural History. Published by Charles Scribner's Sons, New York.

A sudden thought struck me how I might *extricate* myself from the bandit's *clutches*. I was unarmed, it is true, but I was *vigorous*. His companions were at a distance. By a sudden pull, I might *wrest* myself from him and spring up the staircase, *whither* he would not dare follow me by himself. The idea was put into action as soon as *conceived*. The *ruffian's* throat was bare; with my right hand I seized him by it; with my left hand I grasped the arm which held the carbine. The suddenness of my attack took him completely *unawares;* and the *strangling* nature of my grasp paralyzed him. He choked and *faltered*. I felt his hand relaxing its hold and was upon the point of jerking myself away and darting up the staircase before he could recover himself, when I was suddenly seized from behind.

— WASHINGTON IRVING*

ENRICHMENT

Use context clues to unlock the meaning of the italicized words in the lines of poetry below.

1. O wind, *rend* open the heat,
   cut apart the heat,
   rend it to tatters. — HILDA DOOLITTLE†

2. And he *smote* upon the door again a second time;
   "Is there anybody there?" he said. — WALTER DE LA MARE

3. The bride kissed the goblet; the knight took it up,
   He *quaffed* off the wine, and he threw down the cup.
   — SIR WALTER SCOTT

4. The waves beside them danced; but they
   Outdid the sparkling waves in glee:
   A poet could not but be gay,
   In such *jocund* company. — WILLIAM WORDSWORTH

5. Night is a curious child, wandering
   Between earth and sky, creeping
   In windows and doors, *daubing*
   The entire neighborhood
   With purple paint. — FRANK MARSHALL DAVIS‡

* From "The Painter's Adventure" by Washington Irving from *Tales of a Traveller with Selections from The Sketch Book* edited by George Philip Krapp, Ph.D. Published by Scott, Foresman and Company, Glenview, Illinois, 1901.

† From "Heat" by Hilda Doolittle from *Collected Poems of H.D.;* copyright 1925 by Boni and Liveright, Inc. Published by Liveright Publishing Corporation, New York.

‡ From "Four Glimpses of Night" by Frank Marshall Davis. Reprinted from *The Poetry of Black America* edited by Arnold Adoff, published by Harper & Row, Publishers, Inc., New York, 1973.

6. I feel a stirring beneath me and hear buds
   opening,
   The river *chants* thy song and the clouds
   dance to it. — CONSTANCE LINDSAY SKINNER*

USING ENGLISH IN ALL CLASSES

In class, examine your science or social studies text. When you find an unfamiliar word that is made clear by its context, raise your hand. If called upon, say the word; then read the sentence. Ask a classmate to give the meaning suggested by the context and to tell what words are clues.

2. Using Root Words, Prefixes, and Suffixes

TALK IT OVER . . .

What are *root words, prefixes,* and *suffixes?* What relationship do they have to each other? If you do not know, find what the dictionary says about them.

Many words in the English language come from Greek or Latin sources. Knowing even a few Greek and Latin root words, prefixes, and suffixes will unlock for you many English words.

*From "Song of Basket-Weaving" interpreted by Constance Lindsay Skinner. Reprinted from *American Indian Poetry* edited by George W. Cronyn, published by Liveright Publishing Corporation, New York, 1934.

GUIDES FOR USING WORD PARTS TO UNLOCK MEANING

1. Learn common *roots, prefixes,* and *suffixes* such as these.

PREFIXES	ROOT WORDS	SUFFIXES
anti- (against)	**aud** (hear)	**-able, -ible** (able to, able to be)
in-, im-, il-, ir-,	**graph** (write)	**-er, -or** (one who, that which)
un- (not)	**meter** (measure)	**-ion, -sion, -tion** (act of,
mis- (wrong)	**sens** (feel)	condition of)
pre- (before)	**vid, vis** (see)	**-itis** (inflammation of)
re- (back, again)	**vit, viv** (life,	**-less** (without)
tele- (far)	live)	**-ness** (condition of being)

2. Look for familiar parts. Perhaps the only new thing about a word is a prefix or a suffix. For example, in *imperfect,* you can spot *perfect.* If you know that *im-* is a prefix meaning "not," you will quickly see that *imperfect* means "not perfect."

3. In applying the meanings of prefixes, roots, and suffixes, change the form of the root definition if necessary. For example, in the word *vision, vis* is "see," and *-ion* is "act of." "Act of see" is what you get when you put the two together, so you change that to "act of see*ing.*"

4. Remember that context clues will give you extra help in unlocking words. For example, if you met the word *illegible* by itself, you would know from *il-* and *-ible* that it means "not able to be" something or other, but without knowing the meaning of the root (*leg*), you would be stumped. If the word were in a sentence, the context might give you the clue to that root:

Because the ink had faded, most of the words were *illegible.*

Faded is the clue that you need to decide that *illegible* means "not able to be read."

LEARNING ACTIVITIES

A. (1) Go over the following words in class. Give the meaning of each word and show how knowing the prefixes, root words, and suffixes helps you figure out the meaning. (2) Name other words with the same roots.

1. inaudible	6. sensation	11. revive
2. telegrapher	7. auditor	12. visionless
3. invisible	8. tonsillitis	13. mismanage
4. preview	9. television	14. audition
5. sensible	10. audiometer	15. senselessness

B. Many words begin with the following prefixes: *uni-, trans-, sub-, non-, auto-,* and *pro-.* Take turns at giving words that begin with these prefixes. Write the words on the board; see how long a list you can make.

C. (1) Copy the following sentences, supplying prefixes and suffixes from the lists on page 116 to complete the words that have letters missing. (2) Exchange papers for checking. (3) Proofread for careless errors, especially in spelling.

1. The snake lay motion____ in the grass until it ____vived.
2. A reason____ person would admit that my search for the lost mine is use____, but my stubborn____ keeps me going.
3. The weather report ____dicts some ____cipita____ for tonight. Most of the forecasts are reli____.
4. My chief competit____ in the race had just ____covered from an appendic____ opera____.
5. You ____judge Charles. I have watched his ____casts on WNBQ count____ times, and I have never yet ____ceived any ____informa____ from them.
6. Are you ____mune to smallpox?

ENRICHMENT

Using the prefixes, root words, and suffixes in guide 1 on page 116, invent new words. For instance, you might make *sensometer* and *regrapher.* Ask the class to decide what they think your words mean.

3. Using the Dictionary

READ AND THINK ABOUT . . .

Once upon a time Mark Twain, who wrote *The Adventures of Tom Sawyer,* sat in the United States Senate listening to a friend make a long speech. Mark Twain decided the next day to have some fun with this friend.

"Do you know, Senator," he said, "I was surprised at your speech yesterday. You may not believe it, but I own a very old book which has every word of that speech in it!"

The senator was indignant. "That speech," he shouted, "was entirely my own! I'd like to see the book, old or new, that contains it!"

A few days later he received a copy of a much-used dictionary!

Of course that book had every word the senator had used. In fact, if it was an unabridged dictionary, it had all the words that anyone who speaks and writes English generally uses to express ideas.

Context clues and a knowledge of word parts often help you to figure out word meanings. When you need further help, the place to look first is in the dictionary. Perhaps you already have the dictionary habit; if not, now is a good time to get it. Using the dictionary regularly will help you (1) to understand better what you hear or read and (2) to express yourself better.

FINDING THE WORD

THINK IT OVER . . .

To find words quickly, you must know the alphabet. Really knowing the alphabet means more, however, than just being able to say it through quickly from *a* to *z*. It means, for example, knowing, without having to say half the alphabet through first, that *s* comes after *r* and before *t;* that *j* comes before *k*, and *k* before *l*.

GUIDES FOR INCREASING SKILL IN USING THE ALPHABET

1. Learn to say and write the alphabet in sections: *abc, bcd, cde, def, efg, fgh,* and so on through the alphabet. When you can speed through them, go on to groups of four: *abcd, bcde,* and so on.

2. Skim not only the first letter of a word, but the second, third, and so on. For example, suppose you want to find *minimum* in a dictionary.

   a) Find the *m*'s.
   b) Skip over all the *ma* and *me* words.
   c) Skip over all the words that begin with *mic, mid,* and so on until you reach *min.*
   d) Skim the *min* words until you reach *mini.*
   e) Skim those *mini* words (there will not be many) until you find *minimum.*

3. Use the guide words to help you skim. These guide words are the big black words at the top of each page. The guide word at the top of the left column tells the first word on the page. The one above the right column tells the last word on the page.

4. Use the thumb index, if your dictionary has one, to help you turn quickly to the right letter.

LEARNING ACTIVITIES

A. (1) In this exercise, think of the two letters that come *just before* and the two letters that come *just after* each letter given below. (2) Have someone read the letters as given here, while you write them, as rapidly as you can, with the two letters that come before and the two letters that come after them. In other words, for the letter *p* you would write **n, o,** *p,* **q, r.** (3) Exchange papers for checking.

1. __ c __	6. __ m __	11. __ t __	16. __ f __
2. __ r __	7. __ w __	12. __ e __	17. __ p __
3. __ u __	8. __ h __	13. __ s __	18. __ g __
4. __ j __	9. __ o __	14. __ k __	19. __ l __
5. __ d __	10. __ i __	15. __ v __	20. __ n __

B. (1) In your dictionary, locate the following words. (2) Write down (*a*) the number of the page containing each word and (*b*) the guide words on that page. (3) Check work in your small groups.

1. mischief	6. nozzle	11. shank	16. attend
2. porch	7. foundry	12. salable	17. whether
3. expense	8. increase	13. kernel	18. tragic
4. pilot	9. correct	14. earnest	19. restrict
5. wrought	10. quest	15. glove	20. humidor

C. Write these words in the order in which they would appear in the dictionary. When you have finished, exchange papers for checking.

1. carrot	7. grumble	13. graduate	19. candy
2. forgive	8. daughter	14. memorize	20. frighten
3. shoulder	9. shower	15. friendship	21. soldier
4. foreign	10. candidate	16. career	22. memory
5. camera	11. friendliness	17. milling	23. graduation
6. solid	12. millionaire	18. darkness	24. should

LEARNING WHAT THE DICTIONARY TELLS ABOUT A WORD

Here are some kinds of information that the dictionary gives about words. The numbers on the following page are keyed to this list.

1. Spelling
2. Pronunciation: (*a*) respelling; (*b*) key
3. Division into syllables
4. Meanings
5. Part of speech
6. Derivation (history of the word)
7. Forms: (*a*) of plurals; (*b*) of verbs; (*c*) of adjective and adverb comparisons
8. Illustrations
9. Synonyms

LEARNING ACTIVITY

On the sample dictionary page that follows, find the answers to these questions. Make this an oral activity.

1. Name a geographical region of Europe that is now divided among three different countries.
2. Name a tropical bird whose name is Spanish in origin.
3. What word is derived from a German abbreviation?
4. Give a name that is a synonym for *pancake.*
5. What word derives from the Latin word for *whip?*
6. The name of what fabric derives from a Middle English word?

flag·wav ing (flag'wā'ving), *n.* **1** the waving of the flag of one's country to excite patriotic feelings in others. **2** any similar attempt to arouse popular enthusiasm for a cause.

flail (flāl), *n.* instrument for threshing grain by hand, consisting of a wooden handle at the end of which a stouter and shorter pole or club is fastened so as to swing freely. *—v.t.* **1** strike with a flail. **2** beat; thrash. [< Old French *flaiel* < Latin *flagellum* whip]

flair (fler, flar), *n.* **1** natural talent: *a flair for making clever rhymes.* **2** keen perception: *That trader has a flair for bargains.* [< Old French, scent < *flairer* to smell < Latin *fragrare*]

flak (flak), *n.* **1** shellfire from antiaircraft cannon. **2** INFORMAL. criticism. Also, **flack.** [< German *Fl.A.K.*, abbreviation of *Fl(ieger)a(bwehr)k(anone)* antiaircraft cannon]

flake (flāk), *n., v.,* **flaked, flak ing.** *—n.* **1** a small, light mass; soft, loose bit: *a flake of snow.* **2** a flat, thin piece or layer: *a flake of rust.* *—v.i.* come off in flakes; separate into flakes: *Dirty, gray spots showed where the paint had flaked off.* *—v.t.* **1** break or separate into flakes. **2** cover or mark with flakes. **3** form into flakes. [perhaps < Scandinavian (Old Icelandic) *flakna* chip off] *—flake'like',* adj.

flak y (flā'kē), *adj.,* **flak i er, flak i est. 1** consisting of flakes. **2** easily broken or separated into flakes. *—flak'i ly,* adv. *—flak'i ness, n.*

flam beau (flam'bō) ,*n., pl.* **-beaux** or **-beaus** (-bōz). **1** a flaming torch. **2** a large, decorated candlestick. [< French]

flam boy ance (flam boi'əns), *n.* flamboyant nature or quality.

flam boy an cy (flam boi'ən sē), *n.* flamboyance.

flam boy ant (flam boi'ənt), *adj.* **1** gorgeously brilliant; flaming; showily striking: *flamboyant colors.* **2** very ornate; much decorated; florid: *flamboyant architecture.* **3** given to display; ostentatious; showy. **4** having wavy lines or flamelike curves: *flamboyant designs.* [< French] *—* **flam boy'ant ly,** adv.

flame (flām), *n., v.,* **flamed, flam ing.** *—n.* **1** one of the glowing tongues of light, usually red or yellow, that shoot out from a blazing fire. **2** a burning gas or vapor. **3** a burning with flames; blaze. See synonym study below. **4** something like flame. **5** brilliance; luster. **6** a bright light. **7** a burning feeling; ardor; zeal. **8** INFORMAL. sweetheart. *—v.i.* **1** rise up in flames; blaze. **2** grow hot, red, etc.: *Her cheeks flamed.* **3** shine brightly; give out a bright light; flash. **4** have or show a burning feeling. **5** burst out quickly and hotly; be or act like a flame. *—v.t.* subject to a flame; heat in a flame: *flame a test tube.* [< Latin *flamma*] *—flame'like', adj.*

Syn. *n.* **3 Flame, blaze** mean a bright burning or fire. **Flame** applies to a fire burning brightly and quickly: *The dying fire suddenly burst into flame.* **Blaze** applies to a hotter, brighter, and more steady fire: *The whole room was lighted by the blaze in the fireplace.*

fla men co (flə meng'kō), *n., pl.* **-cos.** style of Spanish Gypsy dance, originally of Andalusia, performed with castanets to fast, fiery, vigorous rhythms. [< Spanish, literally, Flemish (applied to the Gypsies' dance celebrating their departure from Germany, later confused with Flanders)]

flam ing (flā'ming), *adj.* **1** burning with flames; on fire. **2** like a flame; very bright; brilliant. **3** showing or arousing strong feeling; violent; vehement.

fla min go (flə ming'gō), *n., pl.* **-gos** or **-goes.** any of a family of large, web-footed, aquatic tropical birds with very long legs and neck, a heavy, bent bill, and feathers that vary from pink to scarlet. [< Portuguese < Spanish *flamenco,* literally, Flemish (from comparing the ruddy complexion of Flemings to the bird's color)]

flam ma bil i ty (flam'ə bil'ə tē), *n.* flammable quality or condition; inflammability.

flam ma ble (flam'ə bəl), *adj.* easily set on fire; inflammable.

Flan ders (flan'dərz), *n.* region in N Europe. It is now divided among Belgium, France, and the Netherlands. See **Burgundy** for map.

flange (flanj), *n., v.,* **flanged, flang ing.** *—n.* a projecting edge, collar, or rim on a wheel, pulley, pipe, or other object, used to keep an object in place, fasten it to another, strengthen it, etc. *—v.t.* provide with a flange. [perhaps ultimately < Old French *flanchir* to bend]

flange
on a railroad
car wheel

flank (flangk), *n.* **1** the fleshy or muscular part of the side of an animal or person between the ribs and the hip. **2** piece of beef cut from this part. See **beef** for diagram. **3** side of a mountain, building, etc. **4** the far right or the far left side of an army, fleet, or fort. *—v.t.* **1** be at the side of: *A garage flanked the house.* **2** get around the far right or the far left side of. **3** attack from or on the side. *—v.i.* **1** occupy a position on a flank or side. **2** present the flank or side. [< Old French *flanc* < Germanic]

flank er (flang'kər), *n.* **1** person or thing that flanks. **2** flankerback.

flank er back (flang'kər bak'), *n.* (in football) an offensive back who lines up on either flank, closer to the sidelines than his teammates.

flan nel (flan'l), *n.* **1** a soft, warm, woolen or worsted fabric having a nap on both sides. **2** a similar fabric made of cotton, especially a strong fabric with a long, soft nap, usually on one side only. **3** **flannels,** *pl.* **a** clothes, especially trousers, made of flannel. **b** woolen underwear. **4** flannelette. *—adj.* made of flannel. [Middle English *flaunneol*]

flan nel ette or **flan nel et** (flan'l et'), *n.* a soft, warm, cotton cloth with a fuzzy nap that looks like flannel.

flap (flap), *v.,* **flapped, flap ping,** *n.* *—v.i.* **1** swing or sway about loosely and with some noise: *The sails flapped in the wind.* **2** fly by moving wings up and down: *The bird flapped away.* *—v.t.* **1** cause to swing or sway loosely. **2** move (wings, arms, etc.) up and down; beat. **3** strike noisily with something broad and flat. *—n.* **1** a flapping motion. **2** noise caused by flapping. **3** a blow from something broad and flat. **4** a broad, flat piece, usually hanging or fastened at one edge only: *His coat had flaps on the pockets.* **5** a hinged section on an airfoil of an airplane, especially a wing, which can be moved to assist a take-off or a landing. [Middle English *flappe*]

flap jack (flap'jak'), *n.* pancake.

flap per (flap'ər), *n.* **1** something that flaps. **2** a young bird just able to fly. **3** a rather forward and unconventional young woman of the 1920's.

Adapted from *Thorndike Barnhart Advanced Dictionary,* second edition, by E. L. Thorndike and Clarence L. Barnhart; copyright © 1974 by Scott, Foresman and Company, Glenview, Illinois. Reprinted with permission.

PRONOUNCING WORDS

When you run into an unknown word in your reading, one of the things that you want to know is how to pronounce the word. In such a case, the dictionary is ready to help you. Notice the following aids to pronouncing words.

1. Syllable divisions are shown by spaces, as in **par ox ysm.**

2. The pronunciation of a word is shown in parentheses after the word, as in **halt** *(hôlt).*

3. The main accent is shown by a heavy mark (′). It tells which part of a word of more than one syllable gets the most emphasis, as in **excerpt** (*n.* ek′sėrpt; *v.* ek sėrpt′).

4. In some longer words, two syllables may be accented, with one syllable being emphasized more than the other and therefore being shown by the heavy accent mark. The lighter accent is shown by a lighter mark (′), as in **energetic** (en′ər jet′ik).

5. How the various letters are pronounced is shown in the key at the foot of the page or at the top right of every right-hand page. For example, ä is the marking for the sound of the *a* in *far;* ė, for the *e* in her; ô, for the *o* in *order.* These marks are known as *diacritical marks.*

LEARNING ACTIVITIES

A. (1) In the key at the top right of the sample dictionary page, find these words: *age, hat, far, equal, let, term, ice, it, open, hot, cup.* (2) Copy those eleven words in a column. (3) Beside each word, write one or more other words containing the same sound as that of the marked vowel. For *āge,* for example, *gate, crane,* and *maple* have the same *a* sound. (4) Compare work in class.

B. (1) Using the pronunciation key in your dictionary, indicate the vowel sounds in each of the following words. (2) Exchange papers with your classmates. (3) Check by looking up the vowel markings of each word as given in your dictionary.

1. foot	5. meal	9. paid	13. wear
2. bone	6. weigh	10. blind	14. turn
3. tool	7. farm	11. meat	15. goal
4. hall	8. seize	12. war	16. rule

C. Find in the dictionary the answers to the following questions. Each question has to do with the respellings and markings that the dictionary gives in the parentheses after the words italicized in the questions. Make this an oral activity.

1. What happens to the *g* in *gentle?*
2. What happens to the *y* in *say?* to the *e* in *late?*
3. What happens to the *ey* in *they?*
4. What takes the place of the *t* in *whistle?*
5. What happens to the *i* in *first?*
6. What happens to the *nk* in *think?*
7. What happens to the *i* and the *a* in *field* and *meat?*
8. What happens to the *c* in *cent?*
9. The respellings of *hallow* and *halo* contain the same four letters. How do their markings differ?

D. (1) Copy each of the following words, putting them all into one column. (2) In your dictionary, find and copy the respelling of each word. (3) Mark the sound of each vowel, and put in the accent marks. (4) Pronounce the words in class to show that you know what the marks mean.

1. invulnerable	4. stabilize	7. tonsorial
2. culinary	5. decorum	8. harbinger
3. masticate	6. multitudinous	9. turbulent

FOLLOW-UP

Notice the words "Used correct pronunciation" on your Speech Chart, page 63. From now on, pay special attention to this point.

USING ENGLISH IN ALL CLASSES

Check through a lesson in another subject to see whether any sentences contain words that you are not sure you can pronounce. Find the words in the dictionary and figure out the pronunciation. Then practice reading the sentences until you are sure of the pronunciation of every word.

DIVIDING WORDS INTO SYLLABLES

As shown in point 1 on page 122, dividing words into syllables is a help in pronunciation. Knowing how to divide words into syllables is also helpful in all your written work, since you often need to break a word at the end of a line.

GUIDES TO DIVIDING WORDS INTO SYLLABLES

1. If you are uncertain where to divide a word, use your dictionary. *Thorndike-Barnhart Advanced Dictionary* (see the sample on page 121) shows syllable divisions by spaces.

    EXAMPLE: par tic i pant (pär tis′ə pənt)

2. In written work, use a hyphen at the end of the line to show that a word is divided. (See guide 7 on page 148.)

3. Divide only between syllables, but never leave a single letter at the end of a line or at the beginning of the next line.

    WRONG: He turned his face a̶
              way. [Do not divide the word.]

    WRONG: We shall need *man-*
              *y̶*helpers. [Do not divide the word.]

LEARNING ACTIVITIES

A. Divide the class into two equal groups. Then see which group can (1) find the most words of more than one syllable in the following paragraph, and (2) divide them correctly. Omit the proper nouns.

> I had heard of some giant bats in the Chillibrillo Valley in Panama, creatures with a wing spread of a yard. They had originally been described by Linnaeus, and a few preserved specimens were in museums, but no living example had ever been exhibited. I engaged some young Hindus in Trinidad, who were keen woodsmen. They found tails of rats and feathers at the hollow bases of giant silk-cotton trees. Such trees average twenty feet in diameter at the ground, and taper up to towering, cylindrical trunks. In the broadened portion they are usually hollow to a height of about twenty-five feet. Investigation by flash lamps disclosed that these tree chambers were the homes of single pairs of giant bats, and that these bats were flesh eaters. When I arrived, I went to the inhabited trees. The beam of the searchlight in each hollow shaft revealed a pair of hanging bats whose bodies looked almost as big as those of opossums. With spliced bamboo poles we dislodged the bats toward us. As we grasped them in heavily gloved hands, their big wings wrapped around us like folds of a thin raincoat. I captured three pairs.
>
> —RAYMOND DITMARS*

* Adapted from *Animal Kingdom: The Way of Life in a Zoo* by Raymond Ditmars; copyright © 1969 by Harper & Row, Publishers, Inc., New York.

B. For further drill, turn to pages 167–170 and copy one of the paragraphs there. Keep as even a margin as you can at the right (one-half inch or more). Doing so will mean that you must divide some words at the end of a line. To help you decide where the divisions come, pronounce the words to yourself so that you can hear each syllable clearly. Exchange papers and check by using the dictionary.

USING ENGLISH IN ALL CLASSES

Go over the most recent paper that you have written for some other class. Look at each word that you divided at the end of a line; check in a dictionary to see whether you did so correctly. If the word is not divided right, make the necessary corrections.

FINDING THE RIGHT MEANING

THINK IT OVER . . .

What does the girl need to to know about the word *keen*? What is the intended meaning of the word here?

As you should have discovered before now, most words have more than one meaning; some words have many, many meanings. When you look up a word that you have met in your reading, you need to choose one meaning out of the different ones given in the dictionary. Here are some guides to help you.

GUIDES TO FINDING THE RIGHT MEANING

1. Read through the various meanings.

2. Choose the meaning that makes the best sense in the sentence in which you found the word.

3. If the word you are looking up is a verb that ends in *ed* or *ing*, drop the ending and find the base word. Choose the best meaning and add *ed* or *ing*, whichever your word had. For example, look at this sentence:

> My father's health had been *deteriorating* for weeks.

The dictionary may give no definition for *deteriorating;* so you look up *deteriorate*. You find that one meaning is *grow worse*. You add *ing* to *grow* and substitute that meaning:

> My father's health had been *growing worse* for weeks.

LEARNING ACTIVITIES

A. Here are some sentences using words that are defined on the sample dictionary page (page 121 of this book). Decide which of the numbered meanings is needed in each sentence. Make this an oral activity.

1. Do you like the *flambeaux* on the wall?
2. *Flag-waving* isn't always sincere.
3. The paint is *flaking*.
4. We had *flank* steak for dinner.
5. My grandmother was a *flapper*.

B. (1) Rewrite the following paragraphs, using other words for the words in italics. Use your dictionary to help you pick out the meaning that makes the best sense for each word. (2) Proofread for careless errors in copying. (3) Read several paragraphs in class or in your small groups. (4) List the various words substituted for the italicized ones. (5) Decide which words give the meaning best.

1. To begin with, the Emperor penguin is a bird, but it is as incapable of *locomotion* in the air as people were before balloons or airplanes were thought of. It can move freely only in water. It is a bird, but unlike most birds, it chooses for its breeding grounds not a *latitude teeming* with insects and grain, with trees to nest in, but instead the most *inhospitable* land in the world, the Antarctic continent. Moreover, its *perversity* is such that, as if to say that we have seen nothing yet, it chooses not the *comparative* mildness of Antarctic summer but the very depth of winter, the

season of 100-mile-an-hour winds, blizzard snows, and temperature of from 40 to 70 degrees below zero, in which to *incubate* its eggs.

—RAYMOND P. HOLDEN*

2. People who have been turned out of their homes make *keen* historians. Forced from the land of their ancestors and onto the open road without a *destination,* they have a way of remembering—often to the minute of the day—the *trauma* of departure. *Etched indelibly* in their memories are the details: a *frenetic* packing; a final, hurried look around an abandoned house; a *wistful,* wishful fondling of familiar possessions that couldn't be taken with them; then, if they were lucky and had wheels instead of just shoe leather and shoulders beneath their possessions, there was the *wrenching* moment of the last, silent, no-looks-back drive out to the nearest highway.

—THOMAS W. PEW, JR.†

USING ENGLISH IN ALL CLASSES

(1) From your next day's assignment in any class, choose and copy a paragraph that has in it at least five unfamiliar words. (If necessary, take more than one paragraph.) (2) Underline the words that puzzle you. Find each word in the dictionary and then select the meaning that fits. (3) Above each puzzling word write the meaning that you chose.

EXPLORING SPECIAL SECTIONS
IN THE DICTIONARY

Some dictionaries have certain special sections. Most dictionaries include brief sections on "How to Use This Dictionary." Such sections are of specific help in getting the most out of dictionary study. Here, for instance, are the main items

* From "Birds of Paradox" from *Wildlife Mysteries* by Raymond P. Holden; copyright © 1972 by Raymond P. Holden. Reprinted by permission of Dodd, Mead & Company, New York.

† From "Route 66: Ghost Road of the Okies" by Thomas W. Pew, Jr., from *American Heritage,* Vol. 28, No. 5, August 1977; copyright © 1977 by American Heritage Publishing Co., Inc., New York.

included in the "Using This Dictionary" section of the *Thorn-dike-Barnhart Advanced Dictionary*:

How to Find Words
How to Use and Understand the Pronunciations
How to Find and Understand Meanings
How to Use This Dictionary for Spelling
How to Use This Dictionary for Writing

LEARNING ACTIVITIES

A. Referring to the pronunciation chart in your dictionary (in the *Thorndike-Barnhart Advanced Dictionary,* this chart is on pages 26 and 27 of "How to Use This Dictionary for Spelling"), copy the various spellings for the following sounds.

1. the *ü* sound
2. the *schwa* (ə) sound
3. the *ō* sound
4. the *g* sound
5. the *n* sound
6. the *z* sound

B. (1) In your dictionary, find the following abbreviations. Some have more than one meaning. (2) Write the abbreviations and their meanings on a sheet of paper. (3) Go over papers orally.

1. agt.
2. alt.
3. amt.
4. b.
5. bal.
6. bbl.
7. chap.
8. dept.
9. fr.
10. k.
11. N.E.A.
12. pk.

C. In your dictionary, find answers to the following questions. Write each answer in a complete sentence. Proofread for careless mistakes in spelling, capitalization, and punctuation. Exchange papers for checking as the answers are read aloud.

1. When was Mary McLeod *Bethune* born?
2. Where and what is *Vesuvius?*
3. When was James *Madison* President?
4. For what is Marie *Curie* famous?
5. What is another name for *Nippon?*
6. How far below sea level is the *Dead Sea?*
7. Which English king named *Edward* was murdered in the Tower of London?
8. How many square miles are there in the state of *Hawaii?*
9. How many *Catherines* were Russian empresses?
10. Who was Katsushika *Hokusai?*

FINDING AND USING SOURCES OF INFORMATION

"I THINK IT'S A BIG RED BOOK."

1. Exploring Reference Books

READ AND THINK ABOUT . . .

You have seen how much information the dictionary can give you. Sometimes, however, you want to know more than the brief facts given in the dictionary. What do you do then?

Knowing where to look for information is important, for then you are pretty sure to find what you need — and are likely to find it quickly. Among the references that will be most useful to you are (1) almanacs, (2) atlases, (3) encyclopedias, (4) the *Readers' Guide,* and (5) books on special subjects.

YEARBOOKS OF FACTS, OR ALMANACS

Yearbooks of facts, also called *almanacs,* contain up-to-date information about many things, such as the name of the football team that won the Rose Bowl game last year, the name of the state that leads in the production of corn, and so on. Two of the best-known almanacs are listed here.

Information Please Almanac
World Almanac and Book of Facts

ATLASES

An *atlas* is a book of maps and other geographical information. It contains not only maps that show the location of countries, cities, and so on, but maps that show natural resources, population facts, temperature and rainfall, surface features, and many other things. The following are atlases especially prepared for school use.

Denoyer's School Atlas
Hammond's World Atlas for Students
Rand McNally's World Atlas, Goode's Edition

ENCYCLOPEDIAS

Encyclopedias usually are sets of books. They give information about thousands of people, places, things, and events. Those listed here are found in many schools.

Britannica Junior Encyclopaedia for Boys and Girls
Compton's Encyclopedia and Fact-Index
World Book Encyclopedia

READERS' GUIDE

The *Readers' Guide to Periodical Literature* (usually shortened to *Readers' Guide*) is an index naming all the articles published in more than a hundred important magazines. (Magazines are called *periodical* literature because they come out at regular periods.)

Here is part of a page from the *Readers' Guide,** showing some of the information given for various topics. The abbreviations that are used are explained at the front of each issue.

LIGHT tables. (See Drawing boards, tables, etc.) — *cross reference*

page numbers — LIGHTING fixtures
Kitchen lighting pointers. Bet Hom & Gard 50:168+ N '72
LIGHTSEY, Ralph. See Lanier, D. jt. auth.

LILIES
author entry — Lilies, a glory; with photographs by I. Penn. Vogue 160:166-9 D '72
(LIN, Yutang) — *title of magazine*
Scrutable Chinese. il por (Newsweek) 80:128-9 D 4 '72 *

subject — (LINCOLN, Abraham)
Lincoln's lost love; letter. April 1, 1838. (il) — *illustrated*
por Am Heritage 23:110-11 Ap '72

LINCOLN, George A. — *date of publication*
Winter fuel shortage: how serious? interview. il por U.S. News 73:73-6 (D 11 '72)

LINCOLN Center for the performing arts, New York
(Opera house) — *subtopic*
title of article — (Touring backstage.) L. Levant. il Opera N 37:32-3 D 23 '72

BOOKS ON SPECIAL SUBJECTS

Books on special subjects, textbooks, for example, contain information about some particular field of knowledge.

* From *Readers' Guide to Periodical Literature,* Vol. 72, No. 20, January 10, 1973; copyright © 1973 by The H. W. Wilson Company, New York.

GUIDES TO THE USE OF REFERENCE BOOKS

1. Get acquainted with the way that encyclopedias are organized. Like the dictionary, the entries in encyclopedias are arranged alphabetically and have guide words at the top of each page. Look for the last name of a person, as in the telephone book.

    a) The first volume of *Britannica Junior* is a ready reference index, alphabetically arranged, of all the different topics covered. It lists for each topic all pages in the entire set that contain information about the topic. The letter *a* after a page number indicates that the information is in the left-hand column; *b,* in the right-hand one.

    b) *Compton's Encyclopedia and Fact-Index* has at the back of each volume an index that lists all the items covered in that volume, plus references to other volumes that also have information on that topic.

    c) *World Book* has a special index volume, *Research Guide and Index,* that accompanies the set. It is organized alphabetically under many subject-matter heads.

2. Learn to use the index that you will find at the back of most atlases, almanacs,* and books on special subjects.

3. Get acquainted with the organization of the *Readers' Guide.*

    a) Main entries give (1) subjects or (2) names of people.

    b) Subheads break subjects into smaller topics. Under "Phonograph records," for example, you might find such entries as "Folk music," "Jazz music," "Opera."

    c) Names of people may refer to (1) authors or (2) people about whom someone has written articles.

LEARNING ACTIVITIES

A. Check your classroom. Does it have a set of encyclopedias, an atlas, and any special subject books besides your regular textbooks?

Hold a discussion about ways to make good use of the reference books in your classroom. Have a chairperson in charge. He or she should look up guide 2 of the Guides for Holding Discussions, page 35.

B. If your school has a library, arrange to take a period or more to find out how many of the references listed on pages 130–131 are contained

---

*The index of the *World Almanac* is at the front of the book.

there. Make note of other special reference books. List on the board all these sources. Decide how they can best be used.

C. Let someone volunteer to call the public library to see whether your class may arrange for a visit there. After the visit, discuss in class the sources of information that you found at the library.

Write a letter thanking the librarian for allowing you to visit. Follow the Guides for Writing Thank-You Letters, page 214, and use the form for business letters, page 216. Choose and mail one of the best letters.

D. In which kind of reference book, other than books on special subjects, could you probably find answers to the following questions? Make this an oral discussion.

1. Where and when was the atom first split?
2. Which baseball player won the American League batting championship last year, and what was his batting average?
3. Which countries of the world lead in coal production?
4. What river forms part of the boundary between Uruguay and Argentina?
5. Who is the United States secretary of state now?
6. Who first played the game of lacrosse?
7. Have there been any important new discoveries in medicine in the past few months?
8. What countries of the world have a very light rainfall?
9. How many voyages to the New World did Columbus make?
10. How are diamonds mined?

E. Here are some entries from the *Readers' Guide*. With the help of the sample on page 131, tell all the information given in each entry. Make this an oral activity. Magazine names that are abbreviated are *Natural History, New Catholic World,* and *National Parks and Conservation Magazine.*

MALI
Native races
Nomads of the Niger. J. P. Imperato. il Natur Hist 81:60-9+ D '72

MALITS, Elena
Yoga is a spiritual discipline. il New Cath World 215:249-51+ N '72

MALLIOS, Harry C.
Symbolic expression: the new battle facing school administrators. bibliog Intellect 101: 117-18 N '72

MALPRACTICE
Yogurt cure; treatment at Feminist women's health center in Los Angeles. Newsweek 80:44 D 18 '72

MAMMOTH CAVE NATIONAL PARK
Mammoth Cave. Holiday 52:26 N '72
Mammoth Cave: a model plan. R. A. Watson. il Nat Parks & Con Mag 46:13-18 D '72

F. In finding answers to the following questions, which key words would you look up in the encyclopedia or in the index of some other book? Number your paper from 1 to 10 and beside each number write the word or words that you would look for first. Compare words in class; then find the answers to the questions.

1. What is the motto of the state of Kentucky?
2. What is the area of Scotland?
3. Which baseball league came first, the National or the American?
4. Who discovered the Hawaiian Islands?
5. What country first tried to dig the Panama Canal?
6. When did the United States Military Academy at West Point first begin admitting women?
7. What new volcano appeared in Mexico in 1943?
8. In what year did the United States set up standard time zones?
9. Can a living person be elected to the Hall of Fame?
10. Where was the great contralto Marian Anderson born?

USING ENGLISH OUTSIDE SCHOOL

Have you a hobby? If so, use the *Readers' Guide* to find magazines or magazine articles about it. In reading them, you may discover people with whom you would like to correspond. In that case, follow the letter-writing guides on pages 203, 207, and 209.

2. Finding Books in the Library

THINK IT OVER . . .

Examining everything on the library shelves in search of a particular book probably is a harder job than you would care to tackle. Luckily, that kind of search is not necessary, for most libraries are arranged in a special way that makes finding books easy.

The plan used by most libraries is the *Dewey Decimal System.* The Dewey system classifies nonfiction books. Storybooks (books of fiction) are not arranged according to the Dewey Decimal System. They are placed in a special "fiction" section and are arranged alphabetically, by the authors' last names.

● THESE ARE FACTS ABOUT THE DEWEY DECIMAL SYSTEM

1. **The Dewey Decimal System divides books into ten large classes, such as** *Religion, Social Sciences, History.*

2. **Each class is assigned a special set of numbers.** Every book about language, for example, will be marked with a number somewhere between 400 and 499. All those books will be put together in one section of the library.

3. **The class number of a book is part of what is known as its "call number."** The call number has two parts:

   a) The upper part is the class number.
   b) The lower part begins with a letter, the first letter of the author's last name.

   The call number is put on the backbone, or "spine," of the book so that it can be seen as the book stands on the shelf.

4. **Books are arranged on the library shelves in regular order from left to right, beginning with the lowest call numbers.** When the upper part of the call number of two or more books is the same, the books are arranged in order by the lower part, as shown by the 373.6 books in the drawing.

| 370 | 373.6 | 373.6 | 373.6 | 373.6 | 375 |
| G | B | B | G | H | B |

LEARNING ACTIVITY

Arrange in a column the following call numbers in the order that books so marked would be found on the library shelves. Make this a chalkboard activity.

702.4	717.3	722.44	717.4	717.1
H	D	M	F	F
792	717.4	722.1	792.1	722.21
A	C	R	A	R

THE CARD CATALOGUE

As you can see, once you know the call number, you will know where to look for a certain book. To find the call number itself, you should look in the *card catalogue*.

● **THESE ARE FACTS ABOUT THE CARD CATALOGUE**

1. **The card catalogue is contained in a cabinet with drawers.**
   a) **On the front of each drawer is a label telling what part of the alphabet the cards in it cover.**
   b) **In the drawer are cards, arranged alphabetically, that give the call number of every book in the library.**
2. **Every book except fiction (storybooks) has three cards:** *(a)* **an** *author* **card,** *(b)* **a** *title* **card, and** *(c)* **a** *subject* **card.**
3. **Books of fiction have** *(a)* **an** *author* **card and** *(b)* **a** *title* **card.**
4. **Each card carries the call number of the book, in the upper left-hand corner. Fiction may have no call number, or may have only the lower part, perhaps with** *F* **(for** *Fiction*) **above it.**

Author Card

The author card is filed alphabetically by the *author's last name*.

```
 *     J
       301.43
          S        Singer, Julia.
                      We all come from Puerto Rico, too.  New
                   York:  Atheneum Publishers, 1977.

                      Summary:  Photographs and brief text
                   describe children at work and play in the
                   villages, towns, and cities of Puerto Rico.

                      1.  Puerto Rico--Social life and customs.
                   I.  Title.

                               ◯
```

*The J above the call number indicates that the book is juvenile literature.

Title Card

   The *title card* is the same as the author card, except that the *title* of the book is typed at the top of the card, above the author's name. The title card is filed in the card catalogue alphabetically by the first word on that top line, unless the first word of the title is *a, an,* or *the*. In that case, it will be filed by the second word.

```
J                We all come from Puerto Rico, too.
301.43
   S             Singer, Julia.
                 We all come from Puerto Rico, too.  New
            York:  Atheneum Publishers, 1977.

                 Summary:  Photographs and brief text
            describe children at work and play in the
            villages, towns, and cities of Puerto Rico.

                 1.  Puerto Rico--Social life and customs.
            I.  Title.

                              O
```

Subject Card

   The *subject card* is the same as the author card, except that the top line tells the *subject* dealt with in the book, such as *baseball* or *butterflies*. There will be a card for each book that the library has on that particular subject.

```
J                PUERTO RICO--SOCIAL LIFE AND CUSTOMS
301.43
   S             Singer, Julia.
                 We all come from Puerto Rico, too.  New
            York:  Atheneum Publishers, 1977.

                 Summary:  Photographs and brief text
            describe children at work and play in the
            villages, towns, and cities of Puerto Rico.

                 1.  Puerto Rico--Social life and customs.
            I.  Title.

                              O
```

LEARNING ACTIVITY

Write answers to the following questions, all based on the card below. Make each answer a complete sentence. Proofread for careless errors. Exchange papers for checking as you go over the questions in class.

624
M
        Macaulay, David.
           Underground. Boston: Houghton Mifflin Co., 1976.

           Summary: Text and drawings describe the subways, sewers, building foundations, telephone and power systems, columns, cables, pipes, tunnels, and other underground elements of a large modern city.

           1. Underground utility lines. 2. Underground construction. I. Title.

---

1. Who is the author?
2. What is the title?
3. Who published the book? When?
4. Under what subject would the book be catalogued?
5. Why is there no *J* above the call number?

GUIDES FOR LOCATING BOOKS IN THE LIBRARY

1. Go to the card catalogue.
   a) If you want a book and know its title, look for that title.
   b) If you want a particular book and know only the name of the author, look for that author's name.
   c) If you are looking for no particular book but want books on a special topic, such as *Circuses,* look under that word.
2. Copy the call number, the title of the book, and the author's name.
3. Find the shelf that holds the books with the upper number of the book that you want.
4. Look for the initial on the lower part of the call number.

LEARNING ACTIVITIES

A. (1) Decide whether you would look for an author card, a title card, or a subject card in each of the following cases. (2) Use the card catalogue to help you locate the books indicated. Copy and read to the class the call numbers, authors, and titles of the books that you find.

1. You are recommending to a friend a book called *Going into Space,* but you have forgotten the author's name.
2. You have heard that a man named Langston Hughes wrote several well-known books of poetry.
3. Chemistry is your hobby. You would like to know what books your library has in that field.
4. You want to get some information about helicopters.
5. You want to find some new books by M. E. Kerr.

B. In the card catalogue, look up the author of a book that you have read this year. Note whether your library has any other books by that person. Report to the class the name of the book that you read, the name of the author, and the call number. Give also the call numbers and titles of other books that the author has written.

C. (1) Using the card catalogue, make a list of six books that the library has on one of these subjects: *aviation, forests, poetry, art, television, politics, stars, inventions, music, travel, photography, physical education.* Copy the title, the name of the author, and the call number of each book. (2) See whether you can locate the books. (3) Leaf through the books to decide on several that you would like to read. (4) Put a star beside each such title on your list. (5) Compare lists in your small groups.

D. The following authors write (or have written) fiction enjoyed by boys and girls. Find out what books the library has by these authors. To do so, divide the names among the class. (If your class is large, two people may report on the same author.) Go over the lists in class. File in your notebook the names of books that you might want to read.

Frank Bonham	Marjorie Kinnan Rawlings
Hal Borland	Mari Sandoz
Ray Bradbury	Zoa Sherburne
Eleanor Cameron	Mary Stolz
B. J. Chute	Jesse Stuart
Howard Fast	B. Traven
Jean Craighead George	John R. Tunis
June Jordan	Margaret Walker
James M. Kjelgaard	Leonard Wibberly
Harper Lee	Maia Wojciechowska
Scott O'Dell	Paul Zindel

3. Getting Acquainted with the Make-up of a Book

Once you have found a book that looks as though it may contain needed information, you can save time by knowing how to use the various parts of the book.

The body of a book is the most important part, of course, but six other parts will help you to use the book efficiently. The first four come at the front; the other two, at the back.

1. The *title page* tells (1) what the name of the book is, (2) who wrote it, (3) who published it, and (4) where it was published. You will need this information if for any reason you want to write to the publisher.

2. The *copyright page* tells when the book was published. The date of publication is important, especially in fields such as science, where new discoveries are always being made.

3. The *preface* (or *foreword*) is the introduction to the book. It usually explains the purpose and tells in general what is covered.

4. The *table of contents* lists in order the chapter titles, usually with subtopics that are covered in them.

5. An *appendix* may follow the main text. It contains such things as explanatory notes, tables, lists of books, or other useful information.

6. The *index* comes last. It lists alphabetically all topics contained in the book and names the pages on which each topic is discussed. It also lists helpful cross references (*See . . .* or *See also . . .*) to other entries.

LEARNING ACTIVITY

(1) Examine this book to find the six parts mentioned above; then use them to find answers to the following questions. (2) Write the answers in complete sentences. (3) Proofread for careless errors. (4) Exchange papers for checking. Tell where you found the answers.

1. How many chapters deal with grammar? What are their numbers?
2. On what page are homophones defined?
3. Which chapter deals with improving reading skills?
4. What is in the appendix?
5. What is the newest date of publication?
6. How are the pages before the body of the book numbered?
7. How many authors has this book? What are their names? Who published it?

4. Making Reports

"I DID BETTER THAN THAT. I JUST COPIED WHAT THE BOOK SAID."

"DID YOU TAKE NOTES ABOUT WHAT YOU READ?"

MAKING A SHORT REPORT

When you are asked to report what is contained in a certain article (in an encyclopedia, a magazine, or a special book), you may make use of several skills: using reference books, the card catalogue, the *Readers' Guide;* taking notes of key words; and outlining. If you need to review any of these skills, use the index of this book to guide you to the right places for help.

GUIDES FOR MAKING A SHORT, ONE-SOURCE REPORT

1. Read the article through once to get the general idea.
2. Write, in your own words, a sentence that tells clearly what the article as a whole is about.
3. Go over the article again and jot down the words or groups of words that are key words. (Review the guides on page 96.)
4. Use those key words to make a topic outline. (See pages 106–107.)
5. Write an interesting opening and a strong closing sentence.
6. In making your report, tell where you found the article.
7. For an oral report, practice at home. Probably you will say things differently each time, but if you put the important key words into your outline, the *ideas* will be the same.

LEARNING ACTIVITIES

A. For your first practice, choose an article about a half-column long in an encyclopedia. Leaf through the book until you find something that looks interesting. Then follow the Guides for Making a Short, One-Source Report. In preparing for an oral report, check your Speech Chart.

After each report is given in class, jot down a note or two about the speaker. Use the Speech Chart, page 63, for points on which to comment. When all reports have been given, take time for each of you to mark his or her Speech Chart on the basis of the notes from classmates.

B. Repeat *A*, only this time write the report, using one of the topics listed below. Check each paragraph by the guides on page 162.

1. armor	6. deserts	11. rainbows	16. kangaroos
2. honey	7. geysers	12. Death Valley	17. Robin Hood
3. rabies	8. locusts	13. scorpions	18. sunstroke
4. tulips	9. marbles	14. pheasants	19. Eskimo dogs
5. stilts	10. pelicans	15. parakeets	20. battleships

REPORTING ON MATERIAL FROM SEVERAL SOURCES

Often, in preparing a report, you are expected to gather material from several sources. In such cases, you should follow a different plan from the one you used for a one-source report. Study the guides that follow.

GUIDES FOR MAKING A LONG REPORT

1. Decide what main points—no more than three or four—you want to cover. Write each main point on a separate sheet of paper and label each with a Roman numeral, I, II, and so on. For a report on *earthquakes,* for example, the first page might be labeled thus:

    I. The causes of earthquakes

    Page 2 might have this label:

    II. The effects of earthquakes

    Page 3 might be labeled thus:

    III. Famous earthquakes

2. Find the material. In addition to encyclopedias, consult other books. Use the card catalogue to find them. (See page 136.) Remember that indexes and tables of contents will save you time. Use the *Readers' Guide* to find magazine articles.

3. Go through these references one by one.

    a) Select only facts that tell about one of your main points.
    b) Jot each fact down on a separate note card, with the name of the source, the name of the author, and the page numbers.
    c) As a rule, put the information into your own words. If you do copy a sentence, use quotation marks and give credit.

4. Separate the cards into piles, one for each main idea. Arrange the facts in each pile in what seems to you the best order.

5. Under each main point, copy from the cards the points that fit it. Write them in regular outline form. (See pages 106–107.)

6. Make a bibliography, or list, of all the sources that you used. This should be put at the end of your report. Arrange the sources alphabetically in the style shown here.

    Hilton, W. F., *Manned Satellites,* pp. 3–45.
    Shatalov, Vladimir, "A Man on a Long Space Flight," *Space World* (October 1972), pp. 30–31.
    "Space Travel," *World Book Encyclopedia* (1967 edition), vol. 18, pp. 560–73.

7. Write the report.

    a) Write it quickly first, without stopping to go back over it.
    b) Go over each sentence and paragraph to be sure that you have written what you want to say.
    c) Check spelling, punctuation, and capitalization.
    d) Copy the report; then proofread it carefully.
    e) Make a cover sheet containing your name, the date, and the title of the report.

LEARNING ACTIVITY

Choose a topic for a report, one assigned in some other class, if possible. If not, you may want to choose one of those listed here.

1. Radar	9. Carrier Pigeons	17. Skin Diving
2. Tornadoes	10. Diamond Mining	18. Hybrid Corn
3. Meteors	11. Flying Saucers	19. Miracle Drugs
4. Whaling	12. Poisonous Snakes	20. Helicopters
5. Comets	13. The Pony Express	21. Indian Houses
6. Archery	14. Peaceful Uses of the Atom	22. Hurricanes
7. Mummies	15. Atomic Submarines	23. Fingerprinting
8. Volcanoes	16. Supersonic Planes	24. Color Television

ENRICHMENT

From the list of topics in the Learning Activity above, select two and prepare a short bibliography for each one. Consult the card catalogue (see page 136), the *Readers' Guide to Periodical Literature* (see page 131), and other reference books (see pages 130–132) for possible sources. For the proper form for your bibliography, see guide 6 on page 143.

Section III:

Writing

MANUSCRIPT FORM

1. Checking the Form of Your Papers

"WHAT DID CORY DO —
POLISH THE FLOOR
WITH IT?"

READ AND THINK ABOUT . . .

Suppose that by some chance you were asked to appear on television. What would concern you most, aside from whatever you were to do on the program? You probably would answer, "How I'd look — that's what!"

In other words, you would want to look your best, knowing that you must face the inspection of many thousands of pairs of eyes.

Something that may never have occurred to you, however, is that whenever you hand in a school paper, you are also up for inspection. What does the appearance of your paper tell the world about *you*?

GUIDES TO PROPER MANUSCRIPT FORM

1. Leave even margins on the sides and at the top and bottom. Your paper should look like a picture set in a frame. See the example on the next page.

2. Unless a different form is used in your school, put the name of the subject on the top line at the left, and your name at the right, with the date below it. The heading should have the same margins as the rest of the paper.

3. Skip a line; then center the title on the next line. Skip another line before you begin your theme.

4. Indent all paragraphs the same distance, at least one-half inch.

5. Write as plainly as you can. Avoid both large, scrawling handwriting and the tiny, cramped-looking kind. (See examples on page 479.)

6. Avoid blots, smudges, and messy cross-outs. If your papers are written in ink, use a good ink eraser.

7. Use a hyphen if you must divide a word at the end of a line. Be sure to put the hyphen at the end of the line, never at the beginning of the following line.

> WRONG: The candidates of both political parties were con xfident of victory.
> RIGHT: The candidates of both political parties were con-fident of victory.

a) Divide only between syllables. (DEFINITION) A *syllable*, you will recall, **is a part of a word pronounced as one sound.** It must always have a vowel (*a, e, i, o, u,* or *y*) and may have one or more consonants (all the other letters of the alphabet). When in doubt about the syllables in a word, use your dictionary. Note the following examples.

ath-lete	hol-i-day
spar-kling	shiv-ered

b) Never carry over a syllable that has in it only one letter. For example, do not divide *copy* (cop'y), since the second syllable has only one letter.

c) Never leave only the first letter of a word at the end of a line. For example, do not divide *about* (a bout'), since the first syllable has only one letter.

d) Never divide words of one syllable.

strength	broil	dealt

English   Elaine Daniels
                                          October 12, 19—

The Hit of the Play

Several summers ago, some friends and I decided to give a play, using our garage as a theater. We did a lot of practicing, but since we had no written play, we just made up our lines as we went along.

On the day that we were to give our performance, we worked like beavers, cleaning our garage, putting up benches, and building a stage. Our curtain was a blanket. It was full of holes, more or less pinned together with large safety pins.

While we were still getting ready, our audience began to arrive. Someone had the bright idea of letting them help us. Soon these helpers were suggesting ideas for the play, and before we knew it, they were in the cast. By the time the play finally began, we had twenty actors—and three people in the audience!

About the middle of the play, my sister walked in and announced, "Elaine, you've got to go to the store."

Even though I explained that we were in the middle of a murder and that I was the victim, it did me no good.

I ran all the way to the store and back. On returning, I found the same act still going on. I rushed up to the stage—and fell flat on my face. It was not really time for my murder, but my fall was too good to waste.

The audience clapped and cheered my "murder." It was worth the price of admission by itself, they declared; and it probably was, for we had taken in exactly one penny—and six safety pins!

LEARNING ACTIVITIES

A. In class, find out whether the form that your teacher wants your papers to have is different in any way from the form that is given in the guides. Take notes on what your teacher's answers are to the following questions:

1. What size of paper are we to use?
2. Are we to write with pen and ink?
3. What information are we to give in the heading? Should there be more than is shown in the example? Exactly where and in what order is the information to be given?
4. Are there to be equal margins on all sides of the paper? How wide are they to be?
5. Where is the title to be written? Shall there be a space below the title?
6. How far shall each paragraph be indented?
7. Are we to write on both sides of the paper?
8. What instructions do we follow when writing on the back or on the second sheet?

B. (1) Copy the following words. (2) Put parentheses around the ones that you would not divide at the end of a line. (3) Mark the other words to show where you would divide them. If you are not sure, use your dictionary. (4) Exchange papers and go over the words in class, explaining the reason for dividing or not dividing each word.

EXAMPLES

(length)   mil|i|tary   care|ful|ness

1. waiting
2. borrow
3. communicate
4. disappoint
5. stretch
6. hospital
7. beyond
8. health
9. breathe
10. grammar
11. yesterday
12. busy
13. waitress
14. honorable
15. dangerous
16. brought
17. gasoline
18. locate
19. wrench
20. remember

2. Making and Using a Writing Chart

Whatever you write should be easy to read and to understand. One practical way to check your skills is to make and use a Writing Chart such as the one on page 151. The chart shows the number and kinds of errors made in an English paper written on September 17.

Writing Chart

Name *Erika Olsen* Date	9/17			
Theme Number	1			
Subject	Eng.			
1. Paragraphs				
a) Good topic sentence?	Y			
b) Good development?	Y			
c) Vivid and exact language?	N			
2. Sentence structure				
a) Errors in grammatical usage?	1			
b) Sentence fragments?	0			
c) Run-on sentences?	1			
3. Mechanics				
a) Errors in spelling?	3			
b) Errors in capitalization?	2			
c) Errors in comma usage?	2			
d) Other punctuation errors?	1			
4. Manuscript form				
a) Correct heading and title?	Y			
b) Correct margins and indention?	N			
c) Satisfactory handwriting?	Y			
5. Grade (*if given*)				
a) Point 1	B			
b) Points 2–4	C			
6. Corrections made	Rw			

Make a Writing Chart like the one on page 151. After you have made it, use it regularly in two ways.

1. Refer to it whenever you write a paper for any class. See what kinds of errors you made last time. Check to see that you avoid such errors in the paper you are about to hand in.

2. Use the Writing Chart as a permanent, continuous record of your improvement.

WRITING IN EVERYDAY SITUATIONS

1. Writing Clear Explanations

"THESE DIRECTIONS SEEM TO BE WRITTEN IN HIEROGLYPHICS."

READ AND THINK ABOUT . . .

How well can you explain in writing how to do something?
Can you always follow written directions for tests?
Are you able to write directions that others can follow easily?

This chapter is designed to make writing directions—and following them—and making explanations in writing easier for you.

PUTTING IDEAS IN PROPER ORDER

To explain something or to give directions clearly, you must not jump around. In other words, you must start at the beginning and go step by step to the end. The order in which you give the supporting sentences in a paragraph is important. Notice the step-by-step order in this paragraph.

> A medicine dropper would not work if it were not for air pressure. When the bulb is squeezed, some of the air is squeezed out of it. After you have put the end of the tube in a liquid, you stop squeezing the bulb. The air pushing down on the liquid outside the tube pushes some of the liquid into the tube to take the place of the air that was squeezed out.
>
> — BERTHA MORRIS PARKER*

GUIDES FOR WRITING CLEAR EXPLANATIONS

1. Be sure you have all the facts and details clear in your own mind.

2. Arrange the facts and details in a step-by-step order. (An outline may be helpful. See pages 106–107.)

3. As you write, follow your step-by-step order exactly.

4. Use simple language. Define any terms your readers may not know.

5. Include any drawings that will aid the reader.

Learn about words!

The following words, taken from Learning Activity *A,* have interesting histories. Use your dictionary to find the story behind each word.

capital article idea magazine

---

* Adapted from *Science Experiences: Elementary School* by Bertha Morris Parker; copyright © 1958, 1952 by Harper & Row, Publishers, Inc., New York.

A. Read the following paragraph and decide how it can be improved. Copy the paragraph, arranging the ideas in a better order. Read your paragraphs in class. Let the Guides for Reading Aloud, page 59, help you.

> A person must read a magazine article carefully in order to outline it. The subpoints in the outline will be the ideas that support the main ideas. Each of the main points in the outline will be a main idea in the article. These points will be labeled with capital letters. These points will be labeled with Roman numerals.

B. (1) Write an explanation to fit one of the following situations, or one suggested to you by them. Use the Guides for Writing a Paragraph, page 162. (2) Exchange papers when you have finished. (3) If the person who reads your explanation does not understand any part of it, he or she should jot down questions on your paper so that you may reword it more clearly. (4) Read the explanations to the class; then discuss them on the basis of the Guides for Writing Clear Explanations.

1. Suppose that you must miss a day or more of school. Send a note to a friend of yours. In the note ask him or her to give your brother certain things for you. Explain in the note just which books and other materials you want. Tell exactly where each one can be found. Ask also for any assignments that you need.

2. You have come down with measles just before a committee of which you are chairperson is to have an important meeting. Send a note to the committee explaining several matters that must be settled at the meeting and the order in which they should be taken up.

3. Your scoutmaster or club leader is well pleased with a project that you have just completed. He or she asks you to write a step-by-step account of your work so that other members may use your explanation as a guide in carrying out a similar project.

2. Writing Directions

In writing directions, keep in mind that you cannot "back up" and begin again to correct any error. Thus, it is important to be completely accurate. Refer to points 2–5 of the Guides for Giving Oral Directions Accurately, page 67.

LEARNING ACTIVITY

Write clear directions to fit one of the following situations, or one suggested to you by one of them. When you have finished, be ready to read your paper to the class. Before anyone's directions are read, look up the Guides to Speaking Clearly and Correctly, page 44. After reading your directions, ask someone to repeat them. To do so calls for careful listening.

1. Your parents are coming for the first time to visit you at camp. Write and tell them exactly how to find the camp and your tent or cabin.

2. You have moved from your old home to a new house in another part of town. Your grandparents are coming by automobile for their first visit since you have moved. Give them careful instructions for finding your house.

3. You are to have work on display in the 4-H Club exhibit at your county fair. You will be on duty there at the time your favorite aunt from the city plans to arrive to visit the exhibit. Write careful directions for getting to (1) the fairgrounds, (2) the 4-H building, and (3) the booth where you will be.

3. Following Written Instructions

In these days of prepackaged foods, hobby kits, and other "do-it-yourself" projects, being able to follow written directions is very important. These guides will provide some help.

GUIDES FOR FOLLOWING WRITTEN INSTRUCTIONS

1. Read the instructions all the way through, perhaps several times, before you begin to work.

2. Ask questions if you do not understand.

3. When you are absolutely sure you know precisely what to do and how you are to do it, follow the directions step by step.

4. Check every step to be sure you have completed each one.

LEARNING ACTIVITIES

A. Work out the following exercise. Do this alone. Pay no attention to your neighbors, and ask your teacher no questions. After you have finished, exchange papers for checking.

Using a ruler, draw on your paper a square, 4 x 4 inches. Divide this square into half-inch squares. Beginning with the upper left-hand square, number the squares across, 1, 2, 3, 4, 5, 6, 7, and so on, but skip every third square. In the first of the skipped squares, print the letter *a;* in the second, *b;* and so on through the alphabet until you have filled every blank square. You may use pencil in making the squares, but fill in the numbers and letters with ink.

In checking, be sure to go over every point in the instructions.

B. Copy the following words in one column on your paper, leaving three blank lines below each word. Then find each word where it appears *first* in your dictionary. Write the page number after the word on your paper. On the first blank line under each word, show how the word can be divided and where the chief accent falls. (You may want to look over the dictionary sample on page 121.) On the second blank line (and the third, if you need it) under each word put down the *first* meaning that you find listed for that word. Use pen and ink and number each word.

If you finish before your teacher tells you to stop, take another sheet of paper and try your hand at writing an original sentence with each word. Underline the word, and number the sentence to correspond with the number of the word on your first paper.

1. discriminate
2. bonanza
3. singular
4. testimony
5. inconsiderate
6. gratitude
7. octogenarian

4. Following Directions in Tests

READ AND DISCUSS . . .

Most tests have directions. Some students just glance at such directions. Other students never even bother to read them at all, because they are sure that they know what is in the directions.

Here are the directions that one teacher gave for one part of a test. Read the directions, and then read the answers that one student wrote.

DIRECTIONS: Copy the sentences in the test. Each sentence contains one wrong answer, which you are to cross out.

1. George Washington was (a) our first President; (b) a great inventor; (c) the husband of Martha Custis.

2. The Battle of Saratoga was (a) fought in Massachusetts; (b) the turning point of the Revolutionary War; (c) fought in 1777.

3. Nathan Hale was (a) hanged by the British; (b) a schoolteacher; (c) a sea captain.

What has the student done that the directions did not say to do? What was *not* done that should have been done?

The student who wrote that paper was bright but failed that test simply by not studying the directions.

It is very easy to make that kind of mistake unless you form the habit of giving careful attention to all test directions.

GUIDES FOR TAKING TESTS

1. Before you begin to write, read the instructions carefully; go over them more than once, if necessary.

2. Ask questions about anything that you do not understand.

3. Answer every question completely, in the form required.

4. Write or print clearly.

5. Go back over the directions, the questions, and your answers to see whether you have left anything out.

6. Proofread for careless mistakes.

LEARNING ACTIVITIES

A. Here are some sample test assignments. Study them carefully. Then answer the following questions about each assignment.

How many different things must the student do?
What errors might be made in carrying out the various parts of the test?

1. Here are remarks made by certain characters in the stories that you have been reading. Below each remark are four names. Circle the name of the character who made the remark. In the blank at the left,

write the name of the selection. Below, write a sentence identifying one of the other three characters named.

2. Here are some incomplete sentences, each of them followed by four possible endings. Copy the sentences, and complete them with true endings. If more endings than one are true, copy those also.

3. Here is a list of characters in the stories you have been reading, followed by several quotations from the stories. Choose the name of the person who made each statement, and write it in the first blank after the quotation. In the second blank, name the person to whom the quotation was said. You may use any name more than once. You need not use all the names.

B. Bring to class any set of test questions that you can find. For example, you might bring tests from other subjects, from *Junior Scholastic* or *Read,* or "intelligence" quizzes from other magazines or from newspapers. Try taking some of the tests in class. Check afterward to see how many people really followed the directions.

PUTTING IDEAS INTO PARAGRAPHS

"WITH ALL THOSE INDENTATIONS IN THE WRITING, THEY MUST HAVE A LOT OF PARAGRAPHS."

1. Writing Good Paragraphs

THINK IT OVER . . .

A page with only one paragraph looks hard to read, but is there a better reason for making paragraphs?

Exactly what is a paragraph?

How do you go about writing a paragraph?

Do you recall what a topic sentence is?

As the preceding questions suggest, paragraphs help readers to follow a writer's ideas. A well-written paragraph reflects well-organized ideas. In this chapter you will learn some of the things that make good paragraphs. You will practice writing paragraphs about a number of different things. The following facts will help you to recall what you learned about paragraphs in Chapter 5. (If you need to do so, review the material in Chapter 5, pages 88–98.)

● THESE ARE FACTS ABOUT PARAGRAPHS

1. (DEFINITION) A *paragraph* is a group of sentences that develops a *central idea*.

2. The central idea of a paragraph is often stated in a *topic statement,* or *topic sentence.*

   a) The topic sentence is usually the first sentence of the paragraph.
   b) It may appear, however, at the end of the paragraph.
   c) It sometimes appears in the middle of the paragraph.

3. In a paragraph, all the sentences should present material that contributes to the development of the central idea. Such a paragraph is said to be *unified.*

Every day you think and talk about many different subjects. Such subjects are called *topics.* When you discuss a topic, you usually have a single, basic idea that you want to communicate about that topic. No one just talks about school, for example. He or she usually has something particular to say about it. "I can hardly wait for school to be out" or "Gym class was fun today" or "I'll be in the eighth grade next fall" are the kinds of specific statements that you might be likely to hear. And often they will provoke a lively discussion.

Likewise, when you plan to write something, you need to have a clear, specific idea—a *central idea*—in mind. Having one helps you to decide what you need to say and what you do *not* need to say in order to communicate your idea clearly. In other words, good writing takes good thinking and planning.

The following guides should help you to plan lively and interesting paragraphs.

GUIDES FOR WRITING A PARAGRAPH

1. Choose a topic. Decide what you want to say about it. In other words, have a clear central idea that is not too broad to be developed in one paragraph.

2. Tell in a topic sentence exactly what the central idea of the paragraph is. While topic sentences may occur anywhere in a paragraph, it is better if you follow the practice of making your topic sentence the first sentence of the paragraph.

3. Develop (expand) the idea expressed in the topic sentence. You may want to do so in one of these ways:

   a) Give *facts* or *examples* to support it.
   b) Give *reasons* to support it.
   c) Relate a brief *incident* (happening) to illustrate it.

4. Stick to the central idea expressed in the topic sentence. Include in the paragraph only those details that support the central idea. In this way your paragraph will have *unity*.

5. Keep the sentences of your paragraph related to each other. Use words and phrases that link ideas together. Some of these words and phrases are *also, after all, besides, as a result, in addition, on the other hand, then, therefore.*

CHOOSING A TOPIC

In planning a good paragraph, it is important, first of all, to choose a good topic. A rule to follow is: Don't write about something that you don't know about or are not interested in. You can't hold someone else's interest if you're not interested yourself.

Your own values and ideas are worth writing about. Almost anyone, if given the opportunity, will find that he or she has lots to say about some things. More important, when you have to write, you learn about yourself. You get rid of half-thought-out ideas and refine your thinking.

LEARNING ACTIVITY

Examine carefully the following list of topics. Discuss each topic in small groups. Pick out several that you might want to write about later. Write them down in your notebook and save them. Add any others that you think of as you discuss these topics.

A visit to the doctor
Friendship
The most unusual person I know
Qualities I admire in others
Qualities I dislike in myself
Someone who influenced me
Sandlot baseball
My favorite trip (book, movie, teacher, relative)

A new house
Spring cleaning
Ways to earn money
Saving money
My first job
A large family is fun
Born accident-prone
Acting is fun

WRITING THE TOPIC SENTENCE

After choosing a topic, you must decide what you want to say about it. That means limiting your topic to a central idea that you can state clearly in a topic sentence. For example, consider the following paragraph.

New York is a city of the sea. The Atlantic Ocean pounds its southern boundary for fifteen miles or more. Quieter waters lap the long straight shoreline of Staten Island and the curving waterfront of Gravesend Bay on the opposite sides of the

Lower Bay. Between them, at the head of the Bay, is the Narrows, where today a bridge has been flung across the gap. Beyond the Narrows lies the Upper Bay.

—SUSAN ELIZABETH LYMAN*

The topic of this paragraph is New York; the topic sentence (printed in italics) states the central idea: *New York is a city of the sea.* Immediately, one's mind forms questions. What is meant by the phrase "city of the sea"? In what way is New York such a city? The sentences that follow support and help to explain in detail what the phrase means and how New York qualifies as a city of the sea.

There are, of course, many other things that the author might have written about the topic of New York. She might have written something about its public transportation system or about its being the center of theater or advertising or music and dance. She chose, instead, to write about New York and the sea.

Like the writer of the example paragraph, you can write a good paragraph when you choose a topic that you know and when you keep your topic limited by a clear, specific topic sentence.

LEARNING ACTIVITIES

A. Read the following examples of topics and topic sentences. Then, for each of the numbered topics, write a topic sentence that expresses a central idea that is clear and specific enough to be developed in one paragraph.

TOPIC: *Weather*
TOPIC SENTENCE: Living on a farm means living close to the weather.
TOPIC SENTENCE: Everyone in our family enjoys a rainy day.
TOPIC SENTENCE: In 1977, the United States suffered the worst drought in its history.

TOPIC: *Shopping*
TOPIC SENTENCE: Our weekly shopping trip to the grocery store is always an adventure.

* From *The Story of New York: An Informal History of the City* by Susan Elizabeth Lyman; © 1964, by Susan Elizabeth Lyman. Published by Crown Publishers, Inc., New York.

Topic Sentence: Buying and wrapping gifts is a pleasure.
Topic Sentence: My aunt always shops in unusual stores.
Topic Sentence: Never go shopping for anything two days before Christmas!

1. Planning a _ _ _ _ _
2. Buying a new _ _ _ _ _
3. My first _ _ _ _ _ _ _
4. Naming our dog
5. Inventions of the future
6. Home responsibilities
7. Careers
8. Spring cleaning
9. Keeping a pet
10. Homesickness
11. Travel
12. Hobbies
13. Reading for pleasure
14. Playing an instrument
15. Chess
16. Experiments in science
17. Learning to cook
18. Respect for animals
19. Favorite sports
20. Women in history

B. Write a topic sentence for a paragraph about your hometown or city (or about another city that you know and like very much). Model your sentence on the statement, "New York is a city of the sea." For example, your sentence might be, "Omaha is a city of the plains," "Denver is a city of the mountains," or "St. Louis is a city of the river."

C. Write a topic sentence for one of the topics you wrote down in your notebook for the Learning Activity on page 162. Keep the topic sentence in your notebook. You will be asked to use it later.

DEVELOPING THE TOPIC SENTENCE

Once you have chosen a topic and have decided on a topic sentence that states your main idea, you need to expand or develop that idea with supporting details. Giving facts or examples, reasons, or an illustrative incident are three good ways to develop your topic sentence. The paragraphs that follow illustrate each of those methods. The topic sentence of each paragraph is italicized.

Facts or Examples

The storm left many grotesque sights. The wreckage of a large motel was buried under tons of fish fertilizer blown from a plant more than half a mile away. Thousands of large rolls of wrapping paper were strewn on the ground near a paper manufacturing plant. An automobile stood on its front wheels with its back wheels balanced on a tree trunk. A boat had been blown halfway through a house and another boat was in a parking lot about three blocks from the beach. Many oceangoing ships weighing thousands of tons had been tossed up on land. As one man said, "The mind cannot accept what the eyes report."

— RUTH BRINDZE*

In this paragraph the topic sentence prepares the reader for examples that support the general, or "umbrella," topic sentence stating the result of a storm: *grotesque sights*. Each of the sentences in the paragraph offers a specific example of the damage done—the wrecked motel, the strewn paper, the overturned car, the two boats and the ships aground. The last sentence offers a comment by a first-hand observer.

Reasons

Egypt's early settlers were very fortunate. They had the Nile, so that water was always close at hand. They needed no shelter from rain, since so little fell. The temperature was always hot, so they did not need houses to keep them warm. The only shelter they needed was shade from the sun. Grains grew wild in the valley for them to pick. In addition, they planted grain seeds for themselves, so that each family had its own food supply. Soon they had fine crops of wheat and barley, and flax which they wove into linen cloth.

— ELIZABETH BARTLETT THOMPSON†

In the preceding paragraph, each sentence following the topic sentence gives a reason why the Egyptians could have been called fortunate. Sufficient water, little rain, warm temperatures, and so on—each is a specific condition, making for a very easy and comfortable life.

* From *Hurricanes: Monster Storms from the Sea* by Ruth Brindze; copyright © 1973 by Ruth Brindze. Published by Atheneum Publishers, New York.

† From *Africa: Past and Present* by Elizabeth Bartlett Thompson; copyright © 1966 by Elizabeth Thompson. Published by Houghton, Mifflin Company, Boston.

Incident

One afternoon not too long ago, a number of scientists at the Carnegie Institute in California were pleased to receive an invitation to tea from Dr. Hirosi Tamiya, a visiting Japanese scientist. With enjoyment, they ate what amounted to a regular meal, with soup, noodles, rolls, tea, and a dessert of ice cream. Some of them were a little startled by the rolls, which seemed to be more suitable for a Saint Patrick's Day party than a gathering of serious-minded scientists. They were a pretty pale green color. Can you guess the reason? The rolls were made with algae. So were the soup, the noodles, the tea, and even the ice cream. *Dr. Tamiya was trying to prove that algae can taste good.*

— LUCY KAVALER*

This paragraph is unusual, both because of the incident described and because its topic sentence is the final sentence. For a paragraph such as this, putting the incident first builds interest and keeps the reader in suspense. But the device can be overdone. Even practiced writers use this kind of paragraph, with the topic sentence last, sparingly.

Learn about words!

The following words, taken from Learning Activity *A* below, have interesting histories. Use your dictionary to find the story behind each word.

region   soil   clock   caterpillar

LEARNING ACTIVITIES

A. In each of the following paragraphs, find the topic sentence. Explain in class how each paragraph is developed (see guide 3, page 162).

1. Although De Soto's expedition seemed to end sadly, it was an important one in the history of North America. He had discovered a great river. He had made the first definite exploration of Florida, Alabama, Georgia, South Carolina, Mississippi,

---

* Adapted from *The Wonders of Algae* by Lucy Kavaler; copyright © 1961 by Lucy Kavaler. Published by the John Day Company and reprinted by permission of Thomas Y. Crowell Co., Inc., New York.

and Arkansas. This beautiful region had riches more important than gold. It had rich soil and a mild climate, which one day would attract thousands of settlers.

—VESTA E. CONDON*

2. Color was more than color; it was symbolism, and, to the Aztec, very real. If red was used as blood, it became the actual equivalent of blood; it *was* blood. Black represented war because black obsidian glass was the cutting edge of battle swords (*maquahuitl*); it was also the symbol of religion: the priests dressed exclusively in it. Yellow was food because it was the color of corn; blue meant sacrifice; and green was royal, because it was the color of the quetzal plumes used only for chieftains. The French symbolists led by Malarmé at the end of the nineteenth century used color in the same way in their poetry, and when they assailed all Paris with the allegories and esotericism of these ancient theurgies, what they believed to be so new was in reality as old as the world itself.

—VICTOR W. VON HAGEN†

3. The day and the clock to us are inseparable partners in time; yet, strangely enough, there have been various definitions of what constitutes a day. Ancient Egyptians reckoned a day from sunrise to sunrise, a practice that was early adopted by Europeans and continued to be a feature of social life until late in the Middle Ages. Evening to evening enclosed the day for devotees of the lunar calendar. In modern astronomy, the day runs a course from noon to noon, while in modern civil life it progresses from midnight to midnight. Employing midnight as the start of a day, the Armed Forces number hours from one to twenty-four, a practice which is used in much of Europe.

—THELMA HARRINGTON BELL AND CORYDON BELL‡

4. Mistakes are worthwhile if you can learn from them. One day, when I was in my first year of Junior League baseball, our team needed a catcher. I foolishly volunteered to catch, al-

* Adapted from *Hernando de Soto* by Vesta E. Condon; copyright © 1950 by Harper & Row, Publishers, Inc., New York.

† From *The Aztec: Man and Tribe* by Victor W. von Hagen; copyright © 1958 by Victor W. von Hagen. Published by The New American Library, New York.

‡ From *The Riddle of Time* by Thelma Harrington Bell and Corydon Bell; copyright © 1963 by Thelma Harrington Bell and Corydon Bell. Reprinted by permission of The Viking Press, Inc., New York.

though I had never caught before in my life and did not know a thing about catching. The one important rule that I did not follow was to keep my right hand doubled up in a fist when the ball came into my glove. A ball came speeding in and hit the tip of the middle finger of my right hand. It felt as if the first knuckle had been shoved into the palm of my hand, although it turned out to be only jammed. Now I always close my fist when catching.

5. Women's clothes were probably more elaborate, bulky, and uncomfortable during the nineteenth century than at any other time in history. Skirts came down to the ground and often trailed along behind. Under her skirt a woman wore five or six petticoats. In summer some of the petticoats were white muslin with frills around the bottom. In winter two or three of the petticoats were flannel. Usually one petticoat was stiffened with horsehair to make the skirt stand out. In the 1860's crinolines were the fashion. A crinoline was a cage made of wire hoops to hold skirts out wide all around. Still later, bustles were the style: skirts were pulled tight across the front but bunched at the back below the waist.

— DOROTHY LEVENSON*

6. In a tropical forest so many creatures live so closely together that every inch of space is a home, a habitat, for something. Baby caterpillars cluster on the undersides of leaves. Spiders spin their webs between trees and vines. Rainwater in broken fruit shells houses mosquito larvae. Grubs bore into palm fruits, and ants seem to crawl on every available exposed surface.

— MARY BATTEN†

7. President John Adams was a defeated and bitter man after the elections of 1800. He had watched his Federalist party splinter and crumble during his four years in office. He was the victim of a vicious, slashing attack by fellow Federalist Alexander Hamilton, who would not support him for reelection.

— BARBARA HABENSTREIT‡

8. The flood of 1903 was unusual in that no rain accompanied it. One hot, sunny morning Don Florencio noticed what appeared to be a cloud of mist rising rapidly from the bushes south of the house along the creek. It was coming fast, with a rushing sound. Suddenly he realized that a wall of water, far wider than the creek banks, was bearing down upon him. One of his laborers was down the creek bed driving some goats to higher ground. Racing his horse, he hurried to get within calling distance of the man, Carlos. The laborer saw Don Florencio and heard his call, but not realizing that the danger was so close, went leisurely on with his work. Suddenly the turbulent water was upon him, and he was borne along with it as it swirled among the bushes. Fortunately, after his first fright, he was able to collect his wits sufficiently to grasp at an overhanging limb and so save his life.

— FERMINA GUERRA*

B. Write a paragraph in which you develop one of the topic sentences below, or one of your own choosing, by means of facts or examples, or incidents.

1. A hobby can be rewarding in many ways.
2. A person who hesitates is lost.
3. Life on a farm is never dull.
4. Opportunities to learn are many in a city.
5. Here's how to do it!
6. First aid can save lives.
7. Vacations are not always carefree.
8. I was the hit of the party.

C. Break up into small groups. Discuss the kinds of reasons you could use to develop the following topic sentences.

1. Gymnastics is an exciting sport for both girls and boys.
2. Grading systems are necessary (unnecessary).
3. The automobile will soon be a luxury and not a necessity.
4. After-school jobs have many advantages.
5. Cheating hurts everyone.
6. Biology (or some other subject) is something everyone needs to study.
7. The quiet student is rarely a dull person.
8. Everyone should play an instrument.

D. From the topic sentence that you wrote for Learning Activity C, page 165, develop a paragraph using any one of the three methods of development that you think will best fit the topic sentence.

---

* From "Rancho Buena Vista" by Fermina Guerra. Reprinted from *Mexican American Authors*, edited by Americo Paredes and Raymond Paredes, published by Houghton Mifflin Company, Boston, 1972.

2. Getting Rid of Unrelated Sentences

"THIS PIECE MUST BELONG TO ANOTHER PUZZLE."

READ AND THINK ABOUT . . .

Just as all the pieces of a puzzle must fit, all the sentences in a paragraph must be related to the topic sentence. In the following paragraphs, the sentences in italics do not belong, because they contain facts that do not fit the central idea being developed.

1. Although most history books do not record it, black Minutemen fought in the first two battles for America's independence, at Lexington and Concord. A Negro named Prince Estabrook fought the British at Lexington, and nine blacks were at Concord: Peter Salem, Cato Stedman, Lemuel Haynes, Cuff Whittemore, Cato Wood, Pomp Blackman, Cato Bordman, and two men known only as Pompey and "Joshua Boylston's Prince," a slave. *Negro troops fought with Andrew Jackson in the Battle of New Orleans during the War of 1812.* Blacks also fought at Bunker Hill, and two crossed the Delaware with General Washington to attack Trenton, New Jersey, on Christmas Day, 1776.

—JOHN HOPE FRANKLIN*

---

* From *An Illustrated History of Black Americans* by John Hope Franklin and the Editors of Time-Life Books, New York; © 1970 Time Inc.

2. The motion of molecules in gases is a dramatic process. Some molecules travel as fast as thousands of feet in a single second. *The speed of light is approximately 186,000 miles per second.* They dart in all directions until they collide with other molecules or the sides of their container. Then they change direction. Picture a room full of Ping-Pong balls that are flying about in all directions. All are in constant motion. Each one travels straight ahead until it hits another ball or the edge of the room. Then it changes direction and travels straight ahead until it collides. So it is with molecules, but, of course, they are very much smaller.

— MARGARET O. HYDE*

Learn about words!

The following words, taken from Learning Activity *A* below, have interesting histories. Use your dictionary to find the story behind each word.

blanket   magnet   attract   chalk

LEARNING ACTIVITIES

A. Two of the following paragraphs have unrelated sentences. In class, explain specifically why the unrelated sentences do not belong in the paragraphs.

1. A great deal of air is caught between the snowflakes in any layer of newly fallen snow. Some snow is much fluffier than other snow; but even in a layer of dry, powdery snow, there is a great deal of air space. Farmers are glad to have snow on their winter wheat fields because it makes a good blanket for young plants. There is so much air in snow that, on the average, ten inches of snow has only about as much water in it as one inch of rain.

— BERTHA MORRIS PARKER†

* Adapted from *Molecules Today and Tomorrow* by Margaret O. Hyde; copyright © 1963 by Margaret O. Hyde. Reprinted by permission of McGraw-Hill Book Company, New York.

† Adapted from *Science Experiences: Elementary School* by Bertha Morris Parker; copyright © 1958 by Harper & Row, Publishers, Inc., New York.

2. Solid particles of any kind, unless they are very, very tiny, can be filtered out of water with filter paper. There are tiny spaces between the fibers of which filter paper is made. Water can go through these tiny spaces, but the particles of chalk and sand are too large to go through them. Those particles are left on the filter paper.

—BERTHA MORRIS PARKER*

3. A magnet will attract practically nothing except iron and steel. Magnets have many different shapes. Magnets attract paper clips, thumbtacks, and nails because these objects are made of either iron or steel. Paper fasteners are made of brass, not iron or steel. Magnets will not attract them. Toothpicks and rubber bands have no metal in them, and, therefore, are not attracted.

—BERTHA MORRIS PARKER*

B. Copy the following paragraph, (1) arranging the sentences in proper order and (2) omitting the two sentences that do not belong.

I can't watch television tonight; I have to study for a biology test. Another time, he gave the impression that the "Mohawks" involved in the Boston Tea Party were actually Indians, not disguised patriots. Every student of history knows that it was Whistling River that Mr. Bunyan straightened out, not Whistling Road! For instance, once he said that Columbus was *trying* to discover America. Our class visited the local newspaper plant the other day. But perhaps his most glaring "boo-boo" was the time he told the class that Paul Bunyan straightened out Whistling Road. Thomas gives interesting class reports, but he often overlooks important facts or twists the truth a bit.

FOLLOW-UP

Go over a theme or other paper that you have written this year in any class. Is the topic sentence in each paragraph easy to locate? Does every sentence support the topic sentence idea? Could you have expressed any topic sentences better? Could you have put any topic sentence in a better location? If your work has any of these weaknesses, it will be good practice for you to rewrite the paper.

* Adapted from *Science Experiences: Elementary School* by Bertha Morris Parker; copyright © 1958 by Harper & Row, Publishers, Inc., New York.

WRITING DESCRIPTIVE PARAGRAPHS

"WRONG SIZE—WRONG COLOR— WRONG STYLE! I MUST HAVE DESCRIBED IT WRONG!"

TALK IT OVER . . .

The girl ordered that sweater over the telephone.

What information must she have given incorrectly, or what must she have failed to include?

You have probably seen a customer outside a shop window pointing out some article to a clerk. Perhaps you yourself have had that experience. When you cannot describe what you want, you have to point to it. Sometimes it is impossible to point, however, because the article is not within view. In that case, you must depend on your ability to describe.

Following are guides for describing that should help you to write good descriptive paragraphs.

GUIDES FOR DESCRIBING

1. Observe carefully; notice details. You cannot give a good picture of something that is blurred in your own mind.

2. Make details exact. Do not be satisfied with general words.

> WEAK: We live in a *white house* with a *fence* around it.
> BETTER: We live in a *little white cottage* with a *low green picket fence* around it.

> GENERAL: She was wearing a *red* scarf.
> EXACT: She was wearing a scarf *of fire-engine red* wool.

> GENERAL: Joe *looked* at me.
> EXACT: Joe *stared* at me.

3. Use vivid picture words that make appeals to the senses, that is, to (*a*) sight, (*b*) hearing, (*c*) taste, (*d*) smell, or (*e*) feeling.

4. Use comparisons.

   a) If you are describing only to identify or to give an actual picture, use real comparisons.

   > The buttons on the coat are *the size of a quarter.*
   > She is about *as tall as I am.*

   b) To give a vivid picture, include imaginative comparisons.

   > He has a voice *like a squeaky door.*
   > A soft *breeze whispered* in my ear.

5. Write your descriptive paragraphs so that they convey to the reader a clear, single idea — a single *dominant impression,* such as of peace, calm, fear, lively activity, and so on. Descriptive paragraphs need not always have topic sentences. They must, however, offer a dominant impression.

1. Observing Details

People very rarely remember everything about what they observe, but most people remember significant details. The careful writer not only pays attention to details, but chooses them so that they create a picture in the reader's mind that is as memorable as the writer's original experience.

Notice the difference between the following two paragraphs. Only one of them gives a real description.

1. In 1935 there was a dust storm in the Great Plains area of the Middle West. It was quite frightening. There were big clouds of dust that made it hard to breathe.

2. The sunlight began to dim hours before sunset and the clean, fresh air acquired a peculiar density as a giant, black dust cloud approached from the northwest. More than a thousand feet high, the cloud swept southeast and extended in a straight line as far as the eye could see, rolling and tumbling like a great wall of muddy water. Hundreds of birds flew in panic before it. People who saw the dust storm coming fled quickly to their homes to tape windows, jam rugs under doors, cover furniture, and hang wet sheets across rooms. Wet towels were held over mouths and noses as the premature but total darkness descended. Homes rattled with the force of the storm, and as the dust sifted in and piled up beneath keyholes, breathing became labored and gave way to choking. Spring, 1935, had come to the southern Great Plains.

— R. Douglas Hurt*

Both paragraphs tell of a dust storm. Why does only one of them give you a clear and memorable picture of the storm? The answer is easy: the second paragraph gives *specific details*.

Look again at the second paragraph. Notice the kinds of details the author has used. They are the kinds that you feel

* From "Dust" by R. Douglas Hurt from *American Heritage*, Vol. 28, No. 5, August 1977; copyright © 1977 by American Heritage Publishing Co., Inc., New York. Reprinted by permission.

come from firsthand observation: the visible approach of the storm, the frantic activity of those in its path.

Notice also how the details contribute to a mood. The scene described begins quietly, with the cloud of dust at a distance. But the sky grows dim; the air grows heavy. Then the writer moves in on the scene ahead of the approaching storm. Details abound—birds flying in panic, people frantically trying to prevent the dust from entering their homes.

Finally there is fear suggested—the fear of being choked to death by the thick dust. This brings what seemed merely a natural event down to a matter of life and death.

LEARNING ACTIVITY

Spend some time in a particular place observing the scene around you. Pick a place that you like—a meadow, a park, a zoo, the cafeteria, a playground—almost anywhere that you can sit and observe. Take careful notes on what you see, what you hear, who comes and goes there. Make your notes as specific and detailed as you can.

After you have completed your notes, discuss them in your small groups. Determine whether you have taken enough notes to help you recapture the scene. If not, go back and observe again. Save your notes for future use.

2. Creating a Dominant Impression

Paragraphs that describe, as well as those that tell a story (that is, *descriptive* and *narrative* paragraphs), sometimes do not have topic sentences. They should have a central idea, however, a feeling or mood that is conveyed by the details of the paragraph. This idea is called the *dominant impression.*

Read the following paragraph. In it the writer takes details about the movement of rivers and uses them to create a general picture of all the rivers moving as one.

> Out across the stretches of America the rivers move on their way to the sea. They run down the mountain slopes, plunging over the rocks, swirling in clear green pools, sweeping along past farms and cliffs and wooded places. Now they lie still under the mist of an early morning, and then they sparkle under the midday sun, and then they move on through the dark at night, until they join at length with other streams, washing other shores; and growing wider and stronger, they are gone at last, merging themselves with the water of the ultimate ocean.
>
> — KATHERINE B. SHIPPEN*

Notice the action words that contribute to the impression of movement: *run, plunging, swirling, sweeping.* Each sentence is longer than the previous one, producing the effect of continuous motion. The end of the paragraph echoes the end of the journey for the rivers. The overall feeling is that the rivers have a destination, like long-distance travelers.

LEARNING ACTIVITIES

A. Reread the paragraph about the dust storm. Make a list of exact and vivid words used. Tell what you think the dominant impression of the paragraph is.

B. Read the following paragraph and answer the questions that follow. As you do so, use the guides on page 175 to help you.

* From "The Strength of the Rivers" from *The Great Heritage* by Katherine B. Shippen; copyright 1947 by Katherine B. Shippen. Published by The Viking Press, Inc., New York.

I woke up early, about half past six, and saw the sun slanting in through the east window. I slid out of bed and tiptoed into the kitchen and opened the back door. The sun was already beginning to warm the chilly early morning air and I could feel the chill and the warmth at the same time. I slipped across the path, wincing as the gravel bit into my bare feet, and stood on the grass, which was cool but not wet, as it had not rained for several days. I admired the view southwest across the valley, the different shades of green, the cloud shadows racing across the fields, and wished that we weren't so busy so that we could spend a day by the river or on the moors. I listened to the early morning noises—the moo of a cow, a dog barking, the twitter of birds in the big sycamore tree. It was good to be alone and rinse my brain clear of the tangle of other people's words and actions.

—HONOR ARUNDEL*

1. What is the dominant impression of the scene described in the paragraph?
2. What is the action described in the paragraph?
3. How observant is the writer? Give examples of vivid, exact details.
4. What senses do the words appeal to?
5. What is the effect of the scene on the narrator?

C. Go over the notes you took in the Learning Activity on page 177. Try to determine from your notes and your memory of the scene just what general feeling or dominant impression you have of the scene. Write a sentence that states that dominant impression. Save your sentence and the notes.

3. Recording Details

When you are describing anything—an object, an animal, a custom, a scene familiar to you, an experience—you need to remember that your readers will not necessarily be familiar with what you are describing. They need help. That is why details are so important. They help the reader to see what you have seen, to feel the way you felt about your experience.

* From *A Family Failing* by Honor Arundel; copyright © 1972 by Honor Arundel. Reprinted by permission of Thomas Nelson Inc., Nashville.

In the following paragraph, the writer gives a vivid picture of the unusual groceries in a food store in New York's Chinatown. Why do you think the author felt it necessary to describe the process of curing eggs?

The windows of food stores are filled with vegetables and groceries not found in the ordinary supermarket. There are lotus roots, fresh ginger, winter melons, victory gourds, bean sprouts, bamboo shoots, water chestnuts, bean curd, taro roots, hairy melons, snow peas, and many other vegetables that are not native to this country. Sugar-cured ducks and whole roast pigs hang from hooks in the stores. They do not hang there for long because they are bought very quickly. Other unusual foods are sea slugs and thousand-year eggs. These eggs are not really a thousand years old; they may be only three months old. Centuries ago, the Chinese found a way to preserve eggs other than by drying or salting them. The eggs are buried in mud mixed with calcium. They age and turn black but do not spoil. They have a very special flavor and are considered a delicious delicacy.

— BETTY LEE SUNG*

*From *The Chinese in America* by Betty Lee Sung; copyright © 1972 Betty Lee Sung. Published by The Macmillan Company, New York.

LEARNING ACTIVITIES

A. Read the following description. Discuss in class the kinds of details and comparisons used by the author. Does the paragraph give you a clear and vivid picture of the trains? Why do you think as you do?

> The train stretched itself out long and low against the tracks and ran very fast and smooth. The drive rods flashed out of the big pistons like blades of light, and the huge counterweighted wheels were blurred solid with the speed. Out of the throat of the stack, the white smoke blasted up in stiff, hard pants, straight up for a yard; then the backward rushing mass of air caught it, trailing out over the cars like a veil.
>
> — FRANK YERBY*

B. Read the following paragraph. Notice the use of detail to convey the sense of life in the forests in late fall. What senses are appealed to in this description? Where does the author use comparisons? Use the guides on page 175 to help you. Make this an oral discussion.

> In my Wisconsin, the leaves change before the snows come. In the air there is the smell of wild rice and venison cooking; and when the winds come whispering through the forests, they carry the smell of rotting leaves. In the evenings, the loon calls,

* From "The Homecoming" by Frank Yerby; copyright © 1946 by John Caswell Smith. Reprinted from *American Negro Short Stories* edited by John Henrik Clarke, published by Hill and Wang, New York, 1966.

lonely; and birds sing their last songs before leaving. Bears dig roots and eat late fall berries, fattening for their long winter sleep. Later, when the first snows fall, one awakens in the morning to find the world white and beautiful and clean. Then one can look back over the trail and see the tracks following. In the woods there are tracks of deer and snowshoe rabbits and long streaks where partridges slide to alight. Chipmunks make tiny footprints on the limbs; and one can hear squirrels busy in hollow trees, sorting acorns. Soft lake waves wash the shores, and sunsets burst each evening over the lakes and make them look as if they were afire.

—Thomas St. Germain Whitecloud*

C. Using the notes and the sentence you wrote earlier, write a paragraph describing your impression of the place you observed. Be prepared to read your paragraph in class.

D. Have someone bring an object to class, such as a china or cloth dog. Place it where everyone can see it. Then write a short description of it. Read your paragraphs in class. Notice how differently people see things. Decide who used exact words and comparisons.

Use your Writing Chart, page 151, and the Suggestions for Good Handwriting, page 479.

E. Write a paragraph in which you describe something that you know well—a house, a store, a pet animal, or a particular place or scene that you remember but that your readers might not know or be familiar with. (Perhaps you are doing an experiment in science class or studying about a particular type of animal or plant.) Make sure that your description helps your reader to become familiar with the details of your subject.

F. Write a paragraph in which you describe a scene from an earlier time in your life. Pick a specific time and a specific place that stand out in your memory as meaningful to you for some reason: because of something that happened to you there or because of something that you did there.

USING ENGLISH IN ALL CLASSES

From time to time in your other classes, you are called on to describe something. When next you must do so, let the Guides for Describing help you to make the description clear and vivid.

* From "Blue Winds Dancing" by Thomas St. Germain Whitecloud from *American Indian Authors* by Natachee Scott Momaday; copyright © 1972 by Houghton Mifflin Company, Boston.

4. Describing People

"OH, SHE'S OF AVERAGE HEIGHT AND HAS DARK HAIR."

"BUT WHAT IS SHE LIKE?"

THINK IT OVER . . .

Which is really more important—what a person looks like, or what kind of person he or she is?

Here is a paragraph that relies on physical details:

> There was nothing small about Tom Evans. He had a huge beak of a nose, a cavern of a mouth, and ears that fairly flapped in the breeze. His feet were the size of snowshoes. A lion-like head covered by a great mane of wiry hair was set on the thick neck that rose from his barrel-like chest. Enormous hands dangled far out of the sleeves that were strained tightly over Tom's bulging muscles. Yes, even his *voice* was big.

This is a good descriptive paragraph about Tom. It gives vivid and specific details, and it conveys a dominant impression.

When you describe people, however, you often want to tell even more about them. You want readers to understand not only what the person looks like but also how he or she thinks and feels. The paragraph about Tom, for example, does not tell you if he was shy or aggressive, awkward or graceful, bold or cowardly. It does not tell you how he feels about himself, how others feel toward him, or what others say about him. Nor does it describe any of his actions.

The following are guides that will help you to describe people.

GUIDES FOR DESCRIBING PEOPLE

1. Describe someone's character by one of the following methods or by a combination of them.

   a) *By appearance.* He was a thin, stoop-shouldered fellow with a sharp, narrow face.

   b) *By actions.* She is the kind who doesn't talk much, but what she does say is worth listening to.

   c) *By what is said.* "I know it," said Hector. "I know I shouldn't say things like that, but they pop out."

   d) *By what someone else says.* "Well," said Elsa, "if I were in a really tough spot, Louisa is the person I'd like to have there with me!"

2. Use vivid and exact words to depict actions and appearances.

3. Be sure that your description conveys a vivid, dominant impression through the various details that you present.

LEARNING ACTIVITIES

A. What sort of person would you say each of the following statements describes? Which methods of describing people are used? Make this an oral discussion.

1. "Aw, what if we do miss the train? There will be another one soon."
2. Mrs. Barry was likely to have good ideas about things—and she was always sure that she knew what people ought to do about them.
3. Mr. Evans was the sort of person who always found time to listen to your troubles.
4. "You'll never get her to stay home from a rodeo!"
5. You couldn't change his mind with a charge of dynamite.
6. "Let's see. Where *did* I put my camera? Maybe it's in this drawer—or, no, it might be in the closet. Well, it *must* be around here somewhere."
7. If you find a stray animal, take it to Madge Olafson. She'll take good care of it.

B. How could you show in a short description, like one of the descriptions in *A*, that a person has one of the following kinds of dispositions? Choose four of the words and then write descriptions that will give the impression without using the words from the list. Try to use each of the four methods given in guide 1 above. Compare work in your small groups.

1. hot-tempered	4. sarcastic	7. brave	10. careless
2. lazy	5. reckless	8. frank	11. timid
3. easygoing	6. stingy	9. loyal	12. friendly

C. Read the following paragraphs, each of which is a description of the writer's mother. Using the questions that follow, discuss in class the differences in the ways that the two writers describe their mothers. Use the Guides for Describing People on page 184 to help you.

1. She can't stand anything phony. She refuses to go to teas, prefers young people to older. She works in the garden, making flowers come up out of the dirt. She wears her hair long, down her back, when she's at home, and up in a braided roll when she goes out. Her back is strong and her hands are gnarly and full of veins. I think she must have worked very hard when she was little to have such hands. Her eyes are huge, frightened, deep, and magnificent; her forehead almost always in a worry design; her mouth too tight and her chin tense. Yet there is an overwhelming strength in her face, and she is one of about five women I can think of who are in her category of beauty. Her figure is excellent. When she runs, on the beach, dressed in blue jeans and a T-shirt, with her hair all down, she looks nineteen. She is fifty-four.

—JOAN BAEZ*

2. But it was Mother who gave me my political education. My mother, my five sisters, and I would talk for hours while we worked, especially when we quilted. It was our own personal women's group. The church and the schools didn't teach us to be independent, so she was really alone in preparing us for life. And she warned us that we would be alone, too, unless we did something to change the society we lived in. We learned from her words, and from her example: whenever there was a family crisis or problem, she always fought it through. She was never defeated. It was my mother who taught us to stand up to our problems, not only in the world around us but in ourselves.

—DOROTHY PITMAN HUGHES†

1. Which of the paragraphs relies more on physical appearance? Which relies on things such as actions and statements?
2. Which paragraph do you think gives a clearer picture of the person? Why?
3. What in each paragraph is the dominant impression you get of the person being described?

---

* From *Daybreak* by Joan Baez; copyright © 1966 by Joan Baez. Published by Delacorte Press, New York.

† From "Daughters and Mothers—Can We Be Friends?" by Ingeborg Day from *Ms. Magazine,* Vol. III, No. 12, June 1975; © 1975 Ms. Magazine Corp., New York.

D. Write a paragraph that will picture the appearance of someone whom you know and that will suggest something about his or her character. Try to get all four methods into your description. If you use quotation marks, do so with care. See the rules on page 232. Read and discuss your descriptions in class. The best ones may be mounted upon the bulletin board, or you may wish to keep yours for possible use in a story.

ENRICHMENT

From your outside reading, find a good paragraph that describes a real person or a character in a story. Try to find one that describes the person's appearance and also what he or she thinks or feels. Be prepared to read your selection to the rest of the class. Explain why you think the selection is a good example. See the Guides for Reading Aloud, page 59.

WRITING PERSONAL NARRATIVES

1. Stating the Theme Idea

An incident can be used to develop the topic sentence of a paragraph by offering a vivid illustration. Similarly, longer stories, or *narratives,* can illustrate or "make" a point.

This practice is actually quite old; even the great storyteller Aesop made sure his readers got the point by adding a "moral" after each of his fables. Of course, his readers were left with the job of pinning the moral to the tale. Here is a famous fable by Aesop.

THE HORSE AND THE OVERBURDENED DONKEY

Two old friends met for the first time in many years as they were traveling on a lonely road. One was a rich man who owned a fine horse with an elegant saddle and shiny stirrups. The other, a poor merchant, had a donkey which was carrying a heavy load of pottery to be sold in the next village. As the men talked of old times, the animals became acquainted.

The horse pranced along bragging of his comfortable life until the unhappy donkey could bear it no longer and interrupted him.

"Ah, my friend, you are so fortunate. I beg you to help one who is not so lucky. I cannot walk another step with this weight on my back. If you would carry some of it, I would be so grateful."

But the horse replied coldly, "I'm sorry but I only carry my master."

Suddenly the donkey collapsed, moaned weakly, and died. The rich man quickly offered his friend the use of the horse. They loaded the pottery sacks around the horse's neck and put the donkey's carcass across his back.

"What a fool I was to refuse to help the donkey," thought the horse. "Now I have to carry not only his burden but his body as well."

Pride brings its own punishment. — AESOP*

* From *Aesop's Fables* retold by Joan Hirschmann; copyright © 1964 by Harlin Quist. A Harlin Quist Book published by Dell Publishing Co., Inc., New York.

Stating the point after the story is over to make sure that the reader gets it is not as effective as building the point into the story itself. The following narrative also makes a strong point. In it the author tells what he has learned from a dramatic event in his life. He does not point out a moral or give advice that he expects other people to follow, but he does explain how a single, highly unusual event "cured" his fear of water. More importantly, the experience taught him how to handle similar problems in later life.

I couldn't swim and I lived in fear of being found out and disgraced.

One day I was walking with a geologist along a narrow mountain path above a noisy stream. We both carried knapsacks filled with specimens of rock. Suddenly the geologist took a false step and the ground gave way under his feet. He tried to catch hold of a bush, missed it, and fell headlong from the steep bank, down into the river. Within seconds I saw him thrashing about in the foaming water, struggling to keep afloat, but his knapsack was dragging him down.

I flung mine off my shoulders, whipped my knife from inside my belt, and jumped in.

It was not till I had swum up to the geologist, cut the straps of his knapsack, and we had both scrambled ashore that I remembered I didn't know how to swim.

And from that day on I have known that the best way of learning something is to take a leap into the unknown without looking back. That way, you either learn or perish.

— YEVGENY YEVTUSHENKO*

The strong point that an author makes — that is, the central idea — is called in literature the *theme*, or the *theme idea*. The theme idea does not always have to be stated in a separate sentence. Indeed, it often is not stated at all by experienced writers. Beginning writers, however, would do well to follow the practice of having a clearly stated theme idea. It may come either at the beginning or at the end of the story.

* From *A Precocious Autobiography* by Yevgeny Yevtushenko translated from the Russian by Andrew R. MacAndrew; English translation copyright © 1963 by E. P. Dutton & Co., Inc., New York.

GUIDES FOR WRITING A SHORT NARRATIVE

1. A good short narrative should illustrate a central idea. The central idea of a short narrative is called the *theme idea*. Be sure that you state your theme idea at the beginning or at the end of your narrative. (It can often help you to create a lively and interesting title.)

2. A narrative usually presents the events of the story in the order in which they occurred in time. Jot down notes about the event or events you want to tell about. Then arrange the events in the order in which they happened.

3. Write a beginning sentence that will catch the interest of your readers.

    a) Begin with an unusual or exciting remark, or state your theme idea.

    b) Use a question, if you like, to get the reader's attention.

4. As soon as possible, tell *who* is concerned, *what* the story is about, and *where* and *when* it happened.

5. Every sentence should build up gradually to the *climax,* which is the most interesting or exciting part of the story.

6. Do not give away your ending.

7. Stop your narrative soon after you tell the climax.

8. Use specific details in describing scenes and people.

9. Leave out facts or comments that have no direct connection with the story.

10. Include conversation if you can. Remember that you will need a new paragraph every time the speaker in a conversation changes. (See Rule 3, page 232.)

11. Create a title that will make people want to read your story. For example, "Chicken-Thief Trap" sounds more exciting than does "My Visit to a Farm." Make certain that the title does not tell so much that it gives away the ending.

12. Read the story critically and revise it. Do not be afraid to cross out certain words or sentences if you can think of better ones. Check your paper against all the items on the Writing Chart, page 151. Make any changes that you think are necessary.

13. Copy the story in ink, being sure to follow the Guides to Proper Manuscript Form, page 148.

14. Proofread for careless mistakes.

LEARNING ACTIVITIES

A. Go to the library and get some books of fables. Find one that you like. (James Thurber has written some delightful modern ones.) Read your fable to your small group and let the members discuss it. After all the fables have been read, let the group decide which fable fits its moral best.

B. Write your own fable and give it a moral. Try writing it in the style of the "once-upon-a-time" stories, but make your moral fit the tale. Let your imagination have free rein, and don't be afraid to be humorous.

2. Ordering the Events of the Plot

The most important part of a narrative is the *plot*—the series of events that make up the story. Those events should have a beginning, a middle, and an end. Keeping the events of your story in the order in which they occur in time is important. Otherwise, a good story often will not build to a climax. (See points 2 and 5 of the guides, page 190.)

The order of time is an order that everyone is familiar with. The physical events of a day are experienced in time; our calendar traces the days and the months of the year in order. Everyone assumes that a story plot follows the order of time, unless there are clues that there is a change in that pattern. Movie plots, for example, are sometimes told as a series of flashbacks from some point in time.

When events are presented out of order, however, confusion can result. Readers may not be sure just when some event took place, or is taking place. In the beginning, it is best if you follow the order of time in your narratives.

In the following story the author tells the events in the order of time. The result is a delightful narrative. It has a beginning that sparks interest, a middle that feeds the reader's curiosity, and an end that includes a humorous climax.

How I Got Carried Away by My Own Music

I love music and I love to bang on the piano. I've taken piano lessons, but the lessons never "took" because I hate to practice. Whenever I get near a keyboard, however, I have an over-whelming urge to play. "Chopsticks" is my best piece; it requires only two fingers instead of ten. Last summer, my love for music caused me several days of pain and almost landed me in a hospital—or worse. This is how it happened.

Just down the road from my grandmother's farm near Green-ville is a little country church. Nestled back from the road it stands, newly white and gleaming, amid the tall pines and crape myrtle and one lone chinaberry tree. It's an old church that had become run-down, but a couple of years ago the members of the church decided to restore it. They refinished the pews, built a new pulpit, and put in new lamps. To top it all off, they got rid of the tinny old upright piano and put in an antique pump organ with gingerbread trim. After seeing that organ, I knew I just had to play on it someday, somehow.

One day late last August, when I was visiting my grandmother, I found my chance. That day everyone was either away from home or busily engaged elsewhere. I stole out to the barn, saddled up my cousin's horse, "climbed aboard" it, and set off down the road to the little church.

I had watched my aunt hide the key away and knew just where to find it. I hitched the horse to the chinaberry tree, unlocked the church doors, went in, and played away on that old organ to my heart's content. As I said before, I play very badly. But pumping on the pedals and thumping on the keys was more fun than anything I had done since arriving at the farm. Since only the horse and I could hear, I really let myself go.

After playing for a good while, I began to realize that I should get back to my grandmother's before I was missed. I closed the organ sadly, locked the church, hid the key again, got on my horse, and started home. The horse, which had behaved itself beautifully on the way to the church, ambling slowly alongside the country road, suddenly picked up speed and "lit out" toward home. Faster and faster it went until I could hardly hang on. I was more frightened than I had ever been before. I was afraid I would fall off the horse and be trampled to death. I was afraid the horse would carry me miles away and I would not know how to get back to the farm. My imagination was working overtime, as I thought of all the things that *could* happen to me. I was not prepared for what did.

When I was halfway home, my aunt, driving back from a shopping trip, saw my plight. She knew it would be dangerous to interfere, but she was afraid for me, too. She slowed down the car and "paced" the horse the rest of the way back. Although she could do nothing, her being nearby gave me courage, and I hung on to the horse all the harder till we reached the house.

There, unexpectedly, the horse came to a sudden stop. I didn't. I toppled over its head on to the hard, red dirt below. The horse looked at me, gave a short snort, and walked away as if to say, "What did you expect? A bed of roses?"

By this time, my aunt had brought her car to a stop and had come running to help me. Yes, I was all in one piece. No, there seemed to be no broken bones. Was I all right? Yes, I guess so, though the next few days were a torment of sore muscles I hadn't even known I had.

The story of my "perilous ride" has been told over and over all year by my parents and my brother and my grandmother and my aunt. But they only know the half of it. They know I rode down the road and then turned back, but they *don't* know where I went that day or why. And I won't tell. If I did, I'm sure someone would say that the horse was only paying me back for the musical ordeal I had put *it* through! And who knows? Maybe that *is* the reason it ran away with me.

—CAROLYN QUINN

LEARNING ACTIVITIES

A. Reread the story of the girl and the horse. Answer the following questions. Make this an oral discussion.

1. What is the theme idea of the story? Where is it stated?
2. What is the connection between the title and the story? Does the title spark your interest? Why or why not?
3. How does the author keep up the suspense as the story develops?
4. List the events in the plot in order.
5. Which paragraphs are devoted to the plot?
6. What does the first paragraph do?
7. What does the last paragraph do?

B. Using the Guides for Describing, page 175, and the Guides for Describing People, page 184, answer these additional questions about the story. Make this an oral discussion.

1. What kinds of specific details are used to make the story and the place where it happened come alive?
2. Find vivid and colorful words that help you visualize the scene.
3. How is the character of the girl revealed through the details of the story? What kind of person is she?

C. Create a title for the story on page 189 about the man who learned to swim.

D. Write a true story of your own. Tell about something that really happened, either to you or to someone you know. The titles below may suggest a story. Read your stories in class, letting the Guides for Reading Aloud, page 59, help you.

Trapped!

More Luck Than Sense

Was It a Dream?

A Half Hour with
   the Baby

Runaway

Admission, One Cent

Fire! Fire!

A Narrow Escape

Look Pleasant, Please

Who's Afraid?

Fare, Please

Thin Ice

Look Before You Leap

FOLLOW-UP

After all the stories written by the class have been read aloud, take a vote to see which ones were liked best. Try to arrange to have these stories read to another class, in an assembly program, or at a P.T.A. meeting.

WRITING A BOOK REPORT

"You're supposed to report on the BOOK, not on what it reminded you of in your own life!"

READ AND THINK ABOUT . . .

Listening to a good story is fun. Reading a good story is even more fun, because you can go back over favorite parts and read them again.

One of the kinds of writing you will be doing a lot of in school is writing book reports. Here are some helpful guides for planning and writing a book report.

GUIDES FOR WRITING A BOOK REPORT

1. Plan carefully what you will cover in the report.

   a) Tell the kind of book: *fiction, biography, travel, science* . . .

   b) Give the exact title and the name of the author.

   c) For *fiction*, do not try to tell the complete story.

      (1) Tell one or two important, amusing, or exciting incidents.

      (2) Tell briefly about the main character or characters.

   d) For *biography, travel, history,* or *adventure* books, tell an event or two.

   e) Give reasons for recommending the book to your classmates. Do not just call it *interesting* or *exciting;* tell why.

2. Arrange in an outline (either sentence or topic) the items called for above. Use that outline in writing the report.

3. Proceed as follows for your report:

   a) Write quickly. Do not go back or stop to check anything.

   b) Write an introductory paragraph.

   c) Write a concluding paragraph that summarizes your report or gives your final feeling about the book.

   d) Reread carefully and revise what you have written to be sure you have expressed clearly what you want to say.

   e) Check all spelling, capitalization, and punctuation.

   f) Copy the report in your best handwriting.

As you write and revise your paragraphs, strive to tie them together. Listed below are two good ways to tie paragraphs together:

1. Make the first sentence of a paragraph connect with the preceding paragraph.

   LAST SENTENCE OF A PARAGRAPH: Jase's wallet with just barely enough money for his summer's expenses was stolen.

   FIRST SENTENCE OF NEXT PARAGRAPH: *About three weeks later,* Jase came across the thief.

   (See also point 5 of the paragraph guides, page 162.)

2. Occasionally make the first sentence of two succeeding paragraphs similar by repeating some parts.

FIRST SENTENCE OF ONE PARAGRAPH: Jim Kjelgaard, author of *Wildlife Cameraman,* studied nature in his boyhood.

FIRST SENTENCE OF NEXT PARAGRAPH: Mr. Kjelgaard shows in *Wildlife Cameraman* how people, depending upon their attitude toward conservation, can help or tear down the balance of nature.

Knowing about an author's life and his or her purpose in writing a book often helps the reader to understand and appreciate the book. If possible, then, learn something of the author's life and purpose. As cautioned in guide 1*c,* page 197, do not try to tell everything; tell just enough to stir interest.

In your report, see whether you can capture the *spirit* of the book. The spirit, or intent, of a book may be one or more of the following:

1. To entertain
   a) with something amusing
   b) with excitement
   c) with suspense
2. To instruct
3. To inspire (a biography, for example)
4. To inform
5. To persuade

LEARNING ACTIVITIES

A. Read the student book report that follows. Then discuss it in class; among other points, consider the questions that follow the report.

The Court of the Stone Children by Eleanor Cameron is a novel of mystery and fantasy. It tells the unusual story of Nina Harmsworth, who has moved with her parents from a small town in California to San Francisco. One of the first friends she makes in her new school is a boy named Gil. When Nina tells Gil of her interest in museums, he tells her about the French Museum and shows her where it is.

Nina is fascinated by the museum's rooms, which were taken from old French homes. Alone in one room, she finds Domi-

nique, a French girl of about her own age. Dominique is dressed in beautiful French clothes of the year 1800, and she welcomes Nina. She tells Nina that these are the same rooms in which she grew up long ago. Nina soon realizes that Dominique is very special, invisible to everyone in the museum except her. The two girls become close friends.

With Dominique's help, Nina solves a 175-year-old mystery involving Dominique's father. He had been falsely accused of murder during the time of Napoleon and had been executed. He had stood up for liberty at a time when liberty was threatened.

The title of the book refers to a courtyard in the museum where Nina and Dominique often meet. In the courtyard are several statues of Dominique's childhood friends. One of them, named Odile, had kept a journal that becomes important in solving the mystery.

The book is not always easy to read, but I liked it anyway because it gave me many ideas to think about. Nina has a special feeling about museums, for instance. Describing this feeling, she says that holding some of the old things "was as if there wasn't any time at all between their lives and mine." Her remark made me realize how museums are special places for keeping alive important facts and ideas about the past.

Another idea I got from the story was why books are important. An official at the museum is writing a biography about Dominique's father. Nina wants to know what good it will do to prove Dominique's father innocent now. "It will do *a* good," Dominique says. "It will set straight one more lie. As for time, that is nothing. But truth is something." That makes books "special places" too. They preserve important facts and ideas about the past in the same way museums do.

The most interesting ideas in the book, however, are those about time. Gil, a schoolmate of Nina's, is working on a project about time, and he has thought a lot about the subject. These thoughts are woven all through the book and play a vital part in the story. "Time Is a River Without Banks" is the title of a painting Nina is attracted to. Dominique explains how she and Nina can exist in different times and at the same time. In a discussion of time, Gil declares, "Prophetic dreams mean that all time — past, present, and future — is one Time."

"It's as if," another character says, "we're ants walking on a tapestry already woven, and having no idea of the whole design but only of the little part we're standing on."

If we think of time as having only one direction, then the story could not be believable. But if "time is only in our heads," as Gil says, then the story can be believable. The way the author wrote the story makes me believe it. In fact, the ideas about time are so interesting that I copied some of them down in my notebook to think about later.

The author of *The Court of the Stone Children,* Eleanor Cameron, has written a number of other books for young people. She was born in Canada, though her parents were English. She moved to the United States as a child and grew up in California. She became a librarian and married and began her writing career by writing stories for her son. She has won several awards for her work, including a scroll from the Mystery Writers of America and two Commonwealth awards.

— GILBERT GRAIL

1. Examine each of the paragraphs in the book report to discover the types of information given. Use the following questions to help you:
   a) Which paragraphs summarize the story?
   b) Which paragraphs discuss the ideas presented throughout the story?
   d) Which paragraph relates information about the author?

2. Do you think the amount of space the writer devotes to each of the topics in the report is well planned? Why or why not?

B. Select a good book to report on and read it carefully. Then choose three of the following topics to cover in your report. Choose topics that fit the type of book you have decided to report on — biography, travel, history, adventure, fiction, and so forth. Decide how much space you want to devote to each topic. One or two paragraphs per topic should be sufficient. Write your paragraphs and combine them into a full-length book report. Observe the Guides for Writing a Paragraph (page 162), and the Guides for Writing a Book Report (page 197).

1. A paragraph about the author
2. A paragraph explaining the author's purpose in writing the book
3. A paragraph telling briefly what the book is about
4. A paragraph about important beliefs, attitudes, or customs
5. A paragraph about the significance of the title of the book
6. A paragraph about the book's setting, or some part of it
7. A paragraph explaining a strong feeling or impression that you gained from reading the book
8. A paragraph (or more) in which you tell the basic facts of the plot and relate a key incident (*for a book of fiction*)
9. A paragraph in which you describe how the central character changed or grew during the time covered in the book
10. A paragraph telling about _____'s contribution to humanity
11. A paragraph telling why you think the book is unusual or worth reading
12. A paragraph telling why you did or did not like the book. Give exact reasons.

WRITING LETTERS

1. Learning Correct Letter Forms

READ AND THINK ABOUT . . .

It is true that *what you say* is the most important part of any letter, but interesting content is not enough. You need to begin by learning correct letter form; then you can concentrate on making the content of your letter interesting.

1. Tell in the *heading* where and when the letter is being written.

617 East Oak Street
Chicago, Illinois 60622
February 2, 19—

   a) Use a comma in these ways:
     (1) Between the name of the town or city and that of the state. Do not insert a comma between the state and the ZIP code number.
     (2) Between the day of the month and the year.
   b) Use no other punctuation.
   c) Capitalize all words in the heading.
   d) Avoid abbreviations.

2. In the *greeting* (or salutation) give the name of the person.

     Rıɢʜᴛ: Dear Luisa,   Dear Mother,
     Pᴏᴏʀ: Dear Friend,   Dear old Pal,

   a) Capitalize the first word and the name of the person.

     Dear Phil and Georgia,   My dear Mitsuko,

   b) Use a comma after the greeting.

     Dear Mother,   Dear Uncle Tom,

3. Divide the *body* of the letter into paragraphs. Begin a new paragraph for each new idea.

4. Capitalize only the first word of the *complimentary close.* Follow the closing with a comma.

     Your loving sister,   Lovingly yours,
     Gratefully yours,   Yours sincerely,
     With much love,   Affectionately yours,

5. Use no punctuation after the *signature.* Sign the name by which the person to whom you are writing calls you.

THE FORM OF A FRIENDLY LETTER

A friendly letter has five parts. When handwritten, it usually is written in indented, or *slant,* style, as shown on the following page.

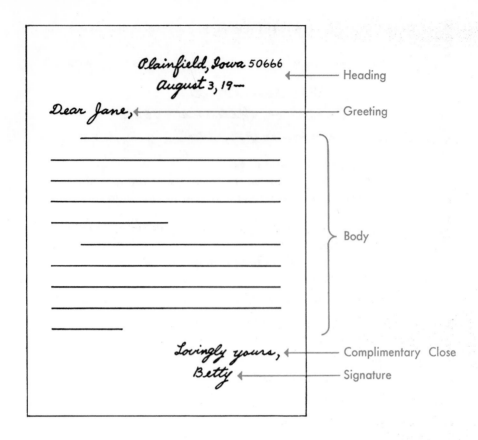

Heading

Greeting

Body

Complimentary Close

Signature

LEARNING ACTIVITIES

A. Arrange and punctuate the various parts of each letter indicated below. For the body, draw lines across the paper to indicate paragraphs, as in the model shown above. Exchange papers for checking as the forms are put on the board and explained.

1. 115 north elm street boston massachusetts 02116 june 16 19— dear uncle myron (*body of letter*) with love jamie
2. rural route 3 blissfield ohio 43805 september 5 19— dear mother and dad (*body of letter*) your affectionate daughter angela
3. pinecliffe colorado 80471 august 4 19— my dear alice (*body of letter*) your loving cousin louise
4. 1627 scott boulevard austin texas 78710 may 10 19— dear oscar (*body of letter*) sincerely yours tomasina
5. rural route 5 clayton kansas 67629 april 4 19— dear zoë (*body of letter*) your friend nick

B. Write two letter models of your own, one for a letter written from a rural address and one from a large city. Have these put on the board for criticism and any needed corrections.

THE ENVELOPE ADDRESS

GUIDES FOR ADDRESSING THE ENVELOPE

1. Indent as shown in the model on this page.
2. Capitalize all words.
3. Do not use abbreviations for names of streets or cities. Abbreviations are hard to read and may cause the letter to be delivered to the wrong address. You may use the post office–approved abbreviations for state names, however. They are two-letter designations, such as: IL (Illinois), NY (New York). Or you may write the state name in full.
4. Put the main address in the lower part of the right-hand half of the envelope. In this location it will not be blotted out when the post office cancels the stamp, and it is well away from the return address, which goes in the upper left-hand corner.
5. Put the ZIP code number after the name of the state if there is room; if not, put it below the name of the city.
6. Use a comma between the name of the city and that of the state. Use no other punctuation except for the period after the abbreviation of a title such as *Mr., Mrs., Dr.*

Here is a model to follow in addressing an envelope.

Harry Wilson
910 Sunset Street
Toledo, Ohio 43610

Mrs. Alfred Edwards
1023 North Oak Street
Cleveland, Ohio 44118

If you do not know the ZIP code number for a certain address, ask at your local post office. All ZIP numbers are contained in the *Directory of Post Offices* supplied to each office by the Post Office Department.

LEARNING ACTIVITIES

A. Draw rectangles to represent envelopes and write the main address and the return address for each of the following:

1. A letter to Miss Carol Elaine Wedemeyer, Rural Route 2, Eugene, Oregon 97401, from Miss Karen Cohee, 2853 Ocean Drive, San Diego, California 92110
2. A letter from Alan Scheer, 7232 Thirtieth Street, Cincinnati, Ohio 45208, to Daniel Bannister, 121 Anne Street, McMinnville, Oregon 97128
3. A letter from Ms. Laurie Nicholson, 439 East Eighty-eighth Street, New York, New York 10028, to Mr. John Devereaux, 205 Edgewood Avenue, New Haven, Connecticut 06511.

B. Draw rectangles on your paper to represent envelopes for the letters in *A*, page 204. Address them, following the model form on page 205. Make up the last name of each writer and the address and full name of the person who is to receive each letter. Exchange papers for checking in class.

C. For further practice in addressing letters correctly, take names and addresses from your daily newspaper. Draw envelope forms and address them. Use your own return address. Go over your work in class.

FOLLOW-UP

Put in your notebook examples of correct letter form and envelope form. Be sure that your teacher has approved them. In the future when you need to write friendly letters, use these forms as guides.

GOOD APPEARANCE IN LETTERS

Using correct letter forms and addressing letters properly are important, but so is the general appearance of the letter. The following guides will help you to write attractive letters.

GUIDES FOR MAKING LETTERS LOOK ATTRACTIVE

1. As a rule, use only black or blue ink and white (or lightly tinted) stationery.

2. Avoid blots and messy cross-outs or erasures.

3. Keep neat, even margins. Allow at least half an inch at sides and top; allow a somewhat wider space at the foot of the page.

4. Write plainly, forming all letters carefully. Avoid writing that is either large and scrawly or tiny and crowded. (See page 479.)

5. Keep lines straight and paragraph indentions even.

LEARNING ACTIVITIES

A. The following letter has many faults, both in form and in appearance. Go over it in class to find those faults. List them on the board.

<blockquote>

643 W. 5th St.
Portland, Me., 04106
July 8 19-

Dear mother

It doesn't seem possible that I have been here at Uncle Edward's for two weeks. There are so many interesting things to do that the days just sail by. I've had a good time every minute. This afternoon we are. ~~doing~~ driving to the seashore for a picnic. According to Uncle Edward we are having it at the same old spot where you and he had so many good times when you were children. ~~Tom~~ Tomorrow I'el write you a long letter ~~till~~ all about the picnic.

your loving son

Jack

</blockquote>

207

B. Rewrite this letter. Arrange it in correct form and include all necessary punctuation and capitalization. The letter contains two paragraphs. Be sure to proofread carefully.

> 2516 north tenth street mobile alabama 36609 september 7 19— dear mother Your letter telling us that Aunt Helen is better and that you probably will be home next week is good news for all of us. We miss you very much, but you mustn't worry about things here at home. Visit with Aunt Helen an extra day or so if you wish to. After all, you don't get to visit her very often. There was some big excitement in the neighborhood yesterday. Little Billy Olivero disappeared for several hours, and everyone up and down the street was out looking for him. Just when his mother was about to call the police, Billy crawled out of their doghouse. No fooling! He'd been asleep in there all the time. Your loving daughter Laurette

C. Draw a rectangle about the size of an envelope. Address the envelope to Laurette's mother: mrs. george myer 1928 east williams street birmingham alabama 35211. Put Laurette's return address on the envelope.

2. Making Letters Interesting

"I CAN'T THINK OF A THING TO TELL HER!"

"JUST PRETEND YOU'RE TALKING."

READ AND THINK ABOUT . . .

How can it be that a person who never runs out of something to say in a conversation feels that he or she has nothing

208

to say in letters? What would the person to whom you are writing like to hear?

Well, Grandfather and Grandmother and your aunts and uncles probably are most interested in hearing about *you* and what you have been doing. When you write to someone near your own age, though, you should write mostly about things that show your interest in *him* or *her*. That is to say, the word *you* should appear in your letters more often than *I*.

If you know the person well, there are many things that you can ask about: pets, hobbies, scouting or 4-H work, books, sports, television, people that you both know, plans for visiting each other, memories of visits that you have had in the past. Remember, this is the body of the letter, the most important part. It is *you* Make your reader know that you are glad to write.

If you are writing to a new friend, ask about some of those same things and tell a little about yourself in connection with them.

GUIDES FOR GOOD LETTER WRITING

1. Bring the other person into the things that you write about. Ask questions about that person and his or her activities; ask for opinions or for advice about ideas that you have.

2. Write as you would talk; that is, avoid stiff, formal language.

3. Make the other person feel that you enjoy his or her friendship.

4. Keep your letter cheerful.

5. Be sure that each sentence has a subject. Do not say, "Hope that you are enjoying your vacation." Say instead, "*I* hope that you are enjoying your vacation."

6. Do not spoil your letter with such worn-out expressions as these:

   How are you? I am fine and hope you are the same.
   Since I have nothing to do, I'll write you a letter.
   Excuse mistakes.
   Well, I guess I'd better close now.
   Hoping to hear from you soon.
   Having wonderful time. Wish you were here.
   My typewriter can't spell.

Read the following letter that one girl wrote to a friend.

Plainfield, Iowa 50666
November 1, 19—

Dear Nina,

Your letter came yesterday. How I wish I could be in your shoes at that rock concert Saturday!

Last Saturday our Scout troop went on an overnight hike to Oakview Park. That's the place where we had our Fourth of July picnic. Remember? The weather was frosty, but that didn't bother us, except that it gave us big appetites. You never saw bacon and eggs disappear so fast!

How are you getting along with your stamp collection? I've been writing to a girl in Venezuela, and she has promised to send me some South American stamps. If there are any special ones you've been wanting, I may be able to get them for you from her.

Are you to have a Thanksgiving vacation? If so, you're invited to spend it here. I hope you can come.

Your friend,
Ilse

LEARNING ACTIVITIES

A. Discuss the letter that Ilse wrote. Why do you think Nina was glad to get it? Check it by the guides on page 209.

B. If you have received an interesting (and not too personal) letter lately, read it to the class. Explain why you think that it is a good letter.

C. Write the letter that you think Nina might have sent in replying to Ilse. If you prefer, write the one from Nina that Ilse was answering. Check your letter by each point on your Writing Chart. The Guides for Good Letter Writing on page 209 will help you to make good scores in *content.* Read these letters in class. Before reading, look over the Guides to a Pleasing, Effective Voice, page 42. Perhaps you will want to vote on the best letters.

D. Write a real letter now to some friend or relative. Check through it to see whether you have followed the guides on page 209. The second guide is, "Write as you would talk." Think of all the things that you tell the family about your school day. Think what you do after school and on Saturdays and Sundays. Tell about those things in detail. Pages 292, 333, 388, and 410 will help you to use vivid words to make your descriptions interesting. Do not forget good paragraphing. (See the Guides for Writing a Paragraph, page 162.)

Ask a friend to give his or her opinion of the letter, or ask your teacher.

Check the form of the letter and its envelope before mailing. Be sure that both are correct.

USING ENGLISH OUTSIDE SCHOOL

A. Probably your school subscribes to magazines that contain letters from boys and girls your age. Try writing a letter to one of those magazines. Tell your age and grade in school; describe your appearance, if you like; discuss your pets and hobbies; ask others who read the magazine to write to you. Your letter may lead to some interesting friendships. Be sure that your letter form is correct; check it by the guides on page 203. Proofread the letter carefully before sealing the envelope.

B. Instead of writing to the magazine itself, you may prefer to write to someone whose letter appears in one of the magazines. It will be especially interesting to write to someone who lives in a different part of the country or in some foreign land. Be sure to check form and appearance before you mail the letter.

FOLLOW-UP

Check your Writing Chart. In what ways are you improving? What are your weakest points?

3. Writing Invitations and Replies

Invitations and replies to invitations are special letters that you will need to write from time to time.

GUIDES FOR WRITING AND ANSWERING INVITATIONS

1. Tell exactly what the invitation is for. Include helpful details, such as naming any special clothes or other items that may come in handy.
2. Make the time and the place definite.
3. Send invitations as early as possible.
4. Make the person feel that you really want him or her to come.
5. Answer any invitation promptly.
6. Show your appreciation, even when you cannot accept.
7. If you refuse an invitation, give a good reason.
8. Keep both invitations and replies short.

Here is an example of a letter of invitation.

> 250 Pearl Street
> Yankton, South Dakota 57078
> July 16, 19—
>
> Dear Leah,
>
> We shall be driving to Sioux City on Friday, July 25, to see the Air Circus. Would you and your brother like to go with us?
>
> We plan to leave at eight in the morning. If you are able to go, we'll stop for you. Tell your mother that we'll be back by ten in the evening.
>
> I surely hope that you both can go with us, for that will make it all the more fun for me. Please let me know at once.
>
> Your friend,
> Benjy

LEARNING ACTIVITIES

A. In your small groups, discuss Benjy's letter. Use the Guides for Holding Discussions, page 35, to help you have a good discussion. Decide how well the letter follows guides 1, 2, 3, 4, and 8 on this page.

B. Write Leah's reply accepting or declining the invitation. Be sure to keep in mind guides 5, 6, 7, and 8 as you write. Follow also the Guides to

Correct Letter Form, page 203. Take turns at reading the replies in class. As letters are read, have them checked both on content and on the reading.

C. Write a letter inviting a friend to go on a camping trip with you and your family. Be sure to proofread for careless mistakes. Exchange letters with a partner. Using the Guides to Correct Letter Form, page 203, and points 1, 2, 3, 4, and 8 of the Guides for Writing and Answering Invitations, check the letter that you receive. When your own paper is returned, correct any mistakes that were found.

D. Write an invitation for some other occasion, and exchange papers with a partner. Write a reply to the invitation that you receive. Read letters in class, using the same plan of checking as in *B*.

4. Writing Thank-You Letters

Most thank-you letters are of two kinds: (1) letters thanking someone for a gift or for a special favor, and (2) "bread-and-butter" letters — letters written after a visit.

GUIDES FOR WRITING THANK-YOU LETTERS

1. Write thank-you letters promptly.
2. Give some particular reason for appreciating the gift or favor.
3. After a visit, write a "bread-and-butter" letter to your host and hostess. Usually that will be the parents of the friend whom you visited. Write also to that friend.
4. Keep the letter short.

A LETTER OF THANKS FOR A GIFT

958 Pine Street
Wilson, North Carolina 27893
June 16, 19—

Dear Aunt Laura,

How did you know that I've been wishing hard for an overnight case all my own? Well, I have — and now, thanks to my thoughtful aunt, my wish has come true.

I had an exciting birthday, with far more gifts than I deserve, I am sure. The gift that is tops, though, is the one from you. I like everything about it — the color, the size, the fittings, and the material. It is perfect!

Thank you again, Aunt Laura.

Your loving niece,
Carol

A BREAD-AND-BUTTER LETTER

Andover, Kansas 67002
September 10, 19—

Dear Mr. and Mrs. Cruz,

New Mexico is now my favorite state, and the people there are the best. I shall never forget all the things that you both did to make my visit enjoyable. The trip into the Red River country was the high spot. I'm still singing that song!

As soon as I get some of these bothersome school assignments out of the way, I'll write Bob a long letter.

Sincerely yours,
Raoul Labonde

214

LEARNING ACTIVITIES

A. Check the two sample letters by the guides on page 214.

B. Here are some sentences from thank-you letters. What criticisms would you make of them? Discuss the sentences in class.

1. I don't feel much like writing, but Mother says I have to get my birthday thank-you letters sent today.
2. Thank you for the billfold. Three other people gave me one, too.
3. I'm sorry that I did not write to you a week ago to thank you for the birthday gift. I forgot all about it.
4. Tell your parents thanks for me. I really enjoyed my visit.
5. Thank you for the sweater. I guess you just forgot that I don't like brown very well.

C. Write a letter of thanks for a birthday gift or a Christmas gift. Check the letter by the Guides to Correct Letter Form, page 203. Read letters in class and discuss them.

D. Write a "bread-and-butter" letter. Proofread for careless mistakes in capitalization, punctuation, and spelling. Go over letters, naming good points and suggesting improvements.

E. Write a letter of appreciation for favors done for you while you were in the hospital. Review the Guides to a Pleasing, Effective Voice, page 42, before reading the letters in class.

USING ENGLISH OUTSIDE SCHOOL

Think of someone to whom you actually owe a letter of thanks for a favor or a gift. Write the letter, following the Guides for Writing Thank-You Letters, page 214, and the Guides to Correct Letter Form, page 203. Address the envelope and mail the letter.

5. Writing Business Letters

THINK IT OVER . . .

In what ways other than in the heading do you have to give exact and correct information in a business letter?

How does the form of a business letter differ from that of a friendly letter?

THE FORM OF A BUSINESS LETTER

Here are the differences between the form of a friendly letter and that of a business letter:

1. The business letter usually is not written in slant style. The example here is in semiblock style; that is, only the paragraphs are indented. Most typewritten letters follow this style.

2. There is an added part, the *inside address.*

3. The salutation is followed by a colon, not a comma.

FORMS FOR BUSINESS LETTER AND ENVELOPE ADDRESS

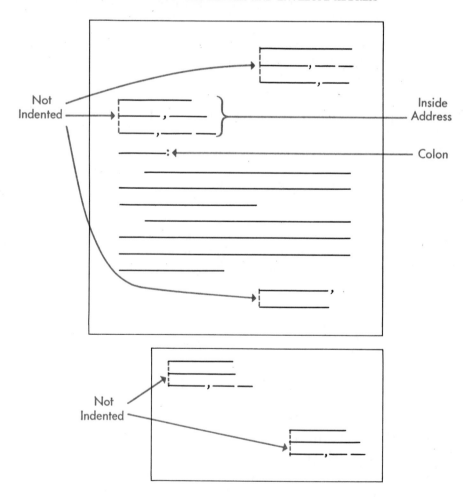

THE CONTENT OF A BUSINESS LETTER

In business letters, the aim should be to present facts clearly, neatly, and briefly. The following guides will be helpful.

GUIDES FOR WRITING BUSINESS LETTERS

1. Get to the point immediately.
2. If the letter is handwritten, use your most careful penmanship.
3. Be polite.
4. Give exact information; do not make it necessary for the receiver to write you for missing facts.
5. If you ask a favor, enclose a stamped, self-addressed envelope.
6. If you enclose money, tell the amount and the form (check, money order, draft).
7. Sign your full name. If you are writing as a club or class officer, put your title below your signature.

Business letters that you might need to write include letters of subscription and letters of request.

SUBSCRIPTION LETTER

432 South Drive
Buffalo, New York 14216
March 3, 19—

Subscription Department
Brown Publishing Company
2 North Apple Avenue
Kansas City, Missouri 64104

Dear Sir or Madam:

Please send *Teen Crafts* magazine to me for one year, beginning with the April issue. This is a new subscription.

I am enclosing a money order for $6.50, your advertised rate for a one-year subscription.

Yours truly,
Blanche Hebert

2427 Maple Street
York, Nebraska 68467
April 12, 19 —

Director, Order Department
Eastman Kodak Company
45 North State Street
Rochester, New York 14604

Dear Sir or Madam:

Please send me your latest catalogue describing flash-bulb cameras. I should appreciate receiving also a price list and an order blank.

Sincerely yours,
Camille Scott

LEARNING ACTIVITIES

A. Check the two sample letters by the guides on page 217. How well do they follow the guides?

B. Write a letter to a magazine publisher, ordering a magazine. Exchange letters with a partner; check form, spelling, capitalization, punctuation, and content. Perhaps you can make this a real letter.

C. Write a letter to a magazine, giving a change of address. Give both the old and the new address. (Most publishers request that you enclose the address label from a copy of the magazine.) In your small groups, take turns at reading and judging the letters.

USING ENGLISH OUTSIDE SCHOOL

Write a letter to a company asking for information or for a catalogue or a sample of some product. The advertising pages of a magazine will suggest a letter that you might like to write. Check the letter by the letter form on page 216 and by the guides on page 217. Have it approved by your teacher before you mail it.

CAPITALIZATION AND PUNCTUATION*

1. Using Capital Letters Correctly

"THE COACH SAID, 'WHEN WE FUMBLED ON THE FIVE-YARD LINE, THE BRUINS CAPITALIZED ON OUR MISTAKE!'"

After Pretest 1 has been scored, go over it carefully to see how to correct your mistakes. Make a record of the kinds of errors that you had. If you made any errors in capitalization, study carefully the rules and exercises that follow.

If you had a perfect score and your teacher excuses you from the instruction and practice that follow, you may enjoy doing the activities in the "Just for Fun" section on pages 242–244.

*Pretest 1 should be taken at this point. All tests called for in the text are contained in a test booklet that may be purchased for each student. The tests also appear in the *Teacher's Guide.* Schools not wishing to buy the booklets may mimeograph the tests.

CAPITALIZING PROPER NOUNS

● FACTS YOU NEED TO KNOW

1. (DEFINITION) A *noun* is a name word.

2. (DEFINITION) A *common noun* **names any member of a** *general group:* boy, day, city, holiday.

3. (DEFINITION) A *proper noun* **names a** *specific* **member of any general group:** John, Friday, Boston, Christmas.

GENERAL:	boy	day	city	holiday
SPECIFIC:	John	Friday	Boston	Christmas

RULES FOR USING CAPITAL LETTERS

RULE 1. Capitalize every proper noun.

COMMON NOUN	PROPER NOUN	COMMON NOUN	PROPER NOUN
boy	John	country	Norway
girl	Mary	nationality	Spanish
day	Friday	holiday	Christmas
month	January	newspaper	*Chicago Tribune*
city	Omaha	organization	B'nai B'rith
state	Nebraska	magazine	*Junior Scholastic*

RULE 2. Capitalize common nouns such as *street, lake, river, mountain, school* **when used as part of a proper noun to name a particular place or thing.**

I swam in the lake. (*The name of the lake is not given.*)
I swam in Lake Michigan. (*The name of the lake is told.*)
We have a new junior high school. (*The name is not given.*)
I attend Irving Junior High School. (*The name is told.*)

COMMON NOUN	PROPER NOUN	COMMON NOUN	PROPER NOUN
river	Missouri River	city	Sioux City
ocean	Atlantic Ocean	avenue	Forest Avenue
day	Labor Day	mountain	Mount Whitney

RULE 3. Do not capitalize prepositions (see the list on page 426), **the conjunction** *and,* **or the articles** *a, an,* **or** *the* **when used as part of a proper noun.**

J. C. Smith *and* Company   "Home *on the* Range"
Cape *of* Good Hope

LEARNING ACTIVITIES

A. Copy the following list of common nouns. After each one write a proper noun that it suggests to you. EXAMPLE: *person — Barbara Mehlen.* Read your lists aloud to see how many different proper nouns the class named. Be sure that each word on your list is capitalized correctly.

1. state	7. airplane	13. store
2. city	8. singer	14. business firm
3. explorer	9. theater	15. baseball player
4. author	10. month	16. automobile
5. film star	11. holiday	17. sports arena
6. restaurant	12. nation	18. zoo

B. Think of a proper noun to use with each common noun in the following list. EXAMPLE: *river — Hudson River.* Write the words in sentences; then read your sentences in class, telling which words you have capitalized. Be sure to apply guides 4 and 7 in the Guides for Reading Aloud, page 59. If you made errors in capitalization, study the rules again so that you understand your mistakes; then correct them.

1. street	5. club	9. sea
2. county	6. canal	10. city
3. mountains	7. junior high school	11. building
4. railroad	8. ocean	12. university

C. (1) Write five sentences with geographical proper nouns of at least three words, one of which should not be capitalized (Rule 3, page 220). Use a map of the world to help you find names to use.

EXAMPLE: The *Strait of Gibraltar* separates Spain and Africa.

(2) Proofread your sentences for careless mistakes. (3) Read your sentences in class. Have someone list on the board the different proper nouns used.

D. Copy Rules 1, 2, and 3 into your notebook, leaving space below each rule for examples. Clip from magazines three examples of each rule and paste them under the rule that applies.

OTHER USES OF CAPITAL LETTERS

Page 220 gives rules for the capitalization of proper nouns. You should make sure that you know certain other uses of capital letters. Study the following rules and examples carefully.

RULES FOR USING CAPITAL LETTERS — Continued

RULE 4. Capitalize the first word of a sentence.

Everyone wanted to go to the game.
Are they coming with us?

RULE 5. Capitalize the first word of a quotation.

Don complained, "No one asked me to go."
"No one," complained Don, "asked me to go."

RULE 6. Capitalize titles used with names of people. Many times these titles are abbreviations. Capitalize initials that stand for names of people.

Mr. and Mrs. R. O. Lopez   Aunt Susan
Dr. Helen A. Crandall   Professor P. K. Bernstein
Lieutenant S. M. Naylor   Superintendent J. B. Bellomo

RULE 7. Capitalize the word *I* and contractions formed with it. (See page 238 if you do not know what contractions are.)

Yes, I plan to go, but I'll have to walk.

LEARNING ACTIVITIES

A. (1) Copy the following sentences, placing capital letters where they belong. (2) Be sure to proofread. (3) Exchange papers with a partner and check your work.

1. the first thing that mr. rogers said was, "where have you been?"
2. lieutenant jane r. dagen was commissioned last year.
3. what i saw, i'll never forget.
4. we have an appointment to see superintendent baynes.
5. marjorie asked, "are you sure that was professor jones?"
6. yes, aunt dorothy and i met the train.
7. the speaker was to be dr. w. l. hanlon of atlanta, georgia.
8. "you should," mrs. ellsworth reminded us, "be in your seats."
9. if ms. franklin calls, tell her i'll be there by 5:30.
10. sitting there, i heard a voice yell, "help!"

B. (1) Write sentences of your own as examples of the seven rules for capitalizing that you have studied. (2) Be sure to proofread your sentences. (3) In class, take turns at putting a sentence on the board, writing all the words with small letters. Call on a classmate to supply the needed capitals.

C. Copy Rules 4–7 into your notebook with Rules 1–3. Clip from old magazines three examples of each of the four added rules and paste them under the rule that applies.

RULE 8. Capitalize the words *Mother, Father, Grandmother,* **and** *Grandfather* **when they are used instead of that person's name. Do not capitalize them when they are preceded by the possessive form of a noun or pronoun:** *John's, Ivy's, my, your, his, her, our,* **or** *their.*

I think that Mother can come.
I think that my mother can come.

RULE 9. Capitalize the first word and all important words in the titles of *books, articles, themes, musical works, poems,* **and** *plays.* **Capitalize a word such as** *a, an, the, and, or, but, of, to, in, on, by* **only if it comes first or last.**

On to Oregon   "The Flag Goes By"
The Prince and the Pauper

RULE 10. Capitalize the name of a school subject when it comes from the name of a country, as *English, French, Spanish, Latin.* (*Latin* comes from *Latium,* a region of central Italy; therefore it needs a capital.)

Do not capitalize names of such subjects as *geography, science, history* **except when used as headings or titles for papers that you hand in.**

My cousin studies history, science, English, Latin, and industrial arts.

RULE 11. Capitalize *East, West, North, South,* **and such words as** *Northwest* **when they indicate a section of the country. Do not capitalize such words when they simply indicate a direction.**

Anya spent last summer in the West and in the Southwest.
Don lives south of the school, but we live northeast of it.

RULE 12. Capitalize references to *religions* **and** *denominations,* **the** *Bible and its parts, other sacred books,* **and the** *Deity.*

The Bible story of Noah and the flood is found in Genesis, in the Old Testament.

In the Koran, the name of the Deity is Allah.

Learn about words!

The following words, taken from Learning Activity *A,* have interesting histories. Use your dictionary to find the story behind each word.

piano   psalm   plastic   theme

LEARNING ACTIVITIES

A. Copy the following sentences, placing capital letters where they belong. In class go over the sentences orally, telling why you used each capital letter.

1. I told grandmother that the bible was on the piano.
2. "mountains at your feet" is an article about the west.
3. The lutheran pastor's sermon was titled "trust in god."
4. My mother knows all about plastics, but she has forgotten most of what she once knew about latin.
5. I read *the gentle tamers* for a history report.
6. The title of her english theme is "where cinnamon comes from."
7. The action in that book takes place in the south.
8. My father walked east five blocks too far.
9. The responsive reading is taken from psalms, in the old testament.
10. Is the musical comedy *the king and i* based on a book?

B. Write two sentences to illustrate each usage that you missed in *A*.

C. Add Rules 8–12 to those in your notebook. Clip from magazines three examples of each rule and paste them under the right rule.

ENRICHMENT

Use each of the following words in *two* sentences. In the first sentence, use it as it is; in the second, use it where it would be capitalized.

EXAMPLE: *lake*   1. Behind our farm is a small *lake*.
2. I spent my last vacation at *Lake* Towanda.

southeast   uncle   band   captain   doctor   mountain

2. Punctuating Sentences Correctly

TALK IT OVER . . .

Understanding the purpose of punctuation is half the battle. Suppose that in a story you came to this last line on a page:

When at last it was time to eat my little dog

You would be surprised and shocked at the idea suggested. Upon turning the page to get the details, however, you would be relieved to find the rest of the sentence: ". . . stood waiting by its bowl."

Where could you put a comma in that sentence to make the meaning clear even before you turned the page?

What is confusing about the following sentences? What marks of punctuation could you insert to make the meaning clear? (Show two different meanings for each sentence.)

The girls plans are a secret. (How many girls?)
Dick my brother needs help. (Are *Dick* and *brother* two people?)

Punctuation marks, correctly used, do two things: (1) they help make the meaning clear, and (2) they help the reader to get the meaning quickly.

If you made any errors on the punctuation part of Pretest 1, you will want to study the rules and exercises that follow.

If you had a perfect score and your teacher excuses you from the work that follows, you may enjoy the "Just for Fun" section on pages 242–244.

PERIODS, QUESTION MARKS, EXCLAMATION POINTS

RULES FOR END PUNCTUATION

RULE 1. Use a period to close a *declarative* sentence, that is, one that makes a statement.

Ice is cold.

When the Pan-American Exposition opened in Dallas, Texas, a $75,000 jeweled lock at the main gate, symbolic of international friendship, was opened by twenty-one girls.

RULE 2. Use a period to close an *imperative* sentence, that is, one that expresses a command or a request.

Water the plants.   Please bring me that book.

RULE 3. Use a question mark to close an *interrogative* sentence, that is, one that asks a question.

Where did John go?   Have you any questions?

RULE 4. Use an exclamation point after an *exclamation*, that is, words that express strong feeling. Sometimes an exclamation is a sentence, and sometimes it is not.

How excited I was! (*a sentence*)   Hurrah! (*not a sentence*)

225

LEARNING ACTIVITIES

A. Copy the following sentences, supplying the correct end punctuation. Exchange papers for checking.

1. Were you at the orchestra concert last Saturday
2. Joan Donaldi, the first cellist, played a solo
3. What a musician she is
4. Her solo came after the intermission
5. Later in the concert, Dee Beech conducted one number
6. Did you notice that she did not use a musical score
7. Bud Foster and Marla Franco are the percussionists
8. There were only four or five empty seats
9. It was a beautiful concert
10. The final piece was a medley of songs from Broadway musicals

B. (1) Write nine sentences about your family or friends, using periods, question marks, and exclamation points three times each. (2) Take turns in class at putting sentences on the board, omitting the end punctuation. Call on a classmate to provide the correct mark for each sentence.

C. Copy in your notebook the four rules for end punctuation, leaving space below each rule for examples. Clip from magazines three examples of each rule. Paste them in your notebook under the rule that applies.

RULES FOR OTHER USES OF THE PERIOD

RULE 1. **Use periods to show abbreviations.** As a rule, avoid abbreviations except for *Mr., Mrs., Ms., Dr.,* or *St.* (when it means *Saint*) before a name and *Jr.* or *Sr.* after one.

Mich.	doz.	Ave.	etc.	Jr.	Mr.
N. Y.	bu.	St.	No.	Sr.	Dr.
Ill.	lb.	Tues.	Co.	Oct.	Ms.

a) The title *Miss* is not an abbreviation and has no period.

My teacher is Miss [*not* Miss.] April Meade.

b) The two abbreviations used to indicate time, A.M. (*ante meridiem* — before noon) and P.M. (*post meridiem* — after noon), should be set off by periods: Be here at 1:30 P.M.

RULE 2. **Use a period after an initial that stands for a name.**

H. C. Bond   P. Anderson   T. Edward Wilson

RULE 3. **Use a period with figures to show** (1) **decimals and** (2) **dollars and cents.** (Note that in reading such a number, "and" shows where the decimal point belongs.)

3.6 (*three* and *six tenths*) $9.40 (*nine dollars* and *forty cents*)

226

LEARNING ACTIVITIES

A. Copy the following sentences, supplying periods where they are needed. Go over the sentences in class.

1. Dr and Mrs J R Griffith bought a painting for $76075 (seven hundred sixty dollars and seventy-five cents).
2. The 5:30 P M train for St Petersburg is late.
3. Among the guests were Ms Lila M Clark and Miss Marie Lane.
4. Two and a half can be written 25.
5. "830 Surrey Ave, Glenview, Ill 60025" was written on the card.

B. (1) Write six advertising signs that you might see in shop windows or along the highway. In them, illustrate the use of periods in abbreviations, initials, decimals, or dollars and cents. (2) Be sure to proofread carefully. (3) In class, read your work aloud. Call on someone to write on the board the abbreviations, initials, and figures that need periods. You may need to say how many periods are to be used.

C. Copy in your notebook Rules 1, 2, and 3. Clip three examples of each rule from magazines. Paste them in your notebook under the rule that applies in each case.

USING COMMAS

READ AND DO . . .

How much do you know about using commas in written work? When you speak, your voice unconsciously puts in comma punctuation. When you read aloud, also, your voice usually points out to listeners where commas are.

Take turns reading aloud one of the following sentences. Call on someone to tell which sentence in each pair you have read.

1. Dick put the dishes away.	1. Mr. Jones, the lawyer is here.
2. Dick, put the dishes away.	2. Mr. Jones, the lawyer, is here.

Take two or three minutes to write a sentence pair similar to the examples. Read them aloud and call for a show of hands as to where the commas are.

The rules in the next two lessons will help you to use commas accurately.*

---

* The use of commas in the parts of a letter is taught on page 203. The use of commas in compound sentences is taught on page 445.

RULES FOR USING COMMAS

RULE 1. Use commas after the various parts of an address. (House number and street form *one* part, as do state and ZIP code number.)

Joy's address is 115 Oak Street, Dayton, Ohio 45400, isn't it?

Sometimes an address ends a sentence. In that case, use only the period (or question mark or exclamation point) at the end.

Were you born in Tampa, Florida?
Write me at 915 Cedar Street, Yankton, South Dakota 57078.

RULE 2. Use commas to set off the year if three parts of a date are given (month, day, year). **Use no commas if only two parts are given. Use no comma after a part that ends a sentence.**

That game was played on October 12, 1978, in a heavy rain.
They visited Florida in January 1978.
That game was played on October 12, 1978.

RULE 3. Use one or two commas to set off a noun in direct address. (DEFINITION) A noun used in speaking directly to a person is called a *noun in direct address.* (This construction is also known as a *nominative of address.*) **Note: Use two commas when other words come both before and after the noun of address.**

John, where did you put that ball of twine?
Where did you put that ball of twine, John?
Where, John, did you put that ball of twine?

RULE 4. Use a comma or commas to set off words used as appositives. (DEFINITION) An *appositive* **is a noun or pronoun that stands next to another noun and means the same person or thing.**

The assembly was conducted by our principal, Mrs. James.
Our principal, Mrs. James, spoke to the students.

If the appositive is one of a group of words, set off the entire group.

The Husky, an Eskimo **dog** used to pull sledges, looks much like a wolf.

LEARNING ACTIVITIES

A. Copy the following sentences, inserting commas where they are needed. Above each comma, write the number of the rule that applies. Exchange papers and read the sentences in class. When you read a sentence, be sure that your voice shows where the commas are.

1. Fred tell Sally that I'll see her in Syracuse New York.

2. Today I saw Ms. Reed our former principal. She left here in May 1977.
3. From Richmond Virginia we went to Greensboro North Carolina.
4. At noon on April 25 1957 the Harbor Freeway was opened.
5. I wonder Mrs. Burt whether you know my aunt Mrs. Stone.
6. Where were you on this particular day June 20 1963?
7. Dr. Riggs the only dentist in town has her office at 112 Elm Street.

B. Write sentences using the following expressions as indicated:

1. the owner of the car (appositive)
2. our next-door neighbor (appositive)
3. Mother (direct address)
4. Miss Benton (direct address)
5. 229 Mill Street Salem Ohio 44460
6. *the date of your own birthday*

RULES FOR USING COMMAS — Continued

RULE 5. **Use commas to separate three or more items in a series.**

Joan, Mary, Lou, and Phil went to the art museum.

Beth plays softball, runs the quarter mile, and is president of the science club.

Note that a comma is used before the *and* that joins the last two items. (Some authorities approve omitting this comma.)

Use no commas when all items in a series are joined by *and* **or** *or*.

We shall move to Georgia *or* Maryland *or* Texas.

RULE 6. **Use a comma when, in reading a sentence aloud, you hear a pause.** The pause may indicate (*a*) a long introductory phrase or (*b*) the insertion of words not really needed.

a) To the audience's great surprise, the bear rode the bicycle backward.
b) There are, of course, several reasons for the action.

RULE 7. **Use a comma after an introductory** *yes, no, well, oh.*

Yes, I plan to go.   Well, I'll think about it.

RULE 8. **Use a comma or commas to separate the exact words of a speaker from the rest of the sentence.**

Mary said, "You may use this pencil."
"I already have one," replied Bill.
"Yes," said Mary, "but you'll need a spare."

Sometimes the sense of the sentence requires some other mark.

"May I borrow a compass?" asked Kristin.
"What a healthy puppy!" remarked Alice.

The following words, taken from Learning Activity *A,* have interesting histories. Use your dictionary to find the story behind each word.

hash   chop suey   spaghetti   game

LEARNING ACTIVITIES

A. Copy these sentences, inserting needed commas. Above each comma, write the number of the rule that applies. Exchange papers for checking with classmates.

1. As soon as you are ready we'll go.
2. Well I am not sure that Tess is going.
3. "Yes" said Al "I like chop suey spaghetti and hash."
4. After the game was over we walked home.
5. Oh we'll have ice cream cake and cookies.
6. Mother said "When you reach home call Mrs. Shapiro."
7. I have friends living in Wisconsin in Kansas and in Oklahoma.
8. "No that man cannot float" said Bea.
9. While you were parking the car I saw Nancy.
10. As soon as I wash dress and eat I'll be ready.
11. "For dessert" said Pam "let's have cake or lemon pie or ice cream. If we have the last I'd like it of course with hot fudge."

B. (1) Write eight sentences, applying each of comma rules 5, 6, 7, and 8 twice. (2) Be sure to proofread for careless mistakes. (3) On the chalkboard, write the sentences without punctuation and call on classmates to tell where commas are needed.

C. Copy in your notebook all eight rules for using commas, leaving space for examples below each rule. Find in magazines and clip three examples of each rule. Paste each example under the proper rule.

ENRICHMENT

Find and read to the class, or to your small group, a paragraph containing eight or more commas. Your audience will listen closely to see how many commas they think are in the paragraph. In preparing to read, apply the Guides for Reading Aloud, page 59.

Look over papers that you are preparing for another class. (1) Check to see that you have used correct end punctuation and that you have placed correctly any other needed periods. (2) Check each comma use by the rules on pages 228 and 229. Insert any other needed commas.

USING QUOTATION MARKS

THINK IT OVER . . .

What is the student really asking for?

Why does a storybook with lots of conversation in it seem more interesting than one without it?

In your writing, how often do you use direct quotations? When you do use them, are you sure of where to place the quotation marks?

What is the difference between direct quotations and indirect quotations?

One good way to make a story lively and interesting is to use *direct quotations*, that is, conversation—the exact words of the people in the story. An *indirect quotation* tells what the speaker said but does not use the speaker's exact words.

DIRECT QUOTATION: Dad said, "Jack, come with me."
INDIRECT QUOTATION: Dad said that Jack should come with him.

RULES FOR USING QUOTATION MARKS

RULE 1. Place quotation marks before and after a direct quotation. (Remember, every direct quotation begins with a capital letter.)

Dan said, "I think that he went home."
Elena asked, "Are you coming with me?"
"I think that he went home," said Dan.
"Come with me!" exclaimed Elena.

Note the commas and other marks used with the quotation marks.

RULE 2. When the explanatory words come in the middle, put quotation marks around each part of the speaker's words.

"I think," said Dan, "that he went home."

Notice that the second part begins with a small letter, because it is part of the whole sentence *I think that he went home.*

"I think that he went home," said Dan. "He was in a hurry."

Here Dan speaks two different sentences; therefore a period follows *Dan,* and *He* begins with a capital letter.

RULE 3. In writing conversation, begin a new paragraph for each change of speaker.

"Bea, who played tonight?" yelled Ann.
"The sophomores played the freshmen," answered Bea. "It was a good game. Karen Haas scored twenty points."
"Who won?" asked Ann.
"The freshmen won, 60–56!" shouted Bea. "Yippee!"

RULE 4. Use no quotation marks with an indirect quotation.

Dan said that Bob had gone home.

RULE 5. Use quotation marks around the titles of *short stories, one-act plays, articles, songs, poems,* **and** *themes.*

Betty's theme is called "On the Way Home."
The poem "Birches" is one of my favorites.

LEARNING ACTIVITIES

A. Copy these sentences, inserting quotation marks. Make new paragraphs for a change of speaker. In class, explain your placement of the marks.

1. Clarence declared that he had seen a face at the window.
2. Wait for me! shouted Bridget.
3. My favorite story is The Ransom of Red Chief.
4. Have you seen Doris? asked Clara.
5. There were only twenty passengers on that plane, remarked Ted. Yes, replied Anita, and five got off at the first stop.
6. Were all the people on time? asked Tom. No, I think all except one were on time, said Felicia.
7. Coach Harkness yelled, Show some speed, team!
8. As the band played The Star-Spangled Banner, we raised the flag.

B. (1) Copy the following sentences, supplying capital letters, quotation marks, and any other punctuation marks needed. (2) Exchange papers for checking. (3) Go over the sentences in class.

1. Some planes said Alexis are still built of wood
2. This play, A Fight to the Finish, is very short but exciting
3. My father Harry announced will furnish a car for the Oakmont trip
4. The game has begun said Harriett both teams are playing hard
5. What is your name the police officer asked
6. The flight attendant said we have been delayed because of a heavy snow
7. I plan to call my theme Baby-sitting in Reverse
8. Jane shouted here comes the parade

C. Change the following indirect quotations to direct quotations. Make this a class activity in which one person dictates the direct quotation for another student to write correctly on the board.

1. Mother announced that I might go.
2. What he said was that he might be able to help us.
3. The nurse insisted that the doctor had just left.
4. Freddy exclaimed that I was being unreasonable.
5. Roberta asked that she be excused early on Tuesday.
6. One man complained that the work was too hard.
7. Elaine said that in her opinion Bill should be the chairperson.
8. Timmy boasted that he was not afraid in the dark.

D. (1) Write four sentences to show that you can apply the rules for using quotation marks. (2) Copy the sentences, omitting all quotation marks. (3) Exchange sentences with a partner and supply the needed marks. (4) Return the sentences for checking.

USING COLONS, UNDERLINING, AND HYPHENS

Here are rules that you should know about using three additional marks of punctuation—the colon, underlining, and the hyphen.

THE RULES

RULE 1. **Use a colon when you write the** *time* **in figures.**

2:30 P.M.   10:30 A.M.   I set the alarm for 6:30 A.M.

NOTE: The use of the colon in business letters is taught on page 216.

RULE 2. **When you write or typewrite, underline titles of** *books, full-length plays, motion pictures,* **and the names of** *magazines* **and** *newspapers.* In print, these appear in italic type. (*This is italic type.*)

(*handwritten*)   *I read King of the Wind twice.*

(*typewritten*)   I read <u>King of the Wind</u> twice.

(*printed*)   I read *King of the Wind* twice.

Last night's *Evening Record* had a review of the musical play *Godspell.*

RULE 3. **Use a hyphen in spelling out** *numbers* **from twenty-one to ninety-nine:** I have visited thirty-two states.

RULE 4. **Use a hyphen when you combine two or more words to put before a noun to describe it.**

I like his never-say-die attitude.
Do you like this navy-blue suit?
A well-known painting hung near the half-open window.

NOTE: The use of the hyphen in dividing a word at the end of a line is covered in guide 7, page 148.

Learn about words!

The following words, taken from Learning Activity *A,* have interesting histories. Use your dictionary to find the story behind each word.

perform   pupil   cousin   iceberg

LEARNING ACTIVITIES

A. Copy these sentences, supplying colons, underlining, and hyphens where needed. Go over your work in class.

1. We got up at 5 15 A.M. in that cold as an iceberg house.
2. My six year old sister has gray blue eyes and a happy go lucky disposition.
3. One good to the last page book that we read in the sixth grade is Runaway Home.
4. Forty two of these men and women performed in old time vaudeville.
5. We had two hours to get there, from 11 30 A.M. to 1 30 P.M.
6. At least twenty five people sent in some well written advice.
7. This hair raising story in the latest issue of Scholastic is true.
8. We saw Fiddler on the Roof last night.
9. The panic stricken pupils could not easily be quieted.
10. May I borrow your month before last National Geographic for forty five minutes this afternoon?
11. A large picture of my twenty seven cousins covered almost a whole page in last night's Daily News.
12. During our longer than usual spring vacation, twenty five members of the Dramatics Club went to see The Importance of Being Earnest by Oscar Wilde, the well known Irish playwright.

B. (1) Write sentences in which you tell something about five books that you have read or about magazines or newspapers that you read regularly. (2) Proofread your sentences for careless mistakes. (3) Read your sentences aloud, asking classmates to tell what words should be underlined and what words in the titles should be capitalized.

C. Make a chart showing how your school day is divided. Express the time in each case in figures. Have several charts put on the board for class discussion.

D. Copy in your notebook the rules for using quotation marks, colons, underlining, and hyphens. Clip examples from magazines and paste each of them under the appropriate rule. Remember that book titles are printed in italics, not underlined.

USING ENGLISH IN ALL CLASSES

Examine papers that you are preparing or have completed for other classes. Proofread each one to be sure that you have followed the rules for proper use of quotation marks, colons, underlining, and hyphens. Make any needed corrections.

"WHERE ARE THE APOSTROPHES?"

My cousins best friends dog does tricks.

THINK IT OVER . . .

How do you make a noun possessive? What do you need to know in order to place each apostrophe (') in the right place in the sentence above?

Where would you put the apostrophe if there were just one cousin? two cousins? if there were one friend? Two friends?

Using Apostrophes to Show Ownership

Often in your writing, you need to show that something belongs to one or more persons. The noun form in which an apostrophe is used to show ownership or possession is called a *possessive noun*. (If you are not sure what a noun is, see page 306.)

Here is the *boy's* cap.   Find *Ann's* book.

If you learn to apply two simple rules, you will never find it hard to write possessive nouns correctly.

RULES FOR USING APOSTROPHES TO SHOW OWNERSHIP

RULE 1. **Form the possessive of any singular noun in this way:**

a) **Write the noun. Do not change any letters. Do not drop any.**

b) **Add** *'s* **to the word.** Notice these examples:

SINGULAR NOUNS:	Lois	son-in-law
POSSESSIVES:	Lois's ring	my son-in-law's job

Remember that a possessive form shows *whose* something is. Do not make the mistake of using it as a plural.

RIGHT: I saw the *boy's* father. [The possessive tells *whose* father.]
WRONG: Both *boy's* helped me. ["Boy's" does not tell *whose* anything is.]

RULE 2. **To form the possessive of a plural noun, follow this plan:**

a) **Write the plural noun.** (For help with plurals, see the rules on pages 253–255.) **Do not change any letters; do not drop any.**

b) **If the plural ends in** *s,* **add only an apostrophe.**

PLURAL NOUNS:	boys	uncles
POSSESSIVES:	both boys' bicycles	my uncles' noses

c) **If the plural does not end in** *s,* **add** *'s,* **just as you would in forming singular possessives.**

PLURAL NOUNS:	children	women
POSSESSIVES:	children's voices	women's group

LEARNING ACTIVITIES

A. Give oral sentences using the possessive form of each of the following nouns. Spell the possessive. If you like, make this a team contest.

1. baby	4. Lincoln	7. Ms. Bruce	10. oxen	13. deer
2. queens	5. artists	8. Bess	11. crow	14. men
3. pupil	6. Charles	9. mice	12. hobo	15. girl

B. (1) Rewrite the following sentences, changing each italicized group of words to the possessive form of the noun. Be careful of your spelling and penmanship. (2) Exchange papers for checking. (3) Go over the sentences in class, spelling orally each possessive used.

EXAMPLE: The name *of the boy* is Don.   The *boy's* name is Don.

1. The pictures *of the boys* are interesting.
2. The totem poles *of the Nootkas* are colorful.
3. The sense of smell *of the dog* is remarkable.
4. The ears *of the horse* pricked up at the strange sound.

5. Have you met the mother-in-law *of Chris?*
6. The books *of Dickens* are still popular.
7. The uniforms *of the police officers* are new.
8. The plans *of the teacher* were definite.
9. Do you celebrate the birthday *of Washington?*
10. The playground *for the students* is being repaired.

Using Apostrophes to Form Contractions

When you are in a hurry, you usually are glad if you can find a short cut that will save you time.

Language has its short cuts, too. One short cut in speaking and writing that you use every day is the *contraction*.

● THESE ARE FACTS ABOUT CONTRACTIONS✻

1. **(DEFINITION) A** *contraction* **is a shortened form in which two or more words are combined by dropping some letters and inserting an apostrophe to take their place.**

you h̶a̶ve = you've	we a̶re = we're	o̶f̶ t̶h̶e̶ clock = o'clock
is n̶o̶t = isn't	I a̶m = I'm	let u̶s = let's

2. **Two contractions change form more than most others.**

will not = won't   shall not = shan't

3. **Some contractions have more than one meaning.** For example, *it's* is the contraction for *it is* as well as for *it has; I'll* is the contraction both for *I shall* and for *I will; I'd* is the contraction for *I had* or *I would.*

4. **Here are the contractions that you probably use most often. The ones that do double duty are underlined in color.**

1. aren't	10. he'd	19. let's	28. there's	37. weren't
2. can't	11. he'll	20. mightn't	29. they'd	38. we've
3. couldn't	12. he's	21. mustn't	30. they'll	39. who's
4. didn't	13. I'd	22. o'clock	31. they're	40. won't
5. doesn't	14. I'll	23. she'd	32. they've	41. wouldn't
6. don't	15. I'm	24. she'll	33. wasn't	42. you'd
7. hadn't	16. isn't	25. she's	34. we'd	43. you'll
8. hasn't	17. it's	26. shouldn't	35. we'll	44. you're
9. haven't	18. I've	27. that's	36. we're	45. you've

✻ Instruction and practice on possessive pronouns confused with contractions will be found on pages 364–365.

LEARNING ACTIVITIES

A. (1) Write the *words* for which the forty-five contractions in the preceding list stand. Write at least two sets of words for each of the contractions underlined in color. *Do not copy the contractions.* (2) Then, with your book closed, strike out the letter or letters that are omitted when you form a contraction of the words. Watch out for the spelling change in No. 40. (3) Write each contraction, putting in the apostrophe correctly. (4) Go over your work in class.

B. (1) Number your paper from 1 to 12. (2) Beside the numbers, write the contractions of the words in italics in each of the following sentences. (3) Exchange papers for checking.

1. I *cannot* read the name.
2. *Are* you *not* going with us?
3. We *have not* finished yet.
4. There *is not* time for a nap.
5. *We shall* do our best.
6. *It is* cold in this room.
7. We *were not* sure of the way.
8. I *do not* have my ticket.
9. He *does not* look like you.
10. *You are* needed at home.
11. *Who is* going with you?
12. Nan *will not* leave today.

C. (1) Copy the following sentences neatly, putting apostrophes where they belong. (2) After each sentence, write the words for which the contractions stand. Do not write in this book. (3) Exchange papers. (4) In class, put the contractions on the board as you go over the sentences.

EXAMPLE: I don't know why they're late. (do not, they are)

1. Theres someone at the door.
2. Its raining harder now.
3. Havent you forgotten something?
4. Youre too late to catch that train.
5. Dont you know whos been taking Jan's place?
6. Whos planning to help Midge?
7. Youve done very well.
8. If were going, we mustnt wait any longer.
9. Doesnt Mary think its been a pleasant place in which to work?
10. Im sure that shes been happy here.
11. I havent read that book, but Ive read other books by that author.
12. Frank says that he cant come now. He wont be late.

D. (1) Write two paragraphs that you might include in a letter to a friend. Use as your topic something that you have done during the past week. Use the Guides for Writing a Paragraph on page 162. In the paragraphs, use at least ten different contractions. (2) Below the paragraphs, list the contractions and, opposite each one, write the words for which it stands. (3) As paragraphs are read in class, jot down any contractions that you hear.

Bring to English class papers for other classes. Check each one for errors in spelling (1) possessive nouns or (2) contractions.

Using Apostrophes to Form Plurals

The sentence underscored in color on page 237 points out that possessive nouns should never be used for simple plurals.

RIGHT: My *mother's* name is Alice.
WRONG: Several *mothers* came.

There are some plurals, however — but never those of nouns — that do contain an apostrophe.

THE RULE FOR FORMING PLURALS WITH AN APOSTROPHE

RULE: **Use an apostrophe and** *s* **to form plurals of these expressions:**

a) **Figures:** There are two *5*'s in our telephone number.
b) **Signs:** How many *+*'s did you have on your paper?
c) **Letters of the alphabet:** I can't tell your *a*'s and *o*'s apart.
d) **Words referred to as words:** Avoid using those *and*'s and *uh*'s.

NOTE: In your own writing, to make clear that those four kinds of expressions are used as words, underline them before adding the *'s*. In printed matter, they are set in italics, as shown in the examples.

LEARNING ACTIVITIES

A. (1) Copy the following sentences, inserting apostrophes where needed. (2) Underline words and expressions that should be italicized. (3) Go over the sentences in class and explain each apostrophe.

1. Do you spell your name with two ps?
2. Your plan contains too many ifs.
3. Were those 6s, or 9s?
4. Jackie's ls look too much like es.
5. Anyway, I have more +s than −s.

B. (1) Write sentences containing the plurals of "and," "7," "m," "+." Remember to underline. (2) Read sentences in class, and write the plurals on the board. Comment on good sentences.

A. Copy these sentences, capitalizing them correctly.

1. tomorrow mother and judge r. o. nicolls have an appointment with principal brown to talk over plans for a new course in history here at logan junior high school.
2. John asked, "did you hear any foreign language in the south?"
3. Mia and Harry take english, geography, arithmetic, and social studies. In addition, Harry takes music, because his father wants him to.
4. when i was in the northwest, i always arose early; but j. b., my friend, slept late every morning.
5. Kirsten added, "be sure to bring your uncle oscar to our christmas party. he can speak swedish with my uncle."
6. my brother studied latin and danish in college, and my sister studied languages, mathematics, and science.
7. my brother's danish teacher was a woman, ms. mary a. hamsum.
8. Clark Gable, who played the part of r. butler in the famous film *gone with the wind,* became a captain in the united states army during World War II.
9. Adele's theme, which she called "rampaging river," told a true story of a flood in the middle west.
10. ever since Frank spent a summer in the southwest, his themes have had such titles as "life in the desert." he even wrote a poem with the title "the song of the coyote."
11. Finally mrs. jones asked, "have you ever read *lassie come home?* i saw the film years ago, and i've seldom seen a better one."
12. dr. a. j. pollard has her office downtown.

B. Copy these sentences, supplying needed punctuation. The number after each sentence or group of sentences tells how many punctuation marks you should insert. A pair of quotation marks counts as one mark. Underlining a title counts as one mark.

1. Tina here is a strange story about an island that almost disappeared said Captain J R Betts Have you read it As he spoke he pointed to the title of the story An Island That Blew Itself Up (12)
2. He and Mrs Betts, of Batavia Java were visiting Mr and Mrs Sanders Tinas parents (8)
3. No I havent Captain Betts Tina replied Ive heard of magicians making rabbits coins and even people disappear In fact, this weeks People has an article on that subject (14)

✱Check Test 1 should be taken at this point. If the results show need for further study, students should do this review practice. They should then take Mastery Test 1.

4. Captain Betts laughed and said Well Tina the magician behind this act wasnt a person Heres the story Krakatoa a little island lies near the western end of Java On August 26 1883 the island blew itself up A series of terrific explosions began at 1030 A M and lasted thirty six hours Dust cinders and bits of rock shot miles into the air High waves walls of water swept along all the neighboring coasts The great waves destroyed 300 villages killed 35,000 people and caused untold damage When the explosions finally ended half the island was gone (30)

5. That sounds like a good book Tina declared I see its called The Earths Changing Surface Do you have any more like it sir (10)

6. Captain Betts answered Yes I have a complete set of books similar to this one (4) *

Word Games to Test Your Thinking

Here is the first of several sets of spare-time activities that you will find in this book. Each such section contains puzzles and exercises for your enjoyment. You may even be assigned these activities if you are excused from some of the regular work in English. You must be a good sport in using these pages. Being a good sport means that you will not write anything in the book. Using a ruler, draw such items as crossword puzzles and checkerboards on your own paper before you try to figure them out.

Scrambled Capital Cities

If you were traveling in the United States and came upon these scrambled city signs, could you figure out in which state capital you were?

---

* Adapted from *The Earth's Changing Surface* by Bertha Morris Parker; copyright © 1958, 1952, 1947, 1942 by Harper & Row, Publishers, Inc.

EXAMPLE: GROOM MY NET would be Montgomery.

1. LEG HAIR
2. SAFE TAN
3. O MY PAIL
4. TAPE OK
5. NET TORN
6. HEN ALE
7. SALT UP
8. DOC CORN
9. SOB NOT
10. ANY LAB
11. LET RIM OPEN
12. SCARE TO MAN
13. JIFFY NO SECRET
14. DIG FERN SLIP
15. TICKET ROLL

Hidden Bowling Terms

Each of the following sentences has hidden in it a bowling term. Can you find them? EXAMPLE: He again looked at *the ad pin*ing to go on such a cruise. (*head pin*)

1. His parents are great bowling fans.
2. A wasp lit on my hand.
3. The Turk eyed me carefully.
4. The baby fell asleep ere I knew it.
5. If illegal methods are used, I shall withdraw.
6. She seemed to be making Ping-Pong her hobby.

A Word Square

The words defined below are four-letter words. Placed one under another, they will spell the same down as across.

1. Something on which to sit
2. Makes mistakes
3. Amount of surface
4. Another spelling of *czar*

Would You Like to Know —?

You may be surprised at the answers that the encyclopedia gives to some of the following questions.

1. What kind of light do *fireflies* produce?
2. What is a *flycatcher*?
3. How do the swimming habits of the *flatfish* differ from those of other fish?
4. Can a *flea* fly?

Valentine Crossword Puzzle

Copy the crossword puzzle on page 244. Do not write in this book. (A HELPFUL HINT: 1, 4, and 29 across make a message that is found on many valentines.)

|1| |■|2|3|■|■| |4|5|
6	7	8	■	■	9	10	11		
12			■	13		14			15
16			■	17	18	■	19		
20		■	21	■	22	■	23		
24		25		■	26		27		
28	■	29			30				31
32	33	■	34		■	35		■	36
37		38	■	39	40		41	■	42
43			44	■	45		■	46	
47			■	48	■	49			
■	50		■	51	52		53	■	54
55			■	56			■	57	

Across

1. To exist.
2. Will ____ be my valentine?
4. Possessive pronoun.
6. Cry of a cow.
9. Past form of *be*.
12. Very little.
14. A wading bird.
16. To perform.
17. Garden tool.
19. To fasten.
20. Roman numeral for *nine*.
21. A closed automobile.
23. Right (*abbr.*).
24. An organ of the body.
26. ____ are red;
Violets are blue.
29. Sweetheart.
32. Associated Press (*abbr.*).
34. Trade-last (*abbr.*).
35. Southwest (*abbr.*).
36. Longfellow's first two initials.
37. A girl's name.
39. Bristles.
42. Pass (*in playing bridge*).
43. Cornhusker state (*abbr.*).
45. Plural of *man*.
46. City in Italy (*place where St. Valentine was put to death*).
47. A piece of furniture.
49. ____ Valentine.
50. Therefore.
51. Georgia (*abbr.*).
53. Preposition.
54. South America (*abbr.*).
55. Nickname for *Elizabeth*.
56. February ____ is Valentine's Day (*Roman numerals*).
57. Ding Dong ____.

Down

1. Preposition meaning near.
3. Conjunction.
5. Biblical form of *you*.
6. 1214 (*Roman numerals*).
7. A cereal grass.
8. A preposition.
9. First person pronoun.
10. Skill.
11. An evening party.
12. Move along on water.
13. Opposite of *here*.
14. A valentine is ____ -shaped.
15. Fish may be caught in these.
18. Officer of the Day (*abbr.*).
21. She ____ sea shells.
22. Sound.
25. A large vessel for liquids.
27. Jumbled New South Wales (*abbr.*).
28. Used by artist.
30. Short messages.
31. Sugar is ____,
and so are you.
33. Polite people say, "____."
36. A book of hymns.
38. Father superior of an abbey.
40. Printer's measure.
41. Indefinite article.
42. Capital of Idaho.
44. First two initials of the author of *Treasure Island*.
46. Egyptian sun-god.
48. For example (*abbr.*).
49. Same as 50 across.
52. Instrument for chopping.
53. Television (*abbr.*).

LEARNING TO SPELL WELL

SPELLING PRETESTS . . .

Before you study this chapter on spelling, it is a good idea to test your present ability to spell certain important words.

(1) Write "Test One" at the top of a sheet of paper; then number it from 1 to 50. (2) On another sheet of paper, write "Test Two"; then number it from 1 to 100. Your teacher will then dictate the words for the two tests. All the words in the first test are spelled according to certain spelling rules; the words in the second test are not.

After they have been returned, study your test papers carefully. How well did you do? Each of the words is a common word that every person is likely to use in even the simplest kind of writing, such as a travel postcard or a thank-you note.

Since the test words are ones that you cannot very well get along without, your own common sense will tell you that you will be wise to master their spelling. Remember, when you get a job, knowing how to spell is often a necessary skill.

FOLLOW-UP

Begin now to keep in your notebook a special section on spelling. (1) Put into it, first of all, any words that you missed on the tests. Arrange them alphabetically, leaving room to insert other words. (2) When a paper is returned, note any spelling errors. Check to see whether the words are already on your list. If so, star them, and then work on them, using the following guides. (3) Add any new words. (4) Before handing in any paper, check carefully to see whether you have used any of your starred words. If you have, make sure that they are spelled correctly.

GUIDES FOR LEARNING TO SPELL TROUBLESOME WORDS

1. Look at the word carefully as you say each syllable distinctly. Note any double letters, silent letters, confusing endings, or other hard spots.
2. Use the word in a sentence. Let the dictionary help you.
3. Repeat each syllable slowly; then close your eyes and recall how the word looks.
4. Compare your picture of the word with the printed word.
5. Write the word without looking at the printed word.
6. Check to see that you are correct.
7. Repeat steps 1–6 three times.

1. Watch Out for Silent Letters!

READ AND DISCUSS . . .

Here is a note found on a lamppost the other day.

> Dear Archie,
>   I waited an our, but I coud not stay any longer. Don't you no that on Wensday we begin corus at to o'clock? You'd better husl!
>
>   George

How many words has George misspelled? What is wrong with them? (Every one has the same kind of error.)

What letters must you insert to correct the misspelled words?

There probably is no foolproof way to make sure that you never leave out any of the silent letters in a word. Here, however, are some pointers that will help you to remember and some activities to give you practice.*

● THESE ARE FACTS ABOUT SILENT LETTERS

1. Silent k, g, **and** w

a) Only a few common words have a silent k, and they have an n after the k, as in *knock.*†

b) Not many common words have a silent g; they have an n after the g, as *gnaw, sign,* or *reign.* (Words with silent *gh* are taught on page 250.)

c) Silent w usually comes only before r, as in *write.*‡ In a few exceptions, the w comes before an h, as in *who, whose, whole.* Still another exception is the word *answer.*

LEARNING ACTIVITIES

A. (1) Write the following words on your paper in two columns, leaving two inches of space between the columns. (2) Beside each word write a word that rhymes with it and begins with *kn, gn, wh* (with the w silent), or *wr.*** (3) Exchange papers for checking before the words are pronounced, spelled aloud, and written on the board.

1. few	7. map	13. dot	19. track	25. clawed
2. list	8. feel	14. pole	20. bench	26. sitting
3. sing	9. life	15. teeth	21. thawing	27. college
4. flat	10. long	16. stone	22. lockout	28. smashing
5. rob	11. deck	17. bright	23. mitten	29. going
6. me	12. clock	18. room	24. chuckle	30. twinkle

---

* Silent e, which gives spelling trouble, as a rule, only in connection with adding suffixes or endings, is covered in the rules on page 258.

† Most *kn*- words are short, simple words from Anglo-Saxon.

‡ Most words with a silent w come from Anglo-Saxon.

** For example, if the word *tree* were on the list, you would write *knee* beside it.

B. The following paragraphs contain twenty incomplete words. To help you, the first letters of the word are given with the number of letters that must be added. (1) Copy the paragraphs, completing and underlining the words that you think are needed. (2) Exchange papers. (3) Check the papers as various students read aloud the sentences in the paragraphs, spelling the words used to fill the blanks. (4) After the papers have been returned, write a sentence using correctly and *underlining* each word that you missed. (5) When your sentences have been checked, file your paper for easy reference.

The day after I had wr (5) a letter re (7) from my job with an auto-wr (6) company, I got up and ate a quick breakfast. Then I strapped an old kn (6) on my back and set out for the country, where I planned to spend the wh (3) day.

I had to walk slowly, having hurt one kn (5) recently. When I felt the gn (5) of hunger, I looked at the watch on my wr (3) . Since it showed noon, I unwr (5) my lunch and ate it under a gn (5) old oak outside a high board fence.

Afterward I looked through a large kn (6) in the fence and saw a neat little farmhouse. Since there was no s (3) saying to keep out, I climbed over the fence and walked up to the house. As I drew near, a large dog, chained to a post, growled and gn (5) its teeth at me. Since there was no kn (5) on the door, I rapped hard on it with my kn (6) . There was no an (4) . I kn (3) down on my good kn (2) to look through the keyhole. This was the wr (3) move, for just then the dog wr (6) out of its collar. It headed straight for me. Forgetting my bad leg, I dashed for the fence and scrambled over it—but I left part of one trouser leg behind me!

● **THESE ARE FACTS ABOUT SILENT LETTERS** — Continued

2. Silent *t* and *d*

   a) Most words containing a silent *t* fall into one of these two classes:

     (1) Those that have an *s* before the *t*, as in *castle*.

     (2) Those that rhyme with *match, sketch, pitch, Scotch,* or *Dutch*. (Words that rhyme with the above but contain no silent *t* are *rich, which, much, such, touch, sandwich, attach, detach,* and words made from them.)

   b) Silent *d* is usually followed by *g*.* Most of the words containing it rhyme with *badge, edge, bridge, dodge,* or *fudge,* or are made from such words.

---

*Exceptions include certain words that begin with *ad*, such as *adjust* and *adjective*.

LEARNING ACTIVITIES

A. (1) See how long a list you can make of words that rhyme with *match, sketch, pitch, Scotch, Dutch, nestle, whistle,* and *rustle,* and contain a silent *t.* (You should find more than twenty.) (2) In class, make a combined list on the board. Arrange the words in columns under the key words *match, sketch,* and so on. (3) Copy the list and file it in your notebook for easy reference.

B. (1) Write a paragraph in which you use the eight important exceptions that have no silent *t* before *ch.* The guides on page 162 will help you to write a good paragraph. (2) Proofread your paper to catch careless errors in spelling and in capitalization and punctuation. (3) Read the paragraphs in your small groups; then choose one of them to be read to the entire class.

C. Repeat *A,* only this time use rhymes for *edge* and *fudge.* (You should find at least ten.)

● **THESE ARE FACTS ABOUT SILENT LETTERS** — Continued

   3. Silent *p, b, l,* **and** *u*

      a) Silent *p* occurs only before *n, s,* or *t,* as in *pneumatic, pneumonia, psalm, psychology,* and *ptomaine.* All such words come from the Greek, and most of them are words that you are not likely to use often.

      b) A silent *b* usually has an *m* before it, as in *dumb.* There are only a few such words that you are likely to need. Exceptions are *debt, doubt,* and words made from them.

      c) There are a number of words containing a silent *l.* The ones that you are most likely to use are the following, or words made from them.

balk	balm	could	half
caulk	calm	should	halves
chalk	palm	would	calf
stalk	psalm		calves
talk	qualm		
walk	almond		
folk			
yolk			

      d) A silent *u* in most cases follows only the letter *g,* as in *guide.* (The purpose of the *u* is, as a rule, to indicate that the word should not be pronounced with a soft *g* [j] sound.)

LEARNING ACTIVITIES

A. (1) In your dictionary, check the words that begin with *pn, ps,* or *pt.* (2) Make a list of ones with which you are familiar. (3) With a partner, practice both oral and written spelling of the words. (4) Put into the spelling section of your notebook those that you need to practice further.

B. (1) On your paper, rule four columns. (2) Over the first column, write *dumb;* over the second, *talk;* over the third, *calm;* over the fourth, *could.* (3) Under the correct headings, write words that have the same two ending letters and that the following explanations describe. Also, write the number of the description next to the appropriate word. (4) Exchange papers for checking as the explanations are read and the words spelled orally. (5) For each word that you miss, write a good sentence using and underlining the word. (6) File these sentences in the spelling section of your notebook.

1. Tree that bears dates
2. Atom __?__
3. "Ought to"
4. What a mule may do
5. Tiny bit of bread
6. Part of a mitten
7. Found inside an egg
8. Large branch of a tree
9. *Shall, should; will, __?__*
10. Lotion (rhymes with No. 1)
11. A base on balls
12. A Bible song (silent *p* and *l*)
13. The stem of a plant
14. What you do on a ladder
15. Used on the hair
16. Used to sketch and write

C. (1) In an oral or a written drill, spell the words that begin with *gu* and rhyme with the following: *scarred, yes, dressed* [two words], *tried, filled, die, wilt.* (2) Write the words, correctly spelled, in the spelling section of your notebook. (3) With the aid of the dictionary, add to the list any other *gu* words that you think will be useful to you.

● **THESE ARE FACTS ABOUT SILENT LETTERS** — Continued

4. Silent *h* and *gh*

a) Silent *h* usually follows *c,* as in *ache, chorus, scheme; r,* as in *rhyme, rheumatism;* or *g,* as in *ghost.* (Almost all such words come from the Greek.)

b) Most words having silent *gh* rhyme with *fight* or *ought.* Other common words containing silent *gh* are these groups:

sleigh	dough	weight	high
weigh	though	freight	sigh
neigh	thorough	straight	thigh

Neighbor and *through* are two other words to remember.

LEARNING ACTIVITIES

A. (1) With the aid of the dictionary, make three lists of words that you think are or will be useful to you. In one list, put words beginning with *ch* (with the *h* silent); in another, those beginning with *rh;* and in the third, those beginning with *gh.* (2) Compare lists in class; then in pairs practice the words on your own lists. (3) File your list in your notebook.

B. (1) Divide the class into two groups. (2) Let one person from each group go to the board and write the words *fight* and *ought.* (3) In turn, each will pronounce a word that rhymes with either of those two words and contains *gh.* He or she will then write it under the proper word. (4) Proceed in the same manner with the other members of the teams. A word correctly spelled by one team cannot be used by the other team. (5) Copy and file any words that are hard for you to remember.

ENRICHMENT

A. With the help of the unabridged dictionary, make a list of words beginning with *kn* or *wr.* Include only words now in your vocabulary or ones that you would like to add to it. After your teacher checks the list, make a "word tree" or some other kind of design in which you group all the related words. (A "group" would be *knit, knitting, knitted, knitter,* for example.) Perhaps your work can be exhibited on the bulletin board.

B. Write a nonsense poem using the twelve words in the rhyming groups in (*b*) of "These Are the Facts," page 250. If your teacher approves your work, you may be asked to read the poem to the class.

REVIEW ACTIVITY

(1) With the help of the points on pages 247, 248, 249, and 250 and of the lists that you have filed in your notebook, make a list of what you think are the hardest silent-letter words. (2) Divide the class into two teams. (3) Choose one person from each team to keep score at the board. (4) Let the first person on one team pronounce a word from his or her list. (5) The first person on the other team must then spell it orally. If the spelling is correct, his or her team scores a point. If not, the one who gave the word spells it correctly. (The giver of the word does not score a point, of course, since the giver can look at the word on his or her paper.) The other side then has a turn at pronouncing a word, and so on. Each word spelled correctly by a team member should be written on the board by the scorer for that team. At the end of the game, the team with the longer list is the winner.

2. Learn to Apply Spelling Rules

RECIEVE

RECIEVE

RECEIVE

THINK IT OVER . . .

Being able to apply certain rules will not make you a perfect speller, because the English language has many words not spelled by rules. Rules can, however, keep you from making the kinds of errors shown in the cartoon. Then you will be free to concentrate on mastering tricky words not spelled by the rules.

Learn about words!

The following words, taken from Learning Activity *A*, page 254, have interesting histories. Use your dictionary to find the story behind each word.

        quart   branch   waltz   circus

SPELLING PLURAL FORMS

Occasionally the irregularity of some plural forms of nouns may disturb you. Luckily, however, only a few nouns have "odd" plurals. The others form their plurals by rules. Before you study those rules, make sure that you know certain things.

● THESE ARE FACTS ABOUT NUMBER

1. (DEFINITION) *Number* **is the difference in the form of a noun or a pronoun that shows whether the word means** *one* **or** *more than one.*

2. (DEFINITION) *Singular* **number indicates** *one.*

3. (DEFINITION) *Plural* **number indicates** *more than one.*

SINGULAR: a boy	an ax	a calf	a goose
PLURAL: six boys	two axes	ten calves	five geese

4. **Most plurals not formed by adding** *s* **or** *es* **to the singular are given in the dictionary after the singular form:** *calf,* **pl.** *calves; lady,* **pl.** *ladies.* **If in doubt, see the dictionary.**

Read the following rules and study the examples. Then do the practice that follows, using these rules.

THE RULES FOR SPELLING PLURALS: I

RULE 1. Add *s* **to the singular to form the plural of most nouns.**

SINGULAR: dog   parent   grandmother
PLURAL: dogs   parents   grandmothers

RULE 2. Add *es* **to most nouns ending in** *sh, ch, s, x,* **or** *z.* When you pronounce the plurals of words with those endings, you cannot help adding a syllable. That added syllable tells you that you need *es,* not just *s.* For example, try saying the plural of *wish.* It comes out as *wish es;* that is, in two syllables.

dish, dishes   dress, dresses   buzz, buzzes
church, churches   box, boxes

RULE 3. Add *s* **to form the plural of nouns ending in** *ay, ey,* **or** *oy.*

valley, valleys   delay, delays   boy, boys

RULE 4. For other nouns ending in *y,* **change the** *y* **to** *i* **and add** *es.*

baby bab~~y~~es babies   berry berr~~y~~es berries

LEARNING ACTIVITIES

A. (1) Number your paper from 1 to 20. (2) Copy each of the following nouns and beside it write its plural. (3) Exchange papers and go over the words in class. As they are spelled aloud, have the words written plainly on the board. (4) File in your notebook any words that you missed. (See the Follow-up activity on page 246.)

1. onion	6. branch	11. glass	16. ditch
2. mouth	7. gallon	12. envelope	17. towel
3. brush	8. quart	13. radiator	18. waltz
4. perch	9. table	14. criminal	19. banana
5. ax	10. wish	15. circus	20. pearl

B. (1) Write a short paragraph in which you use and underline the plural of each of the following nouns. (2) Compare paragraphs by reading them aloud in your small groups. (3) Ask a classmate to spell each plural that you have used. (4) Choose the best paragraph to read to the entire class. (Make sure that you follow guides 1, 3, and 4 of the Guides to Good Listening, page 28.)

1. sky	3. key	5. library	7. tray	9. alley
2. penny	4. party	6. monkey	8. fly	10. puppy

THE RULES FOR SPELLING PLURALS: II

RULE 5. Add *s* to form the plural of most nouns ending in *f*, *ff*, or *fe*.

chief, chiefs   cuff, cuffs   safe, safes

RULE 6. For some words ending in *f* or *fe*, change the ending; drop the *f* or *fe* and add *ves*.

calf, calves   loaf, loaves   wife, wives

If in doubt, say the plural of the word. If you hear the sound of *v*, follow Rule 6. If you hear the sound of *f*, follow Rule 5.

For example, say the plurals of the following words: *gulf, leaf, puff, knife.* Which plurals end in *ves*?

RULE 7. Add *s* to form the plural of most nouns ending in *o*.

solo, solos   radio, radios   studio, studios

Some nouns ending in an *o* that is preceded by a consonant add *es*. Here are some important examples.

echo, echoes   tomato, tomatoes   torpedo, torpedoes

hero, heroes   potato, potatoes   mosquito, mosquitoes

veto, vetoes

LEARNING ACTIVITIES

A. (1) Number your paper from 1 to 15. Copy each of the following nouns and beside it write its plural. (2) Exchange papers. (3) Your teacher will then pronounce the plurals, and you will spell them orally in unison while he or she writes them on the board. Check the paper that you have received. (4) Use the Follow-up activity on page 246 if you miss any words.

1. handkerchief	4. wolf	7. proof	10. belief	13. roof
2. handcuff	5. gulf	8. life	11. leaf	14. safe
3. sheriff	6. knife	9. bluff	12. cliff	15. thief

B. In carrying out this activity, follow the same plan as in *A*.

1. alto	5. silo	9. rodeo	13. mosquito	17. echo
2. potato	6. hero	10. cello	14. torpedo	18. ego
3. trio	7. tomato	11. bolero	15. kangaroo	19. veto
4. piano	8. tattoo	12. photo	16. soprano	20. auto

THE RULES FOR SPELLING PLURALS: III

RULE 8. Spell the plurals of certain words irregularly.

SINGULAR:	man	woman	goose	tooth
PLURAL:	m**e**n	wom**e**n	g**ee**se	t**ee**th

SINGULAR:	mouse	foot	child	ox
PLURAL:	m**ice**	f**eet**	child**ren**	ox**en**

RULE 9. Add *s* **to all proper nouns except those that end in** *s, sh, ch, x,* **or** *z.* **To those exceptions, add** *es.* **Never use an apostrophe.**

Brown, the Brown**s**   Perkin**s**, the Perkin**ses**
Mary, both Mary**s**   Wal**sh**, the Wal**shes**
Molloy, the Molloy**s**   Bur**ch**, the Bur**ches**

RULE 10. For some words, mostly names of certain animals, write the plural just as you do the singular.

one *deer,* many *deer*   one *trout,* many *trout*
one *sheep,* many *sheep*   one *elk,* many *elk*

NOTE: Some words have only a plural form: *tweezers, trousers, scissors, pliers, shears, clothes, slacks, hose.* (Why, do you think?)

RULE 11. For compound nouns (made up of two or more words), **add** *s* **to the important name part.**

son-in-law, son**s**-in-law   car dealer, car dealer**s**
drum major, drum major**s**   major general, major general**s**

NOTE: Compounds made with *ful* add *s* at the end: *cupful***s**.

LEARNING ACTIVITIES

Directions: Activity *A* concerns plurals covered in rules 8–11. Activity *B* covers all the rules for plurals. File any words that you miss, as explained in the Follow-up activity on page 246.

A. (1) Number your paper from 1 to 20. (2) Write the plurals of the words given below. (3) Exchange papers for checking. (4) Take turns at putting the plurals on the board and giving the rule.

1. Sally	6. fish	11. foot	16. father-in-law
2. Harris	7. woman	12. suds	17. moose
3. ox	8. salmon	13. trout	18. teaspoonful
4. mouse	9. Riley	14. handful	19. commander in chief
5. Bess	10. sheep	15. Charles	20. shears

B. (1) Make a list of ten plural nouns, each one of them illustrating a different rule. (2) On another paper, write these plurals, but mix up the letters in each; for example, for *ponies,* you might write *noisep.* (3) Exchange papers. (4) Figure out what each word is and write it beside the mixed-up form. (5) Write the singular form of each word. (6) Go over the papers with your partner.

USING ENGLISH IN ALL CLASSES

Bring into English class any papers that you are preparing for your other classes. Exchange papers with a partner and examine the papers that you receive for mistakes in spelling plural forms. If you are not absolutely sure of a word, check it in the dictionary. Return papers and list in your notebook any words that you misspelled. (See the Follow-up activity on page 246.)

ADDING SUFFIXES AND ENDINGS

To make plural forms, an *s* or *es* was added to some nouns. These letters, which change the form of a word, are called *endings.* Other endings are the *er* and *est* in certain forms of adjectives and adverbs and the *ed, s,* and *ing* in certain verb forms.

A group of letters, such as *-able,* is often added at the end of a word in order to create a new or different word. The verb *read,* for example, can become the adjective *readable.* These letter groups, which change the meaning or function of a word, are called *suffixes*.

THE RULES

RULE 1. Make no other change when you add *s, ed,* **or** *ing* **to a verb that ends in** *ay, ey* **or** *oy**

stay, stays, stayed, staying   obey, obeys, obeyed, obeying

Important exceptions are the past of *say* (*said*), *lay* (*laid*), and *pay* (*paid*), and words based upon them, such as *mislaid, repaid,* and so on.

RULE 2. When you add an ending or a suffix to a word that ends in *y* **preceded by a consonant** (any letter except *a, e, i, o,* or *u*), **change the** *y* **to** *i*†

a) Verb Endings

try, tries, tried   apply, applies, applied

b) Adjective Endings

happy, happier, happiest   icy, icier, iciest

c) Suffixes

pity, pitiful, pitiless   rely, reliant, reliable
happy, happiness, happily

LEARNING ACTIVITIES

A. (1) Number your paper from 1 to 20. (2) Copy the following items. (3) Beside each of them, write the word suggested, which must end in *y*. The first letters are given for you. (4) Beside the word write other words made by adding endings or suffixes. You should have at least three other words. (5) Go over your work in class, putting the words on the board.

EXAMPLE: dangerous: ri— *risky, riskier, riskiest, riskily*

1. not hard: ea   4. rich: we
2. misty: fo   5. awkward: cl
3. beautiful: lo   6. not steady: sh

---

* The idea here is like that of rule 3 for forming plurals, page 253.
† The rule does not apply when adding an ending or a suffix beginning with *i,* such as *ing* or *-ial:* rea*dy*, rea*dying;* reme*dy,* reme*dial.*

7. not on time: ta
8. powerful: mi
9. not ambitious: la
10. not fat: sk
11. not generous: st
12. vacant: em
13. oily: gr

14. fast: sp
15. loud: no
16. fortunate: lu
17. amusing: fu
18. tired: we
19. foolish: si
20. piggish: gr

B. Here are forty words that are likely to be misspelled if the writer does not know the rules for words ending in *y*. Practice spelling these words orally with a partner; then dictate them to each other.

1. business	11. muddier	21. employer	31. colonial
2. steadily	12. dustiness	22. paid	32. geographical
3. dried	13. notified	23. cries	33. spied
4. empties	14. married	24. buried	34. identifies
5. luckily	15. journeyed	25. satisfied	35. pries
6. thirstier	16. oilier	26. destroyed	36. dignified
7. mysterious	17. huskily	27. beautiful	37. carrier
8. victorious	18. hurried	28. glorious	38. trial
9. enjoyed	19. cloudiness	29. funniest	39. plentiful
10. sleepier	20. worrier	30. obeyed	40. tiniest

Adding Suffixes and Endings to Words with Final Silent *e*

THE RULES

RULE 1. In most cases, drop a final silent *e* before an ending or a suffix beginning with *a, e, i, o, u,* or *y*.

writ*e*, wri**ting**   ros*e*, ro**sy**   lov*e*, lo**vable**

Two important exceptions are (1) *dyeing* (coloring), in which the *e* is kept so that the word will not be confused with *dying* (ceasing to live), and (2) *mileage*.

RULE 2. Keep the final *e* if the word ends in *ce* or *ge* and the suffix begins with *a* or *o*.*

noti*ce*, noti**ceable**   coura*ge*, coura**geous**

Keep a silent *e* in most cases if the suffix begins with a consonant; that is, with any letter except *a, e, i, o, u,* or *y*.

tam*e*, tam**ely**   hop*e*, hop**eful**   troubl*e*, troubl**esome**
pal*e*, pal**eness**   lov*e*, lov**ely**   snak*e*, snak**elike**

Exceptions include *true, truly; argue, argument*.

*The *e* is kept to show that the *c* has the sound of *s*, and that the *g* has the sound of *j*.

LEARNING ACTIVITIES

A. (1) Copy the following words in a column. (2) Beside each of them, make new words ending with as many of these suffixes as you can: *-y, -ly, -ness, -able, -ation,* or *-ition.* For some words, only one suffix will fit. (3) Have a combined list made on the board. (4) Check your own paper.

1. stone	5. excuse	9. compose	13. true
2. explore	6. curve	10. lame	14. lace
3. move	7. pure	11. change	15. ripe
4. peace	8. tune	12. large	16. wire

B. (1) Have an oral drill in which you add *ing* to each of the following verbs. (2) Write the words as your teacher dictates them, and beside each, put the word formed by adding *ing.* (3) Exchange papers for checking.

1. divide	5. blame	9. prove	13. line	17. place
2. scrape	6. come	10. trace	14. care	18. give
3. take	7. vote	11. like	15. store	19. behave
4. note	8. save	12. smile	16. close	20. price

Adding Suffixes and Endings to Words with Final Consonants

THE RULES

RULE 1. In adding a suffix or an ending beginning with a vowel (*a, e, i, o, u,* or *y*), **double a final consonant** (except *h* or *x*) **if the word has only one syllable and the consonant has a single vowel before it:** bat, batter. The rule is most useful in spelling the following:

> *a) Verb forms:* stop, stopped, stopping
> *b) Comparisons of adjectives:* thin, thinner, thinnest
> *c) Nouns made from verbs:* swim, swimmer; run, runner
> *d) Adjectives made from verbs or nouns:* fun, funny; fog, foggy

RULE 2. Follow Rule 1 for words of more than one syllable if the word is accented on the last syllable.

> refer (re fer'), referred, referring, referral
> permit (per mit'), permitted, permitting

Note that the words fit the pattern given in rule 1: (1) the endings and suffixes begin with a vowel (*ed, ing, -al*), and (2) there is only one vowel (*e, i*) before the final consonant of the base word.

RULE 3. For most other words, do not double a final consonant when adding an ending or a suffix beginning with a vowel.

> look, looked, looking (The *k* has *two* vowels before it.)
> o'pen, o'pened, o'pening (The accent is on the *first* syllable.)

LEARNING ACTIVITIES

A. (1) Copy the following sentences, putting in the needed form of each word in parentheses. (2) Exchange papers for checking. (3) Tell why each final consonant has or has not been doubled.

1. Are you (plan) to do your (shop) before (meet) Helen?
2. As I (step) inside, the lights (flicker) and grew still (dim).
3. You are (forget) that we haven't (unwrap) the (big) gift of all.
4. The (win) of the contest probably will be Tina. She's no (quit).
5. I'm (begin) to think that I (omit) one line of that poem.
6. He is always (brag) that he is a better (hit) than I am.
7. (Enter) that (swim) race was not my idea. I'm not very (speed).
8. Bill was (sit) on the porch when I (slip) up behind him.
9. I was really (stun) when I saw how much (fat) he is now.
10. After the rain had (stop), the day grew (sun).

B. (1) Add the indicated suffix or ending to each of the following words, doubling the end consonant if necessary. (2) Use the new words in written sentences. (3) Be sure to proofread for careless errors in spelling, punctuation, and capitalization. (4) Exchange papers for checking.

1. war (ior)	3. equip (ment)	5. snob (ish)	7. drug (ist)
2. bit (en)	4. forbid (en)	6. fool (ing)	8. open (ed)

APPLYING THE PREFIXES <u>DIS-</u> AND <u>MIS-</u> AND THE SUFFIX -<u>FUL</u>

In making words with the prefixes *mis-* and *dis-* and with the suffix *-ful,* apply the following rules.

THE RULES

RULE 1. Never double the *s* of the prefixes *dis-* or *mis-*.

dis + appear = disappear   mis + lead = mislead

RULE 2. Keep both *s*'s if the base word begins with *s*.

dis + satisfied = dissatisfied   mis + step = misstep

RULE 3. Never add an extra *l* to the suffix *-ful*.

a cup, a cupful   care, careful

A. (1) As your teacher gives you a word and a prefix, write on your paper the new word made by adding *dis-* or *mis-*. (2) Exchange papers for checking before the new words are spelled aloud and written on the board.

1. obey (dis)	6. miss (dis)	11. state (mis)
2. spell (mis)	7. use (mis)	12. place (mis)
3. approve (dis)	8. spent (mis)	13. lay (mis)
4. take (mis)	9. agree (dis)	14. own (dis)
5. appoint (dis)	10. solve (dis)	15. sent (mis)

B. (1) Add the suffix *-ful* to the following words; then use them in sentences. Apply Rule 2, page 257, if necessary. Use a variety of sentence beginnings. (2) Be sure to proofread. (3) Exchange papers for criticism. (4) Put a star before especially good sentences.

1. hand	4. car	7. pity	10. spoon	13. mouth
2. room	5. cheer	8. peace	11. plenty	14. pocket
3. care	6. wonder	9. sorrow	12. use	15. doubt

SPELLING WORDS WITH IE OR EI

The old rhyme for remembering when to write *ie* and when to write *ei* probably is the best rule for helping you to avoid errors.

THE RULE

Use *i* before *e* except after *c*
Or when sounded as *ā*
As in *neighbor* and *weigh*.

Here are some examples:

field (Use *ie* because the letters follow *f*, not *c*.)
receive (Use *ei* because the letters follow *c*.)
eight (The letters sound like *ā*.)

Some common exceptions that you need to know are these:

their (Remember that *he* and *I* are in it.)
foreign (Remember that it has *ore* in it.)
either and neither (Remember that they have *it* in them.)
height (Remember that *he* and *I* are in it.)

A. Here are sentences containing one or more scrambled words. Some of them when written correctly contain *ei;* the others, *ie.* (1) Make two columns on your paper, one headed *ei* and the other, *ie.* (2) Figure out the words and write each of them under the right heading. (3) Check your own paper as the words are spelled orally and written on the board.

1. Did you (ceevire) a letter from your new (redfin)?
2. The storm brought some (efiler) from the heat, I (vilebee).
3. I paid cash for both books, but in (tenhire) case did I get a (petrice).
4. Write a (firbe) theme about a (firenog) land that interests you.
5. I've gained an inch in (hitheg), but I think I've lost (hegwit).
6. The son of our next-door (grobhine) often gets into (semifich).
7. The (hifet) who stole those (higet) cars is now in prison.
8. This (hildes) is so strong that no arrow can (erepic) it.
9. The (ivel) on that hat is its (hicef) trimming.
10. On (ehtir) trip, they found a (nive) of gold.

B. (1) Using the lists made in *A,* see how many other words related to them you can make. (2) Have a combined list put on the board.

You may prefer to make this a team contest in which you take turns in putting a word on the board and then adding words related to it. Score a point only if each new word is spelled correctly.

3. Watch Out for Troublesome Spellings!

DIFFERENT VOWELS IDENTICAL SOUNDS	IDENTICAL VOWELS DIFFERENT SOUNDS
fir	though
fur	through
were	ought
worm	rough
learn	cough
	bough
	thorough

"AT LEAST IN MATH, A = A."

What do the words on the board show about the spelling of words in the English language?

If each letter had only one sound, spelling would be easy. Unfortunately, however, the same letters or combinations of letters have different sounds. Note the letters in color in the examples below.

tap	city	grow	bead	boot	fill
tape	camp	germ	instead	foot	file
fall			great		machine
far					

How many sounds can you think of for *e?* for *o?* for *u?* for *s?*

Another problem is that the same sounds may be spelled in different ways. Note the letters in color in these words:

tape, great, wait, weigh, stay, they
be, bead, field, seem, gasoline, seize

How many ways can you think of to spell the sound of *i* as pronounced in the word *fine?* of *o*, as in the word *go?*

HELPFUL HINTS FOR SPELLING TROUBLESOME WORDS

1. Find words within the troublesome words. For example, "heard" has an "ear" in it.

2. Pair troublesome words with ones that you know how to spell. The words need not be rhymes, though they may be.

   rain—again, captain, certain, mountain, villain
   song—among, wrong   hide—decide

3. Make a sentence giving a clue; underline the troublesome word and the clue or clues that will help you to spell that word.

   I feel all right, but my work seems to be all wrong.

   Divide the divers into two classes.

4. Keep a special list of troublesome words. Write the trouble spots in red. Practice the words over and over.

   excellent   children   minute   answer   early

After doing the following activities, handle any misspellings as suggested in the Follow-up activity on page 246.

LEARNING ACTIVITIES

A. In each of the following words, you can find one or more words that will help you to remember how to spell the troublesome part. (1) Copy the words on your paper. (2) In each word, find another word and circle it. Be sure to circle only a word that you think will be helpful to you; then write it beside the word containing it. (3) Compare work in class. (4) Change your own list if necessary before putting it into the spelling section of your notebook.

EXAMPLES: soldier   old   doctor or   sleeve eve

1. ache	13. expense	25. meant	37. safety
2. across	14. forty	26. motor	38. search
3. afraid	15. fourth	27. ninety	39. secretary
4. against	16. friend	28. notice	40. sensitive
5. before	17. grammar	29. often	41. separate
6. business	18. holiday	30. only	42. something
7. busy	19. ignorant	31. patient	43. temperature
8. college	20. instant	32. pleasant	44. thrown
9. color	21. invitation	33. ready	45. together
10. country	22. label	34. really	46. toward
11. definite	23. leather	35. recent	47. vacation
12. every	24. many	36. recognize	48. vegetable

B. In the following words, trouble spots are shown in color. In a class discussion, figure out ways of mastering the spelling of these words.

1. absence	6. corner	11. February	16. Saturday
2. almost	7. describe	12. necessary	17. surely
3. always	8. doctor	13. nervous	18. through
4. built	9. doesn't	14. reason	19. until
5. committee	10. exercise	15. remember	20. Wednesday

ENRICHMENT

(*One or two students may volunteer to do this activity.*) (1) Examine in the large dictionary all the words that begin with *ph*. What do you find about their source? (2) Examine the words that begin with *ch* pronounced like *sh*. What do you learn about their source? (3) Make a list of the commonest *ph* and *ch* (sh) words. (4) Make a report to the class. Be sure to use the Guides for Making a Short, One-Source Report, page 142.

4. Watch the Pronunciation!

THINK IT OVER . . .

Many common words are misspelled simply because the user pronounces them carelessly or wrongly. For example, unless you are careful to say *escape*, you are likely to write *excape*.

LEARNING ACTIVITIES

A. What mispronunciations in the following words are likely to lead to misspellings? (1) In a class discussion have the words listed on the board and the trouble spots underlined. (2) Say and spell the words aloud.

1. apologize	6. chocolate	11. hundred	16. perhaps
2. athlete	7. divide	12. Indian	17. permanent
3. athletics	8. government	13. library	18. sentence
4. children	9. congratulate	14. partner	19. surprise
5. chimney	10. history	15. perform	20. strictly

B. (1) As your teacher dictates them, write the words in *A* on your paper. (2) Exchange papers for checking. (3) Write a helpful sentence for each word that you miss. (4) Circle the misspelled part of each word.

5. Watch Out for Homophones and Similar Words!

READ AND TALK ABOUT . . .

What wrong mental pictures do the italicized words in the following sentences suggest?

As they crossed the *planes,* the pioneers saw many buffaloes.
I write in this *dairy* every night.
I ate too much *desert.*

As those sentences suggest, certain words are likely to be confused with other words. Sometimes the confused words sound alike (as in *plains, planes*). Sometimes they just look much alike (as in *dairy, diary*).

● THESE ARE FACTS ABOUT HOMOPHONES

1. (DEFINITION) *Homophones* **are words that have the same pronunciation but that differ in spelling and meaning.**

   May I have a piece of pie?
   Peace is better than war.

2. **Here are some sentences that show how certain confusing homophones should be used.**

   a) How much is the bus fare? I believe in fair play.
   b) Of course I know you. This thread is too coarse.
   c) Steel is made from iron. A good person will not steal.
   d) One pane of glass is cracked. See a doctor about that pain.
   e) It's [It is] time for lunch. The tree lost its leaves.
   f) Your car is ready. You're [You are] late.
   g) I know their names. There they go! They're [They are] here.
   h) Here comes the team! Can you hear me?
   i) Our ship will sail today. These coats are on sale.
   j) I lost a pair of gloves. Will you pare this pear for me?
   k) Who led the parade? My feet feel as heavy as lead.
   l) Whose book is this? Who's [Who is] going with you?

LEARNING ACTIVITIES

A. In class, go over the preceding sentences to make sure that the differences in meaning between the homophones are clear. Give oral sentences of your own to show that you can tell the words apart. What other meanings can you illustrate for *fare?* for *fair?* for *course?*

B. Here is a list of common words that have homophones. (1) Write each word and its homophone or homophones. (2) Have the homophones listed on the board to help you check your paper. (3) Have a team contest in which a member of one team pronounces and spells one of the homophones. A member of the other team must then use that word in a sentence. Score a point for each correct sentence given.

1. beat	5. wait	9. great	13. peak	17. grown
2. bare	6. road	10. lane	14. break	18. toad
3. see	7. sole	11. heel	15. hole	19. vain
4. die	8. pail	12. seem	16. passed	20. seen

● THESE ARE FACTS ABOUT OTHER CONFUSING PAIRS

1. **Certain words are confused because they sound somewhat alike. If you pronounce them right, you will not confuse them.**

   a) Don't **lose** your ticket. Tighten that **loose** bolt.

   b) We have lived here **since** 1970. Use your own good **sense**.

   c) I like cold **weather**. I don't know **whether** I can help.

   d) She is older **than** I. First John sang and **then** Vera.

   e) Are you **quite** sure? The room was very **quiet**.

2. **Some words are confused simply because they look much alike, even though they sound entirely different.**

   a) The child behaved like an **angel**. Measure this **angle**.

   b) We sell milk to that **dairy**. I should write in my **diary**.

   c) Walk **through** that door. He gave us a **thorough** test.

   d) Hang your **clothes** in this closet. The tables had new **cloths** on them.

   e) Take a deep **breath**. It is hard to **breathe** in a stuffy room.

LEARNING ACTIVITIES

A. (1) Study carefully the word pairs given as examples. (2) Close your book. (3) Number a sheet of paper from 1 to 20. As your teacher reads each of the sentences, write the correct word on your paper. (4) Exchange papers for checking as your teacher reads the sentences again and writes the words on the board.

B. (1) For each error that you made in *A*, write the word correctly in a sentence. Use the Suggestions for Good Handwriting, page 479. (2) Check your work and file the paper in your notebook.

ENRICHMENT

Begin a collection of errors that you find in the use of homophones or other words that are confused. Look for them in advertising signs, circulars, newspapers, letters, and similar places. Copy or clip these examples, circling the wrong word and writing above it the word that should have been used. When you have a good collection, report to the class.

CHECK TESTS IN SPELLING

At the beginning of this chapter, you took two Pretests in spelling. You will now take those tests again. Follow the plan for the Pretests, page 245.

 Cumulative Review

CAPITALIZATION

Copy these sentences, placing capital letters where they are needed.

1. rabbi o. d. siegel read from the old testament of the bible.
2. Then mother asked, "who else is in your english class?"
3. the story that betty wrote is called "the best of the bunch."
4. My grandfather and i went over to madison street to visit the new y.m.c.a.
5. The browns have just returned from the west. there they visited mr. and mrs. l. t. jackson in sacramento, california.

PUNCTUATION

Copy the sentences, supplying needed punctuation marks, including underlining.

1. Yes said the teacher Ive seen a big improvement in your spelling
2. When you do not use so many ands and uhs you sound better
3. Mother have you seen my book The Life of Daniel Boone
4. Dr and Mrs John J Rogers of Atlanta Georgia want us to visit them this week next week or Christmas week
5. Fall coats are priced at $4295 (forty-two dollars and ninety-five cents) at the Fashion Shop

Section IV:

Handbook
of
Grammar
and
Usage

GRAMMAR: THE CODE
OF LANGUAGE

1. Language and Communication

"ALL RIGHT, FRISKY —— I'LL THROW IT FOR YOU ONCE MORE!"

TALK IT OVER . . .

Frisky has not actually *said* anything; that is, she has not used *words*. She has communicated an idea, however. How can you tell?

The boy speaks to Frisky, but is it really what he *says,* or what he *does,* that answers the dog?

Do you agree that "language" and "communication" are not necessarily the same? Which one includes the other?

As the drawing suggests, language is purely a human activity. Words and the way in which they are arranged form a code. That code gives human beings the power to express meanings and shades of meanings that mere sounds or gestures could never communicate.

The English language is one code; the French language is another; so is the German; so is each one of the many other languages in the world. Certain codes are alike in some ways, but no two are exactly the same. As an example, you say, "Thank you," but if you were French, you would say, "Merci"; if Spanish, "Gracias"; if German, "Danke"; if Italian, "Grazie"; and so on.

LEARNING ACTIVITIES

A. What different things may a dog be trying to express when it barks? when it growls? when it whines? Is it using language?

B. Suppose you had a parrot or a mynah bird that you had taught to say, "Hello, how are you?" when someone came into the room. Would the bird be communicating? Justify your opinion.

2. English: A Changing Language

"HAST CONNED THY LESSON FOR TODAY?"

"COME ON, BILL! TALK ENGLISH!"

READ AND DISCUSS . . .

Strange as his remark may sound, Bill *is* speaking English — but not in its present-day form. Certainly you can figure out what he means. How would that sentence be worded today?

What word have you substituted for "Hast"? What word must you insert after it? What word would you use instead of "conned"? What has happened to "thy"?

A sentence such as "Hast conned thy lesson for today?" is a good example of how language changes as the years go by. When the greatest English writer, William Shakespeare, was a boy, four hundred years ago, "hast" and "conned" were as much a part of everyday speech as "have" and "studied" are today.

LEARNING ACTIVITIES

A. Find the word *hast* in your dictionary. On the basis of what you discover, decide why Shakespeare would not have been likely to say, "*He* hast conned his lesson."

Now look up the verb *con.* Does it, like *hast,* have the label *Archaic?* (You will remember from Chapter 1 that *archaic* means "no longer in common use.") Examine the definition. Do you agree that *con* is more specific than *study?* Why?

B. Here are other English sentences as Shakespeare might have expressed them. On your paper, "translate" them into modern English. Look up any unfamiliar words in your dictionary.

1. Be thou thyself mine enemy?
2. Methinks the clock hath strucken thrice.
3. I wot not whereof thou dost speak.
4. Mayhap he doth but wish to fright thee.
5. Whence cometh this man? Wast thou who brought him?

C. Many of the changes in the English language down through the years have been in spelling. A great number of words today are the very same words that Geoffrey Chaucer, the first great English poet, used six hundred years ago. The words simply are spelled differently now.

Here are sentences in which the italicized words are spelled as Chaucer would have written them. With the help of the other words in the sentences, figure out the italicized ones. (Reading aloud will help.) Rewrite the sentences, using today's spelling.

1. *Thenne I bigan to thinke* that I *sholde retourne hoom.*
2. He *seyde,* "I *hidde* the *tresor* in a *litel feeld nat ferre fro heer.*"
3. *Oon* of *thise* men *wol helpe yow peynte* the *dores.*
4. *Laste somer* Ed and I *toke* a *journee togidre thurgh* that *contree.*
5. A *longe whyle* ago my *fader yaf* me *som goode avys:* "*Alwey* do your *duetee.*"

3. English: A Patterned Language

"TOMMY WANTS A DRINK OF WATER."

Tommy has not yet learned to use "I" instead of "Tommy" in that sentence, but he *has* learned to say, "Tommy wants a drink of water," and not "Of water a drink wants Tommy," or "Wants of water a drink Tommy."

Though he does not realize the fact, Tommy has already learned an important truth about language: sentences are "patterned." In English sentences, words and groups of words tend to fall naturally into a certain order; that is, into *patterns*. Sentence meaning depends upon the pattern. Consider this sentence, for example: *The boy chased the dog.*

You know that the boy is the one who is doing the chasing; *boy* is, in other words, the "subject" of the sentence. You know that the dog is what is being chased; *dog* is, you know, the "object" in the sentence. The pattern, then, looks like this:

subject + verb + object
boy + chased + dog

What happens if you change the position of the two nouns?

The dog chased the boy.

The pattern (*subject + verb + object*) is the same, but the meaning has changed.

LEARNING ACTIVITY

The pairs of sentences in this activity have exactly the same words. In class explain what difference in meaning the change in word order causes.

1. Everybody likes John. John likes everybody.
2. Freda, change your mind. Freda, mind your change!
3. He supplies ships for the navy. He ships supplies for the navy.
4. Did Ethel vote? Ethel did vote.
5. She rakes leaves. She leaves rakes.
6. Everyone here works. Everyone works here.
7. Those girls are workers! Those workers are girls.
8. The men with her are partners. The men are partners with her.
9. Did you check the date? Did you date the check?
10. He will plan the attack. He will attack the plan.

4. Sentence Structure

The definitions, facts, and examples given here will be helpful to you in your study of the parts of sentences. Refer to them whenever you need to.

● THESE ARE FACTS ABOUT SENTENCES

1. **A** *sentence* **is a group of words that does one of the following things:**

    a) **It may make a** *statement:* The band played a march.

    b) **It may ask a** *question:* Who took the dictionary?

    c) **It may express a** *command* **or a** *request:* Go immediately.
    Please follow me.

2. **Every sentence must have a** *subject* **and a** *predicate* **(***verb***).**

3. **(DEFINITION) The** *simple subject* * **in a sentence is the** *main word* **that tells** *who* **or** *what* **the sentence is about.**

    The little white **dog** ran down the street.

4. **(DEFINITION) The** *complete subject* **is** *all* **the words in the sentence that together tell** *who* **or** *what* **the sentence is about.**

    The little white dog ran down the street.

5. **(DEFINITION) The** *simple predicate* † **is the verb.**

    The little white dog **ran** down the street.

6. **(DEFINITION) The** *complete predicate* **is** *all* **the words in the sentence that together tell something that the subject** *is* **or** *does.*

    The little white dog **ran down the street.**

---

* In this book the term *subject* when used alone refers to the *simple subject.*

† In this book the term *predicate* when used alone refers to the *simple predicate,* that is, the *verb,* sometimes called the *predicate verb.*

SENTENCE PATTERNS

Many verbs must be followed by other words to complete their meaning. Such words are called *complements*. The kind of complement, or "completer," that a verb takes determines the pattern of a sentence.

● THESE ARE FACTS ABOUT COMPLEMENTS

1. **There are four kinds of complements: the** *direct object,* **the** *indirect object,* **the** *predicate nominative,* **and the** *predicate adjective.*

2. **A** *direct object* **receives the action of the verb or shows the result of its action.**

    The girl spoke three languages .   They played tennis .

3. **An** *indirect object* **tells** *to whom (what)* **or** *for whom (what)* **the action of the verb is performed.**

    She gave me the bill.   I told her a story.

4. **A** *predicate nominative* **renames or identifies the subject of the verb.**

    He is our friend .   Mrs. Johannsen is an architect .

5. **A** *predicate adjective* **describes the subject.**

    Mala was happy .   The orange juice is refreshing .

The basic pattern of any simple sentence in English can be described by formulas that show the kind of complement, if any, that the sentence has in its complete predicate.

These sentence patterns are written with letters that stand for the parts of speech that can fill the subject, verb, and complement positions. Here are the symbols used in the patterns:

N: a noun, pronoun, or word group used as a noun
V: a verb
LV: a linking verb (*be, seem, look, appear, feel, . . .*)
A: an adjective or word group used as an adjective

Here are the five basic sentence patterns you will study in the chapters that follow:

Pattern 1: **Noun + verb:** Snow fell. (*subject, verb*)

Pattern 2: **Noun + linking verb + noun:** Books are friends. (*subject, verb, predicate nominative*)

Pattern 3: **Noun + linking verb + adjective:** Helga looks tired. (*subject, verb, predicate adjective*)

Pattern 4: **Noun + verb + noun:** Jamie followed Nora. (*subject, verb, direct object*)

Pattern 5: **Noun + verb + noun + noun:** Alma gave Gina medicine. (*subject, verb, indirect object, direct object*)

USING VERBS IN BUILDING SENTENCES*

I certainly —— you.

How important is the missing word in that sentence?

Why is there no real sentence idea without it?

Which of these words will "make sense" in the blank: *saw, truth, rich, likes, about, stole?*

---

* Pretest 2 should be taken at this point.

1. Recognizing Doing (Action) Verbs

When a runner hears the signal "Go!" what does he or she *do*? What does a football team *do* when the signal "Hike!" is called? What *action* takes place when these commands are given: "Wait!" "Look!" "Listen!"? Such words as those call for doing something and, therefore, each might be called a "doing" word. The grammatical name is *verb*.

A verb is one of the parts of speech. *Parts of speech* are the different classes of words out of which sentences are built.

● THESE ARE FACTS ABOUT VERBS: I

1. (DEFINITION) A *verb* is a word that makes a statement about persons, things, or ideas by showing (*a*) what something does or (*b*) that something exists.

2. (DEFINITION) Verbs that express action are "doing" verbs. They will fit at least one of the blanks, or slots, in these sentences:

   He _____. We _____. She _____ it. They _____ it.

   EXAMPLES: He **laughs**. We **laugh**. She **drives** it. They **drive** it.

3. (DEFINITION) A verb that simply shows existence or condition is a *verb of being*. Such verbs are used as *linking verbs*.*

   EXAMPLES: He **is** an artist. She **seems** fatigued.

4. Verbs can change form or take endings as needed.

You **jump** well.	He **jumps** well.	She **jumped** well.
We often **go**.	He often **goes**.	They often **went**.
I **am** sorry.	He **is** sorry.	They **were** sorry.

5. Every sentence must have a verb.

   The porpoise *tossed* the ball.

   Take out the doing word (*tossed*) and you have no idea what the porpoise did, except that it concerned a ball.

   The porpoise __?__ the ball.

   Did the porpoise *throw it, find it, lose it, drop it, . . . ?* You must have that word *tossed* before you can know what is happening. *Tossed,* in other words, is the verb, the most important word.

---

* The uses of linking verbs will be studied under predicate nominatives and predicate adjectives, pages 323 and 383.

The following words, taken from Learning Activity *C*, have interesting histories. Use your dictionary to find the story behind each word.

immense   nasturtium   tent   luggage

LEARNING ACTIVITIES

A. Many words suggest action, but only verbs say that it actually takes place, has taken place, or will do so. By using the test frames in 2 on page 279, find which of the following words can be verbs.

1. hike   3. runner   5. song   7. yell   9. bought
2. sits   4. rapidly   6. throw   8. argues   10. explosion

B. The following groups of words will not mean much until the blanks are filled with verbs. Copy the sentences, putting a good "doing" word of your own choice in each blank. Do not write in this book.

When you have finished, each group of words will be a sentence. In other words, it *will make sense*. Read your sentences in class to see how many different meanings were given by the use of different verbs.

1. Irene _____.
2. Ted _____ his mother.
3. Sally _____ loudly.
4. Phil _____ into the house.
5. The audience _____ the program.
6. The wind _____ through the trees.
7. The old man _____ slowly.
8. Jean _____ down the road.

C. (1) Copy the following sentences, underlining the verb in each sentence twice. (2) Proofread for careless errors in copying. (3) Exchange papers for checking.

1. An airplane flew over the city.
2. Mother reads many books.
3. Many bright nasturtiums grow in our garden.
4. Yes, my uncle whittled this figure for me.
5. The cat raced to the top of the tent.
6. Mrs. Johnson shipped her luggage to Oregon.
7. Tom brought some magazines to Father.
8. The Ohio River runs into the Mississippi.
9. The fire engine dashed noisily down the street.
10. The rain soaked quickly into the dry earth.
11. Karen climbed to the top of the old maple tree.
12. The baby upset its bowl of cereal.
13. The travelers saw an immense black bear.
14. Laura swam across the pool.
15. Jim missed the football game.

D. Try substituting other verbs for the ones used in the following sentences. List on the board the different verbs suggested for each sentence.

1. The child fed the birds.
2. Alice bought a new bike yesterday.
3. Harry sent the message.
4. The class gave a play.
5. Henry wrote a long letter.
6. Mary builds model planes.
7. The boys walked home today.
8. Gene sings well.

Spot Review

Notice the above title, for you will see it often. Each time it will be the heading for a short check-up to see whether you are remembering and using what you study.

(Based upon the sentences in C of the preceding activities)

1. Why is *Father* capitalized in sentence 7?
2. Why is *uncle* not capitalized in sentence 4?
3. Explain the comma in sentence 4.
4. Why is *River* capitalized in sentence 8?

2. Recognizing Auxiliary Verbs

THINK IT OVER . . .

What is missing in the sentences?

Which of the following words will fit in the first blank? in the second? in the third? Here are the words: *is, was, has, had, does, did, shall, will, should, would, may, might, must, can, could.*

281

6. (DEFINITION) An *auxiliary verb* **is one that helps a doing or a being verb express an idea.** (*Auxiliary* is from the Latin *auxilium,* meaning "aid" or "help.") **The auxiliary signals that the** *main verb* **is coming.**

The sun **has** *broken* through the clouds.

In that sentence, the verb is *has broken,* made up of the helping verb *has* and a form of the doing verb *break.*

7. (DEFINITION) **A main verb with its auxiliaries is a** *verb phrase.*

8. **The verbs used as auxiliaries are so few in number that you can memorize them.** Here they are, grouped in families to help you learn them easily. The verbs in groups I, II, and III can be used as main verbs as well as auxiliaries.

I		II	III	IV	V
is	were	has	do	shall	may
am	be	have	does	will	might
are	being	had	did	should	must
was	been			would	can
					could

9. **Changing the helping verb changes the meaning of a sentence.**

I *shall* walk.	I *could* walk.	I *must* walk.
I *may* walk.	I *did* walk.	I *should* walk.
I *can* walk.	I *do* walk.	I *might* walk.

10. **A doing verb may have one, two, or even three helping verbs.** In verb phrases all but the last verb will be auxiliaries. Note that the final, or main, verb can have different forms.

Dee **will** *go* tomorrow. (*one auxiliary*)
Dee **should have** *gone* today. (*two auxiliaries*)
Dee **might be** *going* soon. (*two auxiliaries*)
Soon Dee **will have been** *gone* a week. (*three auxiliaries*)

LEARNING ACTIVITIES

A. Auxiliaries keep a definite order when two or more of them are parts of a verb phrase. You would never say, for example, "Roy *have should* helped you"; the right order is "should have."

In class, go over the five groups of auxiliaries. See how many two- or three-word combinations you can make from them. Which group cannot be used as auxiliaries with words in any of the other groups?

B. (1) Number your paper from 1 to 20. (2) Find the verb phrase in each sentence and write it after the corresponding number on your paper.

1. The settlers had brought their families with them.
2. Our neighbors are planning a long trip.
3. Joe might agree with you.
4. My brother could have come sooner.
5. The letter may have arrived early.
6. Those poor people do need our help.
7. Your sister must be told about our plans.
8. The new plans should have been explained to us.
9. Flora was polishing the car.
10. The twins were working in the garden.
11. The work is being completed rapidly.
12. Yes, Helen does watch *Nova*.
13. Mother must have left for work very early.
14. Our house can be seen from this corner.
15. Tim has changed his mind again.
16. Georgia did go to the game after all.
17. Jane is planning a trip for next summer.
18. No mail will be delivered tomorrow.
19. Most people would like my Uncle Jack.
20. These volunteers shall be instructed carefully.

C. Go back to the sentences in *B*. Find those with two or more auxiliaries. Can you arrange those auxiliaries in any other sensible order?

● THESE ARE FACTS ABOUT VERBS: III

11. *Has, have, had, do, does,* **and** *did* **can be used as the doing verb in a sentence.** They are auxiliaries only when they come before the main verb.

Sue **has** the tickets.	Joe **does** his best.
We **had** a heavy snow.	Ellen **did** well.
We *have* **had** rain.	

12. *Is, am, are, was,* **and** *were* **can stand alone as verbs of being.** *Be, being,* **and** *been* **can be main verbs of being when preceded by auxiliaries.**

The boys **are** cousins.	Tom *may* **be** late.
The book **was** open.	You *are* **being** coy.

LEARNING ACTIVITIES

A. In an oral activity, see how quickly you can pick out the verbs in the following sentences. They may look like helping verbs, but here they are used as main verbs. Tell which ones are verbs of being and which ones are verbs of action.

1. The book was on the table.
2. The owners of the farm are away.
3. Jerry is my friend.
4. May has a new watch.
5. The team members did their best.
6. Those two days were holidays.
7. A kind word does wonders.
8. The patient had a good doctor.
9. The nights have been colder lately.
10. Angry words often do great harm.

B. (1) Write two sentences for each of the following verbs or verb phrases: *has been, might have, should be, were, could have been.* Use them (*a*) as auxiliary verbs and (*b*) by themselves; that is, without doing verbs. (2) Proofread your sentences for careless mistakes in capitalizing, punctuating, or spelling. (3) Exchange papers in class and underline each verb or verb phrase twice in the sentences that you receive. (4) Return papers and check to see that all the verbs are correctly underlined.

The illustration on this page may suggest things to write about.

FOLLOW-UP

Keep a list of the helping verbs. Test yourself from time to time to see how well you can write them from memory.

3. Recognizing Verbs with Separated Parts

Look at this sentence: *The book could not be found.*

What is the verb? At first glance you might say it is *could not be found.* Which word in "could not be," however, is not an auxiliary? (See point 8, page 282.) What, then, is the verb phrase?

● THESE ARE FACTS ABOUT VERBS: IV

13. **Often the parts of a verb will be separated by other words.**

    The road is already **being repaired**
    Maria **can** almost always **help** us.
    Shana is not **going** tomorrow.

14. **In a question, the parts of the verb are often separated.**

    Has Elena **bought** a ticket?

    Turning a question into a statement helps to locate the verb.

    QUESTION: **Has** Elena **bought** a ticket?
    STATEMENT: Elena **has bought** a ticket.

15. **To turn a statement into a question, you must make certain changes in the sentence.**

    a) If the statement has (1) a verb phrase or (2) a being verb, you need to change only the sentence order.
       (1) Lou **is waiting**   **Is** Lou **waiting**?
       (2) Those boys **are** cousins.   **Are** those boys cousins?

    b) If the statement has a doing verb with no auxiliaries, you (1) will need to insert one of the auxiliaries *do, does,* or *did* and (2) may need to change the form of the doing verb.
       (1) Bears **roam** here.   **Do** bears **roam** here?
       (2) Alice **lives** here.   **Does** Alice **live** here?
       Dean **left** today.   **Did** Dean **leave** today?

16. **Sometimes part of the verb is within a contraction.** (See page 238 for a discussion of contractions.)

    Jack **hasn't gone** yet.   Why **wasn't** the bell **rung**?

The following words, taken from Learning Activity *A*, have interesting histories. Use your dictionary to find the story behind each word.

soldier   muscle   bonfire   ventriloquism

LEARNING ACTIVITIES

A. In an oral activity, find the verb phrase in each sentence. The number of auxiliary verbs is indicated in parentheses.

1. The sun has not shone all day. (1)
2. The scouts have surely watched that bonfire carefully. (1)
3. That soldier may soon see his home again. (1)
4. A visit to the mill can probably be arranged. (2)
5. Harry is just beginning a new book. (1)
6. Gina must always have been reading about ventriloquism. (3)
7. The bell had already rung. (1)
8. The curtain will then be lowered. (2)
9. Jane isn't really living here now. (1)
10. This muscle has evidently been strained before. (2)
11. The speaker's voice is not being heard clearly. (2)
12. Our plans are almost always made at the last minute. (1)

B. (1) Copy the questions below and underline the verbs twice. If it will help you, think of the question in the form of a statement. Do not write in this book. (2) Exchange papers for checking.

1. Why has Jan come with you?
2. What is Mother bringing tonight?
3. In what year did Texas become a state?
4. By what nickname was Andrew Jackson known?
5. Could Jean have come with us?
6. Where was Abraham Lincoln born?
7. When will the game begin?
8. Will your brother tell Sally of the change in plans?
9. Have any letters come for me?
10. How can Frank plan the party?

C. Turn the following ten statements into questions. As you go over them in class, explain the changes that you needed to make.

1. Lucia has always lived in Florida.
2. Carlos found his lost gloves.

3. The books will be delivered tomorrow.
4. Manya's uncle still pitches for the Dodgers.
5. Ms. Burns came here from Canada.
6. The names of the winners were announced last night.
7. The wind blew the roof off that house.
8. Both girls made the basketball team.
9. Everyone except John left early.
10. That plant needs more sunlight.

D. Write five questions of your own, underlining the verbs. You may want to write questions about a hobby, about sports, or about a book that you have read. Read your questions in your small group and ask a member of the group to name the verb in each sentence.

ENRICHMENT

Compose a paragraph of five or more sentences about a motion picture that you have seen recently. For help, refer to guides 2–4 of the Guides for Writing a Paragraph, page 162. In two or more sentences, use verbs with their parts separated by other words.

Read your paragraph in class. Let guides 4, 6, and 7 of the Guides for Reading Aloud, page 59, help you. Ask classmates to jot down each verb that they hear. (This activity will require careful listening. Review guides 1 and 4 of the Guides to Good Listening on page 28.)

4. Telling Time with Verbs

Today I walk.
Yesterday I walked.
Tomorrow I shall walk.

THINK IT OVER . . .

What happens to the verb "walk" in the second and third sentences in the drawing?

The verb form used in a sentence tells the time when an action takes place. It tells (1) whether something is happening in the *present,* (2) whether it happened in the *past,* or (3) whether it will happen in the *future.*

● THESE ARE FACTS ABOUT VERBS: V

17. (DEFINITION) *Tense* **is the grammatical term for the form of a verb that shows the time of the action or state of being that the verb expresses.** The first three forms shown below are *simple tenses;* the next three are called *perfect tenses.*

(*Tense* comes from the Latin word *tempus,* which means "time.") The tense that is used will show when something *is, was,* or *will be* happening.

PRESENT TENSE: Today I *play.*
PAST TENSE: Yesterday I *played.*
FUTURE TENSE: Tomorrow I *shall* (or *will*) play.

PRESENT PERFECT TENSE: Today I *have played.*
PAST PERFECT TENSE: Yesterday I *had played.*
FUTURE PERFECT TENSE: Tomorrow I *shall* (or *will*) *have played.*

18. **All of the tenses are based on the three main parts of the verb, called the** *principal parts:* **the** *present* **form, the** *past* **form, and the** *past participle.* *(See the list of principal parts on page 478.)

Present	Past	Past Participle
dare	dared	dared
play	played	played
go	went	gone

a) (DEFINITION) **Verbs like** *dare* **and** *play* **are called** *regular verbs* **because they form the past and the past participle simply by adding** *d* **or** *ed* **to the present.**

dare + d = dared   play + ed = played

b) (DEFINITION) **Some verbs, like** *go* **in the example, change their spelling to form the past and the past participle, and are therefore called** *irregular verbs.* These verbs will be pointed out throughout this book.

c) **The dictionary gives the principal parts of all irregular verbs. If the parts are not given, a verb is regular.**

*The *present participle* is sometimes included with the principal parts. It is made by adding *ing* to the present: *walk, walking.* Forms of the auxiliary *be* are used with the present participle to make special verb tenses: I *am lying,* I *have been waiting.*

LEARNING ACTIVITIES

A. (1) As your teacher dictates the following regular verbs, write on your paper their principal parts. (2) Exchange papers for checking.

1. rake	4. warm	7. need	10. harm
2. clean	5. form	8. land	11. scout
3. blame	6. pretend	9. excuse	12. test

B. The following verbs are irregular only in that a spelling change takes place as *ed* is added to form the past and the past participle. (1) Write a sentence, at least six words long, using the past of each of the verbs. (Rule 2 on page 257 and rules 1 and 2 on page 259 will help you to spell the words correctly.) (2) Take turns reading your sentences in class or in your small groups, spelling the verb orally. (3) Exchange papers for criticism of spelling, punctuation, and neatness. Note good things as well as bad.

1. carry	3. stop	5. refer	7. hop	9. study
2. bat	4. hurry	6. marry	8. omit	10. cry

5. Forming Tenses

TENSE	= AUXILIARY	+ PRINCIPAL PART
Future	= shall or will	+ present form
Present Perfect	= has or have	+ past participle
Past Perfect	= had	+ past participle
Future Perfect	= shall have or will have	+ past participle

THINK IT OVER . . .

By studying the list of tenses on page 288, you can see that only the present tense and the past tense of a verb show time by themselves. All the other tenses require auxiliaries.

Learn about words!

The following words, taken from Learning Activity *A*, page 291, have interesting histories. Use your dictionary to find the story behind each word.

tennis   season   bus

19. **Remember that the** *present tense* **and** *past tense* **are two of the principal parts of a verb. They do not require auxiliaries.** *

> I **depart** today. I **go** today. (*present tense*)
> I **departed** yesterday. I **went** yesterday. (*past tense*)

20. **The third simple tense,** *the future,* **combines the auxiliaries** *shall* **or** *will* **with the** *present form* **of the main verb.** (*Shall* is used with *I* or *we; will* is used with all other subjects.)

> We **shall depart** tomorrow. (*future tense*)
> I **shall go** tomorrow. (*future tense*)
> You, he, and they **will** all **depart** tomorrow. (*future tense*)

21. **To form the** *perfect tenses,* **the third principal part — the** *past participle* **— is combined with different auxiliaries.**

PRESENT PERFECT TENSE: Use the auxiliary *has* or *have* with the *past participle.*

> He **has** already **departed.**
> They **have** already **gone.**

PAST PERFECT TENSE: Use the auxiliary *had* with the *past participle.*

> You **had departed** by the time I arrived.
> They **had gone** by then.

FUTURE PERFECT TENSE: Use the auxiliaries *shall have* or *will have* with the *past participle.*

> We **shall have departed** by the time you arrive.
> I **shall have gone.**
> Both he and they **will have departed** by the time you arrive.
> They **will have gone.**

22. **(DEFINITION) The orderly arrangement of all the forms and tenses of a verb is called a** *conjugation.* **For the conjugations of** *to be, to have, to do,* **and** *to draw,* **see pages 473–477.**

In forming tenses, remember that *regular verbs* form both their past tense and their past participle by adding *ed* to the present form. *Irregular verbs,* however, may have three entirely different principal parts. You must study them carefully to distinguish between the simple past tense, which never takes an auxiliary, and the *past participle,* which *always requires an auxiliary.*

---

* The present tense may use certain auxiliaries in order to pose a question or to add emphasis to a statement: They *do* agree. *Do* you agree? (See point 15, page 285.)

LEARNING ACTIVITIES

A. In an oral activity, name the verbs in the following sentences and tell their tense.

1. A smiling woman answered the door.
2. The bus will leave early in the morning.
3. Several birthday cards had arrived late.
4. By next June our family probably will have moved to Texas.
5. My father likes pie for breakfast.
6. Will some kind friend help me with this problem?
7. Jack has always lived on Maple Street.
8. Susan found her tennis racket.
9. The plane will have arrived in New York by then.
10. They played chess all afternoon.
11. Has the mail come?
12. Next week Bob will go to St. Louis.
13. Mary had painted scenery every night of that week.
14. The team has lost only one game all season.
15. The girls found no frogs in the pond.
16. Ralph had never seen the play before.
17. Perhaps the snow will have ended by morning.
18. Every year my father bakes a cake for my birthday.

B. (1) Copy the following sentences, putting in the verb tense called for in the parentheses. Write carefully, applying the Suggestions for Good Handwriting, page 479. (2) Exchange papers for checking.

1. Which student (*past of* lock) this door?
2. By tonight Tom (*future perfect of* finish) his trip.
3. No one (*past perfect of* close) his or her eyes that night.
4. The price (*future of* go) up tomorrow.
5. On Saturdays Luis (*present of* help) his father in the drugstore.
6. The children (*present perfect of* decide) on a name for their dog.
7. The president usually (*present of* open) the meeting.
8. The snow (*past perfect of* pile) up in huge drifts.
9. Which boy (*future of* wash) the windows for you?
10. The color in the fabric certainly (*present perfect of* fade).

6. Using Vivid Verbs

TALK IT OVER . . .

How many different verbs can you think of to express the simple action of *walking* down a street? From your observations of people you know, describe different ways of walking. You may have noticed one person *strolling* down the street and another person *strutting*. How else might a person *walk* down the street?

GUIDES FOR USING VIVID VERBS

1. Use strong verbs. "The car *screeched* around the corner," for example, gives a clearer picture than "The car *turned* the corner."

2. Use exact, vivid substitutes for the verb *said*. "She *shouted* at him," for example, gives a more vivid impression than "She *said* to him." (The guide does not mean that you should never use *said*. What it does mean is that many times other words will express your meaning better.)

3. Avoid "big" verbs when simple ones give the meaning that you want to express. "*Chew* your food well," for example, is usually better than "*Masticate* your food well."

LEARNING ACTIVITIES

A. *Run, say,* and *look* are general verbs. (1) Make a list on your paper of exact, vivid words that you might substitute for them. For example, in thinking about *run*, picture to yourself the various ways in which people run and then find the exact word to describe each way: *gallop, scurry, scoot,* and so on. (2) In class, make a combined list on the board. (3) Copy into your notebook vivid, exact verbs for future use.

B. One reason that good writers are good writers is that they use vivid verbs. Here are examples from the works of famous poets. Read them together and then discuss the verb choices. Use the Guides for Choral Reading, page 48. (Be sure to follow discussion guides 3 and 4, page 35.)

1. . . . the wind on the warm sea dozes, . . .
   — ALGERNON CHARLES SWINBURNE
2. . . . the door upon its hinges groans. — JOHN KEATS
3. The high masts flickered . . . — ALFRED, LORD TENNYSON
4. The light white cloud swam over us. — ALFRED, LORD TENNYSON
5. The last red leaf is whirled away. — ALFRED, LORD TENNYSON
6. Pluck strange dirges from the storm
   Sift rare stones from ashes of the moon, . . . — WOLE SOYINKA*
7. The white foam spun behind us. — RUDYARD KIPLING

---

* From "Fado Singer" from *Idanre and Other Poems* by Wole Soyinka; copyright © by Wole Soyinka 1967. Reprinted by Hill and Wang, Inc., New York.

8. How the sleet whips the pane! — MATTHEW ARNOLD
9. Where the grey seas glitter, . . . — GILBERT KEITH CHESTERTON
10. A late lark twitters from the quiet skies . . .
                              — WILLIAM ERNEST HENLEY
11. Time bleeds into dreams children have . . . — OWEN DODSON*
12. All day the wind breathes low . . . — ALFRED, LORD TENNYSON
13. An awful Tempest mashed the air . . . — EMILY DICKINSON†
14. . . . the sunrise glazed the barnyard mud with red; . . .
                              — ELIZABETH BISHOP‡
15. The night wind wailed round the empty room . . .
                              — DANTE GABRIEL ROSSETTI
16. The hot sun bit the garden beds, . . . — WILLIAM MORRIS

C. In class or in your small groups, make a list on the board of vivid verbs that tell different ways in which you might describe the following:

1. The blowing of the wind
2. The running of a stream
3. The flying of birds
4. The shining of sun, stars, moon
5. The sounds made by birds
6. The falling of snow, rain, hail
7. The noises made by automobiles, planes, motorboats
8. The sight and sound of a fire

D. Replace the "big" verbs in these sentences with ones better suited to ordinary conversational speech.

1. Have you perused that copy of *Newsweek* yet?
2. You should cerebrate at least an hour before deciding.
3. Unexpected company always discomposes Mom.
4. I prognosticate a win for our team in Friday's game.
5. Why don't you manifest a little interest in our plans?

FOLLOW-UP

From the lists made in *C*, copy words that appeal to you. File them in your notebook for use in your themes, letters, or other writing.

---

7. Using Standard English

Do "I *done* my best" and "I *did* my best" mean the same thing?

If so, what difference does it make which one is used?

Is there more to language than simply expressing meaning?

There are two main levels of English usage: *standard* and *nonstandard*. Standard English is the kind of language used naturally by well-educated speakers. Nonstandard English is language that such speakers would not normally use. "I *did* my best" is standard English; "I *done* my best," nonstandard.

USING TROUBLESOME VERBS

Nonstandard use of irregular verbs is a common problem. From time to time in this book, practice is provided in the proper use of the principal parts of irregular verbs. Each time, before doing the practice, learn the principal parts. Notice that the third form, the past participle, always has an auxiliary with it. (You may want to review the auxiliary verbs listed on page 282 and the examples of tense formation on page 290.)

USING IRREGULAR VERBS—<u>DO</u>, <u>DID</u>, <u>DONE</u>

RULE. Always use an auxiliary (helping) **verb with** *done. Did* **is the past tense and stands alone.**

Today I **do.**   Yesterday I **did.**   Often I *have* **done.**

LEARNING ACTIVITIES

A. Go over the following sentences orally in class, choosing the standard forms from the parentheses. Repeat the activity several times. If you use the past participle, tell what the auxiliary verb is.

1. Have you (did, done) the assignment yet?
2. Jack should have (did, done) his homework.
3. Flavia (did, done) extremely well on the test.
4. We (did, done) all the puzzles correctly.
5. What has television (did, done) for people?
6. I (did, done) all the reading except the last chapter.
7. Has anything been (did, done) about the mistake?
8. Who (did, done) most of the planning?
9. The hardest job was (did, done) early in the morning.
10. The decorating must be (done, did) well.

B. (1) Write these sentences, filling each blank with the standard form of *do*. (2) Underline twice both the form of *do* that you use and any auxiliary verbs. (3) Exchange papers for checking when the sentences are read aloud. Do not write in this book.

1. Your work should always be _____ neatly.
2. Yes, Beth _____ her best in the last contest.
3. Who _____ this?
4. Terry has _____ very well this time.
5. We _____ this assignment yesterday.
6. Has Mother ever _____ this kind of work before?
7. These papers must not be _____ hastily.
8. I have _____ these exercises every morning for a month.
9. Yesterday I _____ something very foolish.
10. I've never _____ this trick successfully.

C. Write five sentences of six or more words, using *did* or *done* in each of them. Write about something that you have done in connection with your schoolwork, with your clubs, or with any other activity.

Have the sentences read aloud in your small groups. Listen carefully, and be ready to say why a sentence is or is not standard English.

D. Do this drill with a partner. (1) Ask a question using *done* properly. (2) Your partner must answer the question using *did*. (3) He or she must then ask you a question using *done*, which you must answer using *did*. (4) Continue until each has asked and answered five questions.

Spot Review ★

(Based upon the sentences in B of the preceding activities)

1. Account for the comma in sentence 2.
2. How would you spell the plural of the proper noun in sentence 4?
3. Why is *Mother* capitalized in sentence 6?
4. Account for the apostrophe in sentence 10.

USING IRREGULAR VERBS — KNOW, KNEW, KNOWN

RULE. Always use an auxiliary verb with *known;* **never use one with** *knew.* **Remember that** *knowed* **is not standard English.**

Today I know.   Yesterday I knew.   Often I *have* known.

LEARNING ACTIVITIES

A. (1) Write these sentences, filling each blank with the standard form of *know.* (2) Underline twice the form of *know* that you use. Underline in the same way any helping verbs. (3) Read the sentences in class. Do not write in this book.

1. Years ago Mother _____ this city from one end to the other.
2. Mrs. Smith has not _____ Sadie for very long.
3. You should have _____ better!
4. We all _____ the speaker a long time ago.
5. Father _____ nothing of the accident until today.
6. Have you _____ those people long?
7. The results of the contest should be _____ soon.
8. Mary has always been _____ as a good student.
9. The news might not yet be _____ to our friends.
10. I _____ what I want — peach ice cream.
11. They had _____ about the treasure for at least seven years, but they didn't _____ exactly where to find it.
12. I _____ the answer all the time, but I didn't say it.

B. Write five original sentences, using *knew* and *known* properly. You may want to write about friends at school or in your neighborhood. In your small groups, read your sentences aloud. Call on classmates to name the helping verbs used with *known.* Listen carefully to teach your ears to recognize the standard forms.

C. Write sentences on the board, leaving blanks to be filled with *knew* or *known.* Have classmates read the sentences out loud as they fill in the proper forms.

D. Do this activity in pairs. (1) Make up a sentence using *knew.* (2) Your partner must change it to use *known* properly. (3) Then he or she will make up a sentence using *knew,* which you must change in a way that will use *known.*

EXAMPLE: I *knew* the right answer.
           I *should have known* the right answer.

Practice until the proper forms sound right to you.

USING IRREGULAR VERBS — <u>SPEAK</u>, <u>SPOKE</u>, <u>SPOKEN</u>

RULE. Always use an auxiliary verb with *spoken;* **never use one with**
spoke.

Today I speak.   Yesterday I spoke.   Often I *have* spoken.

LEARNING ACTIVITIES

A. (1) Write these sentences, filling the blanks with the proper form
of *speak.* (2) Underline twice the form that you use and any helping verbs.
(3) Read the sentences aloud in class as many times as needed to make the
right forms sound natural. Do not write in this book.

1. Have you _____ to Mother about our trip?
2. You should certainly have _____ first to my mother.
3. In giving that report, Charles _____ clearly.
4. Mary has already _____ to me about the picnic.
5. Not many of Anne's sentences are _____ above a whisper.
6. The last words were _____ very loudly.
7. Is English, Italian, or French _____ in that country?
8. I had already _____ to Alice about the change in plans.
9. Who _____ just then?
10. You might have _____ up sooner.

B. (1) See how many combinations of helping verbs and *spoken* your
class can name. Have these written on the board. (2) Practice reading
them aloud together so that you can hear the proper forms. Here are a
few combinations to start you off: *was spoken, may have spoken, can be spoken,
had been spoken.*

C. (1) Write five original sentences, using *spoke* and *spoken* properly. To
get ideas for your sentences, think about conversations that you have had
recently with friends or members of your family. (2) Read your sentences
aloud in your small groups. (3) Call on classmates to identify any auxiliary
verbs. Listen to hear the standard forms.

Spot Review

(Based upon the sentences in A *of the preceding activities)*

1. Why is *Mother* capitalized in sentence 1 and not in sentence 2?
2. How would you write the plural of the name in sentence 3? in
   sentence 4?
3. Account for the apostrophe in sentence 5.
4. Account for the capitals and the commas in sentence 7.

USING IRREGULAR VERBS—<u>BEGIN</u>, <u>BEGAN</u>, <u>BEGUN</u>

RULE. Always use an auxiliary verb with *begun;* **never use one with** *began.*

Today I **begin**.   Yesterday I **began**.   Often I *have* **begun**.

LEARNING ACTIVITIES

A. Write these sentences, filling the blanks with the proper form of *begin*. Underline twice (1) the form that you use and (2) any helping verbs. Read the sentences aloud in class as often as needed to make the proper forms sound natural. Do not write in this book.

1. Work has finally _____ on the new building.
2. We _____ the long trip back to the ranch at 9:30 A.M.
3. Both women's vacations _____ yesterday.
4. Who _____ this argument?
5. The program must not have _____ on time.
6. The Joneses _____ their trip last week.
7. Our club was _____ as a class activity.
8. Early last Thanksgiving morning a heavy rain _____.
9. Has the new schedule _____ yet?
10. Wars are usually _____ for selfish reasons.

B. Here is oral practice in using *began* and *begun*. (1) Go around the class, saying and completing this sentence: "Yesterday I began . . ." Each ending must be different and must make sense. (2) Repeat the process, only this time complete the following question: "Have you begun . . . ?"

C. Write five sentences similar to those in *A*. Perhaps your hobbies, your pastimes, or your school activities will give you ideas for your sentences. Exchange papers and read the sentences orally, supplying *began* or *begun*. Listen closely to hear whether the standard forms are chosen.

D. Practice the following activity in pairs. (1) Make up a sentence using *began*. (2) Your partner must change the sentence to use *begun*. (3) Then he or she will make up a sentence using *began*, which you must change to use *begun*. (4) Continue this until the proper forms sound right to you.

★   **Spot Review**

(Based upon the sentences in A *of the preceding activities)*

1. Account for the colon and the periods in sentence 2.
2. Explain the location of the apostrophe in sentence 3.
3. Explain the spelling of the proper noun in sentence 6.
4. In sentence 8, why is *Thanksgiving* capitalized?

298

USING IRREGULAR VERBS — <u>SEE</u>, <u>SAW</u>, <u>SEEN</u>

RULE. Always use an auxiliary verb with *seen;* **never use one with**
saw.

Today I **see.**   Yesterday I **saw.**   Often I *have* **seen.**

LEARNING ACTIVITIES

A. (1) Write these sentences, filling the blanks with the proper form of
see. (2) Underline twice the form that you use and any helping verbs.
(3) Proofread for careless mistakes in copying. (4) Read the sentences
aloud to get used to hearing the standard forms.

1. Yesterday I _____ a good new television program.
2. Haven't you _____ that man before?
3. You must have _____ my little sister Lurlene.
4. On his way to school this morning, James _____ two gray squirrels.
5. Who _____ you at last night's game?
6. We've never _____ most of these out-of-the-way places before.
7. My neighbor, Mr. Black, _____ a strange sight last week.
8. Hasn't Marissa ever _____ a circus?
9. Last New Year's Day I _____ an exciting parade.
10. The votes were not _____ by any of us candidates.

B. In an oral activity, complete the following sentences. (1) Use *saw* if
no helping verbs are given; otherwise use *seen.* (2) Add at least three other
words to make a good sentence. (3) Repeat the activity until everyone has
given at least two proper sentences. Speak distinctly; be sure, for example,
that you say "must *have*," not "must *of*" or "must *uh.*"

1. Somebody in that crowd must have . . .
2. As a matter of fact, nobody . . .
3. Have you ever . . .
4. On our trip through Texas, we . . .
5. According to the police report, only one person . . .
6. Even a careless driver surely would have . . .
7. Before her visit to Chicago, Paula had not . . .
8. In my opinion, no one could have . . .

C. (1) Take turns telling about something that you saw this morning on
the way to school. To give your sentences variety, tell *where.*

EXAMPLE: "I saw a sports car parked by the bank."

(2) See how many combinations of helping verbs and *seen* you can name.
Have these written on the board. Remember to include combinations containing *be, being,* or *been;* for example, *can be seen, are being seen, had been
seen.*

D. Write five sentences using *saw* and *seen* properly. Write about things that you once saw and about things that you have seen often. Make your sentences interesting. Read sentences aloud in your small groups. Listen carefully to hear the standard forms.

E. Do this activity with a partner. Ask a question using *seen*. Your partner must answer using *saw*. Then he or she will ask you a question using *seen*, which you must answer using *saw*. Practice until the proper forms really sound natural to you.

★   **Spot Review**

(Based upon the sentences in A *of the preceding activities)*

1. How would you write the plural of the proper noun in sentence 4?
2. Explain the use of the hyphens in sentence 6.
3. What is the reason for the commas in sentence 7?
4. Which sentences contain contractions? What do they stand for?

USING IRREGULAR VERBS — CHOOSE, CHOSE, CHOSEN

RULE. **Always use an auxiliary verb with** *chosen;* **never use one with** *chose.*

Today I choose.   Yesterday I chose.   Often I *have* chosen.

LEARNING ACTIVITIES

A. (1) Copy these sentences, supplying either *chose* or *chosen* and adding at least three other words to make interesting sentences. (2) Underline the verb twice, including any auxiliary verbs. (3) Proofread to catch careless errors. (4) Read the sentences aloud in class.

1. New officers for our club will not be . . .
2. A new president was . . .
3. For the first time in my life, I . . .
4. The members of the picnic committee have not yet . . .
5. Last night the team . . .
6. According to that traffic sign, we should have . . .
7. The poster winners will be . . .
8. On the spur of the moment, Jerry . . .
9. You could not have . . .
10. At that moment new members were being . . .

B. Write five sentences, using *chose* three times and *chosen* twice. Read the sentences aloud in your small groups. As you read, the other members of the group should listen and then jot down *Standard* or *Nonstandard* for each sentence. Afterward, compare notes to see how well you agreed. Have doubtful sentences read again to see who was right.

C. Do this activity with a partner. Make up a sentence using the past form of *choose*. Your partner must change the sentence to use the past participle. Then he or she will make up a sentence using the past, which you must change to the past participle.

Chapter Review*

A. Copy the following sentences, underlining each verb twice. Some of the verbs are one-word verbs; some of the verbs have two or more words. In some sentences the verb parts are separated. Some sentences are questions. Read carefully. Do not write in this book.

1. The organ grinder has a monkey.
2. Three planes have flown over our house today.
3. What is Amanda building in the basement?
4. The actors had been studying their parts for weeks.
5. Has your brother ever been given a part in a play?
6. The rain must not have soaked into the ground.
7. Where did Mother go to college?
8. June's new fishing pole was almost lost in the pond.
9. Hasn't Betty told you the way to the library?
10. Father must not have been ready for dinner.
11. Mince pie couldn't have been his favorite dessert.
12. Does your bicycle have balloon tires?
13. The other car was a red convertible.
14. Where might they have gone for help?
15. Bob has not been studying in his usual corner.

B. Go over these sentences, choosing the proper forms from the parentheses. Read the sentences aloud in your small groups. Listen to hear the standard forms.

1. Have you (spoke, spoken) to Henry yet?
2. I (saw, seen) the accident happen.
3. We should have (begun, began) the meeting on time.
4. What have you (did, done) with the paper?
5. New officers will be (chose, chosen) today.
6. Have you (knew, known) Ms. White long?
7. The show (began, begun) exactly on time.
8. The vase had been (chose, chosen) for the occasion.
9. Spanish is (spoke, spoken) in Mexico.

* Check Test 2 should be taken at this point. If the results show need for further study, students should do this review practice. They should then take Mastery Test 2.

10. Father would have (knew, known) the answer.
11. Maybe the game has not yet (began, begun).
12. Who (did, done) the work on this ship model?
13. Frank could have (spoke, spoken) more clearly.
14. You should have (did, done) something about this request.
15. Roberta (knew, knowed) me a long time ago.
16. Has anyone (saw, seen) Zelda this morning?
17. Susan was (chose, chosen) as class representative.
18. The rain must have (began, begun) during the night.

★ **Cumulative Review**

CAPITALIZATION

Copy these sentences, supplying needed capital letters.

1. Is it true that lindblom high school of chicago, illinois, is the only high school in the middle west to play football in the south?
2. Whenever grandfather comes to our house, mother gets out his favorite book, *the adventures of huckleberry finn.* he likes to sit in the sun just south of the lilac bush and read.
3. Last august mr. i. r. smith, who teaches french and latin in our high school, and coach lambert took a trip to georgian bay.
4. That little store on garnett street is now owned by mrs. j. jones. She calls it jones's general store.
5. He spoke at great length about the history of saudi arabia.

PUNCTUATION

Copy these sentences, supplying needed punctuation.

1. No the Cincinnati Reds didnt lose the World Series in 1976
2. Have you Dick ever heard of Dr Margaret Mead What an exciting life she has led
3. Frieda said that she saw a ship flying a blue yellow and white flag off Miami Florida on June 12 1977
4. In stormy weather Mrs P A Bailey always wears her hip boots
5. The coach exclaimed Al thinks fast makes few errors but cant hit

SPELLING

Copy the following words in a column on a sheet of paper. Beside each word write another word made from it by adding a suffix or ending. These words are spelled by rules.

1. beat	4. time	7. pity	10. cool	13. easy
2. carry	5. swat	8. bake	11. step	14. use
3. enter	6. healthy	9. warn	12. begin	15. fit

Word Games to Test Your Thinking

Get the Hint

All the words defined below rhyme with *hint*.

1. Place where money is coined
2. To spring or leap
3. To close the eyes partly
4. A thin strip of wood
5. To form letters
6. Flash or gleam
7. Fluff of any material
8. One of five identical children
9. Color
10. Stone used in arrowheads

Would You Like to Know—?

Find the answers the encyclopedia gives to the following questions.

1. What causes the humming that gives the *hummingbird* its name?
2. Is the *hawk* related to the eagle?
3. How did the *Hessian fly* get its name?
4. What is unusual about the legs of the *hyena?*

Beheading Puzzle—A City in Indiana

Replace each pair of italicized definitions with two words that rhyme. Then "behead" the first word in each pair; that is, remove the first letter. The ten letters you have removed will spell the name of a city in Indiana.

EXAMPLE: Behead *not happy* and leave *a public notice.* (*sad—ad;* the letter would be *s*)

1. Behead *to run away to get married* and leave *an easy stride.*
2. Behead *valleys* and leave *light-colored beers.*
3. Behead *nearly* and leave *a boxing match.*
4. Behead *at no time* and leave *at all times.*
5. Behead *a backless seat for one person* and leave *an instrument.*
6. Behead *sells* and leave *finishes.*
7. Behead *a standard of perfection* and leave *to distribute cards.*
8. Behead *a shelf-like projection* and leave *a border or margin.*
9. Behead *to gain knowledge* and leave *to gain by labor.*
10. Behead *a hard, heavy wood* and leave *consisting chiefly of bone.*

A Word Square

Each of the definitions below can be written as a four-letter word. Placed one under another, the words will spell the same down as across.

1. A sharp nail on the foot of an animal
2. A citrus fruit
3. The close of a prayer
4. Past tense of *go*

A "Lucky" Crossword Puzzle

Copy the crossword puzzle. Do not write in this book.

Across

1. A U-shaped lucky piece.
9. Fifteen ____'s for the team.
10. ____s grow from acorns.
12. Look ____ me.
14. A ____ in your shoe for luck.
16. Virginia (*abbr.*).
17. A bloodhound is ____-eared.
19. A ____ is man's best friend.
20. Nickname for *Mildred*.
21, 23. ____ ____ clover.
24. Furrow made by vehicles.
25. The wrong kind of luck.
26. Baking-part of a stove.
29. To go by something.
32. Atmosphere.
33. A ship's distress signal.
35. Allow.
36. Rhode Island (*abbr.*).
37. Opening in a fence (*plural*).
39. ____ and fro.
40. Girl's name — mixed up *Nan*.
41. At or near the middle.
43. Happiness birds.

Down

2. Either you ____ I.
3. To knock.
4. A rude structure built for shelter, storage, etc.
5. That which is sung.
6. Cut and dried grass.
7. Okay (*abbr.*).
8. Offspring of a cow.
11. One of two equal parts.
13. Also.
15. Negative word.
16. By way of.
18. ____ than the driven snow.
20. A flat piece of metal given as an award.
22. Present tense of *ran*.
23. Take up liquid with the tongue.
26. Rowing implements.
27. Lucky number (*Roman numerals*).
28. A small bed.
30. To place.
31. Halt.
33. Of sound mind.
34. Prefix meaning *half*.
37. African antelope.
38. A title of respect used in addressing a man.
40. Man's nickname.
42. Doctor of Divinity (*abbr.*).

USING NOUNS IN BUILDING SENTENCES*

1. Recognizing Nouns

"CAN YOU THINK OF SOME NOUNS?"

"NOW'N' THEN I SWIM.
NOW'N' THEN I PLAY BALL.
NOW'N' THEN I WATCH
TELEVISION."

THINK IT OVER . . .

What do *you* know about nouns?

You have learned that a verb is one of the two most important parts of speech that you use. The other is the *noun*. You will learn other parts of speech as you study this book.

* Pretest 3 should be taken at this point.

● THESE ARE FACTS ABOUT NOUNS*: I

1. **(DEFINITION)** *Nouns* are "name" **words. They meet certain tests:**

   a) **A noun fits into one or both of these "slot" sentences:**

   > She wrote something about _____.
   > She wrote something about a (an) _____.

   EXAMPLES: She wrote something about **money**.
   > She wrote something about a **friend**.
   > She wrote something about an **island**.

   b) **A noun can change its form to show plural number:**

   house, house**s**   box, box**es**   man, m**e**n

   c) **A noun can take special words before it:**

a book	**some** idea	**ten** cars	**my** luck
the news	**any** day	**that** face	**this** job

   Such words are known as *determiners.* You will study them in Chapter 20 and Chapter 21.

2. **The nouns easiest to recognize name** (1) PERSONS, **such as** *girl, tailor;* (2) PLACES, **such as** *school, church, town, farm;* **or** (3) THINGS, **such as** *book, dog, table, pie, tree.*

   NOTE: The part of speech of a word is determined by the way that it is used. For instance, *hit* is sometimes a verb:

   > The boy *hit* the ball. [*Hit* shows action.]

   But in this sentence, *hit* is used as a noun:

   > His *hit* was a double. [*Hit* is the name of something.]

LEARNING ACTIVITIES

A. List all the nouns in this paragraph. Exchange papers for checking.

Four playful dogs, followed by a crowd of laughing children, ran out of the yard. Each boy carried a box or a parcel, and each girl had an empty pail or a basket. These young people were going to the woods to gather walnuts. The boys were carrying the lunch. The merry party entered the woods, laughing and shouting. Even the dogs seemed excited, chasing squirrels and chipmunks through the trees.

---

* For information about possessive nouns, see page 236.

B. In an oral activity, tell how you know that the italicized "nonsense" words in the following sentences are used as nouns.

1. The *flibbider* gave us some *calooches.*
2. *Rikbligs* usually like a *gruggle* on their *smirzes.*
3. The first *prokle* made some *zilzies* out of a *bamgan.*

C. Go over these sentences in class, deciding whether each italicized word is a noun or a verb.

1. The *park* is not open today.
2. Where did you *park* the car?
3. *Face* the class as you talk.
4. Jack's *face* was covered with mud.
5. Shall we *run* to school?
6. That *run* won the game for us.
7. The *match* burned my fingers.
8. Your shoes and mine *match.*
9. Do your parents *baby* you?
10. The *baby* soon went to sleep.
11. Do you need *help* with your homework?
12. When will you *help* me hang this picture?
13. Listen closely and you can hear the *murmur* of the brook.
14. When you *murmur,* we cannot understand your words.

D. Write sentences using each of the following words, first as a verb and then as a noun: *work, ring, fight, train, change.* Compare work in class or in your small groups.

E. Copy the following paragraph, filling each blank with a noun. Read your paragraphs in class. Note how differently they turned out!

As soon as I knew that I was alone, I opened the _____. Inside, I found some surprising things. One of the strangest was a _____ with a _____ on one end. Near it were three shiny _____ decorated with little _____. I was about to open one of them when I heard a _____ behind me. I turned around and saw two huge _____ with _____ in their _____. They gave me a _____, took my _____, and then disappeared through the _____.

LEARNING MORE ABOUT NOUNS

Most nouns are easy to recognize because they name things that you can see or touch. Other nouns may be more difficult to recognize because they name less obvious things such as events and ideas.

3. **Some nouns name things that you cannot see, touch, smell, or hear:** *honesty, happiness, beauty, courage, loyalty,* **for example.**

4. **Most nouns can be classed as** *count nouns;* **that is, they can be counted:** *one book, two books, many books.* **Some nouns, however, are** *mass nouns;* **they are not ordinarily countable.** *Spinach* is an example, for you are not likely to say *one spinach.*

   Use the words *a* (or *an*) and *many* to test whether a word is a mass noun. If they do not fit before the word, you have a mass noun. Would you say, for example, "a spinach"? "many spinach (*or* spinaches)"? No; therefore, *spinach* is a mass noun.

5. **Each noun covered by points 1 and 2, page 306, is called a** *common noun,* **because it refers to** *any* **member in its general group. Words that name** *special* **members of a general group are** *proper nouns.* (To review their capitalization, see page 220.)

COMMON NOUNS	PROPER NOUNS
girl	Martha
organization	Scouting/U.S.A.
street	Magee Street
city	Jefferson City

Learn about words!

The following words, taken from Learning Activities *A* and *B,* have interesting histories. Use your dictionary to find the story behind each word.

pizza   barn   chair   yacht

LEARNING ACTIVITIES

A. All words in the following list are nouns. Copy the ones naming things that you cannot see, touch, smell, or hear. Exchange papers for checking.

1. apple	6. kindness	11. simplicity	16. blanket
2. strength	7. cowardice	12. radio	17. tool
3. wickedness	8. bravery	13. duty	18. chair
4. telephone	9. star	14. freedom	19. fun
5. barn	10. sunrise	15. snow	20. yacht

B. Make two columns on your paper. Label one column *Count Nouns;* the other, *Mass Nouns.* By applying the tests with *a, an,* and *many,* put each noun in these sentences into the correct column. Compare lists in class.

1. The music to that song was composed by my uncle.
2. Every farmer in our community harvested a large crop of wheat.
3. Lightning struck the building but did no damage to the machinery inside.
4. With the money, the girl bought a new tire for her bicycle.
5. My sister would like celery on the table at every meal.
6. Scenery along this road gives a person a chance to use a camera.
7. Was this rice cooked in milk or in water?
8. To many people, grass is always greener on the other side of the fence.
9. My cousin had little luck with her latest scientific experiment.
10. His favorite food was spaghetti but now is pizza.

C. Here are quotations from famous authors. (1) Take turns at reading the lines aloud. (2) Call upon someone to name the nouns in the lines read. (3) The listeners should be ready to comment on the reading.

1. The day is done, and the darkness
     Falls from the wings of Night,
   As a feather is wafted downward
     From an eagle in his flight. — HENRY WADSWORTH LONGFELLOW
2. The brightest blade grows dim with rust,
   The fairest meadow white with snow. — OLIVER WENDELL HOLMES
3. Earth hath more silver, pearls, and gold,
   Than eyes can see, or hands can hold. — ANNE BRADSTREET
4. Small feet were pattering, wooden shoes clattering,
   Little hands clapping and little tongues chattering,
   And, like fowls in a farmyard when barley is scattering,
   Out came the children running. — ROBERT BROWNING
5. The ground gripped my feet and my heart was circled by icy walls
   of fear. — RICHARD WRIGHT*
6. All in a hot and copper sky,
     The bloody sun, at noon,
   Right up above the mast did stand,
     No bigger than the moon. — SAMUEL TAYLOR COLERIDGE
7. And on the bay the moonlight lay,
   And the shadow of the moon. — SAMUEL TAYLOR COLERIDGE
8. My life is like a faded leaf,
     My harvest dwindled to a husk. — CHRISTINA ROSSETTI

---

* From "Between the World and Me," by Richard Wright. Copyright 1935 by *Partisan Review.* Reprinted by permission of Paul R. Reynolds, Inc. 599 Fifth Avenue, New York, New York 10017.

Choose one of the nouns named as examples in point 3, page 308. Write a paragraph explaining what that particular word means to you. The Guides for Writing a Paragraph, page 162, will help you.

2. Using Nouns As Subjects

"OH, NO! MARIA, NOT MAVIS, HIT A HOME RUN IN THAT GAME."

"THERE YOU GO—ALWAYS TRYING TO CHANGE THE SUBJECT!"

SUBJECTS AND PREDICATES

Every sentence has a subject and a predicate, as you learned on page 275 of Chapter 17. The *simple subject* is the word that tells *who* or *what* the sentence is about. The *simple predicate* is the *verb*, the word that says what the subject *is* or *does*.

The twins sang.

Who or *what* sang? *twins* (*Twins* is the subject.) What did the twins *do*? *sang* (*Sang* is the verb.)

The *complete subject* is all the words in the sentence that together tell who or what the sentence is about. The *complete predicate* is all the words that together tell what the subject is or does.

complete subject	complete predicate

The red-headed twins sang loudly on the camp bus.

LEARNING ACTIVITIES

A. (1) Have the headings *Subject* and *Verb* put on the board. (2) Go over the following sentences in class. Locate the verb first; write it under the verb heading. Then ask, "*Who* or *what* ... ?" to locate the subject (simple subject); write it under the subject heading.

EXAMPLE: The porpoise tossed the ball.

Subject	Verb
porpoise	tossed

1. My younger brother is a Cub Scout.
2. The heavy snow blocked the road past our farm.
3. My best friend moved away.
4. Our doctor performed an operation.
5. Irene helped with the plans for the Halloween party.
6. The wind howled around the corners of the house.
7. Most people like this town.
8. Beautiful flowers bloomed in the meadow.
9. My favorite uncle comes to our house often.
10. A terrible storm raged through the valley.
11. The cats went into the house.
12. This letter arrived before breakfast.

B. Copy the following sentences, underlining with one line the *simple subject* and with two lines the *simple predicate*. Exchange papers for checking.

1. Tickets for the operetta will go on sale tomorrow.
2. Both boys build model trains.
3. My dog has very good manners.
4. The students from our room walked slowly down the stairs.
5. Mr. Baker bought two dozen oranges.
6. The horses climbed slowly to the top of the mountain.
7. Martha was playing shuffleboard with three friends.
8. Lucia took her little sister Patty to the basketball game.
9. That woman is an electrical engineer.
10. Sharon went with her father to the Metropolitan Opera.

C. If you missed any of the verbs and subjects in *B*, use *C* and *D*, pages 280–281, for more practice. (1) Copy the sentences. (2) Underline each verb with two lines and each subject with one line. (3) Exchange papers for checking.

FOLLOW-UP

Write an original paragraph to show that you know how to use verbs and subjects in sentences. (1) Choose a topic from any that you have listed in your notebook or one suggested by the drawing on this page. Use at least six sentences. The Guides for Writing a Paragraph, page 162, will help you. (2) Exchange papers with a partner. (3) In the paragraph that you receive, underline each verb with two lines and each subject with one line. Call attention to errors in spelling, capitalization, and punctuation as well. (4) Go over your paper with the one who checked it.

MORE ABOUT SUBJECTS AND PREDICATES

The normal sentence order in the English language has the subject followed by the verb. Not all sentences, however, are so arranged. If they were, the English language would be far less interesting. The following points will help you find the subject in sentences that do not follow normal order.

● **THESE ARE FACTS ABOUT SUBJECTS AND PREDICATES**

1. **Sometimes a sentence will be turned around. Such a sentence is said to be in "inverted order."**

    Down the street ran the little white dog.

    The rule for finding the subject still holds.

    a) Find the verb. It is a doing word, *ran*.
    b) Ask, "*Who* or *what* ran?" *Dog* ran; so *dog* is the subject.

2. **Sometimes a sentence is a question.** (For help with finding the verb in a question, review point 14, page 285.)

    Is Jane going with us?

    In this sentence the verb is *is going*. *Who* or *what* is going? *Jane* is going; so *Jane* is the subject.

3. **Sometimes a sentence begins with an introductory** *there*. Do not be fooled into thinking that it is the subject.

    There has been a change in our plans.

    The verb is *has been*. *Who* or *what* has been? *Change* has been; so *change* is the subject.

4. **Sometimes a sentence that is not a question may have words separating the parts of a verb.** (For help with finding the verb when the parts are separated, see point 13 on page 285.)

    The boys have not yet finished their work.

    The verb is *have finished*. *Who* or *what* have finished? *Boys* have finished; so *boys* is the subject.

5. **Sometimes words separate the subject and the verb.**

    A box of Jonathan apples came today.

    The verb is *came*. *Who* or *what* came? At first you might say *apples*. If you stop to think about it, you will realize that what came is a *box*, although it is true that the box had apples in it. Therefore *box* is the subject.*

---

* "Of Jonathan apples" is the kind of word group called a *prepositional phrase.* You will study such phrases on pages 425–433.

LEARNING ACTIVITIES

A. The sentences in this activity are like those just described. Remember that if the verb has two words, the first will be a helping verb. If it has three or more words, all but the last of them will be helping verbs. Any verb after the helping verbs will be a doing verb. The figure in parentheses tells how many words the verb has. (1) Copy the sentences, underlining each verb with two lines and each subject with one line. (2) Proofread for careless errors in copying. (3) Exchange papers for checking. (4) Go over the sentences orally.

1. Near the end of September came several bad storms. (1)
2. Has Alfred been doing good work? (3)
3. The Bernsteins were not expecting visitors. (2)
4. The carpenter accidentally left a keg of nails on the doorstep. (1)
5. There may be a slight delay. (2)
6. The wind had just died down. (2)
7. Near a little wooden cabin on rugged Bear Mountain lived two tame squirrels. (1)
8. How can the Girl Scouts raise money for their camp? (2)
9. A box of books was lying on the teacher's desk. (2)
10. The Browns have often visited Yellowstone Park. (2)
11. In *The Animal World* there are two chapters about snakes. (1)
12. A gift of flowers pleases most people. (1)
13. Does your school have a holiday before the end of the month? (2)
14. Which detective finally solved this case? (1)
15. The committee has just set the time for the picnic. (2)
16. Hasn't the mother of those boys bought a new car? (2)
17. On the table lay the tickets to the game. (1)
18. Did your friend play soccer in college? (2)
19. Those three albums of records must have pleased Ms. Scott very much. (3)
20. There might be a good reason for Joe's absence. (2)

B. If you need more practice in selecting verbs and subjects, use the sentences in *A* and *B*, page 286. Make this an oral activity.

★ **Spot Review**

(*Based upon the sentences in* A *of the preceding activities*)

1. Why is *September* capitalized in sentence 1? Why is *Girl Scouts* capitalized in sentence 8?
2. Why is *The Animal World* italicized in sentence 11?
3. Account for the apostrophe in sentence 9.

USING ENGLISH IN ALL CLASSES

Look over papers that you have written for other classes. Do all the sentences have the subject first and then the verb? If they have, change a few of them so that the verb will come before the subject. Then read your papers in your small groups to see whether your classmates think the changes are an improvement.

3. Recognizing <u>Pattern 1</u> Sentences

As explained in Chapter 17, English is a patterned language. There you saw examples of the five sentence patterns you will study in this book.

In this lesson you will study *Pattern 1* sentences.

● **THESE ARE FACTS ABOUT** *PATTERN 1* **SENTENCES**

1. *Pattern 1* **sentences need only a** *subject* **and a** *verb.*

EXAMPLES: Plants grow.   Rain fell.   Fish swim.

2. *Pattern 1* **sentences fit this formula:** **N** *(noun)* + **V** *(verb).*

  N + V   N + V   N   +   V
Plants grow.   Rain fell.   Accidents happen.

3. A *Pattern 1* **sentence may have other words in it.**

  N   +   V
EXAMPLE: Many tall **plants grow** in our garden.

LEARNING ACTIVITY

Fill out the following *Pattern 1* sentences with details about the subject, the verb, or both. Keep the **N** + **V** pattern, however. Compare sentences in class or in your small groups.

EXAMPLE: Rain fell.
  A soaking rain fell *here just after midnight.*

1. The ice melted.   3. Days passed.   5. The faucet dripped.
2. Visitors arrived.   4. Thunder boomed.

DIAGRAMMING VERBS AND SUBJECTS*

A doctor analyzes a case of sickness; a detective analyzes a criminal case; a chemist analyzes drugs. If you want to feel sure about your speaking and writing, you should be able to analyze the sentences that you use. One way to analyze a sentence is to make a *diagram* of it.

As you go on with your study of grammar, you can learn how to diagram all the words in the sentences that you study. For the present, you need work only with the two necessary parts of any sentence: the *verb* and the *subject*.

Steps in Diagramming Verbs and Subjects

The following example shows the basic steps for diagramming verbs and subjects.

SENTENCE: "The porpoise tossed the ball." *Tossed* is the verb. *Porpoise* is the subject.

1. Draw a straight line, like this:

2. On the right-hand half, write the verb.

3. Draw a vertical line before the verb, extending the line through the horizontal line.

4. Write the subject in front of the vertical line.

Look now at another sentence: "A new house will be built across the street." What is the verb? *Will be built.* Put it into a diagram. *Who* or *what* will be built? *House* will be built; so *hous* is the subject. Put it into the diagram.

---

* This section and all the following sections on diagramming can be used as a supplement to the teaching done earlier in the chapter. These sections on diagramming are so placed that they may be omitted without disturbing the sequence of instruction.

You have found and named the most important words in the sentence. Now look at another sentence, one that expresses a request: "Help me." In this sentence no subject is named. Who is supposed to do the *helping*? It is the person to whom the speaker is talking, that is, *you.* When *you* is the subject, but is not actually named, the subject is said to be "understood." A diagram of a sentence with an understood *you* as the subject looks like this:

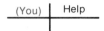

LEARNING ACTIVITIES

A. (1) Diagram the verb and the subject in the sentences that follow. Always find the verb *first.* (2) After you have diagrammed the verbs and subjects on paper, put the diagrams on the board. Explain the diagrams in some regular form: "The verb in this sentence is *tossed,* and the subject is a noun, *porpoise.*" Form the habit of using a definite pattern for explaining diagrams. Always go over diagrams orally.

1. Then Tanya ran rapidly down the street.
2. The wind has been blowing hard.
3. The early settlers traveled in covered wagons.
4. The captives were taken to the bandit leader.
5. Four small children were playing in the park on Elm Street.
6. My Uncle Sebastian has returned from Canada.
7. This team should win handily.
8. The roses were blooming in every garden.
9. Our club will meet in the new clubhouse.
10. Five pictures hung on the walls of the room.

B. For further practice in sentence analysis, diagram the verbs and subjects in the sentences in *A,* page 311.

Diagramming Other Arrangements of Verbs and Subjects

In the sentences that you have been diagramming, (1) the verb parts are not separated, and (2) the verb comes immediately after the subject. On page 313 you saw five other arrangements of verbs and subjects. Whatever the arrangement of the verb and subject in a sentence may be, the pattern of the verb and the subject in a diagram always looks the same. Study the sentences and diagrams that follow.

Down the street came Helga.   Is Naomi going with us?

```
Helga | came                    Naomi | Is going
——————+——————                  ——————+—————————
      |                               |
```

There was silence in the room.

```
There        silence | was
—————————    ————————+——————
                      |
```

(Since *there* is only an introductory word, it is diagrammed separately.)

The Lombardis have not yet left.   The box of apples has come.

```
Lombardis | have left                   box | has come
——————————+——————————                  —————+——————————
          |                                  |
```

LEARNING ACTIVITIES

A. (1) Diagram verbs and subjects in the sentences that follow. If you need help in locating subjects, review points 1–5 on page 313. (2) Have the diagrams put on the board. (3) Go over the diagrams orally, explaining in this way: "The verb in the sentence is *came*, and the subject is a noun, *Helga*."

1. Where was Emilio going with that package?
2. Over the hill came the parade.
3. There will be a short intermission.
4. This bushel of peaches should be canned at once.
5. A bucket of sand was put into the trunk of the car.
6. Will the club help with the plans for the rally?
7. Near the tree sat two gray squirrels.
8. The bark of both trees had been scarred by lightning.
9. Where did the girls go after school?
10. The plumbers have almost finished the repairs.
11. The days of the week pass rapidly.
12. Up the hill ran the cadets.
13. Most members of our class listen carefully.
14. There has been a change in our plans.
15. Does Miranda play badminton?

B. (1) Diagram each verb and subject in *A*, page 314. Be sure to find the verb first. (2) Exchange papers. (3) Put the diagrams on the board. (4) Go over the diagrams orally.

4. Using Compound Verbs and Subjects

● THESE ARE FACTS ABOUT COMPOUND VERBS
AND SUBJECTS

1. **The subject of a sentence may have more than one verb.**
(DEFINITION) **When the subject has two or more verbs, the sentence is said to have a** *compound verb.*

> The *porpoise* **tossed** the ball and **leaped** for its reward.
> The *children* **swam, fished,** and **rode** their bicycles.

2. **The verb in a sentence may have more than one subject.**
(DEFINITION) **When the verb has two or more subjects, the sentence is said to have a** *compound subject.*

> **Hector** or **Lallie** *will do* the dishes.
> The **girls,** their **mother,** and their **uncle** *went* to the game.

3. **A sentence may have both a compound verb and a compound subject.**

> Ann and Idabell stopped and stared.

4. **In a** *Pattern 1* **sentence that has compound parts, the labels will be repeated.**

> Many days and nights came and went.

LEARNING ACTIVITIES

A. (1) Copy the following paragraph. (2) Draw two lines under each part of a compound verb and one line under each part of a compound subject. (3) Exchange papers for checking. Do not write in this book.

> The dog and the cat stood and glared at each other. Which enemy would strike first? Suddenly the cat raised its paw and swung. In a flash Penny turned and raced away. Now the cat crept up and teased Penny again. Penny seemingly paid no attention but suddenly sprang. Round went cat and dog in a fierce struggle. Finally the cat pulled away, dashed up the nearest tree, and was safe. Penny barked angrily for a time but then slunk off. Again, a cat had baffled her.

B. (1) Write ten sentences of your own in which you use compound subjects and compound verbs. (2) Exchange papers. (3) Proofread first for careless errors on the paper you receive. (4) Underline the compound verbs twice and the compound subjects once. (5) Correct any mistakes on your own paper when it has been returned.

ENRICHMENT

Here are quotations from Henry Wadsworth Longfellow's long poem *Hiawatha*. Many of them have compound verbs or subjects; all are in inverted order. The poet has used inverted order to give emphasis to a word or to achieve rhythm. Read the quotations aloud; then restate each one in normal sentence order. Note how they sound much less rhythmical.

1. Round about the Indian village
   Spread the meadows and the cornfields.
2. On the air about him wildly
   Tossed and streamed his cloudy tresses.
3. Then up started Hiawatha,
   And with threatening look and gesture
   Laid his hand upon the black rock.
4. Like a ring of fire around him
   Blazed and fired the red horizon.
5. Down into that darksome cavern
   Plunged the headlong Hiawatha.
6. Weltering in the bloody water,
   Dead lay all the fiery serpents.
7. Winged with feathers, tipped with jasper,
   Swift flew Hiawatha's arrow.
8. At the feet of Hiawatha
   Lifeless lay the great Pearl-Feather.
9. In the Northland lived a hunter,
   With ten young and comely daughters.
10. On their pathway through the woodlands
    Lay an oak, by storms uprooted.
11. On the border of the forest,
    Underneath the fragrant pine trees,
    Sat the old men and the warriors
    Smoking in the pleasant shadow.
12. From the memory of the old men
    Pass away the great traditions,
    The achievements of the warriors,
    The adventures of the hunters.
13. Fearing not the Evil Spirits,
    Forth to hunt the deer with antlers
    All alone went Chibiabos.
14. Then in swift pursuit departed
    Hiawatha and the hunters
    On the trail of Pau-Puk-Keewis.
15. Through the forest, wide and wailing,
    Roamed the hunter on his snowshoes.
16. Homeward then went Hiawatha
    To the lodge of old Nokomis.

DIAGRAMMING COMPOUND SUBJECTS AND VERBS

In diagramming compound subjects and verbs, each part of the compound should be put on a separate line. The conjunction should be written on the line joining the compound elements.

COMPOUND SUBJECT

Hector or *Lallie* will do the dishes.

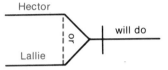

The *girls*, their *mother*, and their *uncle* went to the game.

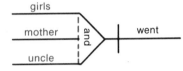

COMPOUND VERB

The porpoise *tossed* the ball and *leaped* for its reward.

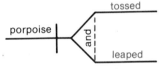

The children *swam, fished,* and *rode* their bicycles.

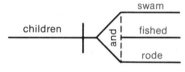

COMPOUND SUBJECT AND COMPOUND VERB

Ann and *Idabell* **stopped** and **stared.**

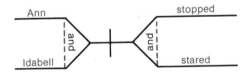

LEARNING ACTIVITIES

A. (1) Diagram the subjects and the verbs in the following sentences. (2) After you have finished, put the diagrams on the board. (3) Explain each diagram orally in this way: "The verb is *will do;* the parts of the compound subject are the nouns *Hector* and *Lallie.*"

1. Jean sawed and hammered all day.
2. Haven't Roy and Harry left for the concert?
3. That private and her captain come from the same small town.
4. Deirdre or her brother cut the grass and trimmed the hedge.
5. Helen and Jack saw and heard the fire engine.

6. This motor bike runs like a dream and doesn't use much gas.
7. Up the mountain climbed the sheep and their shepherd.
8. The apples and the plums looked ripe and tasted delicious.
9. Hasn't Mother or Father seen your drawing?
10. The small cat and the dog ran outside.

B. On the board, diagram all the verbs and subjects in the sentences of the paragraph in *A,* page 319. Two of the sentences have neither compound subjects nor compound verbs. Go over each diagram orally.

★ **Spot Review**

(*Based upon the sentences in* A *of the preceding activities*)

1. Why are *captain* and *private* not capitalized in sentence 3?
2. Why are *Mother* and *Father* capitalized in sentence 9?
3. Explain the use of the apostrophes in sentences 2, 6, and 9.
4. How would you write the plurals of the subjects in sentence 2?

5. Using Nouns As Predicate Nominatives

On page 315, you studied *Pattern 1* sentences (N + V). In this lesson you will learn to recognize *Pattern 2* sentences, which are ones that have nouns used as *predicate nominatives.*

THESE ARE FACTS ABOUT PREDICATE NOMINATIVES

1. **People, animals, and things often have more than one name to explain or identify them, as in these examples.**

   Linda Mendoza is a **doctor.**
   Linda Mendoza is an excellent **surgeon.**
   Linda Mendoza is my **sister.**

   Note that each of the nouns in color follows the verb and is another name word applied to the subject, Linda Mendoza.

2. **(DEFINITION) A noun that follows the verb and renames the subject is a** *predicate nominative, or predicate noun.*

3. **(DEFINITION) Verbs that join a subject and a predicate nominative are called** *linking verbs.* **They are verbs of** (a) *being,* (b) *seeming,* **or** (c) *condition.* **The commonest linking verbs are** *am, is, are, was, were, be, being, become, seem, appear.*

   George Washington **was** our first *President.*
   Jimmy Carter **became** *President* in 1976.
   Glinka **seems** a friendly *puppy.*

4. **A sentence that has a predicate nominative is a** *Pattern 2* **sentence. The formula for it is N + LV + N.**

   Those two boys are cousins.
   $$N + LV + N$$

5. **Predicate nominatives may be compound.**

   My favorite desserts are **pie, cake,** and **ice cream.**
   The formula for that sentence is **N + LV + N, N, N.**

LEARNING ACTIVITIES

A. Going quickly around the room, have each person suggest a predicate nominative for one of the following four sentences. List on the board all the predicate nominatives suggested.

1. That dog is _____.
2. My friend was once _____.
3. That person must be _____.
4. My favorite song is _____.

B. (1) Copy the following sentences. (2) Put parentheses around each predicate nominative. (3) Go over each sentence orally in class, naming the verb and the subject and the predicate nominative.

1. Lewis Carroll is the author of *Alice's Adventures in Wonderland.*
2. Mr. Roberts has been our friend and neighbor for years.

3. Ms. Odette Devall may be our next principal.
4. Benedict Arnold became a traitor to his country.
5. Was the location of the mine a secret?
6. Iris will be the captain of the team.
7. The first arrivals at the party were Joe, Carmela, and Mitsuko.
8. Usually Mrs. Evans seems a happy person.
9. Abraham Lincoln became President in 1860.
10. The state flower of Texas is the bluebonnet.

DIAGRAMMING PREDICATE NOMINATIVES

You are ready now to learn where to put the predicate nominative in a diagram.

Natasha is my *sister*.

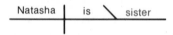

Notice that the predicate nominative is placed on the same line as the subject and the verb. This line you will think of as the *backbone* of any sentence, because it contains the really important words. Notice, too, that the line separating the predicate nominative from the verb is slanted. It points back to the subject to show that the predicate nominative means the same as the subject. The slanted line does not cross the base line.

Here are diagrams of *compound* predicate nominatives.

The winner will be *Lionel* or *Melba*.

Fruits in season now are *pears, peaches,* and *plums.*

LEARNING ACTIVITIES

A. Diagram verbs, subjects, and predicate nominatives in the following sentences. Put them on the board when you have finished. Go over the diagrams orally, giving each part its correct name.

1. That plant is an ivy.
2. Our best musicians are Domingo and Thea.
3. Llamas are the sheep of the Andes.
4. The first prize was a trip to Hawaii.
5. Gold is a valuable mineral.
6. Paul has been my friend for a long time.
7. The signal will be one blast of the whistle.
8. Was Mrs. Barnes ever a member of Congress?
9. Her favorite sports are baseball, golf, and track.
10. Greta could have been president of her class.

B. For further practice, use the sentences in *B*, pages 323–324. Explain the diagrams orally in your small groups.

6. Using Nouns As Direct Objects

The term *direct object* may be new to you. Nouns, you have learned, may be used as subjects of verbs and as predicate nominatives. Another common use of nouns is as objects of a verb, or *direct objects*,* as they are also called. They are found in *Pattern 4* sentences, which you will study in this lesson.

---

*The uses of nouns as objects of prepositions and as indirect objects are covered on pages 426 and 437.

The porpoise tossed the ball.

● THESE ARE FACTS ABOUT DIRECT OBJECTS

1. **(DEFINITION) A direct object receives the action of the verb or shows the result of its action.**

   The porpoise tossed the ball.   The plant sprouted leaves.

2. **To find the direct object in any sentence having an action verb, say the subject and the verb, followed by** *whom* **or** *what.* **The noun that answers the question is the direct object.**

   Porpoise **tossed** whom or what? ball
   Plant **sprouted** what? leaves

3. **If no word answers the question** *whom* **or** *what,* **you know that the sentence does not have a direct object.**

   The dog barked loudly.

   Loudly tells *how* the dog barked, not *what* it barked.

4. **(DEFINITION) A verb that has a direct object is a** *transitive** **verb.**

   The porpoise tossed the *ball.*   The plant sprouted *leaves.*

   "Tossed" and "sprouted" are *transitive* verbs.

---

*An advanced study of transitive and intransitive verbs is presented in later books of the Basic Language series.

5. A sentence with a direct object is a *Pattern 4* sentence. The formula is N + V + N.

N + V + N   N + V + N
Jim saves his money.   My sister likes her new job.

6. Direct objects may be compound.

Manuel raises **ducks** and **geese.**
Our team defeated **Wayne, Dixon, Laurel,** and **Tilden.**

The formula for the second example is **N + V + N, N, N, N.**

LEARNING ACTIVITIES

A. Copy the following sentences, supplying a direct object for each blank. Do not write in this book. In class, read your sentences orally. Note how the different direct objects change the sentence picture.

1. My little brother lost his _____.
2. Yesterday Amy found a _____.
3. Uncle Edward bought some _____.
4. The package contained a _____.
5. For her birthday Jan received some _____.
6. On his farm Mr. Jackson raises _____.

B. Locate the direct objects in the following sentences. Find the verb and the subject first. Then, so that you may be sure that you are selecting the right word, say the subject and the verb, followed by *whom* or *what.* Make this an oral exercise in your small groups.

1. The cat has hidden my silver thimble.
2. The book contained an index.
3. Mr. Jones bought a new tractor and a secondhand hayrack.
4. The burglar stole my typewriter.
5. Katherine Anne Porter wrote *Noon Wine.*
6. Mike baked beans, rolls, and a pie for dinner.
7. Johann Strauss composed many beautiful waltzes.
8. The athletes enjoyed their visit to Mexico.
9. Queen Victoria ruled England for sixty-four years.
10. Does this furnace burn gas?

C. (1) Write ten *Pattern 4* sentences of your own. Use compound objects in at least two sentences; write their formulas above them. You might write sentences having to do with your spare-time activities. (2) Exchange papers with a classmate and ask him or her to name each verb, subject, and direct object. (3) Discuss your papers with your partner.

D. For further drill in finding direct objects, use the sentences in *A*, page 314. Eight of them have no direct object. What is the pattern of those eight sentences? Make this an oral activity.

(Based upon the sentences in B of the preceding activities)

1. Explain the abbreviation in sentence 3.
2. What is the reason for quotation marks in sentence 5?
3. Give the rule for spelling the plural of *waltz* in sentence 7.
4. Explain the capital letters and the hyphen in sentence 9.

DIAGRAMMING DIRECT OBJECTS

Direct objects are diagrammed like predicate nominatives, with one difference.

The porpoise tossed the *ball*.

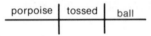

The direct object is also placed on the line with the subject and the verb. Notice, though, that the line between the verb and the direct object is perpendicular, not slanted.

Here are diagrams of *compound* direct objects.

Manuel raises *ducks* and *geese*.

Our team defeated *Wayne, Dixon, Laurel,* and *Tilden*.

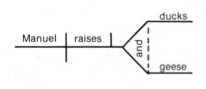

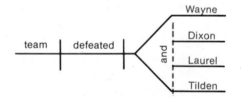

LEARNING ACTIVITIES

A. Diagram verbs, subjects, and any direct objects in the following sentences. Two sentences have predicate nominatives, not direct objects. Diagram them also. Go over the diagrams orally when you have finished.

1. Father has bought a tweed coat and a sleeveless sweater.
2. Have the children finished their work?
3. My mother was once the owner of a restaurant.
4. Our neighbors are building a house.
5. That child needs glasses.
6. One boy in our class has had measles, mumps, and chicken pox.
7. Cecile sold ten tickets in a very short time.
8. Your song will be the first number on the program.

9. The farmers are cutting their wheat, oats, rye, and barley now.
10. Jessie found a flashlight.

B. Diagram the verb, the subject, and the direct object in the sentences in *B*, page 327.

7. Using Nouns As Appositives

READ AND DISCUSS . . .

Are *you* sure what an appositive is? If not, you, too, should turn back to Rule 4 on page 228.

What do appositives and predicate nouns have in common? How are they different? Which italicized word is which in the following sentence?

Our lawyer, *Mr. Greer,* is a busy *person.*

● THESE ARE FACTS ABOUT APPOSITIVES

1. **Appositives are set next to, or near, the words with which they are in apposition, that is, the words that they explain or identify.** In the example above, *Mr. Greer* (the appositive) comes right after *lawyer* (the noun that it explains).

2. **Most appositives are set off by commas or a comma.**

   A new teacher, **Kumiko Ikeda,** has been hired.
   This dish is my favorite dessert, **shortcake.**

   If the appositive is used in a group of words, the entire expression is set off.

   Tim's father, **a tall man with a friendly smile,** met us.
   Paulette won the award, **a trip to Hawaii.**

3. **Appositives may be compound.**

   Mary received two gifts, a **ring** and a **watch**.

4. **Appositives should not be confused with predicate nominatives.** Remember, a predicate nominative completes a linking verb.

   John, my *brother,* came early. (*appositive*)
   John **is** my *brother.* (*predicate nominative*)

5. **Often an appositive helps to make one smooth sentence out of two short, choppy sentences.**

   Astrid is a careful driver. She does not take chances.
   Astrid, a careful *driver,* does not take chances.

LEARNING ACTIVITIES

A. In the following sentences, find the appositives and tell where commas are needed to set them off. Include any group of words containing an appositive. Make this an oral activity.

1. Rome the capital of Italy is also its largest city.
2. A city on the equator is Quito the capital of Ecuador.
3. Paris the capital and largest city of France is on the Seine River.
4. Christiania is the former name of Oslo the capital of Norway.
5. Austin the capital of Texas was named for Stephen Austin founder of the first settlement in that region.
6. Denver the capital of Colorado is called "the mile-high city."
7. The most famous "twin cities" are St. Paul the capital of Minnesota and Minneapolis that state's largest city.
8. Bolivia actually has two capitals La Paz and Sucre.
9. The seaport for Tokyo the capital of Japan is Yokohama.
10. Mexico City the capital of Mexico has a fine climate.

B. (1) Rewrite the following sentences, combining each pair into one sentence by the use of an appositive. (2) Proofread for careless errors in spelling, capitalization, or punctuation. (3) Exchange papers. (4) Read the revised sentences aloud, telling where commas are needed.

1. Gilbert du Motier was the Marquis de Lafayette. He was born in a wild and rocky part of France.
2. During his childhood, he was left mostly in the care of three women. These women were his grandmother and his two aunts.
3. At the age of fourteen, Gilbert began his military career in a famous regiment. This regiment was the Black Musketeers.
4. As a young man, he became interested in a new nation. It was the United States of America.
5. To take him to America, he bought a ship. The name of the ship was the *Victoire.*
6. Two opponents tried but failed to stop him from going. They were his father-in-law and the French government.
7. In America he fought bravely and helped to win the last battle of the Revolution. It was the Battle of Yorktown.
8. Later, during the French Revolution, Lafayette helped to save the rulers of France from an angry mob. These rulers were Louis XVI and Marie Antoinette.
9. When France became a republic, Lafayette refused its highest office. It was the presidency.
10. Declared a traitor, he was captured and imprisoned for five years in two different countries. These countries were Germany and Austria.
11. Lafayette's son, smuggled to America, was cared for by George Washington. That was the man for whom he had been named.

12. In 1824, Lafayette returned to visit the United States and to receive from Congress two gifts. These gifts were two hundred thousand dollars and a township of land.

USING ENGLISH IN ALL CLASSES

Bring into English class the next composition assignment (such as a report) for any class. Write your first draft quickly. Next, see whether you can improve it by using appositives to combine certain sentences.

DIAGRAMMING APPOSITIVES

Appositives are placed inside parentheses and are located next to the words with which they are in apposition.

APPOSITION WITH SUBJECT

Our lawyer, *Mr. Greer,* is a busy person.

APPOSITION WITH DIRECT OBJECT

Paulette won the award, a *trip* to Hawaii.

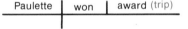

APPOSITION WITH PREDICATE NOMINATIVE

This dog is Princess, our family *pet.*

COMPOUND APPOSITIVES

These gifts, a *ring* and a *watch,* were a real surprise.

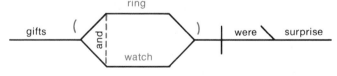

Cleotha has two sisters, *Jane* and *Mavis.*

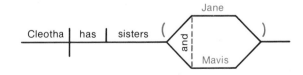

331

Diagram verbs, subjects, appositives, and any predicate nominatives or direct objects in these sentences. Exchange papers for checking as the diagrams are put on the board and explained orally.

1. Sunday, my birthday, was a rainy day.
2. The high scorer in every game has been Arnold, our center.
3. Both persons, my father and my aunt, were born on a farm.
4. Laura plays two games well, baseball and soccer.
5. Our neighbors, the Smiths and the Barrys, are also our friends.
6. Has your sister met our new leader, that tall man in the gray suit?
7. Mrs. Lewis provided the entertainment, slides of her trip to Spain.
8. The speakers were two strangers, a Dane and a Swede.
9. These girls, Sheila and Karen, are new in school.
10. Sitting on the fence were two birds, a robin and a sparrow.

8. Using Vivid, Exact Nouns

READ AND DISCUSS . . .

Here are three pairs of sentences. In each pair, pick out the sentence that you think gives the better picture. Tell why you think so.

Suddenly I heard a loud noise.
Suddenly I heard a loud crash.

I fell asleep to the drumming of rain on the roof.
I fell asleep to the sound of rain on the roof.

In the glass bowl were some lovely yellow tulips.
In the glass bowl were some lovely yellow flowers.

Only one word is different in each pair of those sentences. Name other words that might have been used for the "different" words. As you will see, the picture changes as you change those nouns.

One good way to widen your vocabulary is to learn to use vivid, exact nouns. The following guides suggest how to go about it.

GUIDES TO USING VIVID, EXACT NOUNS

1. Go over written work that you do, at home or at school. Think about each noun. Ask yourself, "Can I find a more exact, or definite, word? Can I find a word that makes a clearer picture?"

2. In your reading, learn to notice the author's choice of nouns. Being aware of what words good writers choose can help you in your own oral and written expression.

3. As a rule, avoid weak nouns like *sound, noise, light, motion.* Find, for example, a noun that names the *special kind* of sound: the *splash* of waves, the *trickling* of a stream, the *rattle* of hail.

4. Avoid a general noun when a specific (exact) one fits:

   GENERAL: Ann was wearing red *shoes.*
   SPECIFIC: Ann was wearing red *sandals.*

   GENERAL: A tall *tree* shades the front of our house.
   SPECIFIC: A tall *elm* shades the front of our house.

   Be as specific as you can. For example, *food* is general; *dessert* is more specific; *pie* is still more specific.

LEARNING ACTIVITIES

A. (1) Write these three headings on your paper: *General, More Specific, Most Specific.* (2) Write each word in the following groups under the correct heading. (3) Go over your work in class. Study the example below, which classifies *carrot, plant, vegetable.*

General	More Specific	Most Specific
plant	vegetable	carrot

1. soldier, person, general
2. money, dime, coin
3. cabin, building, house
4. Nile, river, water
5. plant, grain, wheat
6. doctor, surgeon, person
7. entertainer, violinist, musician
8. shortstop, ballplayer, athlete
9. hammer, object, tool
10. cedar, tree, evergreen

B. Here are some lines from Mark Twain's *The Adventures of Tom Sawyer.* In each line, one of the words in parentheses is the one that the author chose. (1) Copy the lines, putting in the words that you think he used. (2) Exchange papers. (3) Check the words chosen as the sentences are read aloud.

1. . . . a candle was casting a dull (glow, light) upon the curtain of a second-story window.
2. Then there was a wild (yelp, bark) of agony, and the poodle went sailing up the aisle; . . .

3. A tremendous (blow, whack) came down on Tom's shoulders, . . .
4. . . . no sound but the far-off (noise, hammering) of a woodpecker, . . .
5. The boys moved off and disappeared in the (gloom, darkness).
6. . . . a thin blue (breath, column) of smoke rose straight into the air.
7. A (touch, sweep) of chilly air passed by, . . .
8. He did not go skipping and prancing, but moved with a dignified (swagger, walk).
9. . . . the air was drowsy with the (sounds, hum) of study.
10. Then they crept to the door and took a trembling (look, peep).
11. Away off in the flaming sunshine, Cardiff Hill lifted its soft green sides through a shimmering (veil, layer) of heat, . . .
12. Just here the (blowing, blast) of a toy tin trumpet came faintly down the green (paths, aisles) of the forest.
13. The (calling, hooting) of a distant owl was all the sound that troubled the dead stillness.
14. . . . an old-fashioned tin lantern that freckled the ground with innumerable little (spots, spangles) of light.
15. Presently a great (jet, amount) of white smoke burst from the ferryboat's side, . . .

C. Write a paragraph describing a strange, exciting, or frightening experience or dream that you once had. If you cannot think of a real one, make one up. Write the paragraph quickly first; then improve it. To do so, (1) check it by the paragraph guides, page 162; (2) try writing some sentences in inverted order (see page 313); (3) replace any weak verbs or nouns with vivid, specific ones; (4) choose a good title (see page 190).

Copy the paragraph neatly and carefully. In your small groups, pass the paragraphs around. Choose ones that you would like the teacher (or someone else) to read to the entire class. Be ready to tell how these paragraphs might be made better.

9. Using Standard English

MAKING VERBS AGREE WITH NOUN SUBJECTS

THINK IT OVER . . .

Most nouns have two forms: *singular* (referring to *one* of anything, as *pin*) and *plural* (referring to *more than one* of anything, as *pins*). This difference in form is called *number*. (See page 253 if you wish to review singular and plural nouns.) Verbs, too, have number.

Many verbs, however, unlike nouns, have the same form in the plural as in the singular. Here are a few examples:

The girl *swam.*	A change *may come.*
The girls *swam.*	Changes *may come.*
John *had left.*	He *will go* later.
The twins *had left.*	They *will go* later.

Here are some rules about number that can help you to use verbs and subjects together properly.

RULES FOR AGREEMENT OF VERBS WITH NOUN SUBJECTS: I

RULE 1. Use a singular verb with a singular subject. (In the present tense, a singular verb used with a noun subject will end in *s*.)

This *flower* blooms every year.   *George* works hard.

RULE 2. Use a plural verb with a plural subject.

These *chimes* ring every fifteen minutes.

RULE 3. Use a plural verb with compound subjects joined by *and*.

Vito and *Tina* live here.   *Wind* and *rain* damage the crops.

RULE 4. For compound subjects joined by *or, nor, either-or,* or *neither-nor*, follow these rules:

a) **Use a singular verb if both subjects are singular.**

Either *Sally* or *Frances* always helps us.

b) **Use a plural verb if both subjects are plural.**

Neither the *apples* nor the *pears* look ripe.

RULE 5. Use the singular forms *is, was, has,* or *does* with a singular subject.

Tom is my cousin.   That *train* has left.
One *toy* was broken.   *Myron* does careful work.

RULE 6. Use the plural forms *are, were, have,* or *do* with a plural subject.

The *skies* are blue.   Our *teams* have won.
The *books* were mailed today.   Those *girls* do their part.

RULE 7. Use only plural verbs with such subjects as *slacks, shears, tweezers, trousers, pliers, clothes,* for they are always plural.

LEARNING ACTIVITIES

A. Go over the following sentences orally, choosing the proper verbs. Listen carefully to get used to hearing the standard forms.

1. Pam and Karen (was, were) at the zoo yesterday.
2. Mother's scissors (is, are) right here.
3. Neither Mother nor Father (is, are) at home.
4. My sisters-in-law (is, are) golfers.
5. These papers (goes, go) on top.
6. The monkey's eyes (was, were) almost closed.
7. Both families (do, does) need larger houses.
8. The children (has, have) never been in a subway before.
9. The man and his daughter (were, was) wearing boots.
10. Those squirrels (come, comes) here often.

B. (1) Copy the following sentences, choosing the proper verbs. Do not write in this book. (2) Exchange papers for checking as the sentences are read aloud. (3) Go over the sentences more than once so that your ears will get used to the sound of the standard forms.

1. Both a drought and a flood (is, are) hard on crops.
2. Neither buses nor trains (is, are) running today.
3. These books (go, goes) in the next room.
4. Neither the girls nor their parents (has, have) returned.
5. John and his sister (was, were) weeding the garden.
6. Jane and her brother (was, were) at the beach.
7. Your services (is, are) always appreciated.
8. Either George or his cousin (has, have) the key.
9. By the end of the day, the players (was, were) tired.
10. The carpenter and the plumber (does, do) good work.

C. (1) Write eight original sentences in which you use the verbs *is, was, has, does, are, were, have, do.* Use compound subjects in three of your sentences. (2) Take turns at reading the sentences aloud in your small groups. (3) Explain why you chose a singular or a plural subject in each case. (4) Call on a listener to judge whether you are right.

★   **Spot Review**

(*Based upon the sentences in* A *of the preceding activities*)

1. Why are the subjects in sentence 3 capitalized?
2. Explain the spelling of the plural subject in sentence 4.
3. Why does the apostrophe in sentence 6 come before the *s?*

RULES FOR AGREEMENT OF VERBS WITH NOUN SUBJECTS: II

RULE 8. Contractions formed with the verbs named in Rule 5 and Rule 6, page 335, follow the same rules.

a) **Use** *isn't, wasn't,* **or** *hasn't* **with a singular subject.**

b) **Use** *aren't, weren't,* **or** *haven't* **with a plural subject.**

c) **Use the singular form** *doesn't* **with a singular subject.**

That *cat* **doesn't** remember me.

d) **Use the plural form** *don't* **with a plural subject.**

Those *cats* **don't** remember me, either.

Warning! In standard usage, the contraction *ain't* **should not be substituted for** *isn't, hasn't, aren't, haven't.*

Standard: Joe **isn't** coming.   The boys **haven't** left.
Nonstandard: Joe a̶i̶n̶'t̶ coming.   The boys a̶i̶n̶'t̶ left.

LEARNING ACTIVITIES

A. Listed below are twenty subjects. Go around the class, saying each subject four times, with (1) *isn't* or *aren't,* (2) *hasn't* or *haven't,* (3) *wasn't* or *weren't,* and (4) *doesn't* or *don't.* You may want to make this a team contest.

Example: *money:* Money *isn't.* Money *hasn't.* Money *wasn't.*
          Money *doesn't.*

1. trees	5. cities	9. price	13. house	17. weeds
2. river	6. truck	10. expense	14. mice	18. children
3. game	7. crops	11. friends	15. tickets	19. radios
4. teams	8. stars	12. geese	16. parks	20. people

B. Copy the following sentences, using the proper contractions. Read the sentences orally in class.

1. The editors (isn't, aren't) meeting today.
2. The cottage (doesn't, don't) have an extra bedroom.
3. Last night the planes (wasn't, weren't) flying over the house.
4. That dog (doesn't, don't) look like a collie.
5. This road (don't, doesn't) run past the school.
6. My boots (hasn't, haven't) any holes in them.
7. The radiators (ain't, aren't) very hot.
8. The barber's scissors (wasn't, weren't) sharp enough.
9. From the air our farm (doesn't, don't) look large.
10. The neighbors (hasn't, haven't) moved yet.

C. Write original sentences in which you use the contractions from Rule 8. In your small groups, take turns reading your sentences aloud. Tell the rule for each contraction used.

★ **Spot Review**

(Based upon the sentences in B *of the preceding activities)*
1. Account for the apostrophes in sentence 8.
2. What rule regulates the spelling of the subject in sentence 10?
3. What is the *number* of the subject of sentence 8?

Learn about words!

The following words, taken from Learning Activity *B*, have interesting histories. Use your dictionary to find the story behind each word.

extra   scissors   neighbor

RULES FOR AGREEMENT OF VERBS WITH NOUN SUBJECTS: III

RULE 9. Always use a singular verb with a singular subject and a plural verb with a plural subject. *Do so regardless of where the verb comes in the sentence order.*

a) **Do not be fooled by questions in which the verb stands before the subject.**

Is your *compass* a new one?

To be sure that the verb and the subject agree, turn the question into a statement:

Your *compass* is a new one.

b) **Do not be fooled by the introductory word** *there.* **You should find the subject just as in any other sentence.**

There are some apples in the bowl.

What is the verb? *Are.* What are? *Apples* are; so *apples* is the subject. Since *apples* is plural, the plural verb *are* is needed.

c) **Use the contraction** *there's* (*there is* or *there has*), **only if the subject is singular.**

There's [There is] one green *apple* in the bowl. (*Apple* is.)

338

LEARNING ACTIVITIES

A. Copy each of the following sentences, using the proper forms. Do not write in this book. Read the sentences aloud in class.

1. (There is, There are) twenty boys in my class.
2. (There has, There have) been many visitors at the exhibit.
3. (There's, There are) several parks in this state.
4. (Has, Have) your shoes ever been polished?
5. When (was, were) your friends coming?
6. (There was, There were) some letters for you.
7. (Is there, Are there) any eggs in that bowl?
8. (There has, There have) been a reduction in prices.
9. (There's, There are) not one boy here yet.
10. (Has, Have) the furniture been polished?

B. In your small groups, take turns giving sentences orally using *there* as an introductory word and *is, are, was, were, has,* or *have* as the verb. You might tell facts about the downtown part of your city or town. Continue the practice until you are sure that the proper forms sound natural to you.

C. Let half the class write on the board questions beginning with *is, are, was, were, has,* or *have,* followed by *there.* Let the other half write answers to the questions.

Example: *Are there* any apricots in the basket?
There are five apricots in the basket.

RULES FOR AGREEMENT OF VERBS WITH NOUN SUBJECTS: IV

RULE 10. Do not be misled by any words that come between the subject and the verb. (Review point 5, page 313.)

The **superintendent** of both schools **is** Mrs. Day.
That **row** of trees **doesn't** give much shade yet.
Both **parents** of that boy **were** here early.
The **rules** on that page **look** easy.
This **box** of books **isn't** mine.

Learn about words!

The following words, taken from Learning Activity *A* on page 340, have interesting histories. Use your dictionary to find the story behind each word.

pantry   pay   compliment   arrive

LEARNING ACTIVITIES

A. All ten sentences below show the proper verbs. Check by locating the verb and the subject in each sentence. First find the verb; then ask, "Who or what?" to locate the subject. In each case you will see that a singular subject is used with a singular verb, and that a plural subject is used with a plural verb. Read the sentences aloud. Listen carefully to get used to the standard forms.

1. My pay for these services is generous.
2. Have the parents of that child arrived yet?
3. One teacher of the lower grades lives near us.
4. A small package of nuts was on the shelf in the pantry.
5. One apple in the barrel was green.
6. The father of those girls has built many monuments.
7. The location of the mines was a secret.
8. The work of your committee has received many compliments.
9. Was the bundle of papers here?
10. The captains of the teams were chosen today.

B. (1) Copy the following sentences, supplying a proper verb for each of them. (2) Compare work orally in class or in your small groups. The verbs chosen may vary, but each singular subject should have a singular verb, and each plural subject should have a plural verb.

1. A truckload of bricks _____ delivered at our house.
2. Both owners of the store _____ on vacation.
3. The price of these tires _____ been raised.
4. The road signs on the highway _____ me.
5. All houses in this block _____ alike.
6. One copy of these instructions _____n't match the others.
7. Two buttons on the coat _____ loose.
8. The painter of the pictures _____ here often.
9. The objections of this student _____ reasonable to me.
10. A can of baked beans _____ with us on every hike.

C. In an oral activity, go over the following groups of words, completing each of them properly with (1) one of these helping verbs: *is, are, was, were, has, have, do* or *does* and (2) any other needed words. Explain each time why the verb should be singular or plural.

1. A quart of strawberries . . .
2. The bunch of bananas . . .
3. The train on the tracks . . .
4. The poorest people in the world . . .
5. The traffic lights on this corner . . .
6. The best road through the hills . . .
7. The longest pencils on the table . . .

8. The strings of that harp . . .
9. The best players on the team . . .
10. The paper with the scribbles . . .

D. (1) Write five sentences of your own in which the subject is separated from the verb by other words. Use both singular subjects and plural subjects. (2) Proofread carefully for errors in capitalization, punctuation, and spelling. (3) Exchange papers and read the sentences aloud in class.

USING TROUBLESOME VERBS

TALK IT OVER . . .

Following is practice on the principal parts of five troublesome verbs — *give, go, take, bring,* and *write.* Remember that your aim is not just to be able to *write* the standard forms but to *put them into practice.*

USING IRREGULAR VERBS — <u>GIVE</u>, <u>GAVE</u>, <u>GIVEN</u>

RULE. **Always use at least one auxiliary verb with** *given.* **Never use any with the past tense** *gave.*

Today I give. Yesterday I gave. Often I *have given.*

LEARNING ACTIVITIES

A. Copy these sentences, filling the blanks with the proper form of the verb *give.* Underline (1) the form of *give* that you use and (2) any helping verbs. Read the sentences aloud in class.

1. Esther's mother _____ a party for her yesterday.
2. The answer was _____ correctly.
3. Careful attention should be _____ to the appearance of your papers.
4. Who _____ you those flowers?
5. On Monday a short play will be _____ in the auditorium.
6. Father _____ me a bicycle for Christmas.
7. Full directions are _____ on the package.
8. The list of winners is _____ in the morning paper.
9. He has _____ his opinion on that subject already.
10. Toshiro was _____ the prize for flower arranging.
11. Strawberries always _____ me a rash.
12. _____ me some help!

B. Write sentences on the board, leaving blanks to be filled with *gave* or *given*. Call on a classmate to read the sentences and supply the proper forms. When a past participle is used, tell what the helping verb is.

C. (1) Write five sentences, three using *gave* and two using *given* correctly. You might write about presents that you have given for birthdays or for Christmas. (2) In your small groups, take turns at reading these sentences aloud. (3) Have classmates tell what helping verbs you used. Listen carefully to get used to hearing the proper forms.

D. Pretend that your class held an auction last week to raise money for a trip to some historic place. Each of you donated one item or more. Tell what you gave. One person may begin by saying, "I gave an elephant. What did *you* give, Agnes?" Agnes then tells what she gave. It must begin with the letter before or after the first letter of the word given by the previous person. In other words, Agnes might say, "I gave a **d**eer," or "I gave a **f**lagpole." She then asks the question of anyone else she wishes, and so on. You will need to listen closely, for if your gift begins with a wrong letter, you are out of the game. You will be out, too, if you say, "I *give* . . ." instead of "I *gave.*"

★　**Spot Review**

(*Based upon the sentences in* A *of the preceding activities*)

1. Account for the apostrophe in sentence 1.
2. Why is *mother* not capitalized in sentence 1?
3. How do you spell the plural of the last word in sentence 6?
4. What is the subject of sentence 8?

USING IRREGULAR VERBS—<u>GO</u>, <u>WENT</u>, <u>GONE</u>

RULE. **Always use at least one helping verb with** *gone.* **Never use any with the past tense** *went.*

Today I go.　　Yesterday I went.　　Often I *have* gone.

LEARNING ACTIVITIES

A. (1) Copy these sentences, filling the blanks with the correct form of the verb *go.* (2) Exchange papers. (3) Check the papers for careless errors in copying. Circle any that you find. (4) Read the sentences aloud in class. Each time that *gone* is used, name the helping verbs.

1. On Thanksgiving Day Juanita should have _____ to Boston.
2. Antoinette has _____ away to college.
3. Until this year, Ed had always _____ to Florida for a month.
4. Who _____ with you yesterday?
5. The notes for your speech should be _____ over carefully.
6. I'd never _____ to that dentist until yesterday.
7. Everyone has _____ except us.
8. The alarm must have _____ off.
9. Had the Joneses _____ to the station before five o'clock?
10. Where has Loretta _____?
11. The Sunday newspapers were all _____.
12. For our last vacation we _____ to the shore.

B. Write five original sentences, three with *went* and two with *gone*. Use these helping verbs with the past participle: *has, have, had, should have, might have*. In your small groups, take turns at reading sentences aloud. Listen to hear whether helping verbs are used each time with the past participle, *gone*.

C. With a partner, take turns at saying sentences that use *gone* properly. For example, make them the answers to a question: "Has anyone in your family ever gone to Mexico?" Give a separate and complete answer for each member of your family. "My sister has gone to Mexico. My brother Fred has never gone to Mexico." Practice until the correct forms sound perfectly natural.

Spot Review

(*Based upon the sentences in* A *of the preceding activities*)

1. Name three proper nouns in sentence 1. Name a common noun for each of them.
2. How would you spell the words for which the contractions stand in sentences 6 and 9?
3. What is the subject in sentence 5?
4. What rule covers the spelling of the proper noun in sentence 9?

Learn about words!

The following words, taken from Learning Activity *A,* page 344, have interesting histories. Use your dictionary to find the story behind each word.

possession   road   place

USING IRREGULAR VERBS—<u>TAKE</u>, <u>TOOK</u>, <u>TAKEN</u>

RULE. **Always use a helping verb with** *taken;* **never use one with** *took.*

Today I take.   Yesterday I took.   Often I *have* taken.

LEARNING ACTIVITIES

A. Copy these sentences, filling the blanks with the standard form of the verb *take.* Underline that form and any helping verbs. Read the sentences aloud in class. Listen to be sure that the proper forms are given.

1. This photograph of pine trees was _____ on Mount McKinley.
2. Has your family ever _____ a long vacation trip?
3. In 1664 the English _____ possession of New Amsterdam.
4. Samuel Clemens _____ the pen name "Mark Twain."
5. This name was _____ from his experiences on the Mississippi River.
6. We should have _____ the other road.
7. The story of this film is _____ from a famous book.
8. In my opinion, the first speaker should not have _____ so much time for questions from the audience.
9. The two boys had _____ a short cut to the beach.
10. Who has _____ your place on the committee?

B. For each error that you made in *A,* write two sentences using the correct form. Read these aloud to a partner, who will judge their correctness. If you and your partner disagree, ask your teacher to decide.

C. Pretend that your class has just returned from the trip in Activity *D,* page 342. Each of you forgot to take along something that would have come in handy. Take turns completing the sentence, "I wish that I had taken . . ." (or "I should have taken . . ."). You can have fun by naming some unusual items; for example, "I wish that I had taken a polar bear." (If anyone asks *why,* be ready with a good answer.)

★   **Spot Review**

(Based upon the sentences in A *of the preceding activities)*

1. Find and write the proper nouns in sentences 1, 3, and 5. Beside each write a common noun that it describes.
2. Name the subject, the verb, and the direct object in sentences 2 and 8.
3. How would you spell the plural of the subject in sentence 7?
4. Why are *Mount* (sentence 1) and *River* (sentence 5) capitalized?
5. Why is the verb in sentence 1 singular?

USING IRREGULAR VERBS — BRING, BROUGHT, BROUGHT

RULE. *Brought* **is the only proper form both for the past tense and for the past participle.** *Brang* **and** *brung* **are nonstandard forms.**

Today I bring.   Yesterday I brought.   Often I *have* brought.

LEARNING ACTIVITIES

A. Go over the following sentences orally, supplying the standard form of the verb *bring*. Name any helping verbs. Listen to get used to hearing the proper form. Do not write in this book.

1. William _____ his friend to the last party.
2. I should not have _____ my camera.
3. Tobacco was first _____ to England from America.
4. Mary has _____ her share of the money.
5. Lorena was _____ up by her grandmother.
6. Irene _____ back many souvenirs from Hawaii.
7. As usual, Tim and I _____ our binoculars.
8. The dog must have _____ us the neighbor's paper.
9. Has each member _____ a visitor?
10. The rain _____ a little relief from the heat.

B. Take turns at writing sentences on the board, leaving blanks to be filled with the proper form of *bring*. Call on classmates to read the sentences and supply the standard forms.

C. Pretend that your class has had a picnic. It was a great success because of the delicious food. Each person will tell what someone else brought. You must drop out of the game (1) if you use *brang* or *brung* or (2) if you name a food that someone else has already named. As you can see, you will need to listen closely. Stop at the end of five minutes. You may want to make this activity a team contest.

Spot Review

(*Based upon the sentences in* A *of the preceding activities*)

1. Rewrite sentence 2, using a contraction.
2. Write the plural of *party* (sentence 1). Give the rule.
3. Which sentences have direct objects? Name those objects.
4. Why is *grandmother* not capitalized in sentence 5?

USING IRREGULAR VERBS—WRITE, WROTE, WRITTEN

RULE. Always use a helping verb with *written;* **never use one with** *wrote. Writ* **is a nonstandard form.**

Today I write.   Yesterday I wrote.   Often I *have* written.

LEARNING ACTIVITIES

A. Copy these sentences, filling the blanks with the standard form of the verb *write.* Underline that form and any auxiliary verbs. Read the sentences aloud in class.

1. Most of the Declaration of Independence was _____ by Thomas Jefferson.
2. Emily Dickinson _____ the poem "I Like to See It Lap the Miles."
3. Louisa May Alcott _____ many books for boys and girls.
4. *The Adventures of Huckleberry Finn* was _____ by Mark Twain, a great author.
5. He _____ that book after he had _____ *The Adventures of Tom Sawyer.*
6. Have you _____ to your Aunt Mary?
7. Your sentences should be _____ carefully and neatly.
8. Every year many new science books are _____ for children.

B. (1) Jot down the names of at least five books or poems that you have read. (2) Take turns at asking who wrote your selections. For example, say, "Tom, who wrote *Treasure Island?*" (3) The one called upon will say, "*Treasure Island* was written by Robert Louis Stevenson." If the person does not know, he or she should say, "I don't know by whom it was written." In that case, call upon someone who raises a hand. (4) Continue until everyone has asked at least one question and given one answer using *wrote* or *written* properly.

STUDYING CONFUSING PAIRS

The verbs on pages 341–346 are troublesome mostly because the past form is used when the past participle form really should be used, and the other way round. The pairs of verbs in this lesson are troublesome because one verb in a pair is often confused with the other, even though both have different *meanings.* Review the Rules for Telling Confusing Pairs Apart, on the opposite page, before doing the Learning Activities on page 348.

RULES FOR TELLING CONFUSING PAIRS APART

RULE 1. *(Learn, teach)*
Use *learn* **when you mean "to get knowledge"; use** *teach* **when you mean "to give instruction."** You *learn* for yourself, but someone else *teaches* you. You learn *something,* not *somebody.*

My teacher *teaches* me.   I *learn* a new word every day.

RULE 2. *(Sit, set)*
Use *sit* **when you mean "to rest in an upright position"; use** *set* **when you mean "to place or put something."** *Sit* never takes an object; *set* always needs one. ("Object" is explained on page 326.)

Phil *sat* on the bench.   He *set* the **glass** on the table.

For *sit* and *set,* you need to know not only the *present,* the *past,* and the *past participle,* but also the *present participle.*

Present	Present Participle	Past	Past Participle
sit	sitting	sat	sat
set	setting	set	set

RULE 3. *(Lend, borrow)*
Use *borrow* **when you mean "to** *get* **the use of something"; use** *lend* **when you mean "to** *give* **the use of something."**

May I *borrow* your pencil?   I'll *lend* you my pen.

NEVER say, "Will you *borrow* me some notebook paper?"

The following words, taken from Learning Activity *A*, have interesting histories. Use your dictionary to find the story behind each word.

dime   desk   teach   poem

LEARNING ACTIVITIES

A. (1) Copy these sentences, choosing the proper verb from each parentheses. (2) Before choosing the verbs in parentheses, be sure to proofread for careless errors in copying. (3) Exchange papers for checking when the sentences are read aloud.

1. (Lend, Borrow) me your pencil, please.
2. Ernestine (sat, set) the telephone down gently.
3. In which seat were you (sitting, setting)?
4. Who (learned, taught) you that song?
5. Will you (lend, borrow) me a dime?
6. Tom should have (set, sat) the box upon the desk.
7. A good teacher can (teach, learn) pupils to like even the most difficult subject.
8. How long shall I (sit, set) here?
9. Our teacher (taught, learned) us a new poem today.
10. This pen was (borrowed, lent) to me by my cousin.

B. In your small groups, take turns giving sentences that use these confusing pairs of verbs. First each student should give a sentence using *learn* or *learned,* and then one using *teach* or *taught.* Continue with *sit, sat, sitting* and *set, setting;* then with *lend, lent* and *borrow, borrowed.* Listen carefully to be sure that the proper form is used each time.

C. Answer in complete sentences the following questions, using the proper verb forms. Make this an oral activity.

1. Where did you set the books?
2. Why did the dog sit in the sun?
3. Have you ever sat all evening watching television?
4. Which room did Grandmother sit in?
5. When was the last time you set the table?
6. Where did you sit in the theater?
7. What did you set on the desk?
8. Why were the flowers set on the windowsill?
9. Who sat behind you last year?
10. When did you set the chairs around the table?

A. (1) Copy the following sentences. (2) Label each *verb* (v.); label each noun used as *subject* (subj.), *direct object* (d.o.), *predicate nominative* (p.n.), or *appositive* (app.). (3) Identify the sentence patterns. (4) Exchange papers for checking.

1. The rain brought some relief from the heat.
2. Mark is the only boy in his family.
3. The detectives searched the house and the garage.
4. The woman in the middle is Mrs. Elson, our neighbor.
5. Suddenly the roar of an airplane broke the silence.
6. Hamburgers and steaks are my favorite meats.
7. My mother and Jack, my oldest brother, are very good drivers.
8. The package contained two footballs.
9. An honest person would have told the truth about the matter.
10. An angry elephant can be a very dangerous animal.

B. Read the following sentences aloud, choosing the standard forms.

1. The scissors on the table (is, are) sharp and pointed.
2. (Has, Have) your brothers-in-law left?
3. There (is, are) a pie and a cake in the refrigerator.
4. The woman with the two packages (don't, doesn't) like streetcars.
5. The two puppies at the end of the row (was, were) fast asleep.
6. (Is, Are) the potatoes in that sack from your garden?
7. The basket of roses (wasn't, weren't) on the piano.
8. There (has, have) been some lovely days this fall.
9. (Doesn't, Don't) Fred or Kirsten ever wait for you?
10. Five loads of coal (was, were) delivered this morning.
11. There (isn't, aren't) any oranges or lemons left in the refrigerator.
12. (Don't, Doesn't) your father remember that game?

C. Read these sentences aloud, supplying the proper form of each verb.

1. A program was (give) in our school last Friday.
2. We (bring) our books with us this morning.
3. Have you (write) to your Uncle Ned?
4. Teresa (give) me the wrong address yesterday.
5. Lois might have (go) without me.
6. This photograph was (take) in Florida.
7. Everyone had (bring) his or her share.
8. This letter was (write) last week.
9. Carlotta has always (take) her work seriously.
10. Phil has (go) to sleep again.

---

*Check Test 3 should be taken at this point. If the results show need for further study, students should do this review practice. They should then take Mastery Test 3.

D. Read the following aloud, choosing the proper verb form.

1. Will Marilyn (borrow, lend) me her bike?
2. That package has (set, sat) there for a week.
3. Mrs. Darrow (learned, taught) us that poem in one day.
4. Was Dean (setting, sitting) beside you?
5. I (borrowed, lent) my pencil to Mary.

★ **Cumulative Review**

CAPITALIZATION

Copy these sentences, supplying needed capital letters.

1. according to marie's report in english class, many austrians, hungarians, poles, and russians came to america after 1850.
2. at last mother said, "we shouldn't go to kansas city on thanksgiving day. our friends from the west will not be there then."
3. father added, "that settles it. we stay on maple avenue. perhaps uncle jim and aunt clara will spend the holiday with us."
4. hattie and bob, who worked in a clothing store during july and august, saw the film *war and peace* as guests of colonel r. k. clark of the simplex radio company.
5. that quotation, i'm sure, is from the old testament, not from the new testament.

PUNCTUATION

Copy these sentences, supplying needed punctuation.

1. Ive won the contest shouted Mavis
2. I wonder said Henry whether its too late to call Melba
3. Yes Sam has won letters in baseball basketball and football
4. The childrens *oh*s and *ah*s showed their excitement
5. Have you read the novel Island of the Blue Dolphin by Scott O'Dell the author of The Black Pearl

CONTRACTIONS

Write sentences using the correct contractions of the words below.

1. cannot	3. she will	5. will not	7. did not	9. I have
2. there is	4. it is	6. you are	8. who is	10. we are

SPELLING

Here are sentences containing one or more scrambled words. Some of them when written correctly contain *ei;* the others, *ie.* Make two columns on your paper, one headed *ei* and the other, *ie*. Figure out the words and write each of them under the right heading.

1. I don't (veelbie) I have met your (eenic).
2. There were (thige) workers in the (lidef).
3. Our (binehorgs) are painting (rheti) house.
4. Do you think that (ithree) of those boys has lost (twighe)?
5. Her (hifec) problem was her (recief) pride.

TROUBLESOME VERBS

Go over these sentences orally, choosing the standard forms.

1. Helen (did, done) more than her share for last night's meeting.
2. Have you (knew, known) Mrs. Scott long?
3. The last contestant has not yet (spoke, spoken).
4. The game (began, begun) early. You should have (saw, seen) it.
5. Mrs. Vance (knew, knowed) Mother in college long ago.
6. Nobody (saw, seen) us leave.
7. Everything had been (did, done) for the sick puppy.
8. Two boys were (chose, chosen) to carry the flag.

Word Games to Test Your Thinking

Diamond Puzzle

The middle letter is the same in each of the following words. Place the words one under the other so that the middle letters will form a straight row up and down. The number of letters in each word is shown in parentheses. (CLUE: All of the words are spelled with only four letters of the alphabet.)

1. One of the three articles in grammar (1)
2. Past of *sit* (3)
3. One of the 50 divisions of the United States (5)
4. Property (plural) left by a person who has died (7)
5. Places on which to sit (5)
6. To chew and swallow (3)
7. *Same as No. 1*

Alphabet Tree Quiz

Can you figure out what trees the following are? EXAMPLE: *O* plus a stove = *orange*.

1. *O* plus a verb meaning *to have life*
2. *D* plus a word meaning *dined*
3. *P* plus a part of the body
4. *A* plus a sound used to tell someone to be quiet
5. *P* plus a word meaning *every*
6. Part of the body plus NUT
7. An insect plus CH
8. The lower edge of a dress plus LOCK
9. To attempt to throw a rider plus EYE
10. PA plus *animal foot*
11. PE plus a metal container
12. Nickname for *father* plus LAR

Hidden Names of Dogs

Each sentence below has hidden in it the name of one kind of dog.

EXAMPLE: Bill was wearing an ascot tie. (*Scottie*)

1. Was Shep herding the cows?
2. I paired a leader in this class with one in the other class.
3. We need someone who understands children.
4. Terrie ran for help immediately.
5. Will the president appoint Ernest to be the chairperson?
6. While going past Bernard, he noticed that Bernie was crying.
7. You have set terms to which I cannot agree.
8. This pan I eliminated first of all.

Word Square

The words defined below have four letters each. Placed one under the other, they will spell the same down as across.

1. Take dinner.   2. Thought   3. Close by   4. A nobleman

Would You Like to Know — ?

You probably will be surprised at the answers the encyclopedia gives to some of the following questions.

1. What kind of disposition has the *camel*?
2. Where in North America did *chocolate* originate?
3. Is *coffee* native to Central and South America?
4. What causes the tail of a *comet*?
5. Where are a *cricket's* ears located?

A "Cross" Crossword Puzzle

Copy the puzzle. Do not write in this book.

Across

1. Western state.
5. Small island.
7. Necessity for.
9. Thirteenth letter of the Greek alphabet.
10. Adverbial conjunction.
11. What you should put after an abbreviation.
14. A house pet.
16. Every Fourth of July should be safe and _____.

17. Opposite of *shut*.
19. Past participle of *see*.
20. Opposite of *less*.
21. Opposite of *there*.
22. Opposite of *go*.

Down

1. Biblical character who slew his brother Abel.
2. President Eisenhower's nickname.
3. Past of *run*.
4. Helps.
6. Not a day for going to church, but something to eat.
8. _____ egg.
12. A number.
13. In grammar, the word for *time*.
14. Kind of books read by many people, especially children.
15. Army Post Office (*abbr.*).
16. Secret Service (*abbr.*).
18. Northeast (*abbr.*).

USING PRONOUNS IN BUILDING SENTENCES*

1. Recognizing Personal Pronouns

READ AND DISCUSS . . .

Read these sentences:

The porpoise leaped at the ball. The *porpoise* tossed the *ball*.

Now read these sentences:

The porpoise leaped at the ball. *She* tossed *it*.

Which pair of sentences sounds better? Why?

She tossed **it**.

* Pretest 4 should be taken at this point.

1. (DEFINITION) A *pronoun* **is a word that stands for a noun or for a group of words used as a noun.**

   The *porpoise* tossed the *ball.*   *She* tossed *it.*

2. (DEFINITION) **The word for which a pronoun stands is its** *antecedent. Porpoise* and *ball* are the antecedents of *she* and *it.*

3. (DEFINITION) **Pronouns that distinguish the** *speaker (first person),* **the** *person spoken to (second person),* **or the** *person spoken of (third person)* **are called** *personal pronouns.* **Personal pronouns have** *number;* **that is, they can be singular or plural.**

4. **Personal pronouns can be used in the ways that nouns can: as** *subjects, predicate nominatives, direct objects,* **or** *appositives.* (As you will discover later, pronouns and nouns can also be indirect objects and objects of prepositions.)

5. **Personal pronouns differ from nouns in one important respect: a noun stays the same in all the uses named above; a pronoun may change its form depending upon its use.**

Mary went home. (*subject*)	**She** went home. (*subject*)
John saw **Mary.** (*direct object*)	John saw **her.** (*direct object*)

   Both nouns and pronouns change form to show possession.

   That is **Mary's.**   That is **hers.**

   a) **The form of a pronoun that shows how it is used in a sentence is called** *case.* **There are three cases:** *nominative, possessive,* **and** *objective.*

   b) (DEFINITION) **A** *declension* **is an orderly arrangement of the various case forms a pronoun can have. Here are declensions of the personal pronouns.**

Singular	*Nominative Case*	*Possessive Case*	*Objective Case*
FIRST PERSON:	I	my, mine	me
SECOND PERSON:	you	your, yours	you
THIRD PERSON:	he, she, it	his, her, hers, its	him, her, it
Plural			
FIRST PERSON:	we	our, ours	us
SECOND PERSON:	you	your, yours	you
THIRD PERSON:	they	their, theirs	them

   c) (DEFINITION) *Compound personal pronouns* **combine the personal pronouns with** *-self* **or** *-selves.* **They are** *myself, yourself, himself, herself, itself, ourselves, yourselves,* **and** *themselves.* **They are used only as** *reflexives* **(objects) or as** *intensifiers.*

   Bill hurt **himself.** (*reflexive*)   **I myself** saw him. (*intensive*)

Learn about words!

The following words, taken from the Learning Activity below, have interesting histories. Use your dictionary to find the story behind each word.

table   squirrel   chimney   bicycle

LEARNING ACTIVITY

Go over these sentences. Locate each pronoun. Tell (1) what its person is, (2) what its number is, and (3) what its antecedent is, if given. The figure in parentheses tells the number of pronouns in each sentence.

1. Tom found Mary with her mother. (1)
2. You must do it yourself. (3)
3. My sister gave me her pet squirrels. (3)
4. The bird carried a worm in its beak. (1)
5. Their house is near ours. (2)
6. They will repair the chimney themselves. (2)
7. The clock on the table is mine. (1)
8. She herself gave them to us. (4)
9. June's plans are much like theirs. (1)
10. They can't help themselves now. (2)
11. I can repair your bicycle by myself. (3)
12. We ourselves saw him. (3)

★ **Spot Review**

(Based upon the sentences in the preceding activity)
1. Why is *mother* not capitalized in sentence 1?
2. What are the direct objects in sentences 1, 4, 6? How would you spell the plural of the object in sentence 1? in sentence 6?
3. Explain the apostrophe in sentence 9; in sentence 10.

2. Learning the Uses of Pronouns

This section is concerned with how pronouns are used in English sentences. The main point to remember is that all the personal pronouns except *it* and *you* change form according to use.

6. (DEFINITION) *Nominative* **case forms are used as** (*a*) **subjects or** (*b*) **predicate nominatives.** *I, he, she, we,* **and** *they* **are** *nominative pronouns.*

> I saw Mary. (*subject*)
> The owner is she. (*predicate nominative*)

7. (DEFINITION) *Objective* **case forms are used as objects.** *Me, him, her, us,* **and** *them* **are** *objective pronouns.*

> Sonya met me at the station. (*direct object*)
> John found us in the park. (*direct object*)

8. *It* **and** *you* **are used both in the** *nominative* **case and in the** *objective* **case.**

   You should memorize the pronouns that have different nominative and objective forms.

NOMINATIVE:	I	he	she	we	they
OBJECTIVE:	me	him	her	us	them

9. (DEFINITION) *Possessive* **case forms show ownership.**

   a) **When possessive pronouns are used as modifiers, they are called** *determiners;* **that is, they are pronouns used as adjectives.** (See page 385.)

   > This is her book.   This is my watch.

   b) *My, your, our,* **and** *their* **are always used as determiners:** *my* book, *your* car. *His, her,* **and** *its* **are sometimes determiners and sometimes simple pronouns.**

   > I have her book. (*determiner*)   I saw her. (*objective pronoun*)

   Mine, yours, hers, ours, **and** *theirs* **are always used as simple pronouns.**

   > The book is hers, not mine. (*possessive pronouns*)

10. **A pronoun may be an** *appositive.*

    > Only one person, you, can help us.

11. **Pronouns may be compound.**

    > She and I look alike. (*subjects*)
    > The losers were she and I. (*predicate nominatives*)
    > Mother called you and me. (*direct objects*)
    > He has chosen two speakers, **you** and me. (*appositives*)

12. **In sentence patterns, N stands for** *pronoun,* **just as it stands for** *noun.*

N +V	N +V + N	N +LV +N
We left early.	I like them.	It was you!

LEARNING ACTIVITIES

A. In an oral activity, tell how each italicized pronoun in the following sentences is used. Give the pattern for each sentence.

1. *He* never watches television.
2. *You* have met *her* before.
3. *It* is *he*.
4. *They* are not strangers.
5. *She* must be a good friend.
6. *He* invited *me* to the party.
7. *We* have sent the package.
8. *She* helped *us*, Eve and *me*.
9. *I* saw *them* at the movies.
10. The captains are *you* and *she*.

B. (1) Copy the following sentences. (2) Underscore verbs twice and subjects once. The subject may be a noun or a pronoun. (3) Enclose in parentheses and label each pronoun used as a direct object or a predicate nominative. (4) Go over the sentences in your small groups.

EXAMPLE:
                          d.o.
      Will you and she help (me)?

1. Where were you and she?
2. Yes, it was we.
3. The author is she.
4. We were not expecting him.
5. Was it you or he at the door?
6. Did they choose her?
7. In the first game, Val was "it."
8. Down the street they hurried.
9. She has visited us often.
10. How can I help you?
11. Surely the winners were John and he.
12. They saw us at the yacht race.

C. Draw three columns on your paper. Above the first column write *subject;* above the second, *predicate nominative;* and above the third, *direct object.* Go back over the sentences in *B*. Put each pronoun in the correct column. Place the corresponding sentence number next to each pronoun. Check your lists in class.

D. (1) Write six original sentences. In two of them, use pronouns as subjects; in two, as predicate nominatives; in two, as direct objects. (2) Exchange papers and mark each pronoun as you did in *B*.

USING ENGLISH IN ALL CLASSES

Look over papers that you have written for any of your classes. Are there any places where you might better have used pronouns? Rewrite any such sentences. Be sure, however, that it is clear to what noun each pronoun refers.

(Based upon the sentences in B of the preceding activities)

1. What is the tense of the verb in sentence 2? 3? 8?
2. Which sentences are interrogative?
3. Account for the comma in sentence 2.
4. Which sentences contain regular verbs?

DIAGRAMMING PRONOUNS

Pronouns are diagrammed just as nouns are. You may want to review pages 316, 317, 318, 321, 324, 328, and 331.

PRONOUN SUBJECT

He was skating at the rink.

PRONOUN PREDICATE NOMINATIVE

The winner is *you.*

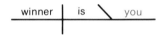

PRONOUN DIRECT OBJECT

Freda met *me* after lunch.

PRONOUN APPOSITIVE

The teacher wants one person, *you.*

COMPOUND SUBJECT AND DIRECT OBJECT

She and *I* saw *you* and *them* in the store.

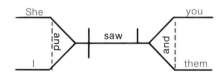

LEARNING ACTIVITIES

A. Diagram verbs, subjects, and any predicate nominatives, direct objects, or appositives in the following sentences. Put the diagrams on the board and explain them orally.

1. It most certainly is she.
2. How can I answer her at this time?

3. I just saw them inside the gym.
4. It could have been they.
5. Did you hear it yesterday?
6. We photographed them in the park.
7. They took us to lunch afterward.
8. It surely must have been you.
9. She unexpectedly invited me to dinner.
10. I need one person, you.

B. For additional practice, use the sentences in *A*, page 358. Go over the diagrams orally in your small groups.

3. Using Standard English

USING STANDARD FORMS OF PRONOUNS

Nouns do not change their form to indicate their use as subjects or objects, but they do to show possession. Pronouns, on the other hand, change their forms for each case, nominative, possessive, and objective.

RULES FOR USING PRONOUNS PROPERLY

RULE 1. **Use the nominative pronouns** *I, he, she, we,* **and** *they* **only as subjects or predicate nominatives.** (Remember that predicate nominatives complete *linking verbs*. To review linking verbs see point 3, page 323.)

They played well. (*subject*)
The players were they. (*predicate nominative*)

RULE 2. **In a compound subject or predicate nominative made up of a noun and a pronoun, be sure to use a nominative pronoun.**

STANDARD: John and I helped.
NONSTANDARD: John and ~~me~~ helped.

(You would not say, "*Me* helped." Neither should you say, "John and *me* helped.")

STANDARD: The altos are Jean and she.
NONSTANDARD: The altos are Jean and ~~her~~.

360

RULE 3. **Use the objective pronouns** *me, her, him, us,* **and** *them* **only as objects.**

A big dog chased me. (*direct object*)

RULE 4. **In a compound direct object made up of a noun and a pronoun, be sure to use an objective pronoun.** *

STANDARD: The dog chased Bill and me.
NONSTANDARD: The dog chased Bill and I.

RULE 5. **In speaking of yourself and others, name yourself last, as a matter of politeness.**

POLITE: John and I agree.
POOR: I and John agree.

POLITE: The dog chased Bill and me.
POOR: The dog chased me and Bill.

LEARNING ACTIVITIES

A. The sentences that follow need predicate nominative pronouns. (1) In an oral activity, go over the sentences, choosing the standard pronoun form in each case. (2) Let half the class read a sentence while the others listen for the proper choice; the others will read the next sentence for the first group to hear and check. Continue in this way for all ten sentences. Do not mark in this book.

1. I agree with Sasha. It was (he, him).
2. It surely wasn't (they, them).
3. Was it (she, her)?
4. No, it was (I, me).
5. It was (we, us) who were chosen.
6. May I speak with May? Is this (she, her)?
7. Was that John calling? Yes, it was (he, him).
8. It must have been (she, her) at the door.
9. Could it have been (they, them) in the car?
10. It was not (I, me), but Jane.

B. Each of the following sentences contains compound subjects, predicate nominatives, or objects. Copy each sentence, choosing the proper form. To help you to decide, drop the other part of the compound.

EXAMPLE: Ray chose Sue and (I, me).
Ray chose (I, me).
Ray chose *me*.

*The proper uses of pronouns in a compound object of a preposition and in a compound indirect object are taught on page 449.

After you have written the sentences, read them aloud and listen carefully to hear the proper forms.

1. The creaking of a door awakened Jack and (I, me).
2. Bella and (he, him) made a huge kite.
3. Will you and (she, her) be ready at nine?
4. Five big geese chased Jerry and (we, us).
5. You and (they, them) were here early.
6. Jane met Ruth and (she, her) at the movie.
7. (She, Her) and (I, me) came too late.
8. That car missed the wagon and (we, us) by inches.
9. At the station (he, him) and (I, me) found the trunk.
10. My uncle and (they, them) once worked in the same office.

C. For each italicized noun or pair of nouns in the following sentences, substitute the proper pronoun. Where the italicized words are "your own name," use *I* or *me;* where they are "you and another person," use *we* or *us.* Decide first whether the pronoun is to be used as a subject, an object, or a predicate nominative. For the nominative and objective pronoun forms, refer to points 6–8 on page 357. Make this an oral practice.

EXAMPLE: Joe and (*your own name*) agree. Joe and *I* agree.

1. Alice and *Lois* will bring the salad.
2. John and *George* planned the program.
3. The tardy students were Louise and (*your own name*).
4. She needs only Jane and (*you and another person*).
5. Hilda called Dee and *Paul.*
6. Laura and (*your own name*) went early.
7. The owners are Mr. Black and *Dr. White.*
8. Miss Williams visited Carol and (*your own name*).
9. Leanna always helps Bill and *Dick and Deirdre.*
10. The new officers are Fred and *Ann.*
11. You and *Dean and Doug* should come early.
12. The first visitors will be you and *Joyce and Audrey.*
13. Sally and (*you and another person*) should wait for Mother.
14. *Lon and Bob* and (*your own name*) went to the movies.
15. Brigham and (*you and another person*) are the winners.

D. (1) Write sentences using the following combinations properly as *subjects, predicate nominatives,* or *direct objects.* (2) Proofread for errors in spelling, capitalization, or punctuation. (3) Exchange papers with a partner. (4) On the paper that you receive, underscore the compound and label it according to the way that it is used. (5) Call attention to any nonstandard uses. (6) Go over the marked sentences orally.

1. May and I	4. Leo and him	7. Allen and them
2. George and they	5. you and he	8. Jack and me
3. Helen and us	6. him and her	9. you and we

(*Based upon the sentences in* C *of the preceding activities*)

1. Write the plural of the italicized word in sentence 1.
2. Account for the periods in sentence 7.
3. Why is *Mother* capitalized in sentence 13?

USING PRONOUNS WITH NOUNS

RULES FOR USING PRONOUNS PROPERLY — Continued

RULE 6. **Before a noun, choose** *we* **if a** *subject* **or a** *predicate nominative* **is needed. Use** *us* **if an** *object* **is needed. As a help, say the sentence without the noun.**

(We, Us) boys went.   (We, Us) went.
We went. [You would never say, "*Us* went."]

He helped (us, we) boys.
He helped (us, we).
He helped *us*. [You would never say, "He helped *we*."]

The cooks were (we, us) girls.
The cooks were (we, us).
The cooks were *we*. [*Us* is not a predicate nominative pronoun.]

LEARNING ACTIVITIES

A. Copy the following sentences, filling the blanks with *we* or *us*. Do not write in this book. Go over the practice orally several times, alone and together, so that you get used to the sound of the standard forms.

1. Shall _____ players wait for you?
2. Have they chosen _____ students?
3. _____ men cannot help your friend.
4. _____ girls have an amateur baseball team.
5. The winners are _____ three violinists.
6. Our guide met _____ tourists at the park gates.
7. The youngest players on the team were _____ two guards.
8. The faculty entertained _____ students at dinner.
9. _____ members of the committee should be there.
10. _____ trombonists often practice separately.

B. Divide the class into teams. Take turns at giving sentences using standard combinations of a noun and *we* or *us,* such as *us swimmers, we students.* Keep a record of the number of misuses by each team. The team with the fewest misuses is the winner. You will need to listen carefully to catch any nonstandard uses.

USING POSSESSIVE PRONOUNS PROPERLY

RULES FOR USING PRONOUNS PROPERLY — Continued

RULE 7. *Never* **use an apostrophe in a** *possessive personal pronoun.* **These pronouns are** *my, mine, his, her, hers, its, our, ours, your, yours, their, theirs.*

> The dog wagged its tail.   That car is like ours.
> Is that book yours?   This ring is hers.
> Our house is gray; theirs is white.

WARNING: Do not confuse the possessive personal pronouns *its, your,* and *their* with the contractions *it's, you're,* and *they're.*

> It's time for dinner. (*It is* time for dinner.)
> You're late again. (*You are* late again.)
> They're coming now. (*They are* coming now.)

If you have trouble deciding between *it's* and *its, you're* and *your, they're* and *their,* substitute in the sentence the words of which the contraction is made.

> The dog wagged (its, it's) tail.

["The dog wagged *it is* tail" does not make sense; use *its.*]

> (It's, Its) time for lunch.

["*It is* time for lunch" makes sense; use *It's.*]

> (It's, Its) been raining all day.

["*It has* been raining all day" makes sense; use *It's.*]

> Give me (you're, your) word.

["Give me *you are* word" does not make sense; use *your.*]

> (You're, Your) just in time.

["*You are* just in time" makes sense; use *You're.*]

> (They're, Their) team won.

["*They are* team won" does not make sense; use *Their.*]

> (They're, Their) my friends.

["*They are* my friends" makes sense; use *They're.*]

LEARNING ACTIVITIES

A. Copy the following sentences, correcting any mistakes in spelling. Do not write in this book. Put the sentences on the board so that everyone can see what changes have been made.

1. Deanna thinks that the box must be your's. It's not mine.
2. This is her's, but our's is not here.
3. Is that you're book or theirs?
4. It's her's, not ours.
5. Collect all toys that are your's, but do not touch theirs.
6. Did the dog lose its appetite?
7. Its their turn, not ours.
8. Their's are not here with his.
9. They're waiting for us.
10. You're riding a new bike today. Its very fast.

B. (1) Write sentences using properly *its, it's; their, they're; your, you're.* (2) Divide the class into two teams. (3) Send the first person of one team to the board. (4) The first member of the other team will read his or her sentences, one by one. (5) The person at the board must spell correctly the pronoun or contraction used.

MAKING VERBS AGREE WITH PRONOUN SUBJECTS

THINK IT OVER . . .

Expressions such as "It (or *He* or *She*) don't" and "They (or *We* or *You*) wasn't" are faults in subject-verb agreement that are sometimes heard in everyday speech. If you find yourself using *don't* when you should use *doesn't,* or *wasn't* when you should use *weren't,* now is the time to rid yourself of such language habits.

The rules for making verbs agree with noun subjects apply also to agreement with pronoun subjects. Those rules are restated here, plus two (*4* and *5*) that deal only with pronouns.

RULES FOR AGREEMENT OF VERBS WITH PRONOUN SUBJECTS

RULE 1. Use a singular verb with the singular pronoun subjects *he,* *she,* **and** *it.* **Use a plural verb with the plural pronoun subjects** *we* **and** *they.*

He **does** live here.	*They* **do** live here.
She **was** at the game.	*We* **were** at the game.
He **has** blue eyes.	*They* **have** blue eyes.
It **is** late.	*We* **are** late.

RULE 2. Use the singular forms *doesn't, isn't, wasn't,* **and** *hasn't* **with the singular subjects** *he, she,* **and** *it.* **Use the plural forms** *don't, aren't, weren't,* **and** *haven't* **with the plural subjects** *we* **and** *they.*

He **doesn't** live here.	*They* **don't** live here.
It **isn't** ready.	*They* **aren't** ready.
She **wasn't** there.	*We* **weren't** there.
He **hasn't** decided.	*We* **haven't** decided.

RULE 3. Never use *ain't* **with any subject, singular or plural.**

RULE 4. Always use a plural verb form with the subject *you,* **whether it means one or more than one.**

You **are** the winner.   *You* **are** the winners.

RULE 5. Use *have, do, was,* **and** *am* **with the pronoun subject** *I.*

I **have** seen him.   *I* **do** want it.   *I* **am** here.   *I* **was** there.

LEARNING ACTIVITIES

A. In an oral activity, take turns at asking and answering the following questions. Make each answer a negative one, using a contraction. In sentences 4, 8, and 12, use *we* in your answer. Your answer must be a complete sentence. Do not mark in this book.

EXAMPLE: (Don't, Doesn't) he need help? He *doesn't* need help.

1. (Don't, Doesn't) it look like rain?
2. (Is, Are) she going with us?
3. (Was, Were) they born in this state?
4. (Wasn't, Weren't) you and your brother at the beach yesterday?

5. (Doesn't, Don't) she know your mother?
6. (Don't, Doesn't) it seem cold in this room?
7. (Was, Were) they angry about the delay?
8. (Wasn't, Weren't) you and Lucille here for the party?
9. (Don't, Doesn't) he live near you?
10. (Wasn't, Weren't) we on time?
11. (Doesn't, Don't) she ever lose a game?
12. (Was, Were) you and he at the assembly?

B. (1) Copy these sentences, choosing the proper forms from the parentheses. (2) Proofread for careless errors in copying. (3) In your small groups, check the verb choices as sentences are read aloud.

1. They (wasn't, weren't) looking for us.
2. (Ain't, Aren't) you going horseback riding?
3. (Doesn't, Don't) he like lobster?
4. You (was, were) busy last night.
5. It (doesn't, don't) make sense to me.
6. We (wasn't, weren't) there at first.
7. (Was, Were) you busy?
8. She (don't, doesn't) like having to wear a cast.
9. He (doesn't, don't) want to sing now.
10. I (wasn't, weren't) planning any games.

C. (1) Write two sentences for each of these pronoun subjects: *he, it, she, you, we, they.* In one sentence of each pair, use *wasn't* or *weren't;* in the other, *doesn't* or *don't.* (2) Divide into two teams. (3) Take turns at reading sentences in class. (4) After reading a sentence, call upon a member of the other team to repeat it. If he or she cannot say the sentence, his or her team will be charged with a miss. The team with the fewer misses is the winner.

USING ENGLISH IN ALL CLASSES

Bring to class papers that you have written for any of your classes. Examine them carefully for agreement of verbs with pronoun subjects. Look especially for any misuses of *don't* with the subjects *he, she,* or *it.*

ENRICHMENT

To the tune of some popular song, write a song of your own that will help your class to remember to say *he doesn't, she doesn't, it doesn't, we weren't,* and *they weren't.* If your teacher approves, put your song on the board for the class to copy and practice singing.

USING TROUBLESOME VERBS PROPERLY

READ AND DO . . .

The next few pages contain practice in using the standard forms of *come, freeze, lie, break,* and *run,* five troublesome irregular verbs.

USING IRREGULAR VERBS — <u>COME</u>, <u>CAME</u>, <u>COME</u>

RULE. Never use an auxiliary verb with the simple past tense *came.*
Use *come* **in two ways:** *(a)* **with an auxiliary verb and** *(b)* **by itself in present time.**

Today it comes.   Yesterday it came.   Often it *has* come.

LEARNING ACTIVITIES

A. (1) Copy each of the following sentences, using the proper form of the verb *come.* (2) Underline the form of *come* that you use. Underline also any helping verbs. (3) Read the sentences in class. Go over them more than once if there is time.

1. The Vikings _____ to the New World long before Columbus.
2. An idea has just _____ to me.
3. Suddenly the moon _____ out from behind a cloud.
4. The children's father had recently _____ home.
5. That box of books has finally _____.
6. The end of the play could have _____ sooner.
7. Many interesting stories have _____ down to us from Colonial days.
8. My sister _____ home from work early.
9. My grandmother had _____ from Rumania thirty years earlier.
10. We should have _____ with you.
11. Mrs. Adams _____ home with a present for each of her children.
12. Mr. and Mrs. Finnerty _____ to visit us last Thanksgiving.
13. Mr. Martinez _____ up from the basement two steps at a time.
14. He had _____ home as soon as possible after the game.
15. They _____ early and stayed all day.

B. Write three sentences using *come* with helping verbs and three using *came.* The illustration on page 369 may give you ideas for sentences. In your small groups, take turns at reading sentences.

(Based upon the sentences in A *of the preceding activities)*

1. Why is *Thanksgiving* capitalized in sentence 12?
2. Why does the apostrophe in *children's* (sentence 4) come before the *s?*
3. Why must you use *has* instead of *have* in sentence 5?

USING IRREGULAR VERBS—<u>FREEZE</u>, <u>FROZE</u>, <u>FROZEN</u>

RULE. **Always use an auxiliary verb with** *frozen;* **never use one with** *froze.* (**Never use** *freezed.*)

Today water freezes.   Yesterday it froze.   Often it *has* frozen.

LEARNING ACTIVITIES

A. Copy these sentences, filling the blanks with the proper form of the verb *freeze.* Underline the verb, including any helping verbs. Read the sentences aloud in class. Do not write in this book.

1. Early in the winter the little streams had _____.
2. The icy wind _____ the buds on the trees last night.

369

3. Commander Byrd's ships _____ fast in the ice.
4. We girls almost _____ at yesterday's game.
5. Ice cubes can be _____ quickly in this refrigerator.
6. Luckily, I've never _____ my ears.
7. Has the ice on the hockey field _____ yet?
8. Wages and prices were _____ during the emergency.
9. Ice safe for skating must be _____ to a certain thickness.
10. A lost mitten was _____ into the ice of the pond.
11. The water in the pond has not yet _____.
12. The rain _____ on the windshield.

B. Write sentences using these helping verbs with the proper form of *freeze: has, had, will have.* In your small groups, take turns at reading your sentences. Listen carefully for the standard forms.

★ **Spot Review**

(*Based upon the sentences in* A *of the preceding activities*)

1. Rewrite sentence 6, replacing the contraction with the words for which it stands.
2. Why does the apostrophe come before the *s* in *Byrd's* in sentence 3?
3. Why is *we girls*, not *us girls*, the proper form in sentence 4?
4. What are the direct objects in sentences 2 and 6?
5. Which sentence has a compound subject?

USING IRREGULAR VERBS—LIE, LAY, LAIN

RULE 1. Always use a helping verb with *lain;* **never use one with** *lay.* **Remember that when you use the forms of** *lie*, **you are talking about** *resting* **or** *sleeping*.

Today I **lie** down. '
Yesterday I **lay** down.
Often I *have* **lain** down.

RULE 2. Use the right present participle, *lying*. (See the footnote on page 288.)

STANDARD: My dog was **lying** on the porch.
NONSTANDARD: My dog was **laying** on the porch.

370

LEARNING ACTIVITIES

A. Copy these sentences, filling the blanks with the proper form of the verb *lie*. Underline each verb, including any helping verbs. In class, read the sentences aloud, more than once if time permits.

1. How long has that sick child _____ in bed?
2. You must _____ still now.
3. Yesterday I _____ on the beach for an hour.
4. Many dangers _____ in the path of the early pioneers.
5. You should not have _____ in bed so late.
6. Are the scissors _____ on that table?
7. My brother should have _____ down after lunch.
8. The bandit _____ in hiding for a week.
9. I must have _____ there for an hour.
10. The boat was _____ at anchor.
11. The troops had _____ in ambush behind the hills.
12. How long did they _____ there?
13. Snow _____ on the mountains all last winter.
14. Were your glasses _____ on the desk?

B. Write sentences on the board, leaving blanks to be filled with *lie, lay, lain,* or *lying*. Call on classmates to read the sentences, using the proper forms and naming any auxiliary verbs.

C. (1) Put these three statements on the board:

    I can lie still.   I am lying still.   I have lain still.

(2) See how many other statements you can make by changing only the helping verbs. Turn to the list on page 282 if you like. Remember, you may combine two or more helping verbs. Make this an oral activity.

D. This is a geography lesson. Number your paper from 1 to 8. Opposite each number write *lie* or *lies*, whichever form is proper for the corresponding sentence. Do not write in this book. Read these sentences orally in your small groups to check your answers.

1. Canada _____ north of the United States.
2. San Diego _____ at the southern edge of the California coast.
3. Many fertile farms _____ in the Mississippi Valley.
4. The Black Hills _____ in western South Dakota.
5. The Pacific and Atlantic coasts _____ thousands of miles apart.
6. South of the Rio Grande _____ the country of Mexico.
7. Which _____ farther north, Maine or Minnesota?
8. Does St. Louis _____ east of Minneapolis?

E. Make out a list of five true geographical statements about your state, using *lie* or *lies* in each sentence. Read your sentences to the class, leaving out the name of the place that you have in mind. The class will try to guess its name.

USING IRREGULAR VERBS—BREAK, BROKE, BROKEN

RULE. **Always use a helping verb with** *broken;* **never use one with** *broke.*

Today it breaks.   Yesterday it broke.   Often it *has* broken.

LEARNING ACTIVITIES

A. Copy these sentences, filling the blanks with the proper form of the verb *break.* Read the sentences aloud and name any helping verbs.

1. Jean and I have not _____ our promise.
2. The sun has not _____ through the clouds all day.
3. The high-jump record was _____ by José Mayo.
4. Three of the eggs in the basket had _____.
5. Eagerly the king _____ the seal on the letter.
6. The strong wind must have _____ this window.
7. Alicia _____ the news to Father this morning.
8. Ground has just been _____ for the new library.

B. Write two good sentences using *broke* and three using *broken.* Use inverted order (see point 1 on page 313) in at least two sentences. In your small groups, take turns at reading the sentences aloud.

★ **Spot Review**

(Based upon the sentences in A *of the preceding activities)*

1. Spell the plural of *library* (sentence 8). Give the rule.
2. Which four sentences contain direct objects? Name these objects.
3. Why is *I,* not *me,* the standard form in sentence 1?
4. Rewrite sentence 2, using a contraction.

USING IRREGULAR VERBS—RUN, RAN, RUN

RULE 1. **Never use an auxiliary verb with the simple past tense** *ran.*

RULE 2. **Use** *run* **in two ways:** (*a*) **with a helping verb and** (*b*) **by itself in present time.**

Today I run.   Yesterday I ran.   Often I *have* run.

LEARNING ACTIVITIES

A. Take turns at completing the following sentences orally, using the proper form of *run* as a part of the sentence and using as many other words as you wish.

1. I have never . . .
2. As a boy, my father . . .
3. Rosa might have . . .
4. That race was . . .
5. After seeing me, the horse . . .
6. The child shouldn't have . . .

B. (1) Find *run* in the dictionary. (2) Write five sentences using different meanings of *run* as a verb. You may use *run* with a helping verb or *ran*. In your small groups, take turns at reading your sentences aloud.

C. (1) Copy these sentences, filling the blanks with the proper form of the verb *run*. (2) Underline each verb, including any helping verbs. Proofread each sentence for careless errors in copying. (3) Exchange papers for checking. (4) Check the verbs as the sentences are read aloud.

1. In my first race, I _____ a poor last.
2. Luisa's sister, a research chemist, must have _____ many experiments.
3. My Aunt Ellen has _____ for Congress twice.
4. Once upon a time, a busy road _____ past our farm.
5. My brother's alarm clock _____ down last night.
6. Have you ever _____ away from home?
7. At the Labor Day picnic last week, the children _____ races.
8. The color in this shirt should not have _____.
9. In the sixth inning of that game, our pitcher _____ into trouble.
10. You must have _____ this machine too fast.

Spot Review

(Based upon the sentences in C of the preceding activities)

1. How would you write the plural of the possessive in sentence 5?
2. How is *chemist* used in sentence 2? Explain the commas.
3. Why do *Aunt* (sentence 3) and *Day* (sentence 7) have capital letters?
4. Why is *have* the proper form in sentence 6?

ENRICHMENT

By yourself or with a friend, make up a jingle to help you remember (1) that *run* is used both by itself (to show present time) and with a helping verb; (2) that *ran* always stands alone. With your teacher's approval, say your jingle for the class.

A. Copy the following sentences. Underline each pronoun and label it according to its use in the sentence: *subject* (subj.), *predicate nominative* (p.n.), *direct object* (d.o.), *appositive* (app.). Proofread to make sure you have made no errors in copying.

1. She and I went to the ball game at Yankee Stadium.
2. The player swung at a ball, hit it, and lofted a high foul.
3. The spectators closest to the ball were Florence and I.
4. The ball landed on a shoulder, mine.

B. Read these sentences aloud, choosing the proper forms.

1. Tom chose Gina and (I, me).
2. Joe and (he, him) are great friends.
3. This is (she, her) speaking.
4. The twins and (we, us) will go with you.
5. Could it be (they, them) standing there?
6. No one called you and (I, me).
7. (We, Us) members of the committee need your help.
8. Will you tell (we, us) adults about the picnic?
9. Father called (we, us) children at six o'clock.
10. Every noon (we, us) students play marbles.
11. The dog wagged (its, it's) tail.
12. Is this book (yours, your's)?
13. The next house is (ours, our's).
14. (They're, Their) car is a new one.

C. Read these sentences aloud, choosing the standard forms.

1. We (wasn't, weren't) waiting for anyone.
2. He (don't, doesn't) ever wear overshoes.
3. You (was, were) wearing jeans last night.
4. (Don't, Doesn't) she speak French?
5. Where (was, were) you last Friday?
6. He (don't, doesn't) believe me.
7. They (was, were) busy in the emergency room.
8. (Wasn't, Weren't) you and Isabel playing ball?
9. It (don't, doesn't) often snow here.

D. Copy these sentences, supplying the proper form of each verb. Go over the sentences orally.

1. That woman (come) to this country forty years ago.
2. (Lie) here until dinnertime.

＊ Check Test 4 should be taken at this point. If the results show need for further study, students should do this review practice. They should then take Mastery Test 4.

3. The dog had (lie) down beside the fireplace.
4. The silence was (break) by a loud crash.
5. At the picnic last Friday, we (run) races.
6. The book (lie) on the table yesterday.
7. I (freeze) the dessert yesterday.
8. Many people have (come) to America from Europe.
9. The man had been (lie) in wait for us.
10. Mr. Blake has (run) for office many times.
11. Last night thieves (break) into Mrs. Gray's store.
12. Now the ground has (freeze) hard.
13. Because of the hot sun, I (lie) in the shade.
14. Christmas Day had (come) again.
15. Whose farm (lie) straight north of here?
16. You (run) that bazaar very well.

Cumulative Review

CAPITALIZATION

Copy these sentences, inserting needed capital letters.

1. mexicans, canadians, and alaskans—all are americans. most of them live on a mainland, north america. people in ireland, england, and scotland live on islands.
2. Finally mother said, "on christmas day, let's show the slides of our trip to the east. we'll write uncle james and aunt alice to come."
3. father added, "that's a fine idea. we'll celebrate right here on good old amsterdam avenue. we'll have a good time."
4. bill and ben, who worked on a farm during june and july, wrote an airplane story that they called "landing in clover."
5. The pilot, captain n. b. dunn, made a forced landing in a clover field near which the boys were working.

PUNCTUATION

Copy these sentences, inserting needed punctuation.

1. Yes Son before I trust you to drive alone said Bobs father Id like to see you park the car
2. Thats easy Bob exclaimed with entirely too much confidence
3. Bob found a busy street tried to back into a parking place and scraped a fender
4. The next day Father Mother and Marge his older sister took Bob to a lonely street and made him practice parking over and over again
5. Then Marge gave him a book called How to Drive a Car by Captain O L Reyburn a member of the local traffic department

CONTRACTIONS

Write the correct contraction of each of these groups of words.

1. will not   3. does not   5. it is   7. you are
2. I will   4. they have   6. are not   8. have not

SPELLING

Copy the following words in a column on a sheet of paper. Beside each word write another word made from it by adding a suffix or ending. These words are spelled by rules.

1. like   5. fool   9. hop   13. quit
2. swim   6. enter   10. skate   14. funny
3. open   7. lucky   11. write   15. refer
4. marry   8. argue   12. play   16. run

POSSESSIVE OF NOUNS

Write the correct possessive form of each of the nouns below and name the thing owned. For each common noun, put *a, an,* or *the* before it. For example, if the word were *team,* you might write *the team's captain.*

1. Joshua   4. bears   7. women   10. Washington
2. oxen   5. children   8. girls   11. father-in-law
3. rabbit   6. Erica   9. authors   12. soprano

VERB-SUBJECT AGREEMENT

Read these sentences aloud, choosing the standard forms.

1. There (isn't, aren't) enough seats in this class.
2. (Hasn't, Haven't) Fritz or Germaine called you?
3. The men in the boat (was, were) fishing.
4. (Don't, Doesn't) the smell of those pies make you hungry?
5. The Chans (has, have) been here before.
6. There (hasn't, haven't) been any rain for twenty days.
7. The pail of blueberries (wasn't, weren't) on the step.

TROUBLESOME VERBS

Read these sentences aloud, using the proper form of each verb.

1. Don has (do) the problem.
2. Have you (give) the answer?
3. I (know) him years ago.
4. The piece was (speak) well.
5. Have you (take) my eraser?
6. Once Bob (bring) us a lion.
7. I've (write) you before.
8. We (begin) work last week.
9. Have they (go)?
10. I have (see) that movie.
11. A queen was (choose).
12. At last he (give) up.
13. Only a pie was (take).
14. Dick had (go) early.
15. Has he (bring) a camera?
16. She has (write) twice.

Word Games to Test Your Thinking

Catch On to the Trick

All the words defined below end in *ick* and rhyme with *trick*.

1. Not well
2. Sound of a watch
3. "Locking" sound
4. Piece of wood
5. A young chicken
6. Not thin
7. Baked block of clay
8. Give a blow with the foot
9. "It must be St. _____."
10. Slight cut
11. Select
12. Part of a candle
13. Fast
14. Smooth
15. A quick light stroke
16. A stack of hay

Forward and Backward Puzzle

Did you ever stop to think that many words are spelled the same forward as backward? Can you figure out the following? An example is *eve*, meaning "the night before."

1. Before (rhymes with *there*)
2. Even (rhymes with *bevel*)
3. Girl's name (rhymes with *banana*)
4. Boy's name (sounds like another word for *car*)
5. Past of *do*
6. A loud noise
7. A nickname for *Mother*
8. A small dog
9. Vigor
10. Distress signal
11. A name for *Father* (not *Pop*)
12. Not speaking
13. A small child
14. Time of day

Would You Like to Know — ?

The encyclopedia answers to these questions may surprise you.

1. What strange weapon of offense has the *octopus?*
2. In what country was *oleomargarine* first produced?
3. What is the real name of the ship nicknamed *Old Ironsides?*
4. Why should *oleander* plants be kept away from little children?
5. In a race between an *ostrich* and a horse, which would win?

"Spelling Demons" Crossword Puzzle

Copy the crossword puzzle. Do not write in this book.

33. Initials of "Honest Abe's" father.
34. One who does.
36. Said when you want someone to keep quiet.
37. A speech in church.
39. Religious holiday.
42. To say again.
43. Comparative form of *dry.*
45. South Carolina (*abbr.*).
46. To try out something.

Across

1. To fail to fulfill someone's hopes.
9. The sixtieth part of an hour.
10. The face of a clock.
11. Present form of *be.*
12. A girl's name.
13. Seven days.
14. Steamship (*abbr.*).
15. A person who has this never embarrasses anyone (rhymes with *fact*).
17. 1,102 (*Roman numerals*).
19. Grass-covered earth.
21. Present of *saw.*
22. Finish.
23. An act of pleading.
25. Payments charged for services.
28. Present tense of *went.*
29. Level; regular; opposite of *odd.*
30. Making use of.
32. Past of the verb *lead.*

Down

1. To change from a solid into a liquid state; to melt.
2. Preposition.
3. A kind of wearing apparel.
4. A book of maps.
5. Opposite of *warlike.*
6. The same (*Latin*).
7. The daughter of one's brother.
8. Opposite of *giving.*
9. Spelled incorrectly.
16. Used in golf (*plural*).
18. An image to which worship is offered.
20. An act.
24. Indefinite article.
26. A kind of duck.
27. Noise made by some sleepers.
31. Jewels.
33. Opposite of *here.*
35. One way to cook meat.
36. Part of a stair.
38. New York City (*abbr.*).
40. A plural form of *be.*
41. "Sing a song of ____pence."
44. Yes (*Spanish and Italian*).

USING ADJECTIVES IN BUILDING SENTENCES*

"ADJECTIVES MUST BE TO KEEP SENTENCES FROM BEING TOO SHORT."

THINK IT OVER . . .

Should adjectives be used "to keep sentences from being too short"?

What *should* determine the use of adjectives?

Have you any idea how much use you yourself make of them?

*Pretest 5 should be taken at this point.

1. Recognizing Adjectives

Recall the sentence "The porpoise tossed the ball." Suppose it read like this:

One clever, agile porpoise tossed *the red* ball.

What does that word *one* tell you? It tells *how many* porpoises. What do *clever* and *agile* tell you? They tell *what kind* of porpoise or what it looked like. What do *the* and *red* tell you? They tell *which* ball the porpoise tossed. The meanings of the nouns *porpoise* and *ball* are affected by those words: *one, clever, agile, the,* and *red.* Such words are used as "adjectives."

One clever, agile porpoise tossed the red ball.

Along with the verb, noun, and pronoun, the adjective is another part of speech. As you study this chapter, keep in mind that you cannot tell what part of speech a word is simply by looking at it. A word that is a noun in one sentence may be a verb in another sentence. In other words, the part of speech a word is depends on the way that it is used in the sentence.

The word "farm," for example, may be used as a verb, as a noun, or as an adjective.

> Did Tess *farm* all last summer? (*Farm* is a verb.)
> Her *farm* is located on Route 40. (*Farm* is a noun.)
> Tess enjoys *farm* life. (*Farm* is an adjective.)

● THESE ARE FACTS ABOUT ADJECTIVES

1. **(DEFINITION)** *True adjectives* **are words that modify** (*affect*) **nouns by describing them, or telling** *what kind.*

    We need tall bookcases.   Red hair suits me.

    True adjectives meet certain tests.

    a) **They will fit into the slots in this sentence:**

    The _____ one seems very _____.
    The tall one seems very tall.
    The red one seems very red.

    b) **They may take** (1) **endings or** (2) **the words** *more* **or** *most* **to show comparison.**

    (1) tall, taller, tallest
    (2) useful, more useful, most useful

2. **Many adjectives are made from verbs.**

    We crossed the frozen lake.   Freezing rain was falling.

3. **Adjectives may be compound.**

    A loud and noisy crowd came.   Has he brown or blue eyes?

LEARNING ACTIVITIES

A. To give a good idea of what adjectives can do, carry out this activity. (1) Here are five nouns: *river, tree, sky, man, coat.* (2) On your paper, write for each of those nouns five adjectives that might be used to describe it. (3) On the board list each noun and all the different adjectives that the members of the class wrote on their papers.

B. Use the tests in point 1 to decide which of the following words can be adjectives.

1. snowy	5. quickly	9. green	13. change
2. about	6. write	10. terrific	14. always
3. help	7. original	11. timidly	15. childish
4. different	8. lovely	12. blank	16. exciting

C. The way that a word is used determines its part of speech. Tell (1) whether each italicized word in these sentences is used as a noun, a verb, or an adjective and (2) how you know.

1. That song is a tale about three *blind* mice.
2. Did those headlights *blind* you?
3. I raised the *blind* to let in the sun.
4. The new store will *open* tomorrow.
5. The bird entered through that *open* window.
6. Come out into the *open.*
7. We are having *fine* weather.
8. The *fine* was a heavy one.
9. Did they *fine* that driver?

D. (1) Write an original paragraph in which you use these nouns: *boy, lake, storm, dog, wind, water.* Be sure to apply the Guides for Writing a Paragraph, page 162. With each noun use one or more adjectives that will give a clear and vivid picture. (2) Be sure to proofread for careless errors; review the Writing Chart, page 151. (3) Take turns reading paragraphs in class or in your small groups. As you listen, jot down adjectives that you think are especially well chosen. Compare notes afterward. The drawing offers ideas for paragraphs.

★ **Spot Review**

(Based upon the sentences in C *of the preceding activities)*

1. Four of the sentences have verb phrases. Name the phrases.
2. Four sentences have direct objects. Name them.
3. Which one is an imperative sentence?
4. Give the pattern for each sentence.

2. Recognizing Predicate Adjectives

"I KNOW IT'S AN ADJECTIVE, BUT WHAT DOES IT MODIFY?"

The porpoise is playful.

THINK IT OVER . . .

Can an adjective come after the verb in a sentence?

Strange as it seems to the girl, *playful* is an adjective in *The dog is playful.* That is a *Pattern 3* sentence, explained in this lesson.

● THESE ARE FACTS ABOUT PREDICATE ADJECTIVES

1. **(DEFINITION) An adjective that completes the verb, or predicate, and modifies the subject is a** *predicate adjective.*

    The porpoise is **clever.**

    The word *clever* comes after and completes the predicate verb, *is;* it modifies the subject, *porpoise.* (It tells *what kind* of porpoise.)

2. **Predicate adjectives complete such linking verbs as** *am, is, are, was, were, be,* **and** *been* **or combinations, such as** *is being, will be,* **and** *have been.*

    The children *were* **sleepy.**

    The weather *has been* **cold** and **wet.**

3. **Predicate adjectives may also complete verbs like** *become, seem, feel, appear, look, taste,* **and** *smell.*

    The fruit *seems* **ripe.**   Mary *feels* **ill.**

4. **Sentences that have predicate adjectives are** *Pattern 3* **sentences. The formula is N + LV + A.**

    N + LV + A
    Today was sunny.

    N + LV + A
    Your desk looks neat.

A. Copy the following sentences. Underline each predicate adjective and draw an arrow to the word modified. Go over your papers orally.

1. This light is certainly brilliant.
2. Mother was late for work.
3. The crowd appeared restless at first.
4. That traffic seems really heavy.
5. Our dog becomes noisy sometimes.
6. The place looks much different now.
7. My sister is skillful at many things.
8. Those flowers smell sweet.
9. Jillana felt better today.
10. We were almost sure of winning.
11. The pages of the book were brown with age.
12. They certainly look healthy.
13. The buttercups in the field are yellow.
14. The room suddenly seemed quiet.

B. Copy the following sentences, completing each one so that it becomes a *Pattern 3* sentence. (Be careful not to use a predicate noun by mistake.) In your small groups, take turns at reading sentences. Notice how the various predicate adjectives change the sentence picture. Do not write in this book.

1. That person certainly looks _____.
2. Our neighbors are _____.
3. Aunt Marietta is _____.
4. The people have become _____.
5. The air smells _____.
6. The children were _____.
7. The house looked _____.
8. Both those books are _____.
9. My head felt _____.
10. I am _____.

C. Write sentences using the following words in *Pattern 3* sentences: *graceful, honest, sleepy, sweet, pleasant, beautiful.* Use a different linking verb in each sentence. Read the sentences in class.

3. Recognizing Adjectival Words: I

Some words that are not true adjectives are used like adjectives; in other words, they modify nouns. *Determiners* form one group of such words. They are *adjectival words,* that is, words that are *used like adjectives.*

1. **(DEFINITION)** *Determiners* **are words that modify nouns but do not fit the tests for true adjectives.**

   a) **Some determiners point out** *which.*

      (1) **The articles** *a, an,* **and** *the* **always do so.**

         A man called.   I ate an apple.   The race is over.

      (2) *This, that, these,* **and** *those* **can do so.**

         This book is mine.   I like those plans.

      (3) *First, second, third,* **and so on can do so.**

         We took the **first** bus.   They live on the **tenth** floor.

   b) **Possessive nouns and pronouns are determiners that tell** *whose.*

      Henry's book is new.   My book is old.

   c) **Numerals** (*one, two, three,* . . .) **are determiners that tell** *how many.*

      I ate two apples.   We need forty-six pens.

   d) **Special determiners limit nouns by telling** *which, how many,* **or** *how much.* **Here are some of them.**

all	both	enough	many	much	several
another	each	every	more	no	some
any	either	few	most	other	such

      Each girl helped.   Both trains left.   I like most foods.

2. **If a noun has both determiners and true adjectives, the determiners always come first.**

   We bought two new tires.   It was a windy, rainy day.

   (*Two* comes before *new; a* comes before *windy* and *rainy.*)

Learn about words!

The following words, taken from Learning Activity *B*, page 386, have interesting histories. Use your dictionary to find the story behind each word.

   lieutenant   mustang   dairy   vacation

LEARNING ACTIVITIES

A. Many words that are used as determiners can also be used as subjects, predicate nominatives, or direct objects. You can recognize the pronouns *his, her,* and *its; this, that, these,* and *those* can also be pronouns. So can many of the words that are listed under subpoint *d* of point *1* on page 385.

Decide which italicized words in the following sentences are used as determiners and which are not. Tell whether the words that are not determiners are used as subjects, predicate nominatives, or direct objects. Make this an oral exercise.

1. *Much* money will be needed for *this* project.
2. Bill has *some* new books. *Several* look exciting.
3. *Many* people remember *her* very well.
4. *This* house must be *his.*
5. May I borrow *those* pliers? I haven't *any* of my own.
6. Where did you hear *that?*
7. *Which* day for the picnic suits you?
8. We can take *either* road. *Both* look very good.
9. *Each* player was a star in *that* game.
10. I don't know *much* about the *other* person.
11. *Most* days lately have had *some* sunshine.
12. *Another* girl has finished *her* report.
13. *Friday's* newspaper has *my* picture in it.
14. *Seventeen* bushels of potatoes were *all* that were left.

B. (1) Copy the following sentences, underlining each adjective or word used as an adjective. (2) Draw an arrow to the noun modified, as in the examples on page 381. (3) Exchange papers for checking. (4) Go over the sentences in class. Tell which words are true adjectives and which are determiners.

1. Three little kittens had white paws.
2. Grandfather's new house has many beautiful rooms.
3. The howling wind drowned our voices.
4. Many women become athletes.
5. Jim's throwing arm has been bothering him.
6. The noisy and excited crowd cheered their team.
7. The tall, thin, smiling lieutenant is my first cousin.
8. Few people have ridden that wild mustang.
9. Those two boys have built several good carts.
10. Aunt Hilda runs a large and spotless dairy.
11. Each team has won four thrilling games.
12. Have you seen Manuel's new camera?
13. These shoes are my favorite ones.
14. Both families have been enjoying their vacations.
15. The frightened child has lost her parents.
16. Every carton was full.

4. Recognizing Adjectival Words: II

Determiners, you have learned, are used like adjectives. This lesson deals with nouns that are used in that way; in other words, with nouns that function as noun modifiers.

● THESE ARE FACTS ABOUT ADJECTIVAL WORDS: II

1. **A word made from a proper noun can modify other nouns. Such a modifier is sometimes called a** *proper adjective.*

   The **American** flag waved in the breeze.

2. **A proper noun itself is sometimes a modifier.**

   Our **South Carolina** home burned.

3. **Common nouns sometimes are modifiers.**

   The package was tied with a **paper** ribbon.

   Automobile accidents are very common.

LEARNING ACTIVITIES

A. Copy the following proper nouns and beside each write the modifying form made from it. If you are not sure of the spelling of any word, look it up in the dictionary. Do not write in this book. Go over the list in class.

1. Canada	3. Japan	5. China	7. Turkey
2. Australia	4. Italy	6. Africa	8. Portugal

B. Copy the following words, and opposite each write the proper noun from which it comes. Check these in class.

1. English	4. Danish	7. Spanish	10. French
2. Norwegian	5. Swedish	8. Brazilian	11. Hungarian
3. Scottish	6. Belgian	9. Roman	12. Welsh

C. Write five sentences using as modifiers words from *B*, or others, if you prefer. Be sure to proofread, using the Writing Chart on page 151. In your small groups, read your sentences. Call on classmates to tell what word each of your choices modifies.

5. Using Vivid, Exact Adjectives

Adjectives can be helpful in making what a person says both interesting and accurate. The trouble with many people is that they use the same adjectives again and again. For example, your father may have said to you last night, "Well, how was the game?" Depending upon which side won, of course, you may have replied with one of these remarks:

"It was great."	"It was terrible."
"It was good."	"It was awful."
"It was keen."	"It was rotten."

The left-hand answers indicate that you enjoyed the game; the other three, the opposite. Not one of them, however, gives a really good picture of what the game was like.

GUIDES FOR USING ADJECTIVES EFFECTIVELY

1. Avoid using such overworked adjectives as *grand, swell, good, keen, awful, nice, terrible,* or *wonderful.*

2. Use words that give an exact, vivid picture. Remember that vivid adjectives can be made from many verbs.

   WEAK: A *bad* hailstorm ruined our wheat.
   VIVID: A *slashing* hailstorm ruined our wheat.

   WEAK: An *old* car pulled up at the curb.
   VIVID: A *battered* car pulled up at the curb.

3. If your library has a dictionary of synonyms, use it to find strong substitutes for adjectives that you overuse.

Learn about words!

The following words, taken from Learning Activity *A,* have interesting histories. Use your dictionary to find the story behind each word.

science   nice   carpenter   minstrel

LEARNING ACTIVITIES

A. Make the following sentences more effective by substituting exact adjectives for the ones in italics. Go over your sentences in your small groups, making a list of the substituted adjectives.

1. It was a *wonderful* motion picture.
2. The trip to Canada was *great*.
3. They had a *grand* time at the minstrel show.
4. The Babins are *swell* people.
5. That certainly was an *awful* storm.
6. Our science teacher is *keen*.
7. We had a *terrible* time finding the carpenter.
8. Iris is a *nice* poodle.
9. The dinner was *terrific*.
10. The party was *neat*.
11. We just returned from a really *super* trip.

B. (1) Study the following sentences, all taken from Mark Twain's *The Adventures of Tom Sawyer*. (2) In an oral activity, point out and have listed on the board the vivid adjectives used by the author. Note that many are made from verbs. Notice also that in one sentence the adjectives follow the noun modified. (3) Point out any vivid nouns or verbs.

1. The balmy summer air, the restful quiet, the odor of the flowers, and the drowsing murmur of the bees had had their effect.
2. Away off in the flaming sunshine, Cardiff Hill lifted its soft green sides through a shimmering veil of heat.
3. The climbing fire lit up their faces and threw its ruddy glare upon the pillared tree-trunks . . . and upon the varnished foliage and festooning vines.
4. One blinding flash after another came, and peal on peal of deafening thunder.
5. The boys cried out to each other, but the roaring wind and the booming thunderblasts drowned their voices utterly.
6. And that night there came on a terrific storm, with driving rain, awful claps of thunder, and blinding sheets of lightning.
7. Potter, pale and haggard, timid and hopeless, was brought in, . . .
8. Tom was a glittering hero once more. . . .
9. The clanging bell had been calling for half an hour.

C. Write five original sentences in which you use adjectives that give a clear and exact picture. For example, describe a race, a fire, a new automobile, a good dinner, a picnic, a hot day, a cold day, a snowstorm, a crowd of people. Remember, adjectives that are verb forms (especially the *ing* ones, such as *blazing*) often are good picture words. Take turns at reading sentences aloud. Have someone list on the board adjectives that seem to the class to be especially good.

FOLLOW-UP

Copy in your notebook the lists of vivid, exact adjectives that the class made in activities *A*, *B*, and *C*. Whenever you have a writing assignment, make use of this list.

USING ENGLISH IN ALL CLASSES

Go over papers that you are preparing for any of your classes. Check to see whether you are using the same vague or worn-out adjectives over and over. If you are, change them to words that give a clearer and more exact picture.

6. Comparing Adjectives

| This porpoise is **happy.** | This porpoise is **happier.** | This porpoise is **happiest** of all. |

If an adjective could not take different forms, such as *happy, happier, happiest,* comparing one thing with another would be almost impossible. Fortunately, adjectives *can* change their form to show various degrees of comparison.

● THESE ARE FACTS ABOUT COMPARING ADJECTIVES

1. **Most adjectives have three degrees of comparison:** (*a*) *positive,* (*b*) *comparative,* (*c*) *superlative.* **The** *positive* **degree states a quality. The** *comparative* **degree compares** *two* **things. The** *superlative* **degree compares** *more than two.*

Positive Degree	Comparative Degree	Superlative Degree
new	newer	newest
funny	funnier	funniest
noble	nobler	noblest

2. **One-syllable adjectives and some two-syllable adjectives** (especially ones ending in *y* or *le*) **add** *er* **and** *est* **to form the comparative and the superlative, as in the examples above.*** (For spelling changes that may take place, see Rule 2, page 257, and Rule 1, page 259.)

3. **Many two-syllable adjectives and almost all those of more than two syllables use** *more* **and** *most.*

Positive	Comparative	Superlative
helpless	more helpless	most helpless
important	more important	most important

4. **A few adjectives are irregular in their comparison.**

Positive	Comparative	Superlative
good	better	best
bad	worse	worst
much, many	more	most
little†	less	least

LEARNING ACTIVITY

(1) In your small groups, divide the following words into two lists: *a*) adjectives that are compared by adding *er* and *est* and (*b*) those compared by using *more* and *most*. (2) Compare lists in class. (3) Have the spelling of the comparisons in the *a* list written on the board. Give for each one the spelling rule that applies.

1. cheerful	6. clumsy	11. honest	16. prompt
2. jolly	7. splendid	12. steady	17. glad
3. flat	8. careless	13. big	18. muddy
4. delicious	9. cool	14. straight	19. simple
5. interesting	10. friendly	15. critical	20. dim

* The dictionary gives the comparative forms of most words that can be compared by adding *er* and *est.*

† The comparison here refers to *little* when applied to an amount: *little* money, *less* money, *least* money. *Little*, referring to *size*, is compared regularly: *little, littler, littlest.*

DIAGRAMMING ADJECTIVES

Here is how to fit adjectives into the diagram pattern.

One clever, agile porpoise tossed *the red* ball.

You have learned that *clever* and *agile* are adjectives modifying the subject, *porpoise,* and that *red* is an adjective modifying the object, *ball. One* is a determiner modifying *porpoise; the* is a determiner modifying *ball.*

Steps in Diagramming Adjectives

1. First, diagram the backbone of the sentence, as usual. Note that the words on the base line are the words of the sentence pattern.

2. Place adjectives on slanting lines below the words that they modify:

COMPOUND ADJECTIVES

A *happy* **and** *playful* porpoise tossed a ball.

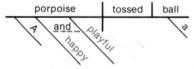

POSSESSIVE ADJECTIVES

Ida's brother often changes *his* mind.

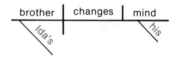

3. Diagram *predicate adjectives* as you do predicate nominatives. Place them on the main line with a slanted line pointing back to the subject.

The chair was *comfortable.*

The delay was *annoying.*

COMPOUND PREDICATE ADJECTIVES

We were *tired* but *happy.*

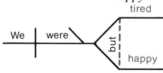

LEARNING ACTIVITIES

A. (1) Diagram the verb, the subject, any direct objects or predicate nominatives, and the adjectives, including predicates, in the following sentences. (2) Exchange papers. (3) Have the diagrams put on the board. (4) Check the papers as each diagram is explained orally. Be sure to follow a definite pattern. For example, one sentence in the sample diagrams might be explained thus: "The verb is an action verb, *changes.* The subject is a noun, *brother.* There is a direct object, the noun *mind. Ida's* is a possessive noun used to modify the subject, and *his* is a pronoun used as a possessive adjective to modify the direct object."

1. That new librarian reads many books.
2. Both girls are busy and happy.
3. Those people are our neighbors.
4. I need four carnival tickets.
5. The old champion has a new title.
6. The speech was long and dull.
7. Sue's young brother is quiet.
8. I have two new records.
9. An acrobat must be alert.
10. This wall is old but strong.

B. For further practice, diagram the sentences in *B* on page 386 and in *A* on page 384. Be sure to explain the diagrams orally.

Spot Review

(Based upon the sentences in A *of the preceding activities)*

1. Account for the apostrophe in sentence 7.
2. Which sentences are *Pattern 3* sentences?
3. Which sentences contain present tense verbs?
4. Compare the adjectives in sentence 6.

7. Using Standard English

USING ADJECTIVES PROPERLY

This section deals with certain common problems in adjective usage. Learn and apply the rules that follow.

RULES FOR USING ADJECTIVES PROPERLY

RULE 1. Use *an* **before a word beginning with a vowel** (that is, *a, e, i, o,* or *u*) **or a vowel sound** (words beginning with silent *h,* as in *heir, honest,* and *hour*).

   an apple   an honor   an egg   an orange

RULE 2. Use *a* **before a word beginning with a consonant sound.**

   a house   a flower   a wreath   a storm

RULE 3. When you speak about *separate nouns,* **be sure to use** *a, an,* **or** *the* **before each. If only one person or thing is meant, do not repeat the article.**

   She needed a stenographer and bookkeeper. (*one person*)
   She needed a stenographer and a bookkeeper. (*two persons*)
   He bought a green and brown coat. (*one coat*)
   He bought a green and a brown coat. (*two coats*)

RULE 4. Use the singular *this* **or** *that* **with** *kind* **or** *sort;* **use the plural** *these* **or** *those* **with** *kinds* **or** *sorts.*

   this (or that) *kind* of shoe   these (or those) *kinds* of shoes
   this (or that) *sort* of skate   these (or those) *sorts* of skates

RULE 5. Do not use *them* **for** *these* **or** *those. Them* **is a personal pronoun** that should be used only as an object.

   STANDARD: Give me those books.
   NONSTANDARD: Give me ~~them~~ books.

RULE 6. Use the *superlative* **form of an adjective only if you are speaking of** *more than two.*

   STANDARD: He is the tallest boy on the basketball team.
   NONSTANDARD: This is the ~~newest~~ of the two books.

RULE 7. Do not use double comparisons; that is, if you add *er* **and** *est,* **omit** *more* **and** *most.*

   STANDARD: I am busier than Dick.
   NONSTANDARD: I am ~~more~~ busier than Dick.

LEARNING ACTIVITIES

A. (*Rules 1 and 2*) Write a list of ten nouns before which you should use the article *an*. Then do the same for *a*. Read your lists in class.

B. (*Rule 3*) In your small groups, go over the following sentences, choosing the proper or clearer forms. Explain your choice in each case.

1. Mrs. Brown is (a physician and surgeon, a physician and a surgeon).
2. On the committee Bob put (a boy and girl, a boy and a girl).
3. I saw (a sailor and a soldier, a sailor and soldier) on the street.
4. Jocelyn was wearing (a red and a blue, a red and blue) jacket.
5. The boys had (a bat and ball, a bat and a ball).
6. Marilyn wants to be (a chemist or biologist, a chemist or a biologist).
7. They are looking for a man to work as (a driver and mechanic, a driver and a mechanic).

C. (*Rules 4 and 5*) Copy these sentences, filling the blanks with *this, that, these, those,* or *them.* Do not write in this book. Exchange papers and check them as you read the sentences orally.

1. _____ sort of desk is more convenient.
2. I like _____ kind better now.
3. Are _____ coats on sale?
4. I bought _____ kind of china.
5. _____ boys went with me.
6. _____ sort of fish lives in fresh water.
7. Those shoes may be a bargain. I don't like _____, though.
8. _____ kinds of matches are more expensive.
9. What did _____ skates cost?
10. I like your glasses. How often have you worn _____?
11. Mother said that _____ kinds of needles are best.
12. Do you ever grow _____ sorts of plants?

D. (*Rules 6 and 7*) (1) Copy the following sentences, using the proper adjective forms. (2) Exchange papers. (3) As they are read aloud, check the sentences for use of the proper adjective forms.

1. Which is the (taller, tallest) of you two boys?
2. I'm (more hungrier, hungrier) at dinner than at breakfast.
3. Of these two jackets, the blue one is the (better, best) value.
4. The (older, oldest) one of those four girls is a senior.
5. Last night we played our (worse, worst) game of all.
6. Is this the (shorter, shortest) of the two roads?

E. Write a paragraph in which you use *this, that, these,* and *those* in the right combinations with *kind(s)* or *sort(s)*. Perhaps thinking about the clothes that you wear will give you an idea for your paragraph. Refer to the Guides for Writing a Paragraph, page 162, as you plan your writing. Read the paragraphs in your small groups. Listen for the proper uses.

USING ENGLISH IN ALL CLASSES

Go over papers that you are preparing for any of your classes. Check to see whether you have misused any adjectives. If so, make the proper changes. If there is one usage that is a particular problem for you, review daily, for at least a week, the rule that applies.

USING TROUBLESOME VERBS

READ AND THINK ABOUT . . .

Knowing the standard forms of irregular verbs is not enough. You must *use* them outside school as well as in the classroom. The next five pages deal with such troublesome verbs as *drink, eat, throw, swim,* and *drive.*

USING IRREGULAR VERBS — DRINK, DRANK, DRUNK

RULE. **Always use a helping verb with** *drunk;* **never use one with** *drank.*

Today I **drink.**　　Yesterday I **drank.**　　Often I *have* **drunk.**

LEARNING ACTIVITIES

A. Copy these sentences, filling each blank with the proper form of the verb *drink.* Underline the verb that you use, including any helping verbs. Do not write in this book. Read the sentences aloud more than once.

1. Have you _____ any milk today?
2. That was my glass of orange juice. Who _____ it?
3. Ruth picked up the glass and _____ the medicine quickly.
4. Someone has _____ my tea.
5. Icy liquids should be _____ slowly.
6. At last Friday's picnic, the boys _____ lemonade.
7. We hurried to the spring and _____ the clear, cold water.
8. Have you ever _____ coconut milk?

B. In an oral activity, let one student read one of the following questions, and then call on another student to answer, using *drank* or *drunk.*

Do not use *did* in answering. Repeat the activity until everyone has had a chance to take part.

1. Did you drink any milk?
2. Has anyone drunk from this glass?
3. Should we have drunk the tea first?
4. Did you drink root beer at the party?
5. How much milk did you drink yesterday?

C. Write five original sentences, two using *drank* and three using *drunk*. In your small groups, take turns at reading the sentences.

USING IRREGULAR VERBS — <u>EAT</u>, <u>ATE</u>, <u>EATEN</u>

RULE. Always use a helping verb with *eaten;* never use one with *ate.* Remember that there is no such standard form as *et* or *aten.*

Today I eat.   Yesterday I ate.   Often I *have* eaten.

LEARNING ACTIVITIES

A. Copy each sentence below, filling the blank with the proper form of the verb *eat*. Underline the form that you use and any helping verbs. In class, read the sentences aloud, more than once if you have time.

1. Pearl _____ her supper quickly and left for the game.
2. Rust had _____ through the iron chain.
3. Who has _____ the last piece of pie?
4. Last night I _____ Chinese food for the first time.
5. Potatoes are _____ in many forms.
6. Mary took the slice of cake and _____ it.
7. The bowlful of cherries was _____ quickly.
8. Our little dog had _____ the children's lunch.
9. John admitted he had never _____ liver.
10. Yesterday my grandmother _____ her breakfast at 6:00 A.M.
11. Before lunch June had _____ several cookies.
12. The hungry animals _____ quickly.

B. Write five sentences, leaving blanks to be filled with *ate* or *eaten.* Take turns at putting your sentences on the board. Call upon some other student to read the sentences, supplying the standard forms.

C. (1) Write two questions using *ate* and two using *eaten.* (2) Choose sides. (3) Alternate in asking a question that must be answered in turn by someone on the other side. The answer must contain *ate* or *eaten.* Score a point for each question or answer that is properly expressed.

(Based upon the sentences in A *of the preceding activities)*

1. Give the rules for the three capital letters in sentence 4.
2. How would you spell the singular of the subject in sentence 5?
3. Why is the verb singular in sentence 7?
4. Explain the location of the apostrophe in sentence 8.

USING IRREGULAR VERBS — THROW, THREW, THROWN

RULE. **Always use a helping verb with** *thrown;* **never use one with** *threw.* **There is no such standard form as** *throwed.*

Today I throw.   Yesterday I threw.   Often I *have* thrown.

LEARNING ACTIVITIES

A. (1) Copy these sentences, filling each blank with the proper form of the verb *throw.* (2) Underline the verb, including any helping verbs. Proofread for careless errors in copying. (3) Exchange papers for checking. (4) Mark the papers as the sentences are read aloud.

1. The pitcher _____ a fast ball often in that game.
2. Suddenly Kathleen _____ the door open and ran out.
3. The rock was _____ with great force.
4. Have you _____ away that large box?
5. Someone _____ this note through the window.
6. The smallest of the children has _____ the ball over the house.
7. The general _____ the best troops into the battle but still lost.
8. Daniel was _____ into the lions' den.

B. Divide the class into two teams. Take turns giving sentences using *threw* and *thrown.* Listen to catch any nonstandard usage. Keep score on the board. Score a point for each proper sentence. Do not score a point, however, if someone gives a sentence that another player has already given. Thus, to help your team, you must listen carefully.

★ **Spot Review**

(Based upon the sentences in A *of the preceding activities)*

1. How do you spell the plural of the final word in sentence 4?
2. Why is *general* not capitalized in sentence 7?
3. Account for the apostrophe in sentence 8.

USING IRREGULAR VERBS—<u>SWIM</u>, <u>SWAM</u>, <u>SWUM</u>

RULE.. Always use a helping verb with *swum;* **never use one with** *swam.*

Today I swim.   Yesterday I swam.   Often I *have* swum.

LEARNING ACTIVITIES

A. (1) Go over these sentences orally, using *swam* or *swum* in each blank. (2) Practice reading the sentences in unison so that you can really hear the standard forms.

1. Yesterday I _____ out to the raft.
2. Have you ever _____ in any races?
3. Terence has never _____ in the ocean.
4. The goldfish _____ slowly around the bowl.
5. Long distances can be _____ by an expert swimmer.
6. Just then a large shark _____ past the ship.
7. Mary _____ in the final race and won it.
8. Has either of the girls _____ across Bear Lake?

B. Write sentences on the board, leaving blanks to be filled with *swam* or *swum.* Call on classmates to read the sentences, supplying the proper forms and identifying any helping verbs.

ENRICHMENT

Make a nonsense rhyme in which you use *swam* and *swum* correctly. Here is an example:

> I swam fast, and Bill swam fast;
> We swam with real perfection.
> But still we lost the race—and *why?*
> We'd swum the wrong direction!

Spot Review   ★

(*Based upon the sentences in* A *of the preceding activities*)

1. Why is *Lake* capitalized in sentence 8?
2. What is the plural of the subject in sentence 4?
3. Why is the verb singular in sentence 8? What is the antecedent of the pronoun in sentence 7?

USING IRREGULAR VERBS — <u>DRIVE</u>, <u>DROVE</u>, <u>DRIVEN</u>

RULE. **Always use an auxiliary verb with** *driven;* **never use one with** *drove.*

Today I drive.   Yesterday I drove.   Often I *have* driven.

LEARNING ACTIVITIES

A. (1) Copy these sentences, filling each blank with *drove* or *driven.* (2) Underline the verb, including any helping verbs. Proofread for careless errors in copying. (3) Exchange papers. (4) Check the verb choices as the sentences are read aloud.

1. The storm _____ many people from their homes.
2. Last summer we _____ to Crater Lake.
3. The owner of those cars has never _____ a truck.
4. We girls _____ to the lake for a picnic.
5. Bernice may not have _____ away yet.
6. Jim _____ the sheep into the pasture yesterday.
7. I had never before _____ this kind of car.
8. Fred has _____ well lately.

B. Dictionaries give many meanings for the verb *drive.* Choose any five meanings and write sentences in which you use either *drove* or *driven.* Do not use any meaning more than once. In your small groups, read sentences aloud.

★   **Chapter Review** ❋

A. Copy the following sentences, underlining all words used as adjectives, including predicate adjectives. Draw an arrow from each adjective to the word that it modifies.

1. She drew four large pictures.
2. One child lost his parents.
3. My dog is a loud barker.
4. The fourth story is short.
5. That cap is a pretty color.
6. We saw an English ballet.
7. Did Edna bring her new skates?
8. Roger must be tired.
9. My father bought these shoes.
10. This banana tastes bitter.

---

*Check Test 5 should be taken at this point. If the results show need for further study, students should do the review practice. They should then take Mastery Test 5.

B. Read the following sentences aloud, choosing the proper forms.

1. Have you seen (those, that) sort of telephone before?
2. (Them, Those) bikes are parked in the wrong place.
3. I must be there in (a, an) hour.
4. (This, These) kind of sweater is my favorite.
5. We needed (a pen and pencil, a pen and a pencil).
6. My job is (more easier, easier) than yours.
7. Which of these two watches is the (better, best)?
8. Mr. Beggs is (a husband and father, a husband and a father).
9. (An, A) orange leaf fluttered to the ground.
10. Did you leave (those, them) magazines at school?

C. Read these sentences aloud, supplying the proper form of each verb in parentheses.

1. For breakfast yesterday I (drink) a glass of milk but no coffee.
2. Have you ever (eat) mushrooms?
3. Tina (throw) hard and struck the batter out.
4. Mr. Smith has (drive) the same car for ten years.
5. I had often (swim) across the pool.
6. Yesterday I (eat) lunch at school.
7. The pitcher should have (throw) a curve.
8. We (drive) to Washington last year.
9. You should have (drink) some tomato juice.
10. She (swim) swiftly to the raft and climbed up on it.

Cumulative Review

CAPITALIZATION AND PUNCTUATION

Copy these sentences, supplying needed capital letters and punctuation.

1. a letter dated december 12 1975 arrived two years late at 4513 north sixth street miami florida 33109
2. no one captain smith passed over the bridge across the sangamon river while private hollis and i were on duty said private bell
3. our leader ann ames has been working with the girl scouts in california new mexico and colorado
4. yes everyone living near the ohio river was afraid of that flood
5. have you asked fred read the book mystery at laughing water molly

PARTS OF THE SENTENCE

Copy these sentences. Label each *verb* (v.), *subject* (subj.), *direct object* (d.o.), and *predicate nominative* (p.n.).

1. The little girl stubbed her toe.
2. That boy is my brother.

3. Did Stella find her notebook?
4. I have polished the silver.
5. Mother has been practicing law since 1972.

VERB-SUBJECT AGREEMENT

Go over these sentences orally, choosing the standard forms.

1. A bunch of grapes (is, are) hanging from the vine.
2. It really (don't, doesn't) make much difference.
3. (Doesn't, Don't) the writer of these stories live in Ohio?
4. There (was, were) five peaches in that bowl this morning.
5. They (wasn't, weren't) at home.
6. He (don't, doesn't) know the tune.
7. The police officer (has, have) just arrived.
8. You (was, were) late this morning.
9. There (isn't, aren't) many cookies left.

PROPER USE OF PRONOUNS

Read these sentences aloud, choosing the standard forms.

1. Ethel invited Ellen and (I, me) to the party.
2. Hector and (he, him) are good friends.
3. Scott and (we, us) found much to talk about.
4. They saw you and (I, me) at the show.
5. (We, Us) Scouts are meeting tonight.
6. Mother heard (we, us) boys.
7. The old cow swished (its, it's) tail.
8. This pen must be (yours, your's).
9. One of those cars is (ours, our's).
10. At the signal, all four elephants raised (they're, their) trunks at the same time.

TROUBLESOME VERBS

Read these sentences aloud, using the proper form of each verb in parentheses. Name any helping verbs.

1. The kittens (lie) in their basket all day today.
2. The water (freeze) in the trough this morning.
3. Who (see) the circus last week?
4. Haven't your parents (go) to the exhibit yet?
5. Each student (do) his or her best in our last contest.
6. The speaker had (come) all the way from Canada.
7. Has Edith (see) her friends?
8. Martha was (take) to the concert in the new car.
9. We (choose) new officers yesterday.
10. My grandfather (give) me his digital watch.

11. Have you ever (run) for office before?
12. The ice almost (break) under the skaters last night.
13. My cousin (do) well in the last race.
14. The truth isn't (know) yet.

Write on your paper the new words made by using the prefix *dis-* or *mis-* or the suffix *-ful*, as indicated.

1. (mis) take	5. peace (ful)	9. (dis) agree
2. spoon (ful)	6. (dis) solve	10. (mis) lead
3. (mis) spell	7. pocket (ful)	11. (mis) step
4. (dis) like	8. (mis) place	12. mouth (ful)

Word Games to Test Your Thinking

His Name Was Tom

Can you name the "Toms" suggested below?

1. This Tom was small enough to stand on the palm of your hand.
2. This Tom was a Mother Goose character who disobeyed the law.
3. This Tom was one of our famous presidents.
4. This Tom was the hero of a book called *Tom _____'s School Days.*
5. This Tom, a Mother Goose character, sang for his supper.
6. Mark Twain made this Tom famous.

Would You Like to Know—?

The encyclopedia answers to some of these questions may surprise you.

1. How do *pythons* kill their prey?
2. Why would you have a hard time buying *pineapple* seed?
3. For what does the *pelican* use its pouch?
4. About how long was *Pompeii* left buried after being destroyed by the volcano Vesuvius?

Another "Spelling Demons" Crossword Puzzle

Copy the crossword puzzle. Do not write in this book.

36. Preposition.
37. Third person pronoun.
39. A girl's name.
40. A riddle or puzzle.
42. A number.
43. A day of the week.

Down

1. The principal character in a story (*plural*).
2. Narrow passageways.
3. Place for sleeping.
4. First person plural pronoun.
5. North Carolina (*abbr.*).
6. A kind of tree.
7. Black substance in chimneys.
8. Move quickly.
11. Joint between the thigh and the lower part of the leg (*plural*).
13. Rowing implements.
14. That which is written.
17. Second note of the scale.
21. A piece of open or cleared ground.
22. One of a pair worn in gliding over snow.
25. Present participle of *make*.
26. Highest card in a deck of cards.
27. Past tense of *enjoy*.
28. Extinct, flightless, large bird of New Zealand.
30. Present tense of *went*.
32. Not closed.
34. Each.
36. 2000 pounds (*plural*).
37. Feminine possessive pronoun.
38. Past tense of *sit*.
39. Same as 33 across.
41. Third person singular form of *be*.

Across

1. Exclamation of surprise.
3. Something to be transacted.
9. Plural of *elf*.
10. A timepiece.
12. First two initials of the author of *Treasure Island.*
13. Exclamation showing pain.
15. A heavenly body that moves around the earth.
16. Contraction of *over*.
18. Present plural of *be*.
19. If you stub your ___, you might say No. 13 across.
20. The hand is quicker than the ___.
21. Day before Saturday (*abbr.*).
23. Initials of the inventor of the electric light.
24. Secret Service (*abbr.*).
25. An error.
28. Film star, ___ West.
29. Frosting.
31. Two things used when fishing (*two words*).
33. Nickname for *Joseph.*
35. Past tense of *pay*.

USING ADVERBS IN BUILDING SENTENCES*

One clever, agile porpoise tossed the red ball high.

1. Recognizing Adverbs

READ AND THINK ABOUT . . .

Compare the above picture with the one on page 380. What word has been added? How does it change the picture?

Words like "high" are *adverbs*, another part of speech. Like adjectives (see page 380), they add to the basic sentence idea by giving exact or vivid details.

---

*Pretest 6 should be taken at this time.

1. (DEFINITION) *Adverbs* **are words used as modifiers to tell** *manner* (how), *time* (when), *place* (where), **or** *degree* (how much).

> She tossed the ball **quickly**. (*manner*)
> She tossed the ball **south**. (*place*)
> She tossed the ball **immediately**. (*time*)
> She tossed the ball **too** far. (*degree*)

2. Adverbs modify, or affect the meaning of, (*a*) *verbs,* (*b*) *adjectives,* **or** (*c*) *other adverbs.*

a) The days go rapidly.

(*Rapidly* tells *how* the days go; so it modifies the verb.)

b) The train was very late.

(*Very* tells *how much* late; so it modifies the adjective.)

c) The porpoise tossed the ball too high.

(*Too* tells *how much* high, or the *degree* of height to which the porpoise tossed the ball; so it modifies the adverb *high.*)

3. A word may be an adverb in one sentence, and another part of speech in some other sentence. To know what part of speech a word is, find how it is used in a sentence.

> The porpoise tossed the ball high.

(*High* is an adverb because it modifies the verb *tossed.*)

> That is a high fence.

(*High* is an adjective because it modifies the noun *fence.*)

4. *Not* **is a special adverb because it really modifies the entire sentence.** *Not* **is usually classed as modifying the verb, however, for the verb carries the basic sentence idea.**

5. Adverbs may be compound.

> He speaks loudly and rapidly.   Marsha works fast but well.

6. Adverbs can shift position in a sentence.

> I **often** agree with her.   I agree with her **often**.
> **Often** I agree with her.   I agree **often** with her.

LEARNING ACTIVITIES

A. Find the adverbs in these sentences and tell what word each one modifies. Make this an oral exercise. Give the sentence patterns.

1. Harold does his work carefully.
2. The club recently won this banner.
3. Yesterday this little baby seemed unusually restless.
4. The snake lay there very quietly.
5. She has called me once or twice.
6. Haven't they often visited here before?
7. Happy children seldom become really unhappy grown-ups.
8. The botanists have never collected finer specimens.
9. They have always been highly critical.
10. You shouldn't decide this important matter too quickly.

B. (1) Write ten sentences using adverbs that tell how you feel about certain things; for example, *hot weather, relatives, homework,* or *getting up in the morning.* (2) Recopy your sentences, but leave a blank for each adverb that you chose. (3) Exchange papers with a partner. (4) Fill the blanks with adverbs. (5) Compare your choices.

C. Shift the italicized adverbs in these sentences to as many other positions as they might sensibly occupy. Make this an oral activity.

1. They lived *then* in Millvale.
2. *Sometimes* we have held our picnic at Stone Lake.
3. You will wait for us, *surely.*
4. The road past our farm is *now* a four-lane highway.

D. In class, give the part of speech of each italicized word.

1. We usually arrive *early.*
2. The *early* train leaves at noon.
3. The *back* of the car was empty.
4. Won't you come *back?*
5. Did Father *back* the car into the garage?
6. Four of us rode in the *back* seat.
7. You must *right* this mistake by yourself.
8. Turn *right* at the corner.
9. That was not the *right* answer.
10. You have the *right* to vote.

E. Modify the basic idea in each of the following sentences by adding one of these adverbs: *not, never, almost,* or *seldom.* Discuss your choices in class.

1. She is there.
2. They have won the race.
3. This road is used.
4. I am late.
5. We had finished.
6. The grass is green.

(Based upon the sentences in A *of the preceding activities)*

1. Which five sentences have direct objects? Name the objects.
2. Why is the verb *lay* correct in sentence 4?
3. How would you compare the adjectives in sentence 7?
4. What is the predicate nominative in sentence 7?

2. Forming Adverbs from Adjectives

● THESE ARE FACTS ABOUT ADVERBS: II

7. Most adverbs are formed from adjectives.

a) **Many adverbs simply add** *-ly* **to adjectives.**

ADJECTIVES:	slow	quick	useful
ADVERBS:	slow**ly**	quick**ly**	useful**ly**

b) **Most adjectives that end in** *y* **change the** *y* **to** *i* **and then add** *-ly.* (See Rule 2b, page 257.)

ADJECTIVES:	laz**y**	happ**y**	might**y**
ADVERBS:	laz**il**y	happ**il**y	might**il**y

c) **Most adjectives that have more than one syllable and end in** *le* **simply change the** *e* **to** *y.*

ADJECTIVES:	nob**le**	favorab**le**	sensib**le**
ADVERBS:	nob**ly**	favorab**ly**	sensib**ly**

8. Not all adverbs are formed from adjectives. *Never, not, here, there, then, when, where, always, very, too,* **and** *now* **are some common adverbs that do not come from adjectives.**

LEARNING ACTIVITIES

A. List the following adjectives and beside each write the adverb formed from it: *easy, large, busy, horrible, heavy, steady, careful, angry, weary, suitable, merry, hungry, equal, strange, considerable.* Go over the words in class and explain the spelling of each adverb.

B. Be prepared to give oral sentences using the adjectives named in *A.* Then give sentences using the adverbs formed from the adjectives; after giving a sentence, spell the adverb.

3. Comparing Adverbs

Since most adverbs are compared by using *more* and *most,* their comparisons are easy to form.

● THESE ARE FACTS ABOUT COMPARING ADVERBS

1. **Adverbs formed from adjectives use** *more* **and** *most* **to express comparison.**

POSITIVE:	slowly	lazily	comfortably
COMPARATIVE:	more slowly	more lazily	more comfortably
SUPERLATIVE:	most slowly	most lazily	most comfortably

2. **A few adverbs, including some words that also may be used as adjectives, add** *er* **and** *est.* Here are some examples.

POSITIVE:	soon	hard	early	fast	high
COMPARATIVE:	sooner	harder	earlier	faster	higher
SUPERLATIVE:	soonest	hardest	earliest	fastest	highest

3. **Some adverbs are compared irregularly.** Here are a few.

POSITIVE:	far	well	little	much	badly
COMPARATIVE:	farther	better	less	more	worse
SUPERLATIVE:	farthest	best	least	most	worst

4. **Adverbs like those in point 8, page 408, cannot be compared.**

LEARNING ACTIVITIES

A. Using the numbered words, make four lists on your paper: (1) of the adverbs that use *more* and *most* in their comparison, (2) of those that use *er* and *est,* (3) of those that are irregular in their forms, and (4) of those that have no comparison. Exchange papers for checking.

1. softly	5. heavily	9. far	13. fairly	17. coldly
2. soon	6. easily	10. high	14. much	18. fast
3. now	7. well	11. quickly	15. never	19. wildly
4. there	8. here	12. closely	16. not	20. quietly

B. For each adverb that can be compared in *A,* give oral sentences using the three degrees. Begin by having someone say a sentence using one of the words in its positive form. He or she will then call on another student to change the sentence so that it contains the comparative form of the same adverb. This student calls upon another student to change the sentence so that it contains the superlative form. He or she then calls upon someone to use another one of the words in its positive form, and so on. You may want to make this a team activity.

4. Using Vivid Adverbs

In each of the pictures above, the boy is walking in a different manner. What vivid and exact adverbs would capture the particular style of each action?

As you will discover, most vivid adverbs often end in *-ly* and tell *how*.

LEARNING ACTIVITIES

A. In an oral activity, have listed on the board as many vivid adverbs as you can think of that show different ways of doing the following: (1) *laughing*, (2) *frowning*, (3) *driving*, (4) *singing*, (5) *dancing*, (6) *working*, (7) *running*, (8) *whispering*.

B. Copy the sentences below, filling each blank with one or more vivid adverbs. Think; do not write just the first word that pops into your head. Read the sentences orally to see how many different adverbs are used.

1. The whistle blew _____.
2. The wind blew _____.
3. Somewhere a dog barked _____.
4. The rain fell _____.
5. The cat sat there _____.
6. The crowd cheered _____.

C. An author often uses adverbs of manner to show how a character feels as he or she makes a remark; for example, "What do you want?" the guard asked *suspiciously.*

Using the adverbs as clues to character, read aloud in class these remarks from Charles Dickens's *Our Mutual Friend.* Read only the quoted words.

1. "Well!" observed R. Wilfer cheerfully, "money and goods are certainly the best of references!"
2. "Nonsense, our age!" cried Bella, impatiently. "What's that got to do with him?"
3. "What did you say?" she asked sharply. "What did you say, Miss?"
4. "Please walk in," said Lavinia haughtily. "Our servant is out."
5. "Oh, I don't know what he said," cried Georgiana wildly, "but I hated him all the same for saying it."
6. "I alone know," returned the man, sternly shaking his head, "that your trumped-up story cannot possibly be true."
7. "Well?" retorted Mr. Venus snappishly. "If you hear it say the words, why don't you answer it?"
8. "My sister Lizzie," said the boy proudly, "wants no preparing, Mr. Headstone. What she is, she is, and shows herself to be."
9. "Ma," said Bella angrily, "you force me to say that I am truly sorry I did come home, and that I never will come home again."
10. "Why didn't you sit down before?" asked Mr. Boffin distrustfully.

D. Adverbs, like adjectives, can be overused, but they can help to sharpen the sentence picture. Here are more sentences, also from *Our Mutual Friend.* Which adverb of each pair in parentheses do you think was the one that Dickens chose? Go over your choices in class. What does his word suggest in each case that the other does not?

1. The white face of the winter day came (slowly, sluggishly) on.
2. At this moment the greasy door is (violently, strongly) pushed.
3. A delicious wind ran with the stream, touching the surface (lightly, crisply).
4. In an instant, with a dreadful crash, flames shot (jaggedly, unevenly) across the air.
5. She rowed in (desperately, hard) for the nearest shallow water where she might run the boat aground.
6. The boat touched the edge of the patch of inn lawn, sloping (slightly, gently) to the water.
7. He now looked at him again—(carefully, stealthily) this time.
8. He sat looking (steadily, straight) before him at the vacant air.
9. Both Mrs. Wilfer and Lavinia were (greatly, ravenously) curious about every article of which the lodger stood possessed.
10. The little dressmaker stood up, humming her song, and nodded to him (brightly, pleasantly).

ENRICHMENT

Choose a book that you are now reading outside your class. Find a passage that illustrates how effective, well-chosen adverbs can add interest to sentences. Read the passage aloud in class, emphasizing the vivid adverbs. Have classmates list the best adverbs.

USING ENGLISH IN ALL CLASSES

A. Clear, exact adverbs are very important in science explanations or experiments. Notice these sentences from two science projects:

1. Do *not* stroke the knitting needle *back* and *forth*. Move the magnet *always* in the same direction.
2. Do *not* tilt the beaker *far enough* to let the pieces of dry ice fall *out*.

Bring your science books to class. Turn to any lesson. See how many important uses of adverbs you can find on one page.

B. Read over any papers that you are preparing for other classes. Make any changes that you think will improve your selection of adverbs.

FOLLOW-UP

From Learning Activities *A* and *B*, copy into your notebook adverbs that you think are especially expressive. Refer to this list when you do original writing. Make your list grow as you discover vivid adverbs in your reading.

DIAGRAMMING ADVERBS

Place an adverb on a slanting line below the word that it modifies, the same way as you do an adjective. As always, the words on the heavy base line are the parts of the basic sentence pattern.

ADVERB MODIFYING THE VERB   ADVERB MODIFYING AN ADJECTIVE

The porpoise tossed the ball *high*.   The train was *very* late.

porpoise	tossed	ball
The	high	the

train	was	late
The		very

ADVERB MODIFYING AN ADVERB	COMPOUND ADVERB

The porpoise tossed the ball *too* high.

The snow fell *thickly* and *softly*.

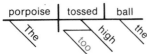

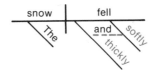

LEARNING ACTIVITIES

A. Diagram all parts in the following sentences. Remember that the adverbs will go below the words they modify. Exchange papers for checking when the diagrams are put on the board. Be sure to explain orally and exactly each part of each diagram, using a regular pattern.

1. The new owner should arrive here soon.
2. My little sister has just had her sixth birthday.
3. We work well together.
4. A very famous writer came here yesterday.
5. Her electric toothbrush does not work very well.
6. I have never taken so many pictures before.
7. Harry walked away slowly and very unhappily.
8. Your work is almost always very neat.
9. Egypt is now our next stop.
10. Have you made that trip often?

B. For additional drill in diagramming adverbs, turn back to the sentences in *A*, page 407. Be sure to go over the diagrams orally.

5. Using Standard English

AVOIDING ADJECTIVE-ADVERB CONFUSION

THINK IT OVER . . .

Nonstandard expression is likely to handicap a person, just as a bowling ball tied to a swimmer's ankle would. Remember that people form opinions of you not only from the *ideas* that you express, but from the *language* in which you express those ideas. Why handicap yourself with nonstandard language habits?

413

THE RULES FOR AVOIDING ADJECTIVE-ADVERB CONFUSION

RULE 1. Use *adjectives* **to modify** *nouns* **or** *pronouns*. **Use** *adverbs* **to modify** *verbs, adjectives,* **or** *adverbs*.

RULE 2. Do not use the adjective *sure* **for the adverbs** *surely, certainly, really*. **Use** *sure* **only if those three words do not make sense.**

Jack is **sure** of the time.
(*Sure* is a predicate adjective modifying the noun *Jack*. It would not make sense to say, "Jack is *surely* of the time.")

I **surely** am going.
(*Surely* is an adverb modifying the verb *am going*.)

RULE 3. Do not use the adjective *good* **for the adverb** *well*.

He had a **good** time.
(*Good* is an adjective; it tells *what kind* of *time*.)

He writes **well.**
(*Well* is an adverb modifying the verb *writes*; it tells *how*.)

RULE 4. Use *well* **as an adjective only when it refers to health.**

I feel **well.**
(*Well* is a predicate adjective modifying the pronoun *I*.)

RULE 5. Use the adverb *badly* **to tell how something is done. Use the adjective** *bad* **in referring to health or feelings and to complete such linking verbs as** *seem, look, taste, smell*.

I played the game **badly** yesterday.
(*Badly* is an adverb modifying the verb *played*.)

I felt **bad** about the news.
(*Bad* is a predicate adjective modifying the pronoun *I*.)

The weather looks **bad.**
(*Bad* is a predicate adjective; it tells *what kind* of *weather*.)

LEARNING ACTIVITIES

A. Copy these sentences, using either *good* or *well* in each blank. Do not write in this book. Read your sentences in class. Tell (1) which you used, an adjective or an adverb, and (2) what word it modifies.

1. Can't you see _____?
2. It was a _____ game.
3. The chowder tastes _____.
4. This biscuit looks _____.
5. Don't you feel _____?
6. I like it very _____.
7. Lucy plays tennis _____.
8. I am not feeling _____.
9. That hot sun feels _____.
10. Both groups did _____.
11. She doesn't seem _____.
12. Ann really sings _____.

B. Copy these sentences, filling the blanks with *bad* or *badly*. Do not write in this book. Go over the sentences orally in your small groups.

1. Rover behaved _____ today.
2. Mary felt _____ about it.
3. Her health has been _____.
4. That pill didn't taste _____.
5. The weather looks _____.
6. I did _____ on the first test.
7. The air smelled _____.
8. The project went _____.

C. Supply the proper form from the words in parentheses in each of the following sentences. Remember, if the word tells *how* in connection with the verb, use the adverb form. Make this an oral exercise. Repeat it several times. Do not write in this book.

1. Selma plays (good, well).
2. The team played (bad, badly).
3. The car runs (well, good).
4. She seems (well, good) now.
5. The egg tasted (good, well).
6. That job was done (bad, badly).
7. Nicole won (easy, easily).
8. I'm (surely, sure) sorry for you.
9. He felt (good, well) today.
10. News (sure, surely) travels fast.

AVOIDING DOUBLE NEGATIVES

READ AND THINK ABOUT . . .

Expressions like "I haven't got no scissors" are not used by careful speakers. Such expressions are called *double negatives.* Since only one negative word is needed to express a negative meaning, double negatives are considered to be nonstandard English.

THE RULES FOR AVOIDING DOUBLE NEGATIVES

RULE 1. Do not use two negative words to limit one idea.

STANDARD: I **never** need help.
STANDARD: I need **no** help.
NONSTANDARD: I **never** need ~~no~~ help.

(Both *never* and *no* give a negative meaning. Only one of them should be used.)

RULE 2. Be especially careful to avoid using *not* **or** *n't, no, never, none, scarcely, hardly,* **or** *nothing* **with another negative word.**

STANDARD: Sue **has no** book.   I **didn't** say **anything.**
STANDARD: Sue **hasn't a** book.   I said **nothing.**
NONSTANDARD: Sue **hasn~~'t~~ no** book.   I **didn~~'t~~** say **nothing.**

415

LEARNING ACTIVITIES

A. Practice the following sentences orally, using the proper words from the parentheses. Do not write in this book.

1. I haven't (none, any) more tickets.
2. This camera isn't (nothing, anything) like mine.
3. I (can, can't) hardly wait.
4. This hasn't (ever, never) happened before.
5. I don't need (no, any) help.
6. We (haven't, have) scarcely any time left.
7. We're not (ever, never) going there again.
8. There has never been (anything, nothing) wrong.
9. Haven't you (no, any) other pencils?
10. You (don't hardly, hardly) look the same.

B. Write five "choice" sentences, similar to those in *A*. In your small groups, exchange papers and read the sentences aloud, making the right choices. Speak distinctly so that everyone in the group gets practice in hearing the standard forms.

ENRICHMENT

Draw a cartoon that shows people getting rid of double negatives in some way, such as by tossing them into a bonfire, putting them down the incinerator or into the garbage disposal unit, burying them, . . . Use as many double negatives as you can: *don't never, haven't no, can't hardly,* and so on. Your work may be displayed on the bulletin board.

FOLLOW-UP

Look back over the rules on pages 414 and 415. Which ones are hardest for you to follow? Pick out one or two that you know are problems; then ask a friend to check your use of the forms covered. Building good speech habits is not really hard—if you really want to do so.

USING TROUBLESOME VERBS

Here are five more verbs that are sometimes used improperly. Most of the problems with these verbs come from using the past tense form when the past participle form is called for. (To review principal parts of verbs, go over point 18, page 288.)

USING IRREGULAR VERBS—<u>RIDE</u>, <u>RODE</u>, <u>RIDDEN</u>

RULE. Always use a helping verb with *ridden;* **never use one with** *rode.*

Today I ride.　　Yesterday I rode.　　Often I *have* ridden.

LEARNING ACTIVITIES

A. Copy each sentence, filling the blank with the proper form of the verb *ride.* Underline the form that you use. Underline also any auxiliary verbs. Practice reading the sentences aloud.

1. We had _____ through some beautiful country.
2. That jockey has _____ many winning horses.
3. Last winter I _____ on a toboggan for the first time.
4. Have you ever _____ on the Metroliner?
5. Florence's bicycle has been _____ many miles.
6. At the rodeo last summer Janice _____ an outlaw horse.
7. In the Bahamas bicycles are _____ by almost everyone.
8. That horse was _____ well in the last race.

B. Write five sentences, two using *rode* and three using *ridden.* You might write about (1) places that you have gone and how you traveled there or (2) rides at an amusement park. Take turns at reading sentences aloud. Call on classmates to identify any helping verbs.

USING IRREGULAR VERBS—<u>FLY</u>, <u>FLEW</u>, <u>FLOWN</u>

RULE. Always use a helping verb with *flown;* **never use one with** *flew.*

Today I fly.　　Yesterday I flew.　　Often I *have* flown.

LEARNING ACTIVITIES

A. Copy these sentences, filling each blank with the proper form of the verb *fly.* Underline that form and any helping verbs. Read the sentences aloud.

1. Billy _____ his first kite on a windy day last spring.
2. Every day much mail is _____ across the country.
3. Have the birds _____ south yet?
4. My aunt has _____ many miles on her job.

5. The swarm of bees has ＿＿＿＿ into the hive.
6. Upon hearing the bad news, Uncle John ＿＿＿＿ into a rage.
7. Supplies were ＿＿＿＿ into Camp Whitney by airplane.
8. The flag of no other country should be ＿＿＿＿ above our own.

B. Choose some city or country in a far-off part of the world. Pretend that your class has just missed a chance to fly to that place. Go around the class, completing in turn one or the other of these sentences:

On that trip we'd have flown over . . .
On that trip we'd not have flown over . . .

USING IRREGULAR VERBS — <u>DRAW</u>, <u>DREW</u>, <u>DRAWN</u>

RULE. Always use a helping verb with *drawn;* **never use one with** *drew.* **Remember that there is no such standard form as** *drawed.*

Today I **draw.**   Yesterday I **drew.**   Often I *have* **drawn.**

LEARNING ACTIVITIES

A. (1) Copy these sentences, filling each blank with the proper form of the verb *draw.* (2) Underline that form and any helping verbs. (3) Proofread for careless errors in copying. (4) Exchange papers for checking when the sentences are read aloud. Listen to be sure that the forms are standard.

1. The children had ＿＿＿＿ water from the well.
2. Yesterday my aunt ＿＿＿＿ these pictures for the magazine.
3. Only one conclusion could be ＿＿＿＿.
4. Either Mary or Irwin has ＿＿＿＿ this sketch.
5. The knight leaped from his horse and ＿＿＿＿ his sword.
6. Names of the winners will now be ＿＿＿＿.
7. The string should be ＿＿＿＿ tightly.
8. We shivered with fear but ＿＿＿＿ closer to the strange sight.
9. The team of horses had ＿＿＿＿ a heavy load up the hill.
10. The same person wrote the book and ＿＿＿＿ the pictures.

B. *Draw* is a verb with many meanings. Open your dictionary to the word; then write sentences using *drew* or *drawn* to illustrate five different meanings. Have sentences put on the board for criticism.

ENRICHMENT

From the sentences in *A,* choose three that show different meanings of *draw.* For each of the three, make a drawing to illustrate the sentence.

LEARNING ACTIVITIES

A. Copy these sentences, filling each blank with the proper form of the
verb *rise.* Underline the verb, including any helping verbs. In class, read
the sentences aloud, first individually and then together.

1. The sun had _____ at five o'clock.
2. The fish _____ to the top of the water and opened their mouths.
3. We should have _____ earlier.
4. Ted _____ from office boy to president of the company.
5. Shirley has _____ from reporter to editor in chief.
6. Have you ever _____ at 3:00 A.M.?
7. The moon had not yet _____.
8. The price of eggs _____ last month to its highest level this year.
9. The woman _____ slowly and went to the door.
10. By noon of that day, the river had _____ two feet.

B. Write five sentences, two using *rose* and three using *risen.* In your
small groups, take turns at reading sentences. Listen both to catch any
nonstandard verbs and to get used to hearing the proper forms.

Spot Review

(Based upon the sentences in A *of the preceding activities)*

1. What is the reason for the colon in sentence 6?
2. Why is there no apostrophe in *its* in sentence 8?
3. Is the subject in sentence 8 singular or plural?

"OFTEN I HAVE STOLEN. YESTERDAY I STOLE. TODAY I AM IN JAIL."

LEARNING ACTIVITIES

A. In an oral exercise, fill each blank with the proper form of *steal*. For each sentence that needs *stolen*, name the helping verbs.

1. This necklace might have been _____.
2. Juliette _____ softly from the room and tiptoed down the stairs.
3. That man's watch was _____ last week.
4. The puppy had _____ one of my shoes.
5. The thief _____ a wallet but did not escape with it.
6. A box of valuable papers has been _____.
7. He _____ up behind me and grabbed my arm.
8. That elephant surely cannot have been _____.
9. The last paragraph was _____ from some famous book.
10. How many bases has he _____ in the games this season?

B. Write five sentences using *stole* and *stolen* properly. Include different meanings of *steal*. In your small groups, take turns at reading sentences.

★   **Chapter Review**✻

A. Copy these sentences. Draw a line under each adverb and from it draw an arrow to the word that the adverb modifies.

1. Soon Marina will be too busy and will need far more help.
2. We shall leave early.
3. Leon answered me nervously but clearly.

✻Check Test 6 should be taken at this point. If the results show need for further study, students should do this review practice. They should then take Mastery Test 6.

4. They are almost ready. Usually they are rather slow.
5. I sometimes walk more slowly.
6. We saw three much larger buildings yesterday.
7. I am too tired now. I must not stay any longer.

B. Read the following sentences aloud, choosing the proper forms from the parentheses.

1. He does his work (good, well) and (carefully, careful).
2. Jonas fielded that ball (perfect, perfectly).
3. I (haven't hardly, have hardly) had time for my meals.
4. She feels (bad, badly) today.
5. Are you feeling (good, well)? You look much better than before.
6. This picnic (sure, surely) has been fun.
7. We sometimes do (bad, badly) on that kind of test.
8. Mr. Di Angelo didn't say (anything, nothing) about a meeting.

C. Read these sentences orally, supplying the standard forms of the verbs in parentheses.

1. Have you ever (ride) in an airplane? I first (fly) last week.
2. Most of the birds had (fly) to warmer lands.
3. Jack (draw) a sketch of our house.
4. The speaker had just (rise) to her feet.
5. We became tired and (steal) quietly away.
6. That picture was (draw) by a great artist.
7. The pony was (ride) by my little sister.

Cumulative Review　　　　　　　　　　　　　　　　　　

CAPITALIZATION AND PUNCTUATION

Supply needed capital letters and punctuation in this conversation.

milton have you seen that black calf since thursday asked paul
no milton replied ive been busy repairing the tractor
there seems to be something wrong with the calfs left front leg paul went on
lets go take a look suggested milton maybe its been cut on some barbed wire
wow look at that gash exclaimed paul wed better call dad

TROUBLESOME VERBS

Go over these sentences orally, supplying the needed verb forms.

1. Yesterday, for the first time, the boy (drink) water from a spring.
2. Last month my grandmother (come) to live with us.

3. Why don't you (lie) down? You should not have (run) upstairs.
4. The lettuce in our garden had (freeze).
5. Has Lois (eat) her breakfast? Where has she (go)?
6. Has the book (come)? You should have (give) it to me.
7. Yesterday the mail carrier (bring) two packages.
8. The dog (lie) on the davenport all last night.
9. Shouldn't you have (write) to Nadia today?
10. Has someone (throw) away yesterday's paper?
11. She (give) me a smile but said nothing.
12. I (run) across a strange story in last night's *Daily News*.
13. The girls should have (drive) more slowly.
14. Are you (lie) on my hat?
15. Have you ever (swim) in a river?
16. Jim has (break) our only teapot. He should not have (take) it.

VERB-SUBJECT AGREEMENT

Read these sentences aloud, choosing the standard forms.

1. She (don't, doesn't) know the correct address.
2. (Was, Were) you waiting long?
3. They (was, were) there early.
4. It (don't, doesn't) matter much to me.
5. In the evening we (wasn't, weren't) at home.
6. (There's, There are) twenty people coming to the picnic.
7. (Wasn't, Weren't) you and Thea born in Elmwood?
8. (Was, Were) you in that picture?

PROPER USE OF PRONOUNS

In an oral activity, choose the standard forms. Explain each choice.

1. Marcus and (he, him) took off (their, they're) caps.
2. Bob and (me, I) walked up to the pup. It offered (its, it's) paw.
3. Were you and (she, her) at the door?
4. The teacher questioned Helen and (I, me).
5. May (we, us) three hikers cut across (your, you're) field?
6. At last Rosalie and (I, me) were ready for the trip.
7. (We, Us) girls remember you and (he, him).

PROPER USE OF ADJECTIVES

Read these sentences aloud, choosing the standard forms.

1. I do not like (this, these) kind of apple.
2. My father is (an editor and publisher, an editor and a publisher).
3. (Them, Those) clowns are doing acrobatic tricks.
4. Give me (an, a) apple.
5. I never watch (that, those) sort of program.

Word Games to Test Your Thinking

Spelling Demons Beginning with C

The blanks in the sentences below can be filled with words unscrambled from the italicized words. Each word begins with the letter *c*. How many can you unscramble? Do not write in this book.

EXAMPLE: Did you see that *eel clog*?
He must go to _____! (*college*)

1. A _____ wears a uniform, but it does not include *a tin cap*.
2. I would not call a *rat nice*, and that's for _____.
3. If the *rich lend* too much money, their _____ may inherit little.
4. *Tony* is a *cur* that lives in the _____.
5. He sings in a _____, *or* some *such* group as that.
6. Dressed in work _____, *she* was leading the *colt* to the barn.

Finding Words in the Word *Triangle*

Many little words can be formed from the letters in the word *triangle*. Figure out those defined below; then see how many others you can find.

1. One who tells falsehoods.
2. Not imaginary.
3. A triangle has three.
4. A stove.
5. Opposite of *small.*
6. A very small insect. (The first letter is silent.)
7. Jack, the _____ killer.
8. Past tense of *ring.*
9. A strong, dazzling light.
10. Opposite of *boy.*
11. A part of a harness.
12. To rule (*homophone for No. 11*).
13. Used by carpenters.
14. Moisture falling from the clouds (*homophone for No. 11*).
15. Rock used in building.
16. Jungle cat.

Would You Like to Know—?

You may be surprised at the answers the encyclopedia gives to some of the following questions.

1. Is it true that the first *tulips* came from Holland?
2. Did William *Tell* really shoot an apple off his son's head?

3. Is it correct to call a *termite* an ant?
4. When were *tanks* first used in warfare?
5. Would you be likely to meet a *tiger* in an African jungle?

Another "Spelling Demons" Crossword Puzzle

Copy the crossword puzzle. Do not write in this book.

Across

1. Needful.
9. This goes around the neck.
10. A rather soft metal.
12. Preposition.
13. A church steeple.
14. Nine times ten.
17. Hotels.
18. East Central (*abbr.*).
19. Pronoun.
20. Cost.
25. Upon.
26. A club used in baseball.
28. Pain.
31. The air inhaled and exhaled in respiration.
33. Small child.
34. To inhale and exhale.

35. Short for *advertisement*.
36. General condition of the body.
37. Is fudge your favorite _____?
38. The night before.

Down

1. Observe.
2. East longitude (*abbr.*).
3. Anything that helps in solving a problem or mystery.
4. Each (*abbr.*).
5. Senior (*abbr.*).
6. Pertaining to the Alps.
7. Part of a harness.
8. Thread spun from wool.
9. A plant from which sugar is obtained.
11. Found in a schoolroom.
15. At that time.
16. Japanese coin.
21. Edgar Allan _____.
22. Certainly.
23. You may take it in a tub.
24. Deadly.
26. To take a bath.
27. Opposite of *here*.
29. Collect on delivery (*abbr.*).
30. Height (*abbr.*).
31. A thin, flat nail.
32. Devour.
34. Short for *Benjamin*.
36. An exclamation.

USING PREPOSITIONS AND CONJUNCTIONS IN BUILDING SENTENCES*

1. Building Sentences with Prepositional Phrases

"I HAVEN'T ANY USE AT ALL IN MY LIFE FOR PREPOSITIONAL PHRASES."

THINK IT OVER . . .

How many prepositional phrases has the boy actually used? What do *you* know about prepositional phrases? How are they useful?

RECOGNIZING PREPOSITIONAL PHRASES

Look at the sentences below. How important are the groups of words in parentheses? Try reading the sentences without them.

> There was a great rush (of feet) (across the deck).
> A belt (of fog) had lifted (with the rising) (of the moon).

---

*Pretest 7 should be taken at this time.

Such word groups are *prepositional phrases,* so named because they begin with a *preposition,* another of the parts of speech. These phrases add important details to the sentence.

● THESE ARE FACTS ABOUT PREPOSITIONAL PHRASES

1. **(DEFINITION) A** *preposition* **is a word that shows relationship between a noun or a pronoun and some other word in a sentence.**

   A *home* **in** *town* suits me.
   A *home* **near** *town* suits me.
   (A home *in* town is very different from one *near* town.)

2. **(DEFINITION) A** *prepositional phrase* **begins with a preposition and ends with a noun or with a pronoun in the objective case:** *in town, with me.*

3. **(DEFINITION) The noun or pronoun that completes a prepositional phrase is called the** *object of the preposition.*

4. **The object of a preposition may have adjective modifiers.**

   A home *in a small town* suits me.

5. **A prepositional phrase may have a compound object.**

   I took a trip *to* **Colombia** and **Brazil** .

6. **Prepositional phrases may be compound.**

   I want a home **on a farm** or **in a small town** .

7. **Here is a list of common prepositions.**

about	at	beyond	from	on	toward
above	before	but (*except*)	in	out	under
across	behind	by	inside	outside	until
after	below	concerning	into	over	up
against	beneath	down	like	past	upon
along	beside	during	near	since	with
among	besides	except	of	through	within
around	between	for	off	to	without

8. **Some words in the above list may be used as more than one part of speech.** Remember, what part of speech a word is depends upon its use. To decide whether a word is a preposition, ask *whom* or *what* after the word. If a noun or a pronoun answers that question, the word is a preposition.

   I came **before** the storm.
   (*Before* what? *storm; before* is a preposition.)

   I have seen him **before** .
   (*Before* what? *nothing; before* is an adverb telling *when.*)

LEARNING ACTIVITIES

A. In a team activity, find the prepositional phrases in these sentences from *The Adventures of Tom Sawyer.* The list of prepositions above will help you. Note how many vivid and specific details the phrases add.

1. Tom drew a line in the dust with his big toe, . . .
2. The master, throned on high in his great splint-bottom armchair, was dozing, lulled by the drowsy hum of study.
3. Tom appeared on the sidewalk with a bucket of whitewash . . .
4. Half an hour later he was disappearing behind the Douglas mansion on the summit of Cardiff Hill.
5. Just here the blast of a toy tin trumpet came faintly down the green aisles of the forest.
6. Then the howl of a far-off dog rose on the night air, and was answered by a fainter howl from a remoter distance.
7. The doctor put the lantern at the head of the grave and came and sat down with his back against one of the elm trees.
8. A figure crept stealthily through a break in the other end of the ruined building, . . .
9. They lay around in the shade, after breakfast, . . . and then went off through the woods on an exploring expedition.
10. Now, for the first time, the deep stillness of the place laid a clammy hand upon the spirits of the children.

B. Go over the following sentences in class. Decide how each italicized word is used: as a *preposition,* a *verb,* a *noun,* an *adjective,* or an *adverb.* If a word is a preposition, name the object.

1. I *like* everything *about* that jacket *in* the window.
2. A *down* pillow *like* this one is really soft.
3. Who painted the *outside* of these bookshelves *before?*
4. I am *about* ready. Wait for me *outside.*
5. He ran *past* in a real hurry.
6. Come *out* and sit *down by* me.
7. The pitcher leaped *up* and caught the ball for the third *out.*
8. Does this team ever kick *before* fourth *down?*
9. The *past* week has slipped *by* too fast.
10. She hurried *down* the stairs and *out* the door.
11. The road *past* our house winds *up* a steep hill.
12. Come *in!* Don't stand *outside* the door.
13. Climb *up* the ladder and *through* the window.
14. I am *through* with this book.
15. The bird flew *off into* the tree.
16. Our clothes were soaked *through.*
17. The player was caught *off* her guard.
18. The *past* seems just like yesterday.

USING PREPOSITIONAL PHRASES AS ADJECTIVES

As pointed out on page 388, expanding a sentence by adding descriptive adjectives helps to create an interesting and accurate sentence picture. Compare the following sentences.

The clever, agile porpoise tossed *the red* ball.

The clever, agile porpoise *with the amiable grin* tossed the red ball high.

What is "with the amiable grin"? What does it tell you? As what kind of modifier is it used?

The clever, agile porpoise **with the amiable grin** tossed the red ball high.

● **THESE ARE FACTS ABOUT PREPOSITIONAL PHRASES USED AS ADJECTIVES**

    1. Phrases used as adjectives modify nouns or pronouns.

       The pears <u>on this tree</u> are ripe.   She helps each <u>of us</u>.

    2. Prepositional phrases used as adjectives may be compound.

       The road <u>past our farm</u> and <u>beyond it</u> is rough.

3. A phrase used as an adjective may modify the object in another prepositional phrase.

We made the trip *by the light* of the moon.

4. Prepositional phrases used as adjectives can be combined into other sentences. For example, you can add the prepositional phrase from the second sentence below into the first as an adjective modifier.

SEPARATE: The tree had no leaves on it.
The tree was *near the barn.*

COMBINED: The tree near the barn had no leaves on it.

LEARNING ACTIVITIES

A. Go over the following ten sentences orally. Find each prepositional phrase that is used as an adjective and name the word that it modifies.

1. I have forgotten the title of that book about birds.
2. The rules of the game demand fair play by one and all.
3. Our work in science covers many things.
4. The immense house on the corner was built recently.
5. That woman in the blue suit is the manager.
6. The grass beneath that tree and near the fence is dying.
7. I know that man with the carnation and the red tie.
8. The girl beside me plays the trumpet.
9. She has always been one of my best friends.
10. Have you a reason for your absence from the meeting?

B. Copy the following sentences. Add to each italicized preposition an object and enough adjectives to fill the rest of the blanks. In your small groups, read sentences aloud to see how the different choices change the picture. Do not mark this book.

EXAMPLE: The man *in* _____ _____ _____ is my father.
The man *in the gray sweater* is my father.

1. That girl *with* _____ _____ _____ always comes early.
2. A letter *from* _____ _____ came this morning.
3. The road *past* _____ _____ was muddy.
4. Grandfather lives in a house *near* _____ _____ _____ _____.
5. The owner *of* _____ _____ _____ gave it to me.
6. The park *near* _____ _____ _____ has a playground.
7. The flowers *along* _____ _____ _____ are zinnias and asters.
8. I put the groceries down *on* _____ _____ _____.

C. Copy the following sets of sentences. In each set, combine the other sentences with the first one by adding the italicized prepositional phrases into the first as noun modifiers.

SEPARATE: The butter melted.
The butter was *on the table.*

COMBINED: The butter on the table melted.

1. The glassware is Norwegian.
   The glassware is *on display.*
2. The dog is named Ruby.
   The dog is *in the backyard.*
3. The sled has runners.
   The sled is *under the Christmas tree.*
4. The clock ticked.
   The clock was *on the wall.*
   The wall was *in the kitchen.*
   [Add the third into the second, and then both into the first.]
5. The reflection was beautiful.
   The reflection was *on the surface.*
   The surface was *of the lake.*
6. The locket contains a picture.
   The locket is *on the gold chain.*
   The chain is *around my neck.*
   The picture is *of my mother.*

USING PREPOSITIONAL PHRASES AS ADVERBS

The clever, agile porpoise with the amiable grin tossed the
red ball high **in the air.**

What do the words "in the air" tell you? What part of speech tells that same thing? Then how is the phrase "in the air" used?

● THESE ARE FACTS ABOUT PREPOSITIONAL PHRASES USED AS ADVERBS

1. **Prepositional phrases may be used as adverbs to tell** (*a*) *how,* (*b*) *when,* (*c*) *where,* (*d*) *how much,* **or** (*e*) *why.* In other words, they tell (*a*) *manner,* (*b*) *time,* (*c*) *place,* (*d*) *degree,* or (*e*) *reason.*

   a) The cat jumped like a frightened rabbit. (*how*)

   b) We left the house at dawn. (*when*)

   c) Meet me on this corner. (*where*)

   d) At least six people saw you. (*how much*)

   e) I wrote for information. (*why*)

2. **Most adverb phrases modify verbs.**

   Kristina ran to first base.

   We were followed by Ted and Leah. (*compound objects*)

   See me at noon or after school. (*compound phrases*)

3. **Adverb phrases can also modify adjectives.**

   Are you ready for the trip?

4. **Prepositional phrases used as adverbs can be combined into other sentences.**

   SEPARATE: The man walked.
   His walk was *down the beach.*

   COMBINED: The man walked down the beach.

LEARNING ACTIVITIES

A. In an oral activity, go over the following sentences. Locate each adverb phrase and name the word that it modifies.

1. The children climbed quickly over the wall.
2. Bernice is helpful in many ways.

3. The money was buried underneath a rock.
4. The children were tired from the game.
5. I have come for my money.
6. Carmela walked along the trail during the shower.
7. We are proud of our team and of its record.
8. The shadows stretched across the pool and the lawn.
9. On the hill stands an old tower.
10. Rafael has gone for the key.

B. Copy the following sets of sentences. In each set, combine the other sentences with the first one by adding the italicized prepositional phrases into the first as verb modifiers.

SEPARATE: The troops marched.
           The march was *across the desert.*

COMBINED: The troops marched across the desert.

1. The crowd rushed.
   The rush was *toward the rock star.*
2. The runner jogged.
   The jog was *around the track.*
3. The Thespians performed.
   The performance was *for the school assembly.*
4. The zookeeper looked.
   The look was *at the new habitat.*
   The habitat was *for elephants.*
   [Add the third into the second, and both into the first.]
5. Our pet skunk Simeon sleeps.
   Simeon sleeps *in a box.*
   Simeon sleeps *in my room.*
6. I found my skates.
   The skates were *on the floor.*
   The floor was *of the closet.*

DISTINGUISHING ADJECTIVE FROM ADVERB PHRASES

Most prepositional phrases can be used either as adverbs or as adjectives. The way a phrase is *used* in the sentence determines whether it is an adverb or an adjective phrase.

The boys ran <u>around the track</u>. (*adverb phrase*)

The fence <u>around the track</u> is high. (*adjective phrase*)

● THESE ARE FACTS ABOUT TELLING ADJECTIVE AND ADVERB PHRASES APART

1. **Adjective phrases tell** *which* **or** *what kind* **and modify nouns or pronouns.**

   The woman with Bill is his aunt. (*which woman*)

   It is a book with many illustrations. (*what kind of book*)

2. **Adverb phrases tell** *how, when, where, how much,* **or** *why;* **they usually modify verbs but sometimes modify adjectives.**

   We traveled in a jeep. (*how;* modifies the verb)

   I'll arrive in an hour. (*when;* modifies the verb)

   He lives in Canada. (*where;* modifies the verb)

   I am older by a year. (*how much;* modifies an adjective)

   She has come for your answer. (*why;* modifies the verb)

3. **A phrase that modifies the object of another phrase is always an adjective phrase.**

   He stood on the top of the hill.

   (*Of the hill* is an adjective phrase modifying *top,* the object in *on the top,* since it tells *which* top. *On the top* is itself an adverb phrase modifying *stood,* because it tells *where.*)

LEARNING ACTIVITIES

A. Go over the following sentences. Locate each prepositional phrase and tell (1) which word it modifies and (2) what kind it is, adjective or adverb. Make this an oral exercise.

1. A group of tourists gathered at the edge of the canyon.
2. In one cage we saw a huge bird from the jungles of Brazil.
3. She divided the equipment among the students in the laboratory.
4. Everyone in the class had finished at the same time.
5. We were awakened by a sudden clap of thunder.
6. Will you go to the hockey game with us?
7. A rosebush with sharp thorns grew beside the fence.
8. The airplane soared above the buildings on the field.
9. My uncle, the owner of the dog, walked slowly past the house.
10. We followed the trail by the marks on the trees.

433

B. Copy the following sets of sentences. In each set, combine the other sentences with the first one by adding the italicized prepositional phrases into the first as noun or verb modifiers.

SEPARATE: The girls and boys·watched the woman.
The watching was *through binoculars.*
The woman was *in the glider plane.*

COMBINED: The girls and boys watched the woman in the glider plane through binoculars.

1. The chief surgeon operated immediately.
The operation was *on the child.*
The child was *in the emergency room.*
2. Jane added tomatoes.
The addition was *to the salad.*
The salad was *in the bowl.*
The tomatoes were *from the garden.*
3. The accountant added the figures.
The figures were *in one column.*
The adding was *to the other column.*
The accountant was *at the desk.*
4. The cat lapped the milk eagerly.
The cat was *in the solarium.*
The lapping was *for two minutes.*
5. The violinist played the concerto.
The violinist was *from Brazil.*
The concerto was *by Mozart.*
The playing was *in a concert hall.*
The hall was *in Boston.*

★   **Spot Review**

(Based upon the sentences in A of the preceding activities)
1. Is the subject in sentence 1 singular or plural?
2. What is the subject in sentence 7? Spell its plural.
3. Why is the subject in sentence 9 not capitalized? Explain the use of the commas.
4. What sentence pattern is sentence 1?

DIAGRAMMING PREPOSITIONAL PHRASES

Like adjectives and adverbs themselves, prepositional phrases are placed below the words that they modify.

Steps in Diagramming Prepositional Phrases

1. Draw a slanting line below the word that the phrase modifies.
2. Write the preposition on the line.
3. Draw a horizontal line from the slanting line.
4. Write the object of the preposition on the horizontal line.
5. Place below the object any words that modify it.
6. Always begin the diagram in the same way. Find the verb and the subject first. Then see whether there is a direct object, a predicate nominative, or a predicate adjective. Last, diagram the modifiers—adjectives, adverbs, and prepositional phrases.

ADJECTIVE PHRASE

The porpoise *with the amiable grin* tossed the ball.

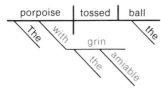

ADVERB PHRASE

The porpoise tossed the ball *in the air.*

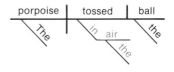

ADJECTIVE PHRASE MODIFYING THE OBJECT IN AN ADVERB PHRASE

The porpoise tossed the ball *over the fence of the aquarium.*

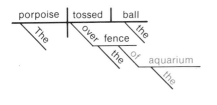

COMPOUND OBJECT OF A PREPOSITION

The porpoise was rewarded *with a herring, a mackerel,* and *two squid.*

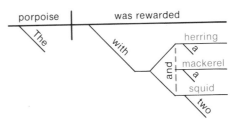

COMPOUND PHRASES

Her performance *in the water* and *in the air* was sensational.

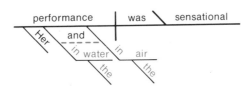

Note that only basic sentence-pattern parts go on the base line.

LEARNING ACTIVITIES

A. Diagram the following sentences. Be ready to explain your diagrams orally. Use a regular order, as in the following sample explanation for the first diagram on page 435: "In this sentence the verb is *tossed*. The subject is the noun *porpoise*. *Ball* is a noun used as the direct object of the verb *tossed*. *The* is a determiner modifying *porpoise*. *With the amiable grin* is an adjective phrase modifying *porpoise*. The preposition is *with;* its object is the noun *grin; the* is a determiner; and *amiable* is an adjective modifying *grin*. *The* is a determiner modifying *ball*."

1. The kite flew over the fence and into some bushes.
2. The trail winds over the hill and through a wide valley.
3. A deep ditch was dug near the boundary of the field.
4. A little puppy with shiny brown eyes barked at Bob and me.
5. The four children listened carefully to every sound.
6. Do you still live in that brick house in the next block?
7. Heaps of wreckage were left after the storm.
8. The real owner of the property is not this stranger.
9. The sound of angry voices came faintly to our ears.
10. We have no time for excuses or delays.

B. If you wish further drill in diagramming phrases, use the sentences in *A*, page 429; *A*, pages 431–432; and *A*, page 433.

USING INDIRECT OBJECTS IN SENTENCES

Both of the following sentences fit the picture.

He gave a watch *to the winner.*   He gave *the winner* a watch.

In the first sentence, *to the winner* is a prepositional phrase in which *winner* is the object. In the second, the preposition is understood, and *winner* is said to be an *indirect object.*

● THESE ARE FACTS ABOUT INDIRECT OBJECTS

1. **(DEFINITION) An** *indirect object* **is really a prepositional phrase in which the preposition** *to* **or** *for* **is understood, not stated. It tells** *to whom* **or** *for whom* **something is done.**

   She sent (to) **me** a gift.
   He made (for) **us** a new lamp.

2. **An indirect object comes between the verb and the direct object.**

   Mr. Jones *gave* the **winner** a *watch.*

3. **An indirect object may have modifiers.**

   He read *his little* **niece** a story.

4. **An indirect object may be compound.**

   She told **Ben** *and* **me** the truth.

5. **Only certain kinds of verbs take indirect objects.** Some that you probably use often are *give, tell, send, get, buy, show, build, do, make, save,* and *read.* **Sentences that have indirect objects are** *Pattern 5* **sentences. Here is the pattern: N + V + N + N.**

   $$N + V + N + N$$
   He has given the winner a watch.

LEARNING ACTIVITIES

A. Copy the following sentences, placing parentheses around each indirect object. Underline with a wavy line each direct object. Go over the sentences in class.

1. Has anyone sent you a notice about the next meeting?
2. Father built us a picnic table.
3. The doctor will send you a bill for his services.
4. I sent Ms. Burns a birthday card.
5. Shall I get you a ticket to the game?
6. Doris bought me two new records.
7. Did Gary tell you and Gregory his secret?
8. Give the man air.
9. The old road saved the hikers much time.
10. Has Elizabeth shown Julius and Rosa her new microscope?

B. Using the topic "Gifts," write an original paragraph that has in it at least five indirect objects. Think of a good topic sentence (see page 162). Review the Guides for Reading Aloud, page 59; then read the paragraphs in your small groups. As you listen, jot down the indirect objects; then compare lists.

C. Rewrite the following sentences so that each sentence has an indirect object in place of the prepositional phrase in italics.

1. I asked a question *of my teacher.*
2. He read a story *to the children.*
3. The Gabriels sent a present *to Ellen.*
4. She bought a leather briefcase *for herself.*
5. I gave a bath *to my dog.*
6. He did a big favor *for his sister.*
7. The artist showed the painting *to us.*
8. They gave a swimming lesson *to David.*

DIAGRAMMING INDIRECT OBJECTS

Indirect objects are diagrammed the same way that prepositional phrases are, except that an (x) is used for the understood preposition.

Mr. Jones gave the *winner* a watch.　　　　He told *Ben* and *me* the truth.

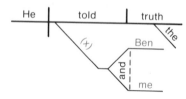

LEARNING ACTIVITIES

A. Diagram the following sentences. Exchange papers for checking when the diagrams are put on the board and explained. Follow a specific, regular order in giving the explanations. See the example in *A*, page 436.

1. The salesperson sold Ellen a diamond needle.
2. The lawyer gave her client good advice.
3. Albert told the teacher his problem.
4. Yesterday I bought myself a new pair of shoes.
5. Has Sadie offered you or Don a ride in her car?
6. Mother should have given Sandra and me more time.
7. The committee awarded each safe driver a certificate.
8. The pitcher threw me a fast ball.
9. I saved you and Gladys two big pieces of watermelon.
10. Has Coach Davis shown you that new play?

B. For additional practice, diagram the sentences in *A* on page 437. Explain the diagrams orally in class.

2. Building Sentences with Conjunctions

BUILDING COMPOUND PARTS OF SENTENCES

One well-put-together sentence can often carry the same meaning as two or three, and do it more economically. Read the following two versions of an incident.

SEPARATE: The nurse cleaned Sam's cut.
The nurse bandaged Sam's cut expertly.
Then the nurse gave him an encouraging smile.

COMBINED: The nurse cleaned Sam's cut, bandaged it expertly, and then gave him an encouraging smile.

Which version sounds better? Why?

When the subjects of any set of sentences are the same, you can usually combine the predicates into one sentence. The result is a sentence that reads more smoothly and builds interest.

What you do is eliminate the repeated subjects and join the predicates to each other with a conjunction. If there are more than two predicates, commas need to be added to keep the different predicates clear.

Effective sentences can also be created by combining other elements—subjects, objects, predicate adjectives, adverbs, or prepositional phrases—from separate sentences to form a compound element in a new sentence. Notice how the subjects in the following group of sentences have been combined in a single sentence.

SEPARATE: Jim ate spaghetti.
Mary ate spaghetti.
Anthony ate spaghetti.

COMBINED: Jim, Mary, and Anthony ate spaghetti.

In the following example, notice how elements from separate sentences are combined to create a single sentence.

SEPARATE: Mary hit a double in one inning.
Mary hit a single in the next.

COMBINED: Mary hit a double in one inning and a single in the next.

● THESE ARE FACTS ABOUT CONJUNCTIONS

1. **(DEFINITION) A** *conjunction* **is a word that** *joins* **one part of a sentence** *with* **another. (A** *junction* **is a place where two things join, and** *con-* **is a prefix meaning** *with.*)

2. **(DEFINITION) Sentence parts, or** *elements*, **that are joined by a conjunction are** *compound elements.*

   SUBJECTS: *John* **and** *I* cut the grass.
   VERBS: Jean *spaded* **and** *weeded* the garden.
   PREDICATE NOMINATIVES: The cashier will be *George* **or** *Lena.*
   PREDICATE ADJECTIVES: The clouds are *large* **and** *black.*
   DIRECT OBJECTS: We saw *Harry* **and** *Fred.*
   ADJECTIVES: She is a *slow* **but** *strong* swimmer.
   ADVERBS: We scored *quickly* **and** *easily.*
   OBJECTS OF PREPOSITION: Wait for *Ann* **and** *me.*
   PREPOSITIONAL PHRASES: Go *up the path* **and** *over the hill.*
   INDIRECT OBJECTS: Julie gave *Pat* **and** *me* a surprise.
   APPOSITIVES: Mrs. Carter, our *principal* **and** *friend*, is ill.

3. **A compound element may have more than two parts.**

   Joe, Irene, and *Jerry* spoke.

   (Joe *and* Irene *and* Jerry spoke.)

4. **Here are some common conjunctions:** *and, but, or,* **and** *nor.* These conjunctions are called *co-ordinate conjunctions. Or* and *nor* are often used as pairs with *either* and *neither.* Other pairs are *both–and* and *not only–but also.*

   Either Alma *or* Eve will go.
   It is *both* cold *and* rainy.

LEARNING ACTIVITIES

A. Locate the compound in each of the following sentences. Tell in which of the ways listed above it is used. Make this an oral exercise.

1. A crowd of boys and girls followed us.
2. I shall choose either Helen or her brother.
3. The happy children laughed and sang.
4. Two hot drinks, cocoa and tea, were served.
5. Our first visitors were Laurette and Caleb.
6. I neither saw nor heard anything.
7. In our garden several small but sturdy trees are growing.
8. Max waited for Libby, Barbara, and me.
9. You must leave quickly and quietly.
10. Nectarines and oranges were bought for the picnic.
11. After the game the boys were tired and hungry.

12. The chipmunk ran across the lawn and into the trees.
13. The gardener gave Rhoda and me some helpful hints.

B. On a separate piece of paper, copy the following sets of sentences. Combine each set into a single, longer sentence. Write that sentence below each set. Be sure (1) to leave out any repeated subjects and (2) to add a co-ordinate conjunction such as *and* or *but* before the final predicate. Read the sentence that results aloud so that you will be sure it sounds smooth.

1. Susan looked out the window at the rain.
   Susan sighed.
   She picked up her book.
   She began to read.
2. The water filled the bathtub.
   The water spilled over onto the floor.
   It leaked through to the apartment below.
3. The flame struggled against the wind bravely.
   It began to flicker.
   It finally went out.
4. Donald trimmed the sails.
   He veered into the wind.
   He headed for home.
5. Audrey dusted the books off.
   She rearranged them slightly.
   Then she saw the key.

C. Copy the following sets of sentences on a sheet of paper. Combine each set to form a single sentence containing compound elements. Write the sentence beneath the set. Use commas when more than two elements are compounded into a series.

1. Jane read those three books.
   Myra read those three books.
   Irving read those three books.
2. The wind was warm.
   The wind was pleasant.
3. Jim writes my cousin letters from Spain.
   He writes me letters from Spain.
4. The seeds were all over the yard.
   The seeds were all over the porch.
   The seeds were all over the car.
5. During the season we had strawberries for breakfast.
   During the season we had strawberries for lunch.
   During the season we had strawberries for dinner.
6. The picnic was paid for by the student council.
   The picnic was paid for by the P.T.A.

7. The horses looked strong.
   The horses looked healthy.
   The horses looked eager to run.
8. The club has a color TV.
   The club has two radios.
   The club has a reel-to-reel tape recorder.
9. The batter swung hard at the curve ball.
   The batter missed.
   He struck out.
10. Luisa dug several holes.
    Luisa planted the seedlings.
    She watered them carefully.
    She watered them lovingly.

DIAGRAMMING COMPOUND ELEMENTS

Compound elements are diagrammed on these pages: verbs and subjects, 321; predicate nominatives, 324; direct objects, 328; appositives, 331; adjectives, 392; adverbs, 413; prepositional phrases, 435; indirect objects, 438.

Here are some additional diagrams to help you.

The storm brought *both* rain
and cold weather.

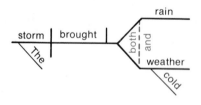

Toby visited in *either*
Iowa *or* Missouri.

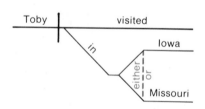

We saw *many* cities and towns.
(*Many* modifies both *cities* and *towns*.)

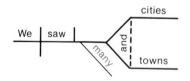

Susan works *not only* neatly
but also quickly.

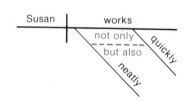

442

LEARNING ACTIVITIES

A. Diagram these sentences; then put them on the board and explain them. Be sure to name the conjunctions and the elements that they join.

1. Spot is a small but reliable watchdog.
2. Jim types rapidly and accurately.
3. The boys raced down the alley and into the park.
4. The day was not only hot but also windy.
5. Dolly often visits both Jones Beach and Coney Island.
6. The crowd whistled and applauded.
7. Either Letty or her cousin will call you.
8. The water at the beach was very rough and cold.
9. The lucky one is neither Tricia nor Bud.
10. Then we stopped at the station for some gas and oil.

B. For further practice, diagram the sentences in *A* on pages 440–441. Be prepared to explain the diagrams orally.

BUILDING COMPOUND SENTENCES

Good writing is economical writing. When two sentences are necessary to state two ideas, you should write two separate sentences. When the ideas are closely related, however, it is more effective to join the two simple sentences with a coordinate conjunction. The result is a *compound sentence.* For example, consider these two sentences:

The train takes eight hours.
The airplane takes only one.

They do not express the contrast as well when they are separate sentences as they do when they are compounded:

The train takes eight hours, but the airplane takes only one.

The two original sentences are still there, but because the ideas are related, the relationship between them is clearer when they are written as a compound sentence. Now read the following sentences:

The porpoise tossed the ball.
The trainer caught it.

The first sentence describes an action. The action leads to another action, which is described in the second sentence. The relationship between the two actions is better expressed when the two sentences are combined in a compound sentence.

The porpoise tossed the ball, **and the trainer caught it.**

● THESE ARE FACTS ABOUT COMPOUND SENTENCES

1. **(DEFINITION)** A *compound sentence* **puts together two or more simple sentences.*** **This combining usually is done by using the conjunctions** *and, but, or,* **or** *nor.*

    The porpoise tossed the ball. The trainer caught it.
    (*two simple sentences*)

    The porpoise tossed the ball, *and* the trainer caught it.
    (*compound sentence*)

2. **Only sentences closely related in thought should be joined.**

    Good: The porpoise tossed the ball, and the trainer caught it.
    Bad: The porpoise tossed the ball, but the water was warm.

---

* Each simple sentence that becomes part of a compound sentence is known as an *independent clause* because it can stand alone.

3. **A comma usually separates the two parts of a compound sentence when they are joined by a conjunction. The comma goes before the conjunction.**

The porpoise tossed the ball, *and* the trainer caught it.

In very short compound sentences, the comma may be omitted, especially if the conjunction is *and*. (Even in such cases, use a comma if you wish to show a pause between the two parts.)

I waited and soon it snowed.

4. **A compound sentence should not be confused with a simple sentence having compound parts.** (See point 2 on page 440.)

To test, divide the sentence before and after the conjunction. Each part of a compound sentence is really a sentence; each has a subject and a verb.

Mike hit a home run, |and| we scored four runs.
(*Each part makes sense. The sentence is compound.*)

The woman rented a car |and| drove to Montreal.
(*Only the first part makes sense. The sentence is simple.*)

My little brother |and| his friend went to the park.
(*Only the second part makes sense. The sentence is simple.*)

Learn about words!

The following words, taken from Learning Activity *A,* have interesting histories. Use your dictionary to find the story behind each word.

cookie   colonel   parade

LEARNING ACTIVITIES

A. (1) Copy the following compound sentences, inserting any needed commas. (2) Draw one line under subjects and two lines under verbs. (3) Enclose conjunctions in parentheses. (4) Exchange papers. (5) Go over the sentences in class. Name the two simple sentences that make up each compound sentence.

1. Karen had planned the barbecue but she could not attend it.
2. Our players did not win the game nor did they score.
3. I leave for New York today and Sis is going with me.
4. Is he a colonel or don't you know?
5. Sara made the motion and Jon seconded it.
6. I should like that but I have a dental appointment.

7. I do not know him but Paul does.
8. We must hurry or the train will leave without us.
9. Hiram baked the cookies and I made the parfaits.
10. Will they watch the parade or haven't they decided?

B. On your own paper, combine each set of sentences below into a compound sentence, using a co-ordinate conjunction and a comma to punctuate the sentence. Choose the conjunction that seems to make the connection between the two statements clearest.

1. The sun is warm.
   The wind is chilly.
2. The telephone rang insistently.
   No one was there to answer it.
3. The fan had been on for over an hour.
   All the windows were open.
4. Daryl put an album on the record player.
   He and his sister started to practice the latest dance step.
5. You practice your exercises.
   I will stop paying for lessons.
6. The book was full of pictures.
   There was very little text.
7. The curtains were fresh and clean.
   The windows seemed to sparkle in the sunshine.
8. The store had a sale on ski equipment.
   The supply was sold out quickly.
9. The waiter came from the kitchen with our orders.
   We soon were eating a long-delayed lunch.
10. The librarian finished explaining about the resource center.
    The students began to examine the books.

DIAGRAMMING COMPOUND SENTENCES

Steps in Diagramming a Compound Sentence

1. Diagram each part as a simple sentence, one below the other.
2. Join the two parts by a dotted line.
3. Write the conjunction on that line.

The porpoise tossed the ball, and the trainer caught it.

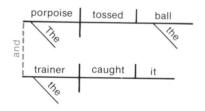

A. Diagram these sentences. Exchange papers for checking when the diagrams are put on the board. In explaining a diagram step by step, give each part its specific name. Begin, "This is a compound sentence."

1. Were you there, or didn't you go?
2. Lee West flew to New York, but she will return by train.
3. Anna played golf, and Ossie swam.
4. They should go, or they will miss a good play.
5. We had planned a picnic, but the forecast indicated rain.
6. The plane left the ground, and we began our journey.
7. Peggy gave the man ten dollars, and he handed her two tickets.
8. Bill was studying English, and Sheila was doing her arithmetic.
9. I had expected the pen, but the skates were a surprise.

B. For additional practice, diagram the sentences in *A*, pages 445–446. Go over the diagrams orally.

3. Using Standard English

USING PREPOSITIONS PROPERLY

He walked around **in** the room.   He walked **into** the room.

"He walked around *in* the room," means that the boy walked while he was in the room, not that he walked from somewhere else into it.

The following rules will help you to use *in* and *into* correctly and to avoid other errors in using prepositions.

RULES FOR USING PREPOSITIONS PROPERLY

RULE 1. Use *into* **for motion from outside to inside; use** *in* **for motion within.**

Sue jumped *into* the water.   She swam *in* the water.

RULE 2. Do not use *to* **or** *by* **as substitutes for** *at.*

STANDARD: He is not *at* home.   I stay *at* my aunt's house.
NONSTANDARD: He is not *to* home.   I stay *by* my aunt's house.

RULE 3. Do not use *off* **or** *off of* **for** *from.*

STANDARD: I bought it *from* him.
NONSTANDARD: I bought it *off* him.

RULE 4. Do not use *off of* **for** *off.*

STANDARD: Get *off* the train.
NONSTANDARD: Get *off of* the train.

RULE 5. Do not use unnecessary prepositions.

Where does she stay *at?*   Where are you going *to?*

LEARNING ACTIVITIES

A. To get used to the sound of the proper forms, practice saying aloud the standard examples of the rules.

B. Copy the following sentences, choosing the correct preposition from those given in parentheses. In class, read the sentences orally several times.

1. Get (off, off of) the roof immediately.
2. Is Eugenia (at, to) home?
3. Get (in, into) the car.
4. Where are you (living, living at)?
5. Luella stayed (at, by) her grandparents' house.
6. I hurried (in, into) the room without knocking.
7. Tom bought the book (off of, from) Nora.
8. For what street are you (looking for, looking)?
9. Where were you (going to, going)?
10. Were many people (to, at) the game?

C. Write sentences to illustrate Rules 1–4. In your small groups, take turns at reading sentences. As others read the sentences, listen to get used to the standard forms.

USING OBJECTS OF PREPOSITIONS
AND INDIRECT OBJECTS PROPERLY

READ AND THINK ABOUT . . .

Look at the following sentences:

> She waved at me.
> She waved at Neal and me.
> Do Neal and me a favor.

"Me" is the proper form in all three sentences. No doubt it sounds right to you in the first sentence, but how about in the other two? It may sound wrong in those sentences, but if you take out "Neal and," you will see that "me" is right.

THE RULES

RULE 1. **Use the objective pronouns** *me, her, him, us, them* **as objects of a preposition. Do not so use** *I, he, she, we, they.*

He sent *for* Joe and me.   The candy was given *to* us volunteers.

RULE 2. **Never use a nominative pronoun** (*I, he, she, we, or they*) **as an indirect object. Use the objective pronouns** *me, him, her, us,* **or** *them.*

Dad saved Gwen and him some cookies.
Miss Bell gave her and me the last pencils.

RULE 3. **In speaking of yourself and others, name yourself last, as a matter of politeness.**

POLITE: He sent for Joe and me.
POOR: He sent for me and Joe.

LEARNING ACTIVITIES

A. Read the following sentences orally, choosing the standard forms. Make this a row contest in which you see which group can say the sentences properly twice in the shortest time.

1. The class gave Pam and (him, he) the prizes.
2. Everyone was ready except (we, us) three.
3. They saved (Grace and me, me and Grace) two seats.
4. This secret is between you and (me, I).
5. Mr. Bie told (them, they) and (us, we) the same story.
6. Will you show Meg and (me, I) your drawing?

7. The librarian will give you and (me, I) the information.
8. It was a vacation for (them, they) and (we, us).

B. (1) Using yourself and some friends as the topic, write five sentences to illustrate the rules on page 449. Begin three sentences with an adverb phrase. (2) Put sentences on the board, leaving a blank for each objective pronoun. (3) Call on classmates to fill the blanks properly.

★ **Spot Review**

(*Based upon the sentences in* A *of the preceding activities*)
1. What is the tense of the verb in sentence 1 and in sentence 7?
2. What part of speech is *ready* in sentence 2?
3. How would you spell the plural of the final word in sentence 5?
4. What are the principal parts of the verb in sentence 5?

USING <u>TO</u>, <u>TOO</u>, AND <u>TWO</u> CORRECTLY

READ AND DO . . .

When you say *to, two,* or *too,* everyone usually understands which word you mean. When you write, however, it is important to remember that each of these three words is spelled differently. If you have trouble distinguishing *to, too,* and *two,* study the following rules and the examples. Then do the activities.

THE RULES FOR USING *TO, TOO,* AND *TWO* CORRECTLY

RULE 1. Use an object with *to;* **it is a preposition:** I went to *town.*

RULE 2. Use *too,* **which is always an adverb, to modify verbs, adjectives, or other adverbs. When it modifies a verb,** *too* **means "also."**

May Harriett *go,* **too**? (*Too* modifies the verb *may go.*)
John is **too** *tired.* (*Too* modifies the adjective *tired.*)
The time is going **too** *fast.* (*Too* modifies the adverb *fast.*)

RULE 3. *a*) **Use** *two* **as an adjective:** Those **two** *children* may go.
         b) **Use** *two* **as a noun:** Two of the boys came early.

LEARNING ACTIVITIES

A. Copy the following sentences, putting in each blank the correct form, *to, too,* or *two.* Check sentences in class. Do not write in this book.

1. I, _____, should like a visit _____ those _____ countries.
2. The boys went _____ town _____ hours ago.
3. Will you go _____ the store, _____?
4. I have _____ tickets _____ the game.
5. _____ girls are swimming _____ the shore.
6. _____ of my friends came _____ the party _____ late.
7. The work is not _____ hard for us _____ students.
8. I am going _____ the library and _____ the bank, _____.
9. _____ trips _____ the park in one day will be _____ many.

B. Write five sentences using *to, too,* and *two* correctly. In your small groups, read sentences aloud. Call on someone to spell the forms needed.

USING TROUBLESOME VERBS

The next few pages contain rules and practice for standard use of the forms of *sing, ring, blow, grow, fall,* and *wear.*

USING IRREGULAR VERBS — <u>SING</u>, <u>SANG</u>, <u>SUNG</u> <u>RING</u>, <u>RANG</u>, <u>RUNG</u>

RULE. Never use an auxiliary verb with *sang* **or** *rang.* **Always use one with** *sung* **or** *rung.*

Today I **sing**.	Yesterday I **sang**.	Often I *have* **sung**.
Today I **ring**.	Yesterday I **rang**.	Often I *have* **rung**.

LEARNING ACTIVITIES

A. (1) Copy each sentence below, supplying the proper form of the verb in parentheses. (2) Underline the complete verb twice. (3) In class, have the sentences read aloud.

1. How long have you (sing) in the chorus?
2. Your alarm clock must have (ring) early.
3. The bell should have (ring) ten minutes ago.
4. This line should be (sing) rapidly.

5. Neither June nor Sammy has ever (sing) on television before.
6. Suddenly a scream had (ring) out from behind the locked door.
7. You've never (sing) better!
8. Many sets of words have been (sing) to this music.
9. Has the bell (ring)?
10. A lullaby should be (sing) softly.

B. Make this a team contest. (1) One after the other, each person on each team will write on the board two sentences, one using *sang* or *sung* and one using *rang* or *rung*. Each sentence must have at least six words in it. The members of a team must go to the board in order, and not more than one person from a team may be out of his or her seat at once. (2) Stop the contest as soon as everyone on one team has written the required sentences. (3) Credit each team with one point for each sentence it has on the board. (4) Go over the sentences orally. Reduce a team's score by one point for every nonstandard verb used.

★ **Spot Review**

(*Based upon the sentences in* A *of the preceding activities*)
1. How would you spell the plural of the last word in sentence 1?
2. What kind of sentence is sentence 7?
3. Is *better* in sentence 7 an adjective or an adverb? How do you know?
4. Why is *has* the proper auxiliary in sentence 5?

USING IRREGULAR VERBS—BLOW, BLEW, BLOWN

RULE. **Always use a helping verb with** *blow;* **never use one with** *blew*. **Remember that there is no standard form** *blowed*.

Today it blows.　　Yesterday it blew.　　Often it *has* blown.

LEARNING ACTIVITIES

A. In an oral activity, practice filling the blanks in these sentences, using the standard form of the verb *blow*. Name any helping verbs.

1. Last night the wind _____ hard.
2. In the storm, the roof was _____ from our garage.
3. The children _____ soap bubbles for an hour this morning.
4. The noon whistles have _____.
5. Has the trouble _____ over yet?

6. Who _____ that whistle?
7. A strong wind had _____ all week.
8. Jan _____ the bugle for taps last night.

B. Write five sentences using *blew* and *blown* properly. Use a vivid adjective or adverb in each sentence. (See pages 388, 410.) In your small groups, take turns at reading sentences. Call on a listener to judge your sentences for standard usage and to name the vivid words.

C. Divide the class into two teams. Take turns at asking and answering questions about a big windstorm. Use one of these questions:

What blew away at your place?   Was anything blown away?

Have fun with your answers. For example, you might say, "The freckles on my sister's nose blew away," or "My dog's bark was blown away." If the person before you uses a nonstandard form, you must reword that sentence before giving your own. Score one point for each proper answer.

Spot Review

(Based upon the sentences in A of the preceding activities)

1. In sentence 1, what is *hard,* an adjective or an adverb? Explain.
2. How would you spell the plural of the subject in sentence 2?
3. Which three sentences have direct objects?

USING IRREGULAR VERBS — GROW, GREW, GROWN

RULE. **Always use an auxiliary verb with** *grown;* **never use one with** *grew.*

Today I grow.   Yesterday I grew.   Often I *have* grown.

LEARNING ACTIVITIES

A. (1) Copy these sentences, filling the blanks with the proper form of the verb *grow.* (2) Underline the verb twice, including any helping verbs. (3) Proofread for careless errors in copying. (4) Exchange papers. (5) Check the verb choices as the sentences are read aloud.

1. The corn _____ several inches last week.
2. I have _____ tired of doing nothing.

3. Bananas are _____ in a hot, damp climate.
4. The grass _____ well last spring.
5. This property has _____ in value.
6. Where were these oranges _____?
7. We _____ oats in this field last year.
8. A younger man would not have _____ tired.
9. How you have _____!
10. My mother _____ up on a farm.

B. Pretend that each of you had a garden last year. Go around the class, telling what you grew and what you wished later that you had grown instead. Be ready to explain why, if anyone asks you. No crop may be named more than once.

★ **Spot Review**

(*Based upon the sentences in A of the preceding activities*)

1. In sentence 4, is *well* an adjective or an adverb? Explain.
2. How would you spell the plural of the subject in sentence 5?
3. What kind of sentence is sentence 9?

USING IRREGULAR VERBS — <u>FALL</u>, <u>FELL</u>, <u>FALLEN</u>

RULE. Always use a helping verb with *fallen;* **never use one with** *fell.*

Today I **fall**.   Yesterday I **fell**.   Often I *have* **fallen**.

LEARNING ACTIVITIES

A. Copy these sentences, supplying the standard forms of the verb *fall*. Underline the verb twice, including helping verbs. Go over your work orally.

1. The baby had just _____ asleep.
2. The responsibility for last month's play _____ upon Jean and me.
3. By morning the river should have _____ a foot or more.
4. Rain has _____ steadily for hours.
5. Yes, the Fourth of July _____ on Monday last year.
6. She might have _____ heir to a large fortune.
7. The picture must have _____ from its hook.

B. Go around the class rapidly, giving sentences with *fell* and *fallen*. See how long it takes for everyone to use each word properly.

USING IRREGULAR VERBS—<u>WEAR</u>, <u>WORE</u>, <u>WORN</u>

RULE. Always use an auxiliary verb with *worn;* **never use one with** *wore.*

Today I **wear**.　　Yesterday I **wore**.　　Often I *have* **worn**.

LEARNING ACTIVITY

In an oral activity, practice the following sentences, using *wore* or *worn* in each blank. When you use *worn*, name the auxiliary verbs.

1. These two colors shouldn't be _____ together.
2. Marie _____ a new kind of slack suit yesterday.
3. This pair of shoes surely has _____ well.
4. My red coat has been _____ often.
5. At the party last Friday, those boys _____ shirts just alike.
6. Everyone had _____ jeans except Bea and him.
7. Are skirts being _____ longer this year?
8. This coat can be _____ either in summer or in winter.

Spot Review ★

(Based upon the sentences in A *of the preceding activities)*

1. Why are *surely* and *well* the proper forms in sentence 3?
2. Why should you say *those* boys, not *them* boys, in sentence 5?
3. Why is *him* the correct pronoun in sentence 6?

Chapter Review✶

A. (1) Copy these sentences; proofread to be sure you have copied accurately. (2) Underline each prepositional phrase and draw an arrow to the word modified. (3) If the phrase is used as an adjective, write *adj.* after the sentence. If it is used as an adverb, write *adv.* (4) Put parentheses around each indirect object. Name the sentence patterns.

1. The children were playing in the street.
2. The librarian gave Lucy a list of new books.

✶ Check Test 7 should be taken at this point. If the results show need for further study, students should do this review practice. They should then take Mastery Test 7.

3. We did the work with great care.
4. After supper we played games.

B. (1) Copy each of the following sentences; proofread to be sure you have copied accurately. (2) Put parentheses around each compound element. (3) Decide how each is used in the sentence. After the sentence, put one or more of these marks: *v.* for compound parts used as verbs; *subj.*, as subjects; *d.o.*, as direct objects; *p.n.*, as predicate nominatives; *p.a.*, as predicate adjectives; *o.p.*, as objects of a preposition; *i.o.*, as indirect objects; *adj.*, as adjectives; *adv.*, as adverbs; and *pr. ph.*, as prepositional phrases.

1. Miriam lost or mislaid her book.
2. The owners are Mr. Eisenberg and Mr. Colucci.
3. A new and better plan was offered by Phil and Stella.
4. Martha or Alice will give you and Ann the money.
5. We saw many lakes and rivers.
6. John writes slowly but neatly.
7. Father was tired and cold from the ride.
8. Mickey hit the ball over the fence and into the street.

C. Number your paper from 1 to 5. After each number, write *Compound* for each compound sentence and *Simple* for each simple sentence.

1. We were watching television, but they were studying.
2. Frank and Kevin are making a salad in the kitchen.
3. The dentist did not pull the tooth, nor did he even fill it.
4. We had better run, or we'll miss part of the game.
5. The reporter wrote the story and gave it to the editor.

D. Read the following sentences aloud, choosing the proper forms.

1. Gloria crawled (in, into) the wagon.
2. Please get (off, off of) the steps.
3. Ruth visited last week (by, at) her cousin's house.
4. Is Joe (at, to) home? I borrowed this book (from, off) him.
5. Where did you (stay at, stay)? Where will you (go, go to) next?
6. Did the (two, too, to) boys go (to, too, two) town, (too, to, two)?

E. Read these sentences aloud, choosing the standard pronouns.

1. Mr. and Mrs. Armand gave a party for Cecile and (me, I).
2. That job is not for (me and you, you and me).
3. Between you and (me, I), there should be no secrets.
4. Mrs. DaSilva gave you and (him, he) good advice.

F. Read these sentences aloud, supplying the proper form of each verb.

1. Have you ever (sing) in public?
2. The corn has not (grow) well this year.
3. He had (wear) a hat, but it had (fall) off.
4. The noon whistles have (blow), and the bell has (ring).

456

PARTS OF THE SENTENCE

Copy these sentences, leaving extra space between lines. Label *verbs* (v.), *subjects* (subj.), *predicate nominatives* (p.n.), *direct objects* (d.o.), *appositives* (app.), *adjectives* (adj.), and *adverbs* (adv.).

1. Is that watermelon ripe? Our first one was a beauty?
2. My plant has a new leaf.
3. The tree, a tall pine, was swaying wildly.

TROUBLESOME VERBS

Read these sentences aloud, supplying the standard form of each verb.

1. I (eat) a sandwich, (drink) some milk, and then went to school.
2. My feet had almost (freeze). Why had I (come) without boots!
3. The man had (drive) up in a cart. It was (draw) by a mule.
4. Why have you (ride) that horse? You have (break) your word.
5. We had (steal) away to the beach and had (swim) out to the float.
6. Have the prices of plane tickets (rise)? I've not (fly) lately.
7. That rock should not be (lie) there. Who (throw) it?

PROPER USE OF PRONOUNS

Go over these sentences aloud, choosing the standard forms.

1. My dog and (I, me) like (your, you're) woods.
2. One day (we, us) boys were fishing in (their, they're) pond.
3. Alfred and (he, him) watched the kitten chasing (its, it's) tail.
4. Yes, it was (she, her), and she saw (we, us) boys.
5. Can it be (they, them)? That car is (there's, theirs).

PROPER USE OF ADJECTIVES AND ADVERBS

Read these sentences aloud, choosing the standard forms.

1. (This, These) kind of plum tastes (good, well).
2. Morton has (sure, surely) found (a, an) interesting book.
3. How (good, well) does he sing?
4. Hedda hasn't (ever, never) liked (them, those) rugs.
5. (Them, Those) gloves (sure, surely) are pretty.
6. Elana (has, hasn't) hardly ever felt (bad, badly).

VERB-SUBJECT AGREEMENT

Read these sentences aloud, choosing the standard forms.

1. She (don't, doesn't) know me. It (don't, doesn't) matter, though.
2. (Was, Were) you at the party? Neither Josh nor I (was, were).

3. The noise of the explosions (doesn't, don't) carry far.
4. A bushel of peaches (has, have) just been delivered.
5. Neither the McDevitts nor the Lums (was, were) there.

Figure out the scrambled *ie* or *ei* words in the following sentences.

1. The hospital (pteitan) was very (tique).
2. The (fithe) dropped a (dankrichfeeh) as he ran off.
3. I (veelibe) you (gihew) more than I do.

Word Games to Test Your Thinking

Alphabet Addition or Subtraction

EXAMPLES: Take *n* from *close by* and leave *part of the body.* (near-ear).
Add *p* to *automobile* and have a *kind of fish.* (car-carp).

1. Take *a* from *once more* and leave *profit.*
2. Take *s* from *talk* and leave the *top of a mountain.*
3. Take *t* from a *pronoun* and leave *stockings.*
4. Take *p* from *gave wages to* and leave *help.*
5. Add *s* to a *female deer* and have a *form of* "do."
6. Add *y* to a *public vehicle* and have *not idle.*
7. Add *m* to a *chum* and have a *kind of tree.*

Would You Like to Know—?

Find the answers that the encyclopedia gives to these questions.

1. How did *Death Valley* get its name?
2. Were the first *dams* built to supply power or to irrigate land?
3. When was *daylight-saving* time first used?
4. You have heard the expression "dead as a *dodo*." Was there ever a real creature of that name?
5. Is the *dragonfly* a harmful, or a useful, insect?

"I" Before "E" Puzzle

Copy the crossword puzzle. Do not write in this book.

Across

1. Your sister's daughter.
4. Part of something.
8. A preposition.
9. Credit (*abbr.*).
10. Used to fish with.
12. Pertaining to a chorus.
14. Opposite of *give*.
16. A preposition.
19. Textile used to stiffen or shape clothes.
21. Eisenhower's nickname.
23. One's relatives.
24. Legal term meaning *unless*.
26. Contraction of *even*.
27. Anything that happens.
29. Six (Roman numerals).
30. "Anchors ___" (Navy song).
31. Half an *em*.
32. Ending that forms the comparative of adjectives.
33. George (*abbr.*).
35. Fastened to a horse's bit.
36. If you are polite, you will say, "Yes, ___," to a man.

Down

1. Short sleep.
2. Pronoun.
3. Company (*abbr.*).
4. Make angry.
5. Period of history.
6. Used after the salutation in a business letter.
7. Nickname for *Edward.*
9. Part of the jaw.
11. To mislead or trick.
12. The part of a room overhead.
13. The medicine helps to ___ the pain.
15. Same as 9 across.
17. One who lives near you.
18. Eleven (Roman numerals).
20. Units in baseball.
22. Past form of *know.*
25. Fishing net.
28. "Now and ___" means the same as *occasionally.*
30. Present form of *be.*
34. East Indies (*abbr.*).

CORRECTING SENTENCE
ERRORS*

1. Avoiding Sentence Fragments

READ AND THINK ABOUT . . .

A listener probably would want to ask, "What about it? What happens at the sound of your voice?"

"At the sound of my voice," you see, is only *part* of a sentence — a sentence that might express many things, all different:

---

* Pretest 8 should be taken at this time.

The mountains echo *at the sound of my voice.*
At the sound of my voice, the neighbors complain.
The crowd cheers *at the sound of my voice.*
At the sound of my voice, start running.

A complete *sentence* may make a statement; it may ask a question; it may state a request or a command; or it may make an exclamation. "At the sound of my voice" does none of those things.

In speaking, as in a conversation, you need not always express yourself in complete sentences. You will be *thinking* a complete sentence but will leave unsaid parts that can be understood.

"When do you plan to rake the leaves, John?"
"In the morning." [*I plan to rake them* in the morning.]

The words "In the morning" do not express a complete thought. Then how do you know what words are missing? You know *because the question that goes before makes them clear.*

You have learned that it takes a verb to make any sense of what you say. (See pages 278–279.) You might call the verb the *motor* of a sentence because it is what makes the sentence go. A group of words trying to be a sentence without a verb is as useless as an automobile without a motor. A motor, however, is not much good unless there is a guiding force, a driver, behind it. The guiding force behind a verb is its subject.

If either the verb or the subject is missing, a group of words is only a part of a sentence, that is, a *fragment.*

Learn about words!

The following words, taken from Learning Activity *B* on page 463, have interesting histories. Use your dictionary to find the story behind each word.

cloud   parasol   terrier   tall

1. **Every complete sentence must have a** *subject* **and a** *verb* **(predicate).** Short as they are, each word group below has a subject and a verb. Each group *makes sense,* as a sentence must do.

   Birds sing.   Stars shine.   Time passes.   Darkness fell.

2. **(DEFINITION) A group of words that lacks a verb, a subject, or both a verb and a subject is a** *sentence fragment.*

   The *boy* in the middle. (*A subject, but no verb.*)
   Waited in the hall. (*A verb, but no subject.*)
   For an hour or more. (*No verb or subject.*)

3. **Sometimes fragments can make sense.** For example, the italicized words below carry little meaning in themselves. However, if you hear them in a conversation, those words make sense because they are answers to questions that have just been asked. The missing parts are understood.

   QUESTION: What did John want from you?
   ANSWER: *A dollar.* [He wanted a dollar.]
   QUESTION: Where is he now?
   ANSWER: *At the game.* [He is at the game.]

4. **In your written work and in your speaking, when you need to make sure that your meaning is clear, you should use complete sentences.**

5. **Sometimes a fragment in written work is simply a matter of incorrect punctuation and capitalization.**

   WRONG: I like to watch television. In the evening.
   RIGHT: I like to watch television in the evening.

6. **Sometimes, a group of words may have a subject and a verb and still be only a sentence fragment.**

   After Hazel had made the candy.

   That group of words has a verb, *had made,* and a subject, *Hazel.* It is not a sentence, however, because it does not give a *complete* thought. You want to know something more — *what happened after Hazel had made the candy.* In other words, the main idea is missing. For a complete sentence, that main idea must be added:

   After Hazel had made the candy, **Don washed the dishes.***

---

* This is what is known as a *complex sentence.* You will study more about this kind of sentence next year.

LEARNING ACTIVITIES

A. Make this an oral activity. (1) Take turns telling which of the following groups of words are sentences and which are only fragments. (2) Add words that will turn the fragments into sentences. (3) Tell whether you added a verb (or part of a verb), a subject, or both. Each member of the class should listen to see whether he or she agrees and should be ready to tell why or why not.

1. Looks like mine.
2. The dog jumped the fence easily.
3. Only two or three cows.
4. Always waits for me.
5. Running around the corner in a hurry.
6. Those two girls moved here from Akron.
7. Don't wait for me.
8. Walking along slowly on the muddy streets.
9. Harold and the other members of the team.
10. Birds singing in the trees outside my window.

B. (1) Number your paper from 1 to 14. (2) If a group of words below is a sentence, write *S*. (3) If it is a fragment, write *F*. (4) Make the fragments into complete sentences. (5) Read the sentences in your small groups. (6) Explain what you did to make the fragments into sentences.

1. Sometimes Uncle Marvin took all of us to the zoo.
2. The woman with the parasol is my aunt.
3. Singing at the top of her voice.
4. Opened the door carefully and peeked through.
5. That terrier has been barking for an hour.
6. Don't forget your gloves.
7. Everywhere, even in the tall grass beside the road.
8. Buzzed around in the morning sun.
9. At exactly ten o'clock every morning.
10. Through the cloud the sun was shining.
11. After a long wait in the station.
12. Always makes nine free throws out of ten.
13. Had the boys ever seen a deer before?
14. Early in the morning of every day but Saturday.

C. The following paragraph contains some sentences and some sentence fragments. (1) Rewrite the paragraph, using complete sentences. Sometimes you may be able to add a fragment to a sentence that comes before it. In some cases you may have to add new words to change a fragment into a sentence. Work carefully. Be sure that every sentence makes sense. (2) Proofread to catch careless mistakes in capitalization and punctuation. (3) Go over the rewritten paragraphs in class, putting some of the best ones on the board.

I like to go into the woods to look for persimmons. In the fall. Have you ever seen a persimmon? It is a small, orange-red fruit. With from six to eight seeds. It is from half an inch to an inch in diameter. The tree is sometimes fifty feet high. The persimmon has a harsh taste. Before a frost. After a frost it is sweet and tastes good. According to some people, a persimmon would ripen anyway. Even without a frost. Persimmon trees grow mostly in the South.

D. (1) Copy the following groups of words. (2) Write *S* beside each complete sentence and *F* beside each fragment. (3) Make complete sentences of all the fragments. If you put the fragment first, use a comma after it. Compare work in class.

1. Before he went to school.
2. While I sat in the car.
3. You should take this pen.
4. Since she moved to Texas.
5. We sent him on a journey.
6. If we build a new chapel.
7. Because I was hungry.
8. His temperature is normal.
9. As I said in my letter.
10. So that we could leave early.

2. Avoiding Run-on Sentences

Some people run sentences together when they are in a hurry or excited about something. In conversation this is not a big problem, but in written work it can lead to misunderstanding on the part of the reader. It can also be very tiring to follow.

● THESE ARE FACTS ABOUT RUN-ON SENTENCES

1. **(DEFINITION) A** *run-on sentence* **is one in which two or more sentences are written incorrectly as one sentence.**

2. **Run-on sentences are of two types:**

   a) **Those run together with no separating punctuation**

   The sky kept getting darker and darker soon snow began to fall.

   b) **Those run together with a comma or commas**

   John came early, the others were late.

3. **Run-on sentences can be corrected in these ways:**

   a) **The ideas can be made into separate sentences**

   The sky kept getting darker and darker. Soon snow began to fall.

   b) **The ideas can be combined into a good compound sentence**

   John came early, **but** the others were late.

4. **Another incorrect grouping of sentences may come from overuse of** *and*'**s,** *and-so*'**s, or** *but*'**s. (DEFINITION) Stringing unrelated sentences together with conjunctions is called** *overco-ordination.*

   Last Friday's football game didn't get started until almost four-thirty, *and* soon it began to get dark, *and so* the other team wanted to quit playing, *but* since we were six points behind we wanted to keep on, *and so* finally after arguing about it we agreed to play ten more minutes, *and* in a little while we made a touchdown *and* kicked the point practically in the dark, *and so* we won by one point.

This paragraph is easier to read and to understand when it is broken up into separate sentences.

   Last Friday's football game didn't get started until almost four-thirty. Soon it began to get dark. The other team wanted to quit playing. Since we were six points behind, we wanted to keep on. Finally, after arguing about it, we agreed to play ten more minutes. In a little while we made a touchdown and kicked the point practically in the dark. We won by one point.

The sentence fragment fails to give clear meaning because it does not express a complete thought. The run-on sentence fails to give clear meaning because it runs together too many separate thoughts. The following guides will help you to get rid of run-on sentences in your own writing.

GUIDES FOR CORRECTING RUN-ON SENTENCES

1. Break run-on sentences into separate sentences, correctly capitalized and punctuated. When possible, combine the ideas into a good compound sentence.

RUN-ON: Our neighbors in the big white house across the street have a great many pets, that is why their house is very popular with all the boys and girls in the neighborhood, in fact, my little brother Tommy spends more time there than at home.

IMPROVED: Our neighbors in the big white house across the street have a great many pets, **and** that is why their house is very popular with all the boys and girls in the neighborhood. **In** fact, my little brother Tommy spends more time there than at home.

2. When you can, correct run-on sentences by combining two or more parts into compound elements.

RUN-ON: Eric was running fast, and he did not notice the hole in the road, and so suddenly down he went, but luckily he did not break his leg.

IMPROVED: Eric **was running** fast and **did** not **notice** the hole in the road. Suddenly down he **went** but luckily **did** not **break** his leg. (*compound verbs*)

RUN-ON: Dick will go to camp this summer, so will Ted.

IMPROVED: **Dick** and **Ted** will go to camp this summer. (*compound subject*)

RUN-ON: Mr. Olson is the owner of this plane he is also the pilot.

IMPROVED: Mr. Olson is the **owner** and **pilot** of this plane. (*compound predicate nominative*)

RUN-ON: Larry collects stamps, he also collects pencils.

IMPROVED: Larry collects **stamps** and **pencils.** (*compound direct object*)

3. Use appositives to combine parts of run-on sentences.

RUN-ON: Joe Denny has won many golf medals, he is my cousin.

IMPROVED: Joe Denny, **my cousin,** has won many golf medals.

LEARNING ACTIVITIES

A. Some of the following groups of words are run-on sentences. Others are correct. (1) For a correct sentence, simply copy the number and write

"Correct" after it. (2) Rewrite each run-on sentence by applying the preceding guides; use correct end punctuation and capitalization. (3) Compare sentences in class. Read the sentences aloud so that you can show by your voice where a sentence ends.

1. John Flynn is a new member of our class he came here from Florida.
2. Follow me, the doctor can see you now.
3. Beth ran the distance in three minutes.
4. We didn't hear the bell, and so we kept on playing, but in a short while the teacher came out, and he called us in, and then he kept us after school.
5. Helen made Mother's birthday gift, it was a leather jacket.
6. Today Bill baked a chocolate cake he also baked some cookies.
7. Ms. Egly takes her vacation in June she usually goes to the mountains.
8. Judie is diagramming the sentences in her notebook, and Lynn is diagramming them in his notebook also.
9. Bill rewrote his paper three times before the end of that tiresome day.
10. Ronnie paid attention to the coach's advice, and so she practiced jumping over and over, and she did leg exercises every night, and finally she could jump higher than anyone else on the team.
11. Come early, we must finish before nine o'clock.
12. The twins are good students, they are also fine athletes and excellent musicians.
13. Pat could not back the long car into the parking space.
14. The lights should be turned out, electricity costs money.
15. Please turn off the radio it bothers me.

B. Study the following paragraph carefully; then decide how you would get rid of the run-on sentences in it. Go over the paragraph in class.

> Bathing in the ocean is real sport there's a trick in plunging into the waves, though. The waves are likely to knock you down they are powerful. The best thing to do is to go out about chest deep and watch the waves come in and then wait for a smallish one, you can jump up and ride it, and so in that way you can avoid being knocked down. Sometimes a very large wave may come along, in that case you should dive right through it, and you will come up beyond it.

C. The following paragraph has both run-on sentences and sentence fragments. (1) Rewrite the paragraph, using complete sentences. You may need to add words to change some of the fragments into sentences. (2) Be sure to proofread your paragraph for careless mistakes. (3) Read the paragraph aloud, letting your voice show where each sentence ends.

> One day while bathing in the surf. I had a rough experience.
> I tried to ride a high wave. Taking a deep breath, I jumped high,

a second later I was dragging the ocean floor. Knocked down by the wave. Finally I came up, blowing and sputtering, and my back was to the ocean, and so I couldn't see anything coming. Crack! Down I went again this time the wave carried me along and pitched me onto the beach. There I lay. With my hands and knees scratched and bleeding.

USING ENGLISH IN ALL CLASSES

Look for run-on sentences in papers that you have written for other classes. Bring these to class. Read them aloud and then explain how you would correct them.

 Chapter Review٭

A. Copy the following groups of words. Write *S* beside each complete sentence and *F* beside each fragment. Then add words that will turn the fragments into complete sentences.

1. Late in the afternoon.
2. Grass glistening with dew.
3. The cabinet door was open.
4. Rains almost every day.
5. Have they raked the yard?
6. Reading quietly in a chair.
7. The records lying on the table.
8. If there is no game today.

B. Rewrite each of the following run-on sentences, using correct punctuation and capitalization.

1. We walked through the fields it was a beautiful fall morning.
2. Sheila suggested a picnic, I wanted to go fishing.
3. One of the volumes of the encyclopedia is missing, I'll bet I know who's using it.
4. Close the window it's getting windy.

C. The following paragraph has both run-on sentences and sentence fragments. Rewrite the paragraph so as to correct these errors. You may

---

٭ Check Test 8 should be taken at this point. If the results show need for further study, students should do this review practice. They should then take Mastery Test 8.

need to add a word or two to change some of the fragments to complete sentences.

> Saturday the telephone rang promptly at 9:30 A.M. It was Sylvia. Bright and cheerful, as always. She called to remind me that the swimming club's practice that day was an hour earlier than usual. I told her that I was ready. Waiting for her to come by. Just then Mom came in to remind me about my violin lesson that afternoon, I said I wouldn't forget. My brother Marcus then stuck his head in the front door to ask if I would mind helping him with his homework. I smiled and said I would do it. If I could find time between practice sessions and lessons. Then Dad came in from the kitchen to say that he needed someone my age to play the part of a young artist in the community theater play he was directing. He wanted to know if I had time. I broke out laughing, he asked me what I was laughing about. I replied, "Oh nothing it's just a typical Saturday around here."

Cumulative Review*

CAPITALIZATION

Copy these sentences, supplying needed capital letters.

1. "well," mabel asked, "isn't jacksonville in the south?"
2. Last saturday the flying aces, our new club, held a model-plane contest in the large field on the west bank of davis creek.
3. In geography class yesterday, we learned that the source of the arkansas river is in the rocky mountains.
4. just before the thanksgiving holidays, judge r. t. mahoney spoke to the students of field junior high school on the subject "the joys of debate."

PUNCTUATION

Copy these sentences, supplying needed punctuation.

1. Jan added that on December 15 1962 the city of Chicago Illinois opened the Dan Ryan Expressway to the public.
2. Samantha asked Didnt you see any horses cattle or pigs on your uncles farm Manya
3. Be sure to look up Dr J R Byers a good friend of mine Ive known him for twenty five years.
4. Mens and womens coats arent on this floor said the clerk.

* After this final review, take the Last Test in the test booklet.

VERB-SUBJECT AGREEMENT

Go over the following sentences orally, choosing the standard forms from the parentheses.

1. (Was, Were) you in school yesterday?
2. That sort of movie (doesn't, don't) appeal to me.
3. (Don't, Doesn't) Jessica want a score card?
4. Either James or Theda (is, are) in the house.
5. It (don't, doesn't) matter to them.
6. They (was, were) waiting for me at the corner.
7. The list of names (is, are) posted on the board.
8. That box of books (look, looks) heavy.
9. (Is, Are) there many people in the room?

TROUBLESOME VERBS

Go over the following sentences orally, choosing the standard forms from the parentheses.

1. Who (sits, sets) here? Where has he (gone, went)?
2. Will you (borrow, lend) me that lamp? Just (set, sit) it here.
3. I (lay, laid) there for an hour. Nobody (saw, seen) me.
4. John (come, came) up to me and (begun, began) a long speech.
5. I've neither (saw, seen) her nor (wrote, written) to her.
6. Merle has (rode, ridden) off. I might have (knew, known) it!
7. Who (give, gave) you that book? I wouldn't have (chose, chosen) it.
8. The collie (brung, brought) in the paper and then (run, ran) into the kitchen.
9. When was the race (run, ran)? Was the record (broke, broken)?
10. I've (taken, took) many trips, but I've never (flew, flown).
11. Have you (ate, eaten) here before? The prices have (rose, risen).
12. We had (drove, driven) to the lake and had (swum, swam) for an hour.
13. I had (drawn, drawed) a walk and later had (stole, stolen) home.
14. Who (learned, taught) you that song? I've (sung, sang) it often.
15. It's (grown, grew) cold! I should have (wore, worn) a coat.
16. The temperature had (fallen, fell), and the lake had (froze, frozen).
17. Who (drank, drunk) my iced tea? You must have (done, did) it.
18. The bell had (rung, rang), and the whistle had (blew, blown).

PROPER USE OF PRONOUNS

In an oral activity, choose the standard forms. Explain each choice.

1. Leaders will be you and (him, he). (You're, Your) our choice.
2. (We, Us) two came early. (It's, Its) the first time!
3. (I and Rhea, Rhea and I) have been looking for you and (him, he).
4. Wait for Ruth and (me, I). Did you forget (us, we) girls?

5. Dad gave (he, him) and (me, I) some chemistry books.
6. (Him, He) and (I, me) usually walk to school together.
7. Is this sweater (yours, your's)? I really like (its, it's) color.
8. Sally and (she, her) will be here later. (Their, They're) busy now.

Go over these sentences orally, choosing the standard forms.

1. Don't do (anything, nothing) now. Wait at least (a, an) hour.
2. Are (them, those) books yours? They (sure, really) look exciting.
3. Mrs. Gambetti hasn't (no, any) ticket. I'm (certainly, sure) sorry, too.
4. You (surely, sure) played (well, good) in that game.
5. Ed is hardly (ever, never) ill, but today he feels (bad, badly).
6. I don't feel (good, well). I haven't eaten (nothing, anything).
7. We can win (easy, easily). Just ask (them, those) other debaters.

Go over these sentences orally, choosing the standard forms.

1. She is not (to, at) home. Where has she (gone, gone to)?
2. He fell (off of, off) that bicycle. He had borrowed it (off, from) me.
3. The (two, too, to) girls were (too, to, two) late for the concert.
4. Did you visit (at, by) your aunt's farm, (too, two, to)?
5. Where will you (stay, stay at)?
6. She jumped (in, into) the car and drove away.

(1) Number your paper from 1 through 6. (2) Read each of the following groups of words. (3) If a group is a sentence, write *S* on your paper after the corresponding number. If it is a sentence fragment, write *F*. If it is a run-on sentence, write *RO*. (4) Make sentences out of the fragments and run-ons.

1. It is fun to pick wild berries in the woods.
2. Black and red berries on green vines.
3. Some people don't like to pick berries, they're afraid of snakes.
4. When Bob saw a small snake on a vine.
5. Gooseberry and blackberry bushes have sharp thorns.
6. Picking berries and hearing them drop into a pail.

MASTERY TESTS IN SPELLING

At the beginning of Chapter 16, you took two Pretests in spelling. At the end of that chapter, you took Check Tests. Take those tests again as Mastery Tests. Follow the plan for the Pretests, page 245.

APPENDIX

Conjugation of <u>TO BE</u>

Principal Parts

Present: be   *Present Participle:* being
Past: was   *Past Participle:* been

Present Tense

SINGULAR	PLURAL
1. I am	we are
2. you are	you are
3. he * is	they are

Present Perfect Tense

SINGULAR	PLURAL
I have been	we have been
you have been	you have been
he has been	they have been

Past Tense

1. I was	we were
2. you were	you were
3. he was	they were

Past Perfect Tense

I had been	we had been
you had been	you had been
he had been	they had been

Future Tense

1. I shall be	we shall be
2. you will be	you will be
3. he will be	they will be

Future Perfect Tense

I shall have been	we shall have been
you will have been	you will have been
he will have been	they will have been

* *She* and *it* and singular nouns are used just as *he* is.

CONJUGATION OF <u>TO HAVE</u>

PRINCIPAL PARTS

Present: have   *Present Participle:* having
Past: had   *Past Participle:* had

Present Tense

SINGULAR	PLURAL
1. I have	we have
2. you have	you have
3. he * has	they have

Present Perfect Tense

SINGULAR	PLURAL
I have had	we have had
you have had	you have had
he has had	they have had

Past Tense

1. I had	we had
2. you had	you had
3. he had	they had

Past Perfect Tense

I had had	we had had
you had had	you had had
he had had	they had had

Future Tense

1. I shall have	we shall have
2. you will have	you will have
3. he will have	they will have

Future Perfect Tense

I shall have had	we shall have had
you will have had	you will have had
he will have had	they will have had

* *She* and *it* and singular nouns are used just as *he* is.

Conjugation of TO DO

Principal Parts

Present: do
Past: did

Present Participle: doing
Past Participle: done

Present Tense

SINGULAR	PLURAL
1. I do	we do
2. you do	you do
3. he * does	they do

Present Perfect Tense

SINGULAR	PLURAL
I have done	we have done
you have done	you have done
he has done	they have done

Past Tense

1. I did	we did
2. you did	you did
3. he did	they did

Past Perfect Tense

I had done	we had done
you had done	you had done
he had done	they had done

Future Tense

1. I shall do	we shall do
2. you will do	you will do
3. he will do	they will do

Future Perfect Tense

I shall have done	we shall have done
you will have done	you will have done
he will have done	they will have done

* *She* and *it* and singular nouns are used just as *he* is.

Conjugation of <u>TO DRAW</u>

Principal Parts

Present: draw *Present Participle:* drawing
Past: drew *Past Participle:* drawn

ACTIVE **PASSIVE**

Present Tense

SINGULAR	PLURAL	SINGULAR	PLURAL
1. I draw	we draw	I *am* drawn	we *are* drawn
2. you draw	you draw	you *are* drawn	you *are* drawn
3. he * draws	they draw	he *is* drawn	they *are* drawn

Past Tense

SINGULAR	PLURAL	SINGULAR	PLURAL
1. I drew	we drew	I *was* drawn	we *were* drawn
2. you drew	you drew	you *were* drawn	you *were* drawn
3. he drew	they drew	he *was* drawn	they *were* drawn

Future Tense

SINGULAR	PLURAL	SINGULAR	PLURAL
1. I *shall* draw	we *shall* draw	I *shall be* drawn	we *shall be* drawn
2. you *will* draw	you *will* draw	you *will be* drawn	you *will be* drawn
3. he *will* draw	they *will* draw	he *will be* drawn	they *will be* drawn

Present Perfect Tense

SINGULAR	PLURAL	SINGULAR	PLURAL
1. I *have* drawn	we *have* drawn	I *have been* drawn	we *have been* drawn
2. you *have* drawn	you *have* drawn	you *have been* drawn	you *have been* drawn
3. he *has* drawn	they *have* drawn	he *has been* drawn	they *have been* drawn

* *She* and *it* and singular nouns are used just as *he* is.

Past Perfect Tense

SINGULAR	PLURAL	SINGULAR	PLURAL
1. I *had* drawn	we *had* drawn	I *had been* drawn	we *had been* drawn
2. you *had* drawn	you *had* drawn	you *had been* drawn	you *had been* drawn
3. he *had* drawn	they *had* drawn	he *had been* drawn,	they *had been* drawn

Future Perfect Tense

SINGULAR	PLURAL	SINGULAR	PLURAL
1. I *shall have* drawn	we *shall have* drawn	I *shall have been* drawn	we *shall have been* drawn
2. you *will have* drawn	you *will have* drawn	you *will have been* drawn	you *will have been* drawn
3. he *will have* drawn	they *will have* drawn	he *will have been* drawn	they *will have been* drawn

SYNOPSIS OF PROGRESSIVE FORMS
(first person, singular)

	ACTIVE	PASSIVE
Present	I *am* drawing	I *am being* drawn
Past	I *was* drawing	I *was being* drawn
Future	I *shall be* drawing	
Present Perfect	I *have been* drawing	
Past Perfect	I *had been* drawing	
Future Perfect	I *shall have been* drawing	

SYNOPSIS OF EMPHATIC FORMS
(second person)

	ACTIVE
Present	You *do* draw
Past	You *did* draw

THE PRINCIPAL PARTS OF TROUBLESOME VERBS

Present Tense	Past Tense	Past Participle	Present Tense	Past Tense	Past Participle
attack	attacked	attacked	lie	lay	lain
beat	beat	beaten	ride	rode	ridden
become	became	become	ring	rang	rung
begin	began	begun	rise	rose	risen
blow	blew	blown	run	ran	run
break	broke	broken	see	saw	seen
bring	brought	brought	set	set	set
burst	burst	burst	shake	shook	shaken
choose	chose	chosen	shrink	shrank, shrunk *	shrunk
climb	climbed	climbed			
come	came	come	sing	sang, sung *	sung
do	did	done			
drag	dragged	dragged	sink	sank, sunk *	sunk
draw	drew	drawn			
drink	drank	drunk	sit	sat	sat
drive	drove	driven	sneak	sneaked	sneaked
drown	drowned	drowned	speak	spoke	spoken
eat	ate	eaten	spring	sprang, sprung *	sprung
fall	fell	fallen			
fly	flew	flown	steal	stole	stolen
freeze	froze	frozen	swim	swam	swum
give	gave	given	take	took	taken
go	went	gone	tear	tore	torn
grow	grew	grown	throw	threw	thrown
know	knew	known	wear	wore	worn
lay	laid	laid	write	wrote	written

* The first form is preferred.

Suggestions for Good Handwriting

1. Slant all letters in the same direction.
   Do not write this way.

2. Make your writing a good size.
   Do not write too large. Do not write too small.

3. Write on a straight line.
   Do not have some letters high and others low.

4. Avoid crowding your writing.
   See how hard to read this kind of writing is.

5. Make capitals and tall letters tall.
   Do not make them the size of the small letters.

6. Keep small letters even in height.
   Notice how uneven these letters are.

7. Use dots, not circles, above i's and j's; really cross t's.
   This just isn't the way to do it.

8. Be sure to close the letters a, d, g, k, o, and s.
   Not closing them makes the words look
   bad and hard to read.

9. Loop the letters b, e, f, g, h, j, k, l, p, q, y, z.
   Never let a loop cut through a word above or below.

   You make your writing hard to read if you
   loop carelessly and have letters crossing other lines.

10. Make the final stroke of a, but not of o,
    touch the line.
    Do not make them hard to tell apart.

11. Round the tops of m's and n's.
    They must not look like w's or v's.

INDEX

Foreword of a book, 140
Form of written papers, 147-50
Fragments, sentence, 460-64
  in conversation, 461
  practice in correcting, 463-64, 468-69,
    471
Freeze, froze, frozen, 369-70
Friendly letters, 206-15
  addressing envelope of, 205-206
    example, 205; guides, 205
  form and appearance of, 203-208
    example, 204; guides, 203
  interesting, 208-11
    example, 210; guides, 209
  invitations and replies, 211-13
    example, 212; guides, 212
  thank-you letters, 213-15
    examples, 214; guides, 214
From, not *off* or *off of,* 448
-ful, spelling words with, 255, 260-61

G

Give, gave, given, 341-42
Go, went, gone, 342-43
Good and *well,* 414
Greek word parts, 115-17
Groups, working in small, 31, 33, 36,
    39, 60, 73, 96-98, 102-104,
    105, 110, 119, 126-27, 170,
    177, 184, 191, 212, 230,
    289, 293, 295, 296, 297,
    300-301, 307, 315, 327, 334,
    336, 338, 339, 340, 342,
    343, 348, 358, 367, 371,
    372, 373, 382, 384, 387,
    391, 395, 400, 415, 416,
    429, 437, 453
Grow, grew, grown, 453-54
Guides
  adjectives, using effectively, 388
  alphabet, skill in using, 119
  book reports, 197
  business letters, writing, 217
  choral reading, 48
  context, learning words from, 112
  conversation, carrying on, 37
  describing, 175
  describing people, 184
  directions, giving, 69
  discussions, holding, 35
  dividing words into syllables, 124
  electing officers, 79
  envelope, addressing, 205

Guides—*Continued*
  explanations, giving clear oral, 67
  explanations, writing clear, 154
  finding right meaning of words in
    dictionary, 126
  friendly letter, content of, 209
  instructions, following
    oral, 70
    written, 156
  introductions, making, 75
  invitations and replies, writing, 212
  key words, using as a study help, 96
  letter appearance, 207
  letter form, 203
  library, locating books in, 138
  listening, good skills in, 28
  listening and viewing, 32
  listening to learn, 31
  manuscript form, 148
  narrative, writing, 190
  nouns, using vivid, 333
  outlining, 106-107
  paragraph, writing a, 162
  reading, improving habits of, 87
  reading aloud, 59
  reference books, use of, 132
  reports, long, 143
  reports, short, 142
  run-on sentences, correcting, 466
  speaking clearly and correctly, 44
  spelling troublesome words, 246
  summarizing, 100
  telephoning, 72
  tests, taking, 158
  thank-you letters, writing, 214
  verbs, using vivid, 292
  voice, effective, 42
  word parts, using to unlock meaning,
    116
Guide words
  in dictionary, 119
  in encyclopedias, 132

H

Handwriting, suggestions for good, 479
Hardly, in double negatives, 415
Heading for letter
  business, 216
  friendly, 203
Heading for paper, 148
Hear and *here,* 266
Helping verbs. *See* Auxiliary verbs
Homophones, spelling, 265-68; defined,
  266

Plural number, 253, 306, 334–35
  defined, 253, 334
  forming plurals, 253–56
  plural forms in dictionary, 120
  See also Number
Poetry
  choral reading of, 46–59
  practice in writing, 251, 367, 373, 399
Positive degree
  of adjectives, 391
  of adverbs, 409–10
Possessive case, pronouns in, 355, 357
  standard usage of, 364–65
Possessive nouns, 236–38; defined, 236
  as determiners, 385–86
  diagramming, 392–93
  practice in forming, 237–38, 376
Possessive pronouns, 355, 357
  distinguishing from contractions,
    364–65
Posture, good, 40–41
Predicate
  complete, 275, 310–11; defined, 275,
    310
  simple, 275, 310–11; defined, 275
Predicate adjective, 276, 383–84;
    defined, 276, 383
  diagramming, 392–93
  in *Pattern 3* sentences, 277, 383
  practice in recognizing, 384, 386, 393,
    407, 413, 450, 456
Predicate nominative, 276, 323–24;
    defined, 276, 323
  diagramming, 324–25
  noun as, 322–25
  in *Pattern 2* sentences, 277, 323
  practice in recognizing, 323–24,
    324–25, 332, 349, 358,
    359–60, 361–62, 374, 386,
    393, 401–402, 408, 413, 436,
    456, 457
  pronoun as, 357
Preface of a book, 140
Prefixes, 115–17
  spelling words with *dis-* or *mis-*,
    260–61
Prepositional phrase, 425–36; defined,
    426
  as adjective, 428–30, 432–34
  as adverb, 430–32, 432–34
  as compound element, 426, 440–41
  with compound object, 426
  diagramming, 434–36
  practice in recognizing, 427, 429,
    431–32, 433, 455–56
  between subject and verb, 313–14

Prepositions, list of, 426;
    defined, 426
  standard usage of, 447–48
  understood with indirect object,
    436–37
  diagramming, 438
President of club, duties, 79
Principal parts of verbs, 288, 289,
    290–91; list of, 478. *See
    also* Irregular verbs, rules
    and practice
Pronouns, 354–67; defined, 355
  antecedent of, 355–56; defined, 355
  as compound elements, 357–58
  diagramming, 359–60
  number of, 253, 355
  personal, 354–60; defined, 355
    case of, 355, 357
    compound, 355
    declension of forms of, 355; defined,
      355
  person of, 355
  possessive, 357
    confused with contractions, 364
    used as determiners, 357, 385–86
  practice in recognizing, 356, 358,
    359–60, 374, 386
  standard usage of, 360–67
  used as determiners, 357, 385–86
  verb-subject agreement, 365–67
Pronunciation, 44–46, 265; guides, 44
  dictionary as aid, 120, 122–23
  words misspelled because of faulty,
    265
Proofreading written work, 29, 33, 82,
    104, 110, 113, 126–27, 128,
    140–41, 143, 158, 190, 208,
    211, 213, 215, 218, 221,
    222, 227, 230, 231, 235,
    249, 260, 280, 284, 299,
    314, 319, 330–31, 341, 348,
    362, 367, 373, 374, 382,
    387, 398, 400, 418, 455,
    456
Proper adjectives, 387; defined, 387
Proper nouns, defined, 220, 308
  capitalizing, 220–21
  forming plurals of, 255–56
Proper usage. *See* Standard usage, rules
    for
Punctuation, 219–40
  apostrophe, 236–40, 364; rules for,
    237, 240
  colon, 234–35; rule for, 234
  comma, 227–31; rules for, 228, 229
  in envelope address, 205